Teacher Learning in Small-Group Settings

Teacher Education Yearbook XVII

EDITED BY CHERYL J. CRAIG
AND LOUISE F. DERETCHIN

Published in partnership with the
Association of Teacher Educators

ROWMAN & LITTLEFIELD EDUCATION
Lanham, Maryland • Toronto • Plymouth, UK
2009

Published in partnership with the
Association of Teacher Educators

Published in the United States of America
by Rowman & Littlefield Education
A Division of Rowman & Littlefield Publishers, Inc.
A wholly owned subsidary of The Rowman & Littlefield Publishing Group, Inc.
4501 Forbes Boulevard, Suite 200, Lanham, Maryland 20706
www.rowmaneducation.com

Estover Road
Plymouth PL6 7PY
United Kingdom

ISSN: 1078-2265
ISBN-13: 978-1-60709-001-4 (cloth: alk. paper)
ISBN-10: 1-60709-001-5 (cloth: alk. paper)
ISBN-13: 978-1-60709-002-1 (pbk.: alk. paper)
ISBN-10: 1-60709-002-3 (pbk.: alk. paper)
ISBN-13: 978-1-60709-003-8 (e-book)
ISBN-10: 1-60709-003-1 (e-book)

Teacher Education Yearbook XVII

EDITORS

Cheryl J. Craig, University of Houston
Louise F. Deretchin, Educational Consultant

Contents

List of Illustrations   ix

Foreword   xi
   Paul C. Paese

Introduction   xiii
   Cheryl J. Craig, Louise F. Deretchin

DIVISION 1: TEACHING

Overview and Framework   3
   Cheryl J. Craig, Louise F. Deretchin

1   Conversations and Collaborations in Communities of Learning: Professional Development That Matters   5
   Mary Kooy

2   Constructing Practice through Conversation in Professional Learning Groups: Variations on a Theme   23
   Lily Orland-Barak

3   What Makes *Some* Learning Communities So Effective, and How Can I Support My Own?   40
   Ellen Ballock

4   Commingling Action Research and PLCs: An Illustration of Key Components   54
   Diane Yendol-Hoppey, Nancy Fichtman Dana

5   Posing Questions: Teacher Research Groups in Search of Answers   66
   Michaelann Kelley, Karen North, Cheryl J. Craig

6   Creating Learning Communities: An Interrogation of a
    Sustainable Professional Development Model   88
    Anne Rath

Summary and Implications   120
    Cheryl J. Craig, Louise F. Deretchin

DIVISION 2: TEACHER EDUCATION

Overview and Framework   125
    Cheryl J. Craig, Louise F. Deretchin

7   Cohort Learning and Complexity Thinking: The Case of the
    CITE Teacher Education Programme   127
    Anthony Clarke, Gaalen Erickson
8   Seminars as Small-Group Learning Sites in Teacher Preparation 146
    Jacque Ensign
9   Preservice Candidates "Looking at Student Work" in a
    Professional Development School Setting   161
    Kami M. Patrizio
10 Tracing Learning in Collaborative Reflection Meetings of Student
    Teachers   178
    Paulien C. Meijer, Helma Oolbekkink-Marchand
11 Cracks in the Mirror: Discovering Teacher Candidates' Strategies
    for Resisting Reflection   200
    Don Halquist, Sue Novinger
12 Exploring Significance and Benefits of Group Learning for
    Developing Cultural Competence with Teacher Candidates   226
    Nancy P. Gallavan
13 Beginning Teachers' Inquiry in Linguistically Diverse Classrooms:
    Exploring the Power of Small Learning Communities   242
    Barbara J. Merino, Rebecca C. Ambrose
14 "It Could Take Forty Minutes; It Could Take Three Days":
    Authentic Small-Group Learning for Aboriginal Education   261
    Joanne Tompkins, Jeff Orr

Summary and Implications   278
    Cheryl J. Craig, Louise F. Deretchin

DIVISION 3: HIGHER EDUCATION

Overview and Framework   285
    Cheryl J. Craig, Louise F. Deretchin

15 The Somehow of Teaching: Small Groups, Collaboration and
   Self-Study of Teacher Education Practices   287
   Mary Lynn Hamilton
16 The Research Issues Table: A Place of Possibilities for the
   Education of Teacher Educators   303
   Anne Murray Orr, Bosire Monari Mwebi, Debbie Pushor, Carla
   Nelson, Janice Huber, D. Jean Clandinin, Ji-Sook Yeom, Pam
   Steeves, Florence Glanfield, M. Shaun Murphy
17 Voices from a Reflective Space: Teacher Educators Reflect on
   Practice   321
   Helen Burchell, Janet Dyson
18 The Faculty Academy: A Place for Grounding and Growth   343
   Lillian Benavente-McEnery, Blake Bickham, Christa A. Boske,
   Andrea Foster, Michele Kahn, Carrie Markello, Susan McCormack,
   Denise McDonald, Heidi C. Mullins, Angela López Pedrana, Joy C.
   Phillips, Rita P. Poimbeauf, Chris Witschonke, Cheryl J. Craig

Summary and Implications   367
   Cheryl J. Craig, Louise F. Deretchin

Afterword   369
   Cheryl J. Craig, Louise F. Deretchin

Illustrations

Tables

2.1	Degrees of Control and Openness in Professional Conversations	28
2.2	Practices of Professional Conversation: Forms of Talk as Related to Structure, Process, and Outcomes	29
9.1	The Larger Case-Study Context	164
9.2	The Reflective Taxonomy: Assessment Tool Connecting Theoretical Typology and Practical School Environment	166
10.1	Concerns of Beginning Teachers	180
10.2	Concerns of Student Teachers Expressed during Regular Meetings for Collaborative Reflection	184
10.3	Categories of Interaction Used in the Present Study, Frequencies, and Percentages	185
10.4	Expected Learning Outcomes Versus Perceived Learning Results for Collaborative Reflection of Student Teachers	187
10.5	Relation between Concerns, Steps Taken in the Discussion of Concerns, and Perceived Learning Results	188
12.1	Twelve Benefits of Group Learning for Developing Cultural Competence from Teacher Interns	235
13.1	Comparison of Case to Section Cohort	248
13.2	Data Sources	249

Figures

4.1	Inquiry-oriented PLC Cycle	61
5.1	4-by-4 Foundation Curriculum	83
5.2	Computer Science at the Hub of Inquiry	84
9.1	Pre-intervention Capstone Course Design	168
9.2	Post-intervention Portfolio Course Design	170

10.1   Pattern of Discussion in Meeting Concerned with Boundaries
       on Teaching Responsibilities   189
10.2   Pattern of Discussion in Meeting Concerned with Students and
       School Context   190
12.1   Survey Exploring Group Learning for Developing Cultural
       Competence   231

Foreword

Paul C. Paese
University of Bridgeport

Paul C. Paese, Ph.D., is professor and dean of education in the School of Education and Human Resources at the University of Bridgeport. He serves as president of the Association of Teacher Educators (2008–2009) and has been a member since 1986. Dr. Paese was formerly at Texas State University (1980–2008) where he served as associate dean for fourteen years and was a professor in the Department of Health, Physical Education, and Recreation. While in Texas he served in many leadership positions including president of the Consortium of State Organizations for Texas Teacher Education and executive director of Texas ATE. His research and publications have been in a number of areas including supervision, professional development schools, teacher effectiveness, international programs for teacher preparation, analysis of teaching, and fitness/health of school-age children.

As president of ATE, I am delighted to participate in launching *Teacher Learning in Small-Group Settings: Teacher Education Yearbook XVII*, which fittingly blends with the theme of my presidency, *the global imperative: educating and assessing the whole child, teachers, and community*. As Goodlad (1979) suggested, public education should educate the whole child and avoid rote teaching that may raise test scores but fail to produce healthy, fulfilled, participatory citizens. If we are to educate the whole child, then the preparation of teachers necessarily must model the use of small-group settings that foster critical/reflective teaching! What strikes me as particularly significant about the chapters contained in this volume is how the group of authors, fifty in all, took the same seed of an idea and developed it in directions one could never have predicted nor imagined.

Small-group learning situations are an effective and cogent way to educate all learners holistically because they are able to focus on the entire range of skills from the affective to the psychomotor to the cognitive domains. Small-group settings lend themselves to addressing a wide variety of approaches more thoroughly and at a greater depth than in other settings, resulting in a higher quality of learning for all. As readers flip through the pages of this volume, they will learn about book clubs, critical friends groups (CFGs), collaborative reflection meetings, small seminars, cohorts, and professional development schools. But they will also come to know about self-study undertaken in group settings, the research issues table, a number of field-based projects, and the Faculty Academy. At the same time, the research methods include teacher research methods, self-study approaches, critical pedagogy, survey research methods, case study methods, narrative inquiry, and reflective analysis in the postmodern tradition. Further to this, educators from all over the nation made scholarly contributions to the yearbook, along with an impressive number of international colleagues whose insights have added to the quality of the volume.

In closing, editors Cheryl J. Craig and Louise F. Deretchin have done a superb job of weaving diverse pieces of research into a cohesive whole. As with previous yearbooks, volume XVII is certain to affect the field. What potentially might be considered a mundane topic has been made profound through the collection of essays assembled here. I would also like to encourage all of you to go beyond the volume's focus on just teacher learning and think about how to use these small-group approaches in a variety of ways in your own academic environments with all types of learners. The key is that the more any learning situation addresses the whole child or person, the more efficacious it is as an educational process!

Reference

Goodlad, J. I. (1979). *What schools are for.* Bloomington, IN: Phi Delta Kappa International Foundation.

Introduction

Cheryl J. Craig
University of Houston

Louise F. Deretchin
Educational Consultant

Cheryl J. Craig, Ph.D., is a professor in the Department of Curriculum and Instruction, College of Education, University of Houston, where she coordinates the Teaching and Teacher Education program and is the director of elementary education. Her research centers on the influence of school reform on teachers' knowledge developments and their communities of knowing. Her book *Narrative Inquiries of School Reform* appeared in 2003 (Information Age Publishing). Dr. Craig is the coeditor of the Association of Teacher Educators' Yearbooks XV, *International Research on the Impact of Accountability Systems* (Rowman & Littlefield Education, 2007); and XVI, *Imagining a Renaissance in Teacher Education* (Rowman & Littlefield Education, 2008).

Louise F. Deretchin, Ph.D., is an educational consultant, former director of higher education for the Houston A+ Challenge (formerly the Houston Annenberg Challenge), former director of Medical Informatics Education at Baylor College of Medicine, a fellow in the Association of Teacher Educators Leadership Academy, a founding member of the Texas Higher Education Coordinating Board Houston P–16+ Council, and cofounder of Regional Faculty, whose purpose is to take a regional approach to directing the growth of educational systems. She has been coeditor of the Association of Teacher Educators' Yearbook since 2006 and has taught university graduate courses and at elementary schools. Her work focuses on creating collaborations among colleges, the business community, and school districts to improve teacher education, teaching, and learning.

Having imagined a renaissance in teacher education in ATE's *Teacher Education Yearbook XVI*, the theme of volume XVII shifts to a more fine-grained topic—teacher learning in small-group settings. Despite ongoing attempts to standardize teaching, teacher education, and higher education, one highly promising though not universally successful pocket of innovative activity remains: that of small-group sites of inquiry and the activities and interactions in which teacher candidates, teachers, teacher educators, and others in higher education engage.

The international collection of essays contained in this volume offers a comprehensive look at how small groups are being employed in the field of education today and the purposes for which they are being used. Where teaching is concerned, readers of the chapters in Division 1 of this volume will come to know how teachers experience professional development in book clubs, critical friends groups (CFGs), and teacher research groups and how action research has been used by teachers in a particular curriculum reform project. In Division 2, where teacher education is concerned, readers are afforded an insider view of what is happening in various cohorts and other small-group configurations throughout the nation and the world, particularly with respect to diversity. In addition, a sense of who benefits and what is learned by teacher candidates and teacher educators is conveyed. Finally, in Division 3, readers will catch a glimpse of what is occurring in higher education and how professors learn to be teacher educators, contributing members of the academy, and collaborative colleagues in their efforts to support and enhance student learning along the educational continuum.

Teacher Learning in Small-Group Settings: Teacher Education Yearbook XVII provides a rich compilation of small-group learning sites throughout the nation and the world. We come to know what is happening in the United States, from New York to California and from Washington State to Texas, as well as points in between. We also learn what is taking place in Canada, Britain, Ireland, Israel, and the Netherlands. Furthermore, one group collaboration involved a professor from South Korea, and a second professor from South Korea on sabbatical leave served on the editorial advisory board for this book.

The panoramic sampling of small-group learning in teaching, teacher education, and higher education we offer would not have been possible without the efforts and cooperation of the participating authors, reviewers, and editorial panel members. As editors, we recognize the many ways that others contributed to the quality of this volume. Lastly, we invite readers to savor and learn from the essays that their colleagues dotted around the nation and the world have chosen to share.

Division 1
TEACHING

Overview and Framework

Cheryl J. Craig

Louise F. Deretchin

Teacher Learning in Small-Group Settings opens with the six chapters in Division 1, all of which cohere around the teaching theme. We begin with the teaching theme because teachers' practices and the contexts within which they teach in many ways set the stage for what happens in teacher education (Division 2) and higher education (Division 3).

Chapter 1, authored by Mary Kooy, is titled "Conversations and Collaboration in Communities of Learning: Professional Development That Matters." In it, Kooy provides a strong argument for why large-group teacher learning does not work. She explores product- and process-oriented communities of learning and shows why small groups such as book clubs do work. For Kooy, optimum teacher-directed learning begins in the induction years and continues along the career continuum.

Written by Lily Orland-Barak, Chapter 2, "Constructing Practice through Conversation in Professional Learning Groups: Variations on a Theme," presents three contrastive cases of teacher conversation taking place in small-group settings. Orland-Barak asserts that such conversations assist teachers in coming to terms with the standardization that envelops their pedagogical practices.

"What Makes *Some* Learning Communities So Effective, and How Can I Support My Own?" is the title of Chapter 3, which is authored by Ellen Ballock. In it, Ballock explores critical friends groups (CFGs) in the beginning stages of collaborative work and CFGs that are more established. Her contrasting cases reveal important differences in how a CFG's work is perceived and valued by teachers.

Chapter 4, penned by Diane Yendol-Hoppey and Nancy Dana, focuses on "Commingling Action Research and PLCs: An Illustration of Key Components." Yendol-Hoppey and Fitchman Dana employ three theoretical constructs con-

3

cerning how teachers use and produce knowledge as a way to frame what happens when action research is undertaken in small learning communities. Six mathematics teachers and a math coach in an elementary school setting form the focus of their research attention.

"Posing Questions: Teacher Research Groups in Search of Answers" is the title of Chapter 5, which is written by Michaelann Kelley, Karen North, and Cheryl Craig. The chapter describes two teacher research groups in two urban high schools, both of which cross content area lines. The essay shows how collaborative reflection and writing serve as logical extensions of the schools' respective CFG work and teacher research endeavors. At the same time, each school subscribes to a particular way teacher professional development is pursued in its specific teacher research group settings.

Finally, Chapter 6, "Creating Learning Communities: An Interrogation of a Sustainable Professional Development Model," is contributed by Anne Rath. In this essay, Rath tells of her work with six primary teachers who participated in an action research project funded by the Irish National Teachers Organization, the largest teacher's union in Ireland. In that project, the teachers reconnected with the values and practices that initially attracted them to the teaching profession. This finding, among others, suggested a sustainable professional development model that was deeply relevant to the teachers in the study and pertinent to their growth and development.

All in all, the six chapters in Division 1 present a rich picture of small-group activity in the teaching field, its purposes, and its outcomes. Combined, they offer a kaleidoscope of possible teaching practices.

CHAPTER 1

Conversations and Collaborations in Communities of Learning
PROFESSIONAL DEVELOPMENT THAT MATTERS

Mary Kooy
University of Toronto, Toronto, Canada

Mary Kooy, Ph.D., is a researcher at the University of Toronto, Toronto, Canada. Her research interests include teacher learning and development, communities of learning, and dialogic and constructivist theory.

ABSTRACT

An unparalleled era of accountability, standards, and comprehensive school reform in the past decade has placed pressures on teachers—key to any school change—to participate in professional development. Traditional "one-shot" workshops are not up to the task; no evidence of carry-through is substantial. New models of small professional groups of teachers provide stories of hope and are critical to transforming the learning landscapes of both teachers and students. This chapter compares and explores theories and models of teacher development considered product oriented (communities of practice operating within schools) and process oriented (communities of learning, generally off-site) and demonstrates how a longitudinal study with two groups of teachers (novice and experienced) became a dialogic and relational learning environment for collaboratively transforming teacher thinking and praxis. I also argue that teacher-directed learning and development in small teacher communities can begin with induction and that such experiences appear to positively inform and shape teacher knowledge and development.

The concept of "perturbation"—*a deviation of a system, moving object, or process from its regular or normal path caused by an outside influence*—characterizes the state of education in many jurisdictions and contexts. A tide of reform initiatives calling for strengthened standards for student teachers and increased account-ability through student testing continues unabated. Since any reform and change depends on teachers who are at the heart of actualizing change efforts (Fullan, 2001; Fox & Fleischer, 2001), improving teacher knowledge and skill becomes increasingly important.

Efforts to legislate or introduce teachers to new expectations, goals, and practices have failed to account for the learning experiences required by teachers (Clark, 2001; Kooy, 2006b). Reform initiatives inevitably become lost in trans-lation from policy and program to classroom practice. Many teachers feel ill-equipped to create pedagogies that support the new cognitive skills students require. Recognizing the teacher's critical role in shaping students' educational experiences (Hawley & Valli, 1999, p. 128) and realizing that highly skilled teachers most positively affect student learning and performance (Ancess, 2001; Elmore & Burney, 1999), it follows that improvement in schools happens only through the improvement of teaching (Capers, 2004).

Sarason (1990), almost twenty years ago, observed that: "It is virtually im-possible to create and sustain over time conditions for productive learning for students when they do not exist for teachers" (p. 45). The recognition of the key role of teachers led scholars and policymakers to demand quality professional development (Borko, 2004).

Although exemplary and highly effective models of teacher learning exist (e.g., Au, 2002; Ball & Cohen, 1999; Clark et al., 1996; Cochran-Smith & Lytle, 1999; Cochran-Smith, 2003; Cochran-Smith & Lytle, 2004; Cochran-Smith & Zeichner, 2005; Darling-Hammond, 1998, 2005; Darling-Ham-mond & Sykes, 1999; Grossman, Wineburg, & Woolworth, 2000a, 2000b), the "one-shot" workshop remains the mainstay of most professional "learning" for teachers—in spite of a history of its ineffectiveness in translating the knowl-edge transmitted into school practice.

We face a complex conundrum: Change and reform initiatives focus on change in learning experiences for students, but, if the current "one-shot" work-shop model persists, reforms will stay as policy or program, and effective expres-sions of practice will continue to elude. The new directions for teacher learning point to, as Dewey observed "breaking with the crust of conventionalized and routine consciousness" (cited in Lieberman & Miller, 2001, p. 11). The tension threatens to undermine or even bypass a new and revitalized interest in re-professionalizing teaching through collegial opportunities for professional learn-ing. Bridging the two paradigms requires ongoing, sustained support and learn-ing experiences for teachers.

To address the issues, I provide an overview of professional learning for teachers; the theoretical framework on teacher learning and development, research, and models of teacher learning; a brief introduction to a longitudinal study on teacher development (Kooy, 2006b); and what we continue to learn in efforts to support and develop professional teachers who maintain active and effective learning lives.

The Context: Situating Professional Development

Much of what constitutes conventional approaches to formal teacher professional development is antithetical to research findings on effective learning. The default "one-shot workshop"—with experts transmitting and teachers "receiving"—perpetuates a transmission model of learning (Barnes, 1995), which is premised on fixing what is wrong with teachers: correcting skill, content, values, knowledge, and attitudes (Clark & Florio-Ruane, 2001).

The traditional teacher workshops tend to be events dealing with decontextualized information that fails to resonate with teachers' perceived needs (Clark, 2001). Typically, an "expert" delivers new content and information. The persistence of the model—its repeated reifications—implicitly sanctions practices (learner as passive recipient, knowledge as packaged, teachers needing "fixing" by experts) that may even conflict with the "expert" position and perspective. The model also assures that whatever legislated changes and reforms teachers are expected to implement cannot be troubled or disputed as these would incur unwelcome perturbations.

The urgency of the demands for change and reform, particularly in the United States, has spawned an industry built on current catchphrases (e.g., technology applications and programs, collaborative learning, guided reading, and courses on video). Costly texts, media, and programs for schools accompany many such programs. Currency marks both the "catchword" and economic benefits for the consultants and companies involved. The "training" process, generally of the "one-shot" workshop variety, promises a quick fix to the ailing system and provides evidence for improvement. The workshops have, as Sykes (1996) observed, ". . . entered educational parlance as shorthand for superficial, faddish, in-service education that supports a mini-industry of consultants without having much effect on what goes on in schools and classrooms" (p. 464). While impact, at first blush, seems ineffective, the economic benefits will keep the purveyors pursuing the purse strings. The benefits to the industry are just too lucrative.

Dismissing the "one-shot" workshop too lightly ignores its persistence and perpetuations in teacher education. It does not seem to want to go away, in spite of evidence indicating that little, if any, benefit accrues from the experiences (Clark, 2001). Why does it stay when teachers almost universally discount the value? The need and policies for professional development have increased significantly in recent times. We can only think that those responsible for planning generally resort to the default workshop model because alternatives may not be apparent. The simple answer may be that traditions die slowly; the more complex response probes deeper.

Steps toward creating awareness of the subtle and even insidious underbelly may move thinking forward. While learning may evade on a surface level, teachers, like their students, do learn, although it may not result in the intended outcome. What they get is teaching techniques, not the deep understanding of the discipline or pedagogies for learning needed to implement reforms envisioned by policymakers. When teachers continuously assume the position of passive learner, "receiver" of information or instructions, the narrative suggests that teacher knowledge has no role, that teachers are empty vessels, that whatever is being proposed cannot be actively questioned or deconstructed. Not surprisingly, this is the outcome that "travels" (Franke, 2005) to classrooms. While teachers may not specifically recognize this, they do almost universally express a lack of interest in conventional professional development related to the nature of the workshops themselves (Clark & Florio-Ruane, 2001; Kooy, 2006b). Nonetheless, the tradition persists.

Theoretical Framework

SOCIAL THEORIES OF LEARNING AND TEACHER DEVELOPMENT

Accepting new educational reforms on a deeper level requires that teachers unlearn some (conventional) practices, learn new concepts of teaching, and have substantial understanding of the subject matter itself. To meet this challenge, teachers need extensive learning opportunities that actively engage them in the practices and experiences they create for their students.

Since the 1990s, teacher learning has been conceived of as a constructivist, reframing process in which, through concrete experience, collaborative discourse and self-reflection, teachers' knowledge is transformed into new conceptual models while links between the old and the new are created (Zellermayer, 2001, p. 40). Recent models of teacher development reflect new conceptions of how teachers learn (Black & Ammon, 1992; Van Zoest & Bohl, 2002; Clandinin, 1993; Kooy, 2006a; Rogoff, Matusov, & White, 1996). Social theories of learning prove helpful, particularly Vygotsky's (1992) "zone of proximal development" (p. 189) and the social construction of knowledge.

Making sense of what goes on around us—and our part in it—occurs by actively constructing a world for ourselves (Vygotsky, 1992; Bruner, 1986). The models we create of how the world functions help us understand our lives and guide our actions, although this does not happen in isolation. Bakhtin's (1986) dialogical theory proposes that thinking and learning depend on multiple voices, each stemming from the voices that came before and blending with the voices already in place. The social interactions both construct and change knowledge (Bakhtin, 1986; Vygotsky, 1992). Knowledge develops and is continually modified in the light of new experiences (Dewey, 1938). New understandings emerge from this interplay (Grimshaw, 1989; Grumet, 1991; Rommetveit, 1992).

What teachers know, how they know it, and what is to be done with their knowledge remains a significant gap for those eager to learn from teachers and about teacher development. In a dialogic teacher community, participants take risks and engage in reflective assessment (Zellermayer, 2001; Bakhtin, 1981). They construct a dialogic approach to theory, making it "internally persuasive . . . half ours and half someone else's" (Bakhtin, pp. 345–346). In this way, theories become dynamic and lead to productive dialogue and generative reflection (Ritchie & Wilson, 2000, p. 18) leading teachers to adopt critical stances for greater understanding not only of their own work but also of the body of research (Berliner, 2003). Disciplined inquiry supported by substantial professional discourse (Darling-Hammond, 1998; Hord, 2004; Ritchie & Wilson, 2000) generates a symbiosis between theory and practice (Miller, 1990).

PROFESSIONAL DEVELOPMENT IN SMALL GROUPS

The past two decades have seen considerable interest and research of collaborative inquiry into the work and professional lives of teachers as a means of re-valuing teachers' positions in educational practice and developing their teacher identities (Darling-Hammond & McLaughlin, 1999; Hindin et al., 2007). The co-construction of knowledge of such collaborations makes linking current knowledge to school practices; dialogical exchange of issues, ideas, and solutions; and the inclusion of teachers in inquiry possible (Mason, 2003).

A community of learners provides a prime route to sharing knowledge constructed by teachers and, thus, offers a particularly suitable context for effecting teacher and school change (Fullan, 2001; Stein & Brown, 1997). Community, rather than merely a group of teachers, includes relationships (community building) developed through shared experiences, knowledge, and practices—the things teachers have in common (Dewey, 1916, p. 5). These groups—Rogoff (1994) aptly names them "communities of practice" (p. 153)—become social gathering points for studying the ongoing evolution and restructuring of teacher knowledge, theories, and epistemologies.

Minimally, this calls upon teachers to resist what Dewey (1927), as cited earlier, called "the crust of conventionalized and routine consciousness" (p. 183). In creating constructs for peer conversations in communities of learning, teachers can interactively construct meaning (Greenleaf & Katz, 2004; Vygotsky, 1978). The most successful teacher professional development activities are long-term and sustained (Kooy, 2006b). Darling-Hammond and McLaughlin in the closing chapter of *Teaching as the Learning Profession* (1999) make the observation that, "If teachers' norms and knowledge are crucial, we also know that changing teachers' knowledge, beliefs, and norms of practice requires long-term learning opportunities based in practice as well as research" (p. 380).

The opportunity to move from learning *from* others to learning *with* others allows teachers to develop new knowledge as their perspectives "interpenetrate" and "interanimate" each other. Their interpretive frameworks are modified, expanded, and realized—particularly through conflict, disagreement, and contrasting perspectives (Nystrand, 1997). Indeed, authentic communities cannot exist unless participants learn to renegotiate and expand their views that understandably occur over sustained periods of time (Clark, 2001; Lieberman & Miller, 1999) and represent the core of educational reform and instructional improvement (Cole & Knowles, 2000; Gordon, 2004; Hollingsworth & Sockett, 1994; O'Donnell-Allen, 2001).

Recent research confirms that sustained professional development affects both the successful translation of reforms and policies into practices, and, subsequently, student learning (Desforges, 1995; Elmore, 1996; Fiszer, 2004; Fox & Fleischer, 2001; Fullan, 2001). Teachers experience the social interactions and learning practices they are expected to translate into effective classroom practices. If sustained professional development changes teachers and prepares them for change in the schools and improvement in student learning, then professional development becomes a de facto concern for schools and school districts (Gordon, 2004).

Orland-Barak and Tillema (2006) suggest that research in collaborative inquiry falls into the familiar "process and product" tracks (p. 10). Process-oriented inquiry examines knowledge that is dynamic, changing, evolving, and might be called "communities of learning," whereas product orientation focusing on the outcomes of professional learning for understanding and knowledge building might be called "communities of practice" (Rogoff, 1994). In some ways, the on-site and off-site inquiries provide similar parallels; that is, on-site (school-based) communities may be seen as "communities of practice" (product orientation) while off-site groups may be called "communities of learning" (process orientation).

School-Based Communities of Practice

A growing body of research documents the effects of professional learning communities on elementary and secondary teachers as being of critical importance to changing school cultures and student learning experiences (i.e., Borko, 2004; Hord, 2004; McLaughlin & Talbert, 2006). Positioned between the "macro" (system level directives) and the "micro" realities of teacher classrooms, they seem ideally situated to interpret and mediate policies, programs, and initiatives coming from the larger system. Within a school, learning communities offer "the possibility of individual transformation as well as the transformation of the social settings within which individuals work" (Grossman, Wineburg, & Woolworth, 2001, p. 948). Benefits of this arrangement include the development of relationships, sharing goals for the school, and formation of networks of support. A collaborative culture within schools leads to higher levels of teacher expertise in the schools (Fiszer, 2004). Borko (2005) conducted significant studies representing this perspective.

Teachers in Borko's study reported that the researcher/staff dialogue, as they worked with children in the classrooms, helped them understand the nature of observations and incorporate classroom observations of student performance into their assessment (Borko, 2005). Most studies on professional learning communities occur with teacher groups in specific school sites (Hord, 2004; McLaughlin & Talbert, 2006). Such sites, with their professional learning communities, develop fertile ground for building shared practice in schools.

Off-Site Communities of Learning

While on-site approaches offer obvious advantages, Moon, Butcher, and Bird (2000) argue that knowledge is situated and the development of professional learning is one of context and purpose. Situating learning experiences outside schools allows "various settings for teacher learning [to] give rise to different kinds of knowledge" (p. 15). Some theoretical and practical evidence exists to support the benefits of "distributed learning communities" (Lave & Wenger, 1991; Lieberman, 2000; Rogoff, 1994) consisting of teachers from multiple school sites (Darling-Hammond, 1998; Darling-Hammond & Ball, 1997). An example of a distributed learning community is The National Writing Project. It represents an effective national program for the teaching of writing. Its website notes that "The National Writing Project is the premier effort to improve writing in America. NWP's network of sites, located on nearly two hundred university campuses, serves more than 135,000 educators annually. Through its professional development model, "NWP develops the leadership, programs, and research needed for teachers to help students become successful writers and learners" (http://www.nwp.org/cs/public/print/resource/2399). Other projects to develop more enduring learning communities and relationships such as the WEST project (Women Educators of Science and Technology) operate off-site to provide a safe place for sharing personal and professional lives (Cavazos, 2001).

Yet, the paucity of existing communities of practice operating in elementary and secondary schools and the importance of sustained teacher-driven learning (Darling-Hammond, 1998; Flecknoe, 2000)—particularly its effects on the quality of student learning—suggest the importance of establishing a multitude of off-site learning communities. It is important to remember, however, that "the process of integrating ideas and practices learned outside the classroom into one's ongoing instructional programme is rarely simple or straightforward" (Putnam & Borko, 2000, p. 16).

"Telling Stories": Inquiry into a Community of Learning

Making a professional learning community available for teachers outside their school contexts required creating a context for using new forms of discourse among teachers as a professional tool. I integrated the social construct of a book club with a professional learning community (Clark et al., 1996; Clark, 2001; Clement & Vandenberghe, 2001; Kooy, 2006a, 2006b). The current book club phenomenon is well documented (Kooy, 2006b; Long, 2003; McMahon & Raphael, 1997; Marshall, Smagorinsky, & Smith, 1995) and widely proclaimed. The investigations of the phenomenon transpire primarily outside of educational contexts (see especially Long's exhaustive study, 2003).

The potential for interactive dialogue and sustained learning through community experiences makes the book club construct a particularly viable, dynamic site for (English) teacher inquiry and learning. As members gather around texts, they negotiate meaning; develop their thoughts; "internalize the voices of the other members" (Marshall, Smagorinsky, & Smith, 1995, p. 119); and form and deepen friendships (Cardwell, 2002; Kooy, 2006a; Long, 2003; Marshall, Smagorinsky, & Smith, 1995)—the marks of a dialogic learning community. Within interpretive communities where narratives intersect and interact, teachers are able to expand their imaginative capacities, re-create the stories of their professional lives, and reconstruct their professional knowledge (Beattie, 1995; Clark, 2001; Kooy, 2006a, 2006b; McIntyre, 1998).

I initiated the off-site professional learning community study in 2000 with two groups of teachers, novice and experienced, that met as book clubs using teacher-selected books as a medium for meaningful dialogue through stories of reading, teaching, and learning. The study, rooted in narrative approaches that reach beyond phenomenon, serves as a method for undertaking and understanding the complexities of the teaching landscape (Clandinin & Connelly, 1999, p. 4) since they offer a way to bring forth the stories of professional practice that teachers carry (Carter, 1990, 1993; Connelly & Clandinin, 1990). Through narrative inquiry, I explore the ways stories, told and read, and the contexts in which they occur, influence and shape teachers' knowledge and contribute to their development.

The study has two phases. Phase 1 began with two teacher book clubs (nine novice teachers and seven experienced teachers) that met separately every five to six weeks in each academic year. They planned, selected texts, and met as book clubs five to six times annually for three years (2000–2003). In addition, the teachers generated literacy autobiographies, responded to surveys on reading and teaching texts, participated in interviews and online conferences. All group meetings (including interviews) were videotaped. The book club meetings continued informally from 2004–2006.

Phase 2 began in 2006 (to 2010) with the original "novice" teacher group in year seven of their teaching. The study aims to inquire into the effects of sustained communities of learning on school practice and culture. Moreover, the study examines the liminal space between learning (professional development) and teaching (school practices) to seek insight into if and how teacher learning "travels" (Franke, 2005) from the learning to teaching. In 2006, five teachers established book clubs in their schools: teacher (3), mother-daughter (1), and a student group (1). The research teachers meet as a focus group/book club for a full day five times annually to collaboratively examine, analyze, and find direction, understanding of, and extensions for the research. Book clubs and focus group meetings are videotaped. Research funding supplies the books and food for each group in the schools and in the teacher focus group. Data in both phases consists of interviews, surveys, literacy autobiographies, book club online conference sites, and videotapes and transcripts of each book club in the schools and the teacher focus group meetings.

THE TEACHER PARTICIPANTS

Phase 1 of the study included two small cohorts of experienced (seven) and novice teachers (nine). As researcher, I participated in the book clubs. In 2000, the experienced teacher group volunteered while the novice teacher group, students in my pre-service English Methods class, proposed to participate in the research at the close of their teacher education year. The teachers in the study are white, middle-class women, most either first- or second-generation European immigrants.

PROCESS AND PROCEDURES

Phase one book club meetings (six annual) included reading the text and preparing informal jottings of observations, issues, and questions. Both groups set an informal book club discussion model as guide. Meetings took place in a comfortable lounge in the faculty building on relatively quiet Saturday mornings. Study funds provided "brunch and books." Group and individual interviews occurred at two points of each academic year. Each teacher prepared an extensive literacy autobiography tracing her life as a reader. Surveys and questionnaires highlighted common features of the teacher readers (e.g., most influential book). Videotaping occurred at each book club meeting and group interview.

Findings and Discussions

Teachers "caught in the action" (Lieberman & Miller, 2001)—even novice teachers—generate perturbations of conventional approaches to teacher learning and development (Kooy, 2006a, 2006b). I report three key findings of the study that reflect the importance and effects of professional learning communities: (1) sustained, social contexts; (2) social construction of knowledge; and (3) professional learning as teacher development.

1. COMMUNITIES OF LEARNING AS SUSTAINED, SOCIAL CONTEXTS

The teacher book clubs of the study mirror Lieberman and Miller's (1999) model that "the underlying processes of teacher growth include developing a professional community and combining inside and outside knowledge, through an ethic of collaboration" (p. 66). Sustained collaborations developed collegiality, relationships, and interdependency. The teachers noted that "the social aspects were very important" and that they provided ". . . people to talk to, human resources that can help in my work as a teacher," and "we need to learn from each other." Relationships developed: "We come together as very good friends," and "It's relationships, not a mandated class, that makes the learning possible." "Without my good book club friends," one noted, "I would not have the time or the energy to think about the important issues and questions for me." The social process of the book club—the story exchanges—made "the invisible, visible and create[d] a richer, more complex picture of women as learners" (Long, 2003, p. 188). A collegial support network emerged through space and time for thinking aloud with others about shared induction issues (Rust & Orland, 2001).

The book club provides open and deliberate dialogue of school realities and a space to articulate vulnerabilities ("How long can I stay in this profession?" "Does this ever end?"). The teachers looked to their book club peers to salvage and revive their doubtful spirits (Elbaz, 1991; Kooy, 2006a). Unlike many professional counterparts who have left the profession altogether (Croasmun, Hampton, & Herrmann, 1997; Gold, 1996), these teachers acknowledge that remaining in the profession is, in no small part, due to their book club participation.

2. SOCIAL CONSTRUCTION OF KNOWLEDGE

The teachers co-constructed "telling stories" that reflect dynamic and increasingly textured views of teaching (Clandinin & Connelly, 2000). This points to a critical finding: Teacher knowledge was actively provoked, and teachers became mutually responsible for the knowledge they created and carried (Kremer-Hayon, 1987). One noted: "I was like a leech, listening and absorbing their dialogue as I heard their different perspectives on the book."

She pointed out:

> On the surface, the book club may appear casual and informal, but the learning is real, authentic. It's a human web of people and ideas with opportunities to compare and exchange stories. The *human* resources allowed me to think in new ways to be and teach in my classes.

"Each time I come, I add another thread to my web of knowledge," another teacher noted.

3. PROFESSIONAL LEARNING AS TEACHER DEVELOPMENT

Through multiple stories and interactive dialogues, the teachers altered their teaching knowledge and epistemologies (Clandinin & Connelly, 2000; Kooy,

2006a). Another noted: "I feel that through our conversations, my knowledge of literature and teaching has really widened, and consequently, so has my understanding of the world." Much of the collaborative dialogue led teachers to rethink teaching: "The comparing and exchanging help me think about my teaching," one teacher observed. Another suggested: "This [book club] experience translated so well for me when I thought about the classroom and the varying perspectives and opinions that my students bring to the texts that we read and view as a class." Another noted: "Professionally, I enjoy seeing how others react to various elements of a text. It helps to remind me of the diversity of reactions within my own classroom. Listening to the others reminds me of the need to create space for students to talk and to model and teach them the value of listening to one another." The group process seems to contribute to identity formation through valuing the multiple perspectives evident (Orland-Barak & Tillema, 2006).

The teachers expressed their evolving understanding of teaching. They indicate that they "replaced the 'Q & A' model of teaching a novel to focus on small-group talk and discussion in my classes." Without fail, they note, each was "encouraged to try new ideas" through the dialogue in the book club. Others suggest: "I took fabulous new ideas to make changes to my teaching repertoire," or "incorporated literature circles in my classes. I'm known as the literature circle queen in my school." One teacher was able to "get students to talk about books in different, unstructured ways that are much more educational." Another found: "The book club emphasized the power of collaborative discussion and enforced the power of choice in reading—for me first and now, my students." Others noted that they gained new teaching strategies, and recognized, as one teacher remarked, that: "I am willing to do here what my students do in class. I share my experiences with them. This has changed my perceptions of English teaching." In light of convincing evidence that teachers actively participating in professional learning become better, more skilled teachers who, in turn, improve learning in their classrooms (Borko, 2004; Florio-Ruane, 2001; Clark, 2001), this by-product of the book clubs is worth pursuing in more detail.

At face value, the teachers attest to the transformative possibilities through their communities of learning. Their evolving and collaborative efforts seem to infiltrate their epistemologies and practices. To explore further, the second phase of the study aims to operationalize aspects of this work: How then does co-constructed, new teacher knowledge "travel" as Franke described from a community of learning (process) to school classrooms (product)? Even within a sustained and dialogical community, individual teachers apply their new knowledge in different ways and to differing degrees. How reliable is self-report? Are the roles they play in the group reliable indicators of their revising classroom practices? How are the two paradigms reflexively active and informed? Is the bridge only suggestive? These issues continue to occupy educational researchers and psychologists (Greeno, Collins, & Resnick, 1996).

Closing Words

The current situation in research of small groups in teacher learning and development is anything but monolithic. The multitude of iterations, interpretations, and research programs provide a rich bricolage of dynamic and new insights into teacher learning and development as a social and sustained process. The future of sound research will weave together the considerable body of insights into teacher and student learning, professional development, and teacher knowledge to create richer, denser forms of professional development that support reforms and student learning for those interested in the ways teachers learn, develop, and practice their profession (Baumfield & Butterworth, 2007; Capers, 2004; Greenleaf & Katz, 2004; Darling-Hammond & Sykes, 1999).

References

Ancess, J. (2001). Teacher learning at the intersection of school learning and student outcomes. In A. Lieberman & L. Miller (Eds.), *Teachers caught in the action: Professional development that matters* (pp. 61–78). New York: Teachers College Press.

Au, K. (2002). Communities of practice: Engagement, imagination, and alignment in research on teacher education. *Journal of Teacher Education, 56*(3), 222–227.

Bakhtin, M. (1981). Discourse in the novel. In M. Holquist (Ed.), *The dialogic imagination: Four essays by M.M. Bakhtin* (C. Emerson & M. Holquist, Trans.). Austin: University of Texas Press.

Bakhtin, M. (1986). *Speech genres and other late essays* (V. McGee, Trans.). Austin: University of Texas Press.

Ball, D., & Cohen, D. (1999). Developing practice, developing practitioners: Toward a practice-based theory of professional development. In S. Lytle & L. Darling-Hammond (Eds.), *Teaching as the learning profession: The handbook of policy and practice.* Hoboken, NJ: Wiley.

Barnes, D. (1995). *Communication and learning revisited: Making meaning through talk.* Portsmouth, NH: Boynton/Cook Heinemann.

Baumfield, V., & Butterworth, M. (2007). Creating and translating knowledge about teaching and learning in collaborative school-university partnerships: An analysis of what is exchanged across the partnerships, by whom and how. *Teachers and Teaching: Theory and practice, 13*(4), 411–427.

Beattie, M. (1995). *Constructing professional knowledge in teaching: A narrative of change and growth.* New York: Teachers College Press.

Berliner, D. (2003, August). Professional development of teachers in the USA: How to do it wrong! Paper presented at the meeting of the *European Association for Research on Learning and Instruction Conference*. Padua, Italy.

Black, A., & Ammon, P. (1992). A developmental-constructivist approach to teacher education. *Journal of Teacher Education, 43*(5), 323–335.

Borko, H. (2004). Professional development and teacher learning: Mapping the terrain. *Educational Researcher, 33*(8), 3–15.

Borko, H. (2005). Professional development for all teachers: Achieving excellence and equity in the era of accountability, *American Educational Research Association Annual Meeting*. Montreal, PQ.

Bruner, J. (1986). *Actual minds, possible worlds*. Cambridge, MA: Harvard University Press.

Capers, M. (2004). Teaching and shared professional practice: A history of resistance; a future dependent on its embrace. In S. Hord (Ed.), *Learning together, leading together: Changing schools through professional learning communities* (pp. 151–162). New York: Teachers College Press & National Staff Development Council.

Cardwell, N. (2002). Teaching through relationships and stories. In N. Lyons & V. Kubler LaBoskey (Eds.), *Narrative inquiry in practice: Advancing the knowledge of teaching* (pp. 76–86). New York: Teachers College, Columbia University.

Carter, C. (1990). Teachers' knowledge and learning to teach. In W. R. Houston (Ed.), *Handbook of research on teacher education* (pp. 291–310). New York: Macmillan.

Carter, C. (1993). The place of story in the study of teaching and teacher education. *Educational Researcher, 22*(1), 5–12.

Cavazos, L., & Members of WEST. (2001). Connected conversations: Forms and functions of teacher talk. In C. Clark (Ed.), *Talking shop: Authentic conversation and teacher learning* (pp. 137–171). New York: Teachers College Press.

Clandinin, D. J. (1993). *Learning to teach, teaching to learn: Stories of collaboration in teacher education*. New York: Teachers College Press.

Clandinin, D. J., & Connelly, F. M. (2000). *Narrative inquiry: Experience and story in qualitative research*. San Francisco: Jossey-Bass.

Clark, C. (2001). *Talking shop: Authentic conversation and teacher learning*. New York: Teachers College Press.

Clark, C., & Florio-Ruane, S. (2001).Conversation as support for teaching in new ways. C. Clark (Ed.), *Talking Shop: Authentic Conversation and Teacher Learning* (pp. 1–15). New York: Teachers College Press.

Clark, C., Moss, P. A., Goering, S., Herter, R. J., Lamar, B., Leonard, D., Robbins, S., Russell, M., Templin, M., & Wascha, K. (1996). Collaboration as dialogue: Teachers and researchers engaged in conversation and professional development. *American Educational Research Journal, 33*(1), 193–231.

Clement, M., & Vandenberghe, R. (2001). How school leaders can promote teachers' professional development: An account from the field. *School Leadership and Management, 21*(1), 43–57.

Cochran-Smith, M. (2003). Learning and unlearning: The education of teacher educators. *Teaching and Teacher Education, 19*(1), 5–23.

Cochran-Smith, M., & Lytle, S. L. (1999). Relationships of knowledge and practice: Teacher learning in communities. *Review of Research in Education, 24*, 249–305.

Cochran-Smith, M., & Lytle, S. (2004). Practitioner inquiry, knowledge, and university culture. In J. Loughran, M. L. Hamilton, V. LaBoskey, & T. Russell (Eds.), *International handbook of research of self-study of teaching and teacher education practices*. Amsterdam: Kluwer Academic Publishers.

Cochran-Smith, M., & Zeichner, K. (Eds.). (2005). *Studying teacher education: The report of the AERA panel on research and teacher education*. Mahwah, NJ: Lawrence Erlbaum Publishers.

Cole, A., & Knowles, G. (2000). *Researching teaching: Exploring teacher development through reflexive inquiry*. Boston: Allyn & Bacon.

Connelly, F. M., & Clandinin, D. J. (1990). Stories of experience and narrative inquiry. *Educational Researcher, 19*(5), 2–14.

Croasmun, J., Hampton, D., & Herrmann, S. (1997). Teacher attrition: Is time running out? http://horizon.unc.edu/projects/issues/papers/Hampton.asp.

Darling-Hammond, L. (1998). Teacher learning that supports student learning. *Educational Leadership, 55*(5), 1–8.

Darling-Hammond, L. (2005). Teaching as a profession: International lessons in teacher preparation and professional development. *Phi Delta Kappan, 87*(3), 237–240.

Darling-Hammond, L., & Ball, D. L. (1997). Teaching for high standards: What policymakers need to know and be able to do. National Educational Goals Panel. Available at http://www.negp.gov/Reports/highstds.htm.

Darling-Hammond, L., & McLaughlin, M. W. (1999). Investing in teaching as a learning profession: Policy problems and prospects. In L. S. Darling-Hammond & G. Sykes (Eds.), *Teaching as the learning profession: Handbook of policy and practice* (pp. 376–411). San Francisco: Jossey-Bass.

Darling-Hammond, L., & Sykes, G. (Eds.). (1999). *Teaching as the learning profession: Handbook of practice and policy*. San Francisco: Jossey-Bass.

Desforges, C. (1995). How does experience affect theoretical knowledge for teaching? *Learning and Instruction, 5*(4), 385–400.

Dewey, J. (1916). *Democracy and education*. New York: MacMillan.

Dewey, J. (1927). *The public and its problems*. New York: Holt.

Dewey, J. (1938). *Experience and education*. New York: Collier MacMillan.

Elbaz, F. (1991). Research on teacher's knowledge: The evolution of a discourse. *Journal of Curriculum Studies, 23*(1), 1–19.

Elmore, R. (1996). Getting to scale with good educational practice. *Harvard Educational Review, 66*(1), 1–26.

Elmore, R., & Burney, D. (1999). Investing in teacher learning: Staff development and instructional improvement. In L. S. Darling-Hammond & G. Sykes (Eds.), *Teaching as the learning profession: Handbook of policy and practice* (pp. 263–291). San Francisco: Jossey Bass.

Fiszer, E. P. (2004). *How teachers learn best: An ongoing professional development model*. Toronto: Scarecrow Education.

Flecknoe, M. (2000). Can continuing professional development for teachers be shown to raise pupils' achievement? *Journal of In-Service Education, 26*(3), 437–457.

Florio-Ruane, S. (2001). *Teacher education and the cultural imagination: Autobiography, conversation, and narrative*. Mahwah, NJ: Lawrence Erlbaum.

Fox, D., & Fleisher, C. (2001). Editorial: The power of teacher inquiry: Toward meaningful professional development and educational reform. *English Education, 33*(3), 187–189.

Franke, M. (2005). Professional development for all teachers: Achieving educational excellence and equity in the era of accountability. Paper presented at the American Educational Research Association Annual Meeting. Montreal, PQ.

Fullan, M. (2001). *The New Meaning of Educational Change* (3rd ed.). New York: Teachers College Press.

Gold, Y. (1996). Beginning teacher support: Attrition, mentoring, and induction. In J. Sikula (Ed.), *Handbook of research on teacher education* (2nd ed., pp. 548–594). New York: Simon & Schuster Macmillan.

Gordon, S. (2004). *Professional development for school improvement.* Toronto: Pearson Education.

Greenleaf, C., & Katz, M. (2004). Ever newer ways to mean: Authoring pedagogical change in secondary subject area classrooms. In A. F. Ball & S. W. Freedman (Eds.), *Bakhtinian perspectives on language, literacy, and learning* (pp. 172–202). Cambridge: Cambridge University Press.

Greeno, J., Collins, A., & Resnick, L. (1996). Cognition and learning. In D. Berliner & R. Calfee (Eds.), *Handbook of Educational Psychology* (pp. 15–46). New York: MacMillan.

Grimshaw, A. (1989). *Collegial discourse: Professional conversation among peers.* Norwood, NJ: Ablex.

Grossman, P., Wineburg, S., & Woolworth, S. (2001). Toward a theory of teacher community. *Teachers College Record, 103*(6), 942–1012.

Grossman, P., Wineburg, S., & Woolworth, S. (2000a). What makes a teacher community different from a gathering of teachers? An occasional paper. Center for the Study of Teaching and Policy and Center on English Learning and Achievement. Seattle: University of Washington, 64 pages.

Grossman, P., Wineburg, S., & Woolworth, S. (2000b). In pursuit of teacher community. *American Educational Research Association Annual Meeting*, New Orleans, LA.

Grumet, M. (1991). Lost places, potential spaces and possible worlds: Why we read books with other people. *Margins, 1*(1), 35–53.

Hawley, W., & Valli, L. (1999). The essentials of effective professional development: A new consensus. In G. Sykes & L. Darling-Hammond (Eds.), *Handbook of Teaching and Policy* (pp. 127–150). New York: Teachers College.

Hindin, A., Morocco, C., Mott, E., & Aguilar, C. (2007). More than just a group. *Teacher and Teaching: Theory and practice, 13*(4), 349–376.

Hollingsworth, S., & Sockett, H. (1994). Positioning teacher researcher research in educational reform: An introduction. In S. Hollingsworth & H. Socket (Eds.), *Teacher research and educational reform: Ninety-third National Study of School Evaluation yearbook.* Chicago: University of Chicago Press.

Hord, S. (Ed.). (2004). *Learning together: Leading together.* New York & Oxford, Ohio: Teachers College Press & National Staff Development Council.

Kooy, M. (2006a). The "telling" stories of novice teachers: Constructing teacher knowledge in book clubs. *Teaching and Teacher Education, 22*(6), 661–674.

Kooy, M. (2006b). *Telling stories in book clubs: Women teachers and professional development.* New York: Springer.

Kremer-Hayon, L. (1987). Women teachers' professional development: General and personal perspectives. *Educational Review, 39*(1), 3–13.

Lave, J., & Wenger, E. (1991). *Situated learning: Legitimate peripheral participation.* Cambridge: Cambridge University Press.

Lieberman, A. (2000). Networks as learning communities. *Journal of Teacher Education, 51*(3), 221–227.

Lieberman, A., & Miller, L. (1999). *Teachers transforming their world and their work.* New York & Alexandria, VA: Teachers College Press & Association for Supervision and Curriculum Development.

Lieberman, A., & Miller, L. (2001). *Teachers caught in the action: Professional development that matters.* New York: Teachers College Press.

Long, E. (2003). *Book clubs: Women and the uses of reading in everyday life.* Chicago: University of Chicago Press.

Marshall, J., Smagorinsky, P., & Smith, M. (1995). *The language of interpretation: Patterns of discourse in discussions of literature.* Urbana, IL: National Council of Teachers of English.

Mason, L. (2003). Personal epistemologies and intentional conceptual change. In G. Sinatra & P. Pintrich (Eds.), *Intentional conceptual change* (pp. 199–237). Mahwah, NJ: Lawrence Erlbaum.

McIntyre, J. (1998). *Personal and professional renewal: Exploring relational learning among consultants within a group context.* Unpublished doctoral dissertation, University of Toronto.

McLaughlin, M., & Talbert, J. (2006). *Building school-based teacher learning communities: Strategies to improve student achievement.* New York: Teachers College Press.

McMahon, S., & Raphael, T. (1997). *The book club connection: Literacy, learning and classroom talk.* Newark, DE: International Reading Association.

Miller, J. (1990). *Creating spaces and finding voices: Teachers collaborating for empowerment.* New York: State University of New York.

Moon, B., Butcher, J., & Bird, E. (Eds.). (2000). *Leading professional development in education.* London: Routledge/Falmer.

National Writing Project. Retrieved February 7, 2008, from http://www.nwp.org/cs/public/print/doc/about.csp.

Nystrand, M. (1997). *Opening dialogue: Understanding the dynamics of language and learning in the English classroom.* NY: Teachers College Press.

O'Donnell-Allen, C. (2001). Teaching with a questioning mind: The development of a teacher research group into a discourse community. *Research in the Teaching of English, 36*(2), 161–211.

Orland-Barak, L., & Tillema, H. (2006). The "dark side of the moon": A critical look at teacher knowledge constructed in collaborative settings. *Teachers and Teaching: Theory and Practice, 12*(1), 1–12.

Putnam, R., & Borko, H. (2000). What do new views of knowledge and thinking have to say about research on teacher learning? *Educational Researcher, 29*(1), 4–15.

Ritchie, J., & Wilson, D. (2000). *Teacher narrative as critical inquiry: Rewriting the script.* New York: Teachers College Press.

Rogoff, B. (1994). Developing understanding of the idea of the community of learners. *Mind, Culture and Activity, 1*(4), 209–229.

Rogoff, B., Matusov, E., & White, C. (1996). Models of teaching and learning: Participation in a community of learners. In D. Olson & N. Torrance (Eds.), *The handbook of education and human development* (pp. 388–414). Oxford, UK: Blackwell.

Rommetveit, R. (1992). Outlines of a dialogically based social-cognitive approach to human cognition and communication. In A. H. Wold (Ed.), *The dialogical alternative: Towards a theory of language and mind* (pp. 19–44). Oslo: Scandinavian Univ. Press.

Rust, F., & Orland, L. (2001). Learning the discourse of teaching: Conversation as professional development. In C. Clark (Ed.), *Shop talk: Authentic conversation and teacher learning* (pp. 82–117). New York: Teachers College Press.

Sarason, S. (1990). *The predictable failure of educational reform.* San Francisco: Jossey-Bass.

Stein, M., & Brown, C. (1997). Teacher learning in a social context: Integrating collaborative and institutional processes with the study of teacher change. In E. Fennema & B. Nelson (Eds.), *Mathematics teachers in transition* (pp. 155–191). Mahwah, NJ: Lawrence Erlbaum.

Sykes, G. (1996). Reform of and as professional development. *Phi Delta Kappan, 77*(7), 464–467.

Van Zoest, L., & Bohl, J. (2002). The role of reform curricular material in an internship: The case of Alice and Gregory. *Journal of Mathematics Teacher Education, 5*(3), 265–288.

Vygotsky, L. S. (1978). *Mind and society: The development of higher psychological processes.* Cambridge, MA: Harvard University Press.

Vygotsky, L. (1992). *Thought and language.* Cambridge: The Massachusetts Institute of Technology Press.

Zellermayer, M. (2001). Resistance as a catalyst in teachers' professional development. In C. Clark (Ed.), *Talking shop: Authentic conversation and teacher learning* (pp. 40–63). New York: Teachers College Press.

CHAPTER 2

Constructing Practice through Conversation in Professional Learning Groups

VARIATIONS ON A THEME

Lily Orland-Barak
University of Haifa, Israel

Lily Orland-Barak, Ph.D., is senior lecturer and head of the Department of Learning, Instruction and Teacher Education at the Faculty of Education in the University of Haifa, Israel. Her main research interests are in the area of mentoring and mentored learning, second-language teacher education, and curriculum development. She has led curricular innovations and reforms in the area of mentoring and EFL, and is presently involved in the design and implementation of educational reforms in these two areas both at the national and international levels.

ABSTRACT

In response to global educational reforms toward privatization, high-stakes accountability of processes, and outcomes and standardization, professional conversation frameworks for teacher learning in Israel are gradually being recognized as particularly valuable means for enhancing and sustaining a motivated professional community that can withstand these pressures and challenges. Describing three contrastive cases that range from close to more open frameworks of professional conversation, I argue that, despite differences in structure, process, and outcomes, practices of professional conversation in Israel share "variations on a theme." Grounded in social learning theory, they portray a feminist narrative to communities of practice, one that surfaces ideologies of diversity, embodied knowledge, and attends to the influence of structures of power. Such a narrative operates as a social–professional backbone to assist participants in

23

managing the external standardized outcomes-narrative to which they must respond in their work.

Introduction and Purpose

Influenced by global educational reforms toward privatization and high-stakes accountability of processes and outcomes, national educational policy in Israel has, over the past few decades, moved toward decentralization along with the standardization of the assessment of curriculum, teaching, learning, and, most recently, teacher education programs. Paradoxically, or rather in response to the above controlling shifts, professional conversation frameworks for teacher learning are gradually being recognized as particularly valuable means for enhancing and sustaining a motivated professional community that can stand up to these pressures and challenges. Mostly, they are viewed as relevant and authentic spaces for participants to critically, collaboratively, and supportively examine their roles and practices as shaped by accountability systems and often competing political agendas of educational reforms (Orland-Barak, 2005a).

Drawing on three contrastive cases of professional conversation groups in the context of graduate and in-service teacher education programs in Israel, I describe how they distinguish in terms of content, design, processes, and expected outcomes. I argue that, despite these differences, practices of professional conversation in Israel are characterized by, as the title of this paper suggests, "variations on a theme." Grounded in social learning theory, they portray a feminist narrative to communities of practice (Griffiths, 1995)—one that imbues ideologies of diversity, values embodied knowledge, and attends to the influence of structures of power. Such a narrative operates as a social–professional backbone to assist participants in managing the external standardized outcomes-narrative to which they must respond in their work.

Professional Learning in Conversation: Situating the Local Practice

Parallel to the surge of accountability measures to control growing decentralizing policies, there is a strong call in the Israeli educational system for advancing the academization of the teaching profession, creating possibilities for advancement within the teaching domain. This has resulted in the design of various academic programs (some of which are partly funded by the Ministry of Education) geared to formally accrediting schoolteachers, principals, coordinators, mentors, and curriculum developers who hold various pedagogical and leadership roles. These programs, instituted in academic settings, align with applied science, instructional orientations to professional learning, or they align with more constructivist, reflective, and collaborative approaches (Carr & Kemmis, 1986).

Programs that identify with the former stress a commonsense view of professional development, one that foregrounds the skillful use of pedagogical knowledge and technical skills for applying theoretical principles to educational situations (Carr & Kemmis, 1986). Professional competence in these frameworks is, thus, evaluated by the professional's effectiveness in achieving certain prescribed goals, namely functioning effectively in leading interventions to assist teachers to raise pupils' achievements. This more instrumental view of professional learning in Israel is rooted in a growing discontent with pupils' low achievements in certain school areas, despite the large budgets invested in in-service programs.

By contrast, programs that identify with constructivist, collaborative approaches emphasize the development of the teacher as professional and follow a personal growth, developmental agenda to professional learning. Rooted in sociocultural theories of professional learning, they suggest a view of knowledge development as socially constructed, rooted in activity and conversation, and embodied in social and cultural practices (Bereiter, 2002; Craig, 2007; Wenger, 1998). Such an orientation to professional learning as a social, communicative act reflects an understanding of the need to attend to the conflicts and dilemmas intrinsic in the multiple functions, accountabilities, and isolation that shape the character of leadership roles in the Israeli educational system (Orland-Barak, 2005b). The frameworks of professional learning in conversation discussed in this chapter align with this latter orientation.

Professional Learning in Conversation: Theoretical Situating

In recent years there has been a focus on community settings as fostering teacher development. This line of work draws on Wenger's notion of "communities of practice" (Wenger, 1998) and its application to diverse situations, such as classroom communities, communities of teachers focused on disciplinary learning, the professional development of teachers, and mentoring processes (e.g., Clark, 2001; Craig, 2007; Little & Horn, 2007; Zellermayer & Munthe, 2007).

In fostering collegiality and professional communication among teachers, the presence of a collaborative group in which positions can be argued and clarified and work can be shared, has proven critical to professional growth and to prospects for educational change (Little & Horn, 2007). The examination of practices, purposes, and values by educators has particular value in linking theory and practice and supporting professional development (Cochran-Smith & Lytle, 1999; Elbaz-Luwisch & Kalekin-Fishman, 2004).

The dialogic view of learning underlying the above contexts is represented in the ideas of Vygotsky (1962, 1978) and Wertsch (1998), whereby individual learning is considered to be mediated by social discourse. Professional conversation, thus, speaks to an orientation to learning as created in dialogue and of utterances as dialogically constituted as people enter into conversation with one another (Bakhtin, 1981) creating a professional discourse of practice. Of a sociocultural constitution, such a discourse embeds the acts, values, ideologies, beliefs, identities, and local and professional languages that shape participants' professional identity and conceptions of their practice (Gee, 1992; Marsh, 2002; Freeman, 1993).

INQUIRY INTO PROFESSIONAL CONVERSATION

For the past two decades the scholarship of teacher learning has advocated the potential of collaborative dialogic-oriented models for engaging teachers in the sharing and co-construction of knowledge through "serious talk" (Feldman, 1999)—whereby participants bring forward, share, and seek new knowledge that can lead to new understandings. Recently there has been a growing interest in gathering data on how teacher conversations support and stimulate development of higher order reasoning and increase knowledge-building in the profession.

Research programs have focused on how teachers articulate and learn from their own experiences through conversation and storytelling (Noddings, 1991; Florio-Ruane, 1991); how participants develop new ideas (Pfeiffer, Featherstone, & Smith, 1993); how voice, knowledge, and action operate in the discourse of conversational groups (Bailey, 1996); and how talk, power relations, and cross-cultural factors operate to sustain teacher conversations (Little & Horn, 2007). Engeström (1994) posits the notion of situated understanding at the workplace as mediated by conversation, collaboration, and identification of problems in current practices, all of which create "shared objects of activity." Recently, there is a growing tendency to focus on how shared knowledge construction is viewed by participants and how participants' beliefs on the nature of professional knowledge influence their evaluations of such collective rethinking in their practice (e.g., Lewis & Ketter, 2002; Tillema & Orland-Barak, 2006; Zellermayer & Munthe, 2007).

Recent feminist perspectives to social learning in communities of practice extend the above agendas of inquiry on to professional conversation, to attend to embodied relationships, to issues of diversity, and to the sociopolitical structures of power that play out in the "here and now" of communities of practice (Greene & Griffiths, 2003; Griffiths, 1995). In this extended view, participants engage in dynamic embodied relations that are of a personal, professional, and political character and operate in a particular time and place.

Attending to issues of diversity within feminist perspectives would speak to issues of belonging and becoming, and to the contradictions and the difficulties that one finds in being part of a practice and becoming someone identified with it (Griffiths, 1995). Sociopolitical structures of power within feminist perspectives attend to the power relations and the power structures that constrain who may belong in any social sphere. Attending to these constraints would imply operating against the assumption that practices are neutral (an assumption that, according to feminists, marks masculinity).

PROFESSIONAL LEARNING IN CONVERSATION: LOCAL PROFILES OF "TALK"

The various forms of professional conversation practices in Israel can be positioned within the above sociocultural perspectives to communities of learning in dialogue. These range from more controlled frameworks (which I will refer to as talking "close") to more open ones (talking "open"). Degrees of control and openness (as illustrated in Table 2.1) would vary in terms of structure, process, and outcomes (e.g., topic, tasks, assessment, duties, expectations, composite of participants, facilitative roles, and boundaries of talk and text).

Let us now focus on three illustrative cases. Each case depicts a professional conversation framework at the close, open, or semi-close/open end of the continuum. To facilitate comparison across contexts, I present the three practices in relation to the above mentioned dimensions of structure, process, and outcomes in Table 2.2.

Taken together, as I elaborate in subsequent sections, the diverse range of dialogic frameworks, whether of a more close or open nature, reflect a strong feminist narrative to professional conversation. Such a narrative, which attends to issues of diversity, embodiment, and structures of power, functioned to assist participants in voicing dilemmas and controversies brought about by the external standardized outcomes-narrative to which they must be accountable in their work.

CASE ONE: TALKING "CLOSE"

As can be seen from Table 2.1, the graduate conversation course that was closer to the talking "close" end of the continuum was characterized by a set structure

Table 2.1   Degrees of Control and Openness in Professional Conversations

Talking "Close"	Talking "Open"
Structure	
Formal courses	Informal gatherings
Course professor as mediator/mentor	Participants mediate each other
Fixed texts (articles, cases)	Texts as oral incidents/stories
Homogeneous audience:	Heterogeneous audience:
Subject-matter specific	General, interdisciplinary
Women educators	Men and women
Experts or novices	Novices and experts
Monocultural	Multicultural
Process	
Talk focused on integrating theory and practice	Talk grounded in "here and now" practice
Task-oriented talk	No predetermined task
Talk on professional issues	Talk on personal and professional
Talk around defined topics	Talk as emergent
Outcomes	
Specific learning outcomes	No predetermined outcomes
Knowledge construction made public	Knowledge construction as private

and format for the conversation session, at a given set time, place, within a formal assessed course. Participants were all mentors of teachers, yet the group was heterogeneous in terms of ethnic backgrounds (both from the Jewish and Arab sectors), disciplinary backgrounds, expertise, and gender. Participation was compulsory, so commitment, duties, and expectations were set in advance through the course outline. The mentor of the conversation group was the course professor, who determined the syllabus and mediated the discussions. She was also the final assessor of the course. The conversation group was task-oriented, and the types of texts brought to the conversation floor were decided upon by the course professor. There were expected learning outcomes set by the course syllabus, which were made public through the publication of the papers in a professional journal.

Issues of Diversity, Identity, and Power in Talking "Close"

Inquiry into the content of the course as a platform for co-constructing knowledge revealed that despite its rigid structure, process, and outcomes, participants' talk revolved around issues of diversity, of professional and personal identities, and of the power and control of external agendas exerted over the work of the

Table 2.2   Practices of Professional Conversation: Forms of Talk as Related to Structure, Process, and Outcomes

	Structure	Process	Outcomes
Talking "close"			
Graduate academic M.A. track on mentoring.	Case-based pedagogy course.	Conversations around connections between theoretical ideas and local practices.	Set in advance by the course syllabus. Cases made public through their publication in a professional journal.
Formal certificate of qualification in addition to the general master's degree.	Selected articles by course professor in mentoring.	Discussions on connections between the research literature on mentoring and the context of mentors' practice.	
	Participants discuss their practices and present them to the group.	To illustrate the genre of case writing, two published cases are analyzed and discussed during the sessions.	
Talking "open"			
Ministry of Education professional development in-service program.	Starting point from participants' expressed need to meet regularly in the company of the project leader and an academic researcher and facilitator.	Topic of each session left open to encourage the mentors to freely voice dilemmas and stories from the field, and to collaboratively reflect on their roles as mentors and as teachers.	Participants' expressed sense of professional development. Awareness of dualities and accountabilities in the passage from teacher to mentor.

Table 2.2   (Continued)

	Structure	Process	Outcomes
Ongoing support of in-service mentors by teachers from different disciplinary backgrounds and levels of expertise.			Pedagogical insights and management of dilemmas in mentoring. Awareness of differences across mentoring contexts.

Talking ''open-close''

| Structured course is not part of a formal academic track. Accreditation of mentors with a formal certificate granted by the Ministry of Education. | Two-year course designed around a major conversational component interspersed with guest lecturers on different topics on mentoring. Mentors asked to present cases of their professional histories as mentors to the group. | During their presentations, they are encouraged to employ various mentoring strategies to present their professional histories. The conversations following the presentations focus on the strategies that mentors use to activate the group based on the content of their professional histories. | Written professional histories submitted at the end of the course around passages, critical people, and phases and events that mentors attribute to their professional development. The format of the stories is left open and unstructured. |
| Mentors of teachers from different disciplinary backgrounds with at least three years of expertise. | Professional and research literature less stressed. | | |

mentor (Orland-Barak, 2002). Mentors spoke about concerns over issues of accountability and boundaries of roles in their practice, bringing forth the image of the mentor as "juggling" in different contexts of practice, while trying to comply with conflicting messages in terms of how to behave, what to say, and how to intervene. The conversations fore grounded the strong sense of vulnerability that mentors often experience in their work by being constantly called upon to mediate between their personal understandings and the external requirements of the job (Orland-Barak, 2002).

Participants also voiced issues of professional identity as related to how their beliefs and practices as teachers of children played out in their mentoring interactions, and how the social, political, and organizational "forces" that played out in the context of their work actually shaped and dictated their mode of intervention. The mentors striving to distinguish their practice as mentors from their practice as teachers during the sessions were strongly reflective of their struggle with issues of boundaries of roles and professional identities.

Thus, the university teacher education course, although representing a course at the more controlled end of the conversation continuum, constituted a valuable context for voicing dilemmas inherent in their field experiences that are often silenced by the system. Paradoxically, it seems that the lifting of these voices could be attributed to the close academic character of the course, which "demanded" from participants to exhibit a critical stance toward the narratives of their field experiences as a criterion for assessment at the end of the course. Thus, the fact that they were given a grade based on the depth of their reflections and on the genuineness and elaboration of their dilemmas encouraged them, in their words, to "think deeper" and to generate confrontation, disagreement, and challenge during the sessions. As they commented, they knew they were going to be evaluated not on the basis of a right or wrong action but on the questions, controversies, and disagreements that their cases triggered on the conversational floor. Furthermore, being "constrained" to convey their stories within the boundaries of a case and within the time limitations of the course session eventually compelled the mentors to elaborate on a thought-provoking and controversial argument that would trigger critical discussion around issues of identity, power relations, and diversity. The heterogeneous composite of the participants from different content areas, backgrounds, and levels of expertise positioned the conversation, in this sense, at a more open end of the continuum, enhancing a feminist narrative around issues of diversity.

CASE TWO: TALKING "OPEN"

We now turn our attention to a contrastive professional conversation case at the "talking open" end of the continuum: a professional course, cosponsored by the

Ministry of Education and the Faculty of Education at a major university, designed to provide ongoing support to mentors of novices. The focal group, in-service mentors of teachers from different disciplinary backgrounds and levels of expertise, had expressed their enthusiasm and readiness to meet regularly, once a month in the company of the project leader and an academic researcher and facilitator. Thus, the content of each session was left open, allowing participants to freely raise any dilemmas and stories from the field as a starting point for the conversations.

Issues of Identity and Power in Talking "Open"

Inquiry into the forms and meanings that the professional conversations took in this open framework (Orland-Barak, 2005a) revealed that talk revolved around specific problems and possible strategies for managing them through critical examination of how these might differ across contexts and, in turn, affect their perception of roles and their professional identities as mentors. The different dialogues that emerged during the conversations depicted more "internally persuasive discourses" (Bakhtin, 1981), privileging independent thoughts and experimentation and scrutiny of experience. In the process, participants engaged in more critical representations of their practice as related to the power exerted by the "authoritative discourses" that dictated their daily practice as mentors. As with the previous case, participants discussed struggles with accountability to the mentee, to the project's agenda, or to people involved directly with the mentee at school. Specifically, they voiced a strong moral obligation toward the mentee's well-being, which often led them to intervene in prescriptive ways that they perceived as incongruent with the reflective, non-prescriptive agenda of the mentoring project to which they were accountable.

CASE THREE: TALKING "CLOSE" AND "OPEN"

This case portrays an "in between" case of a structured course (similar to the first case) but which, by contrast to the first course, was not part of a formal academic track toward a master's certificate, although it accredited mentors with a formal certificate. Similarly to the previous courses, the two-year course was designed around a major conversational component, interspersed by guest lecturers on different aspects of the practice of mentoring. As a requirement for the course, mentors were encouraged to write their professional stories on the passage from being a teacher to becoming a mentor, focusing on events, critical persons, and events that shaped mentors' professional development. By contrast to the first case, the format of the stories was left open and unstructured. The conversations following the presentations focused both on the process (i.e., the strategies that mentors used for activating the group) and on the content of their professional histories and cases.

Issues of Power in Talking "Close" and "Open"

The conversations around the stories surfaced issues of power as related to the critical role that the school principal plays in the mentor's success or failure to function as agent of change in the school. A predominant recurrent theme in the stories was the complex nature of the relationship between the mentor and the school principal, especially in regard to the dilemmas that emerge between being "loyal" to the schoolteachers on the one hand and accountable to the school principal on the other hand. Learning to work through these dilemmas was seen as a major condition for developing a professional identity as mentors.

Variations on a Theme: Professional Conversation as Inherently Feminist

Although different in degrees of openness and closeness of structure, process, and outcomes, the content of the conversations in three illustrative cases surface variations on a prevalent "feminist theme"—one that attends to issues of diversity, to relational aspects of knowledge construction and identity, and to the influences of structures of power and dominant authoritative discourses.

PROFESSIONAL CONVERSATION AS A RELATIONAL PRACTICE

Professional conversation in community of practice in Israel, whether of a more controlled or open nature, is relational. As such, it is marked by embodiment and by dynamic and permeable boundaries that allow for articulating the various identities constituted in participants' work such as being a teacher, a mentor, and a parent. These multiple identities depict the various discourses to which participants see themselves belonging and that "need not, and often do not, represent consistent and compatible values" (Gee, 1992, p. xix). The relational and fluid character of the conversations yielded a shared discourse of practice (Freeman, 1993) characterized by accountability and boundaries of roles inherent in the various conflictive "identity kits" that mentors carry (Gee, 1992, p. 142).

PROFESSIONAL CONVERSATION AS A PRACTICE
OF DIVERSITY

Professional conversation in the Israeli context is also strongly marked by diversity, reflective in the active engagement of participants from different cultures and practices in the same conversation floor. Such diversity allows for a range of views to develop and comfortably coexist within the external constraints of the practice. In this shared conversational floor, participants welcomed opportunities to engage in professional conversations with other professionals who did not necessarily share the same content area of specialization. The learning value intrinsic in discovering similarities and shared concerns, despite the diverse disciplinary affiliations of participants, reinforces the design of professional conversations around interdisciplinary aspects of the practice. In this sense, diversity constituted an important condition for the participants to examine the constraints and permutations of their own mentoring contexts, as compared to other participants in the group. For example, in the Arab sectors, mentors voiced a less conflictive position in regard to the place of their own voice within the system than did mentors in the Jewish sector. This was attributed to the hierarchical and more traditional structure of the educational system in the former, whereby boundaries of roles are more clearly defined. Furthermore, mentors in the Arab sector shared their frustration in regard to the less encouraging prospects in the Arab educational system to foster change and, consequently, to the limited feasibility of their mandate as agents of change.

The diverse interdisciplinary composite of the participants in the various groups helped to learn about other mentoring practices and to become aware that the practice of mentoring is shaped by similar conflicts and dilemmas across institutional and cultural contexts, and subject areas. Thus, the diversity of the group in terms of content areas, backgrounds, and levels of expertise was perceived as an asset to the participants' learning. Diversity allowed for a less hierarchical space to develop, one that did not compromise the idiosyncratic identity of its members.

PROFESSIONAL CONVERSATION AS POLITICAL

A feminist perspective to professional conversation perceives communities of practice as reproducing, to a great extent, the power relations that exist outside the community. One might expect then, that by virtue of their diversity, the professional conversations would somehow replicate similar power relations that are manifested in the larger social and professional contexts of participants. Yet, as mentioned earlier, talk was characterized by a symmetrical discourse amongst participants which, in turn, prompted them to engage in shared scrutiny of their practices as influenced by external structural power relations. Thus, the conversations can be described as political in the sense of *talk about* power (rather than of reproducing external power relations into the community). Participants surfaced a strong sense of vulnerability in their work, which had "political and moral roots . . . linked to matters of interest and values . . . [as participants] . . . find themselves permanently forced to make decisions with moral consequences in their dealing with the multiple, diffuse, and even contradictory demands by their different clients [teachers, principals, and inspectors] . . ." (Kelchtermans, 1996, pp. 307–314). Caught in these contradictory messages, the mentors' stories (both in the Jewish and Arab sectors) revealed that their choice for complying with one voice over another was often determined by their need to be professionally recognized by the system, rather than by their personal moral, ethical, or pedagogical stance on the issue. These choices can be described as a form of politics of identity, a struggle between recognition by others and self-recognition (Calhoun, 1994, p. 20).

What accounts for professional conversations in the Israeli context as being variations on an inherently feminist theme? I offer several interpretations.

A Feminist Response to an Educational Context of Contrived Collegiality

Understanding the predominance of a feminist orientation to professional conversations turns our attention to views of social learning in community as interpreted against their historical, social, cultural, and institutional conditions, resources, and constraints of the practice (Wenger, 1998, p. 79). Taken to our context, and regardless of whether the professional conversations emphasized "process" or "product," they all operated *as a response* to the larger institutional context of "contrived collegiality" (Hargreaves & Dawe, 1990). In such a context, practitioners are "required" to engage in a kind of "collaborative culture of learning." Furthermore, inspectors and project leaders are the ones who appoint mentors and agents of reform, defining their roles, their mandate, and their degree of accountability to the system. Thus, even when considering the more open end of the continuum (e.g., talking "open" groups), the environment was contrived to foster collegiality, closer to what Grimmett and Grehan (1992) would describe as "an organizationally induced type of contrived collegiality." This "induced type of contrived collegiality" along with the "demand" to adopt a critical stance toward practice yielded a discourse of practice that functioned as a kind of rescue board to survive and voice the pressures of outside expectations. Thus, the depth and richness of participants' talk was probably enhanced by the infrastructure of engagement that "expected" from them to be controversial and challenging to other members of the group (Rodgers, 2002, p. 857).

An Infrastructure of Engagement: Conversations about What Really Matters among Experts

An additional interpretation to the inherently feminist character of professional conversations, especially at the closer end of the "talking continuum," can be attributed to the infrastructure of engagement that characterized the frameworks (Wenger, 1998). These allowed for ample physical space, mutual access in time and space, and joint tasks, prompting the articulation of a critical stance toward pedagogical and moral dilemmas, role conflicts (Wenger, 1998, p. 237), and collegial relationships in the larger professional community (Little & McLaughlin, 1993, p. 6). Thus, the infrastructure of engagement allowed practitioners to use the conversation space to talk about "what really matters to them as professionals" (Tillema & Orland-Barak, 2006)—in our case—issues of a feminist conversational character pertaining to dilemmas and conflicts around diversity, identity, and power. This sustained, progressive, feminist discourse constituted a kind of distributed knowledge construction process (Bereiter, 2002), to arrive at situational understandings of participants' practice.

The predominance of talk around identity, power, and diversity over instrumental problem-solving talk may also be related to the fact that the infrastructure of engagement was comprised mostly of experienced practitioners who had taken upon themselves additional roles in the educational system. As characteristics of experts, and in trying to make sense of new role passages, they were open to ideas advanced by others, to critical scrutinizing of their practices, and to pushing and challenging each other. As they shared intents and dilemmas of professional identity in their role passages, they were more open to scrutinizing practice (Tillema, 2005).

Putting It All Together

The nature of talk that emerges from professional conversation groups in Israel uncovers, then, tensions between authoritative and internally persuasive discourses, alongside potential benefits of an infrastructure of contrived collegiality for stimulating a feminist discourse amongst experienced teachers and mentors.

Implications for Teacher Education

The need for safe professional spaces for dialogue, collaboration, documentation of experiences, and for managing conflicts of accountability seems imperative in an educational context where accountability to policy makers and standardization are strongly embedded in the character of the practice. These "safe spaces" allow for conveying less "neat" representations of practice, without fearing that certain ideas might impinge on their professional status in the eyes of the group or of the facilitator.

These illustrative cases suggest that conversation groups are potentially valuable arenas for critically examining instrumental and conceptual aspects of professionals' practice. They also suggest that the content and quality of talk resides less in the use of closer or open frameworks and more in participants' collaborative process of challenging each other to arrive at solutions to specific problems, to develop new ideas, to examine approaches across practices, and to articulate and frame dilemmas of practice.

Experienced teachers, mentors, and project leaders' positive dispositions toward professional conversation frameworks as opportunities for learning suggest their potential for professional development. For the Israeli context, it constitutes a challenging opportunity for developing professionally beyond the immediate, present, instant, and pragmatic action that usually characterizes the practice of teaching (Elbaz, 1983). In this sense, Dewey's notion of possessing an attitude that values the personal and intellectual growth of oneself and of others as central to developing reflective practice (Dewey, 1933) seems particularly apt for the population of these conversational groups.

The illustrative cases presented in this chapter suggest that educational practices within educational systems of accountability and standardization can benefit from contrived collegiality frameworks to advance feminist narratives of practice. These narratives open a window into how global educational reforms play out in the relational, political, and diverse character of local practices.

References

Bailey, F. (1996). The role of collaborative dialogue in teacher education. In D. Freeman & J. G. Richards (Eds.), *Teacher learning in language teaching* (pp. 260–281). New York: Cambridge University Press.

Bakhtin, M. (1981). *The dialogic imagination: Four essays by M. M. Bakhtin* (Trans. M. Holquist & C. Emerson). Austin, TX: University of Texas Press.

Bereiter, C. (2002). *Education and mind in the knowledge society.* Mahwah, NJ: Lawrence Erlbaum Associates.

Calhoun, C. (Ed.). (1994). *Social theory and the politics of identity.* Oxford: Blackwell Publishing. (Cited in Kelchtermans, G. (1996). Teacher vulnerability: Understanding its moral and political roots. *Cambridge Journal of Education, 26*(3), 307–323.).

Carr, W., & Kemmis, S. (1986). *Becoming critical.* London: Deakin University Press.

Clark, M. C. (2001). *Talking shop.* New York: Teachers College Press.

Cochran-Smith, M., & Lytle, S. L. (1999). The teacher research movement: A decade later. *Educational Researcher, 28*(7), 15–25.

Craig, C. (2007). Story constellations: A narrative approach to situating teachers' knowledge of school reform in context. *Teaching and Teacher Education, 23*(2), 173–188.

Dewey, J. (1933). *How we think*. Buffalo, NY: Prometheus Books. (Original work published in 1910).

Elbaz, F. (1983). *Teacher thinking: A study of practical knowledge*. New York: Nichols Publishing Co.

Elbaz-Luwisch, F., & Kalekin-Fishman, D. (2004). Professional development in Israel: fostering multicultural dialogue among Jewish and Arab Israeli teachers. *Journal of Inservice Education, 30*(2), 245–264.

Engeström, Y. (1994). Teachers as collaborative thinkers. In I. Carlgren (Ed.), *Teachers' minds and actions*. London: The Falmer Press.

Feldman, A. (1999, April). *Conversational complexity*. Paper presented at the meeting of the American Educational Research Association Annual Meeting, Montreal, PQ.

Florio-Ruane, S. (1991). Conversation and narrative in collaborative research: An ethnography of the Written Literary Forum. In C. Witherell & N. Noddings (Eds.), *Stories lives tell: Narrative and dialogue in education* (pp. 234–256). New York: Teachers College Press.

Freeman, D. (1993). Renaming experience/reconstructing practice. In D. Freeman & J. G. Richards (Eds.), *Teacher learning in language teaching* (pp. 221–242). New York: Cambridge University Press.

Gee, J. (1992). *The social mind: Language, ideology, and social practice*. New York: Bergin & Carvey.

Greene, M., & Griffiths, M. (2003). Feminism, philosophy, and education: Imagining public spaces. In N. Blake, P. Smeyers, R. Smith, & P. Standish (Eds.), *The Blackwell guide to the philosophy of education*. Oxford: Blackwell Publishing.

Griffiths, M. (1995). *Feminisms and the self: The web of identity*. London: Routledge.

Grimmett, P. P., & Grehan, E. P. (1992). The nature of collegiality in teacher development: The case of clinical supervision. In A. Fullan & A. Hargreaves (Eds.), *Teacher development and educational change* (pp. 56–85). London: Falmer Press.

Hargreaves, A., & Dawe, R. (1990). Paths of professional development: Contrived collegiality, collaborative culture, and the case of peer coaching. *Teaching and Teacher Education, 3*(6), 227–241.

Kelchtermans, G. (1996). Teacher vulnerability: Understanding its moral and political roots. *Cambridge Journal of Education, 26*(3), 307–323.

Lewis, C., & Ketter, J. (April, 2002). *Learning as social interaction: Interdiscursivity in a teacher and researcher study group*. Paper presented at the American Educational Research Association Annual Meeting, New Orleans, LA.

Little, J. W., & Horn, I. S. (2007). "Normalizing" problems of practice: Converting routine conversation into a resource for learning in professional communities. In L. Stoll & K. S. Louis (Eds.), *Professional learning communities: Divergence, detail, and difficulties* (pp. 79–92). Maidenhead, England: Open University Press.

Little, J. W., & McLaughin, M. W. (1993). Perspectives on cultures and contexts of teaching. In J. W. Little & M. W. McLaughin (Eds.), *Teachers' work: Individuals, colleagues, and contexts* (pp. 1–19). New York: Teachers College Press.

Marsh, M. M. (2002). The shaping of Ms. Nicholi: The discursive fashioning of teacher identities. *Qualitative Studies in Education, 15*(3), 333–347.

Noddings, N. (1991). Stories in dialogue: Caring and interpersonal reasoning. In C. Witherell & N. Noddings (Eds.), *Stories lives tell: Narrative and dialogue in education*. New York: Teachers College Press.

Orland-Barak, L. (2002). What's in a case? What mentors' cases reveal about the practice of mentoring. *Journal of Curriculum Studies, 34*(4), 451–468.

Orland-Barak, L. (2005a). Convergent, divergent, and parallel dialogues in mentors' professional conversations. *Teachers and Teaching: Theory and Practice, 12*(1), 13–33.

Orland-Barak, L. (2005b). Lost on translation: Mentors learning to participate in competing discourses of practice. *Journal of Teacher Education, 56*(4), 355–367.

Pfeiffer, L., Featherstone, H., & Smith, S. P. (April, 1993). *"Do you really mean all when you say all?" A close look at the ecology of pushing in talk about mathematics teaching*. National Center for Research on Teacher Learning, Michigan State University.

Rodgers, C. (2002). Defining reflection: Another look at John Dewey and reflective thinking. *Teachers College Record, 104*(4), 842–866.

Tillema, H. H. (2005). Collaborative knowledge construction in study teams of professionals. *Human Resource Development International, 8*(1), 47–65.

Tillema, H. H., & Orland-Barak, L. (2006). Constructing knowledge in professional conversations: The role of beliefs on knowledge and knowing. *Learning & Instruction, 16*(6), 1–17.

Vygotsky, L. S. (1962). *Thought and language*. Cambridge, MA: The MIT Press.

Vygotsky, L. S. (1978). *Mind in society: The development of higher psychological processes*. Cambridge, MA: Harvard University Press.

Wenger, E. (1998). *Communities of practice: Learning, meaning, and identity*. New York: Cambridge University Press.

Wertsch, J. V. (1998). *Mind as action*. New York: Oxford University Press.

Zellermayer, M., & Munthe, E. (2007). *Teachers learning in communities*. Rotterdam: Sense.

CHAPTER 3

What Makes *Some* Learning Communities So Effective, and How Can I Support My Own?

Ellen Ballock
Towson University

> Ellen Ballock, Ph.D., is an assistant professor in the Elementary Education Department at Towson University in Maryland. Her research interests include professional development schools, professional learning communities, and preservice teacher development.

ABSTRACT

Drawing from a review of research and the findings of a multiple case study, this chapter explores several key distinctions between learning communities that are in the beginning stages of collaborative work and those that are well established and highly effective in the areas of professional community, professional learning, and action and accountability. It also points to the potential benefits of engaging in a reflective process of group analysis and goal setting.

Research from recent decades suggests that collaborative learning communities hold promise for school improvement because collaborative actions (e.g., shared work, frequent and precise discussion of teaching practice, and mutual observation and critique) support teachers in changing their teaching practices in order to better address the needs of all their students (Little, 1982; McLaughlin & Talbert, 1993). Research has documented a connection between a learning community's stage of development and student achievement (Wheelan & Tilin, 1999; Wheelan & Kesselring, 2005). However, the task of replacing traditions of isolation, privacy, and competition with habits of collaboration, collective responsibility, and ongoing inquiry can be a challenging enterprise, "a journey, not a destination, a verb rather than a noun" (Grossman, Wineburg, & Woolworth, 2001). Just as the implementation of any reform or innovation can result in varying levels of success, there are some cases in which groups develop into powerful authentic learning communities and other cases where groups function as learning communities in name only.

The purpose of this chapter is to explore the factors that set apart the truly authentic and effective learning communities. It seeks not only to distinguish the highly functioning communities from the less-developed communities, but also to identify the areas in which all learning communities might focus their efforts in order to facilitate group development. More specifically, this chapter focuses on small learning communities commonly known as critical friends groups (CFGs).

CFGs, first initiated in 1994 in 70 participating schools by the Annenburg Institute for School Reform (Olson, 1998; Dunne, Nave, & Lewis, 2000), are now affiliated with the National School Reform Faculty and include tens of thousands of educators in twenty-six states (NSRF, 2007). A CFG is typically composed of six to twelve professionals who make a commitment to meet together regularly to collaboratively inquire into teaching practice. CFG participants include preservice teachers, novice teachers, veteran teachers, administrators, university professors, and any other interested stakeholders. CFG meetings frequently use structured protocols for looking at student work samples or other data, discussing relevant texts, and working through dilemmas of practice (Dunne & Honts, 1998; Dunne, Nave, & Lewis, 2000; Bambino, 2002).

Strong foundational principles and practices guide these learning communities, but there is still variability in the implementation and effectiveness of CFGs (Dunne & Honts, 1998). The following narratives, fictional composites derived from actual CFG cases in the literature, serve to illustrate the attributes and experiences of two different CFGs. The first composite describes a CFG just beginning as a professional community, while the second composite describes a more highly developed and experienced CFG.

Composite 1. CFG members at Middleburg Elementary School are glad they have made the commitment to set aside time to meet together regularly this year. They are developing a new appreciation for their colleagues as they discover that others in their group share similar passions and offer unique insights and expertise. They are also relieved to find out they are not the only ones with questions about their teaching practice. These individuals describe a typical CFG meeting as collaboration focused on problems that arise with students, analysis of successes in their teaching, and discussions of texts through the use of protocols. Intrigued by the difference they see in their conversation when it's structured by a protocol, teachers in these CFGs are eager to try out many other types of protocols to see how they would work. However, they fail to mention that they still feel insecure about putting their own students' work out for others to look at and that their coach frequently ends each meeting by asking, "Would *anyone* be willing to bring work for the group to look at next time?" The coach of this group is trying to balance two important roles. First, she is working on logistics: helping participants to follow the established norms, to stick to the protocols, to discern between clarifying and probing questions, and to distinguish between observations and judgments. Second, she is working to help the group develop a vision for collaborative work. She tries to find texts that will raise questions about teaching and learning to help the group find direction for shared work, and she supports group members in identifying questions within their practice that they might bring to the group for examination.

Composite 2. CFG members at Deer Woods Elementary School describe their work together as a commitment to ongoing professional learning. While some years they have supported each other in their own individual year-long inquiries into teaching practice, other years a shared inquiry drove their collaborative work. To support these inquiries, they read research together, examine student data, consider appropriate standards for student work, and analyze lesson plans, assessments, and units. Deeply internalized norms of respect for one another and much experience in working together have helped them to develop that optimal balance between safety and risk needed for learning. They speak very candidly with one another, asking challenging questions, pressing one another for clarification, and looking for each other's underlying assumptions. They are not afraid to challenge one another. On the other hand, they encourage and support one another in such a way that members feel they can expose even their deepest questions and concerns about their practice without fear of judgment. To maintain their mutual accountability to ongoing learning, this CFG's coach continually challenges the group members to report back to the group the ways they are learning and growing through their inquiries and in what ways this learning is impacting their students. Because the group members have such clearly defined learning goals, they have not found it difficult to document their own learning and that of their students through lesson plans, student work samples, student achievement data, and other artifacts. Though they have grown significantly as a group, the members of this CFG strive never to become complacent or stagnant in their work together. Their coach continually encourages them in monitoring their collaborative work, and as a group they are considering how they might seek further perspective from parents, students, and community members. Since they have learned so much, they are also talking as a group about how they can take action at the district level in order to effect change.

These narratives describe two vastly different CFGs. This chapter will elaborate on the distinctions between the CFGs represented in these composites by examining three facets of CFG growth and development: professional community, professional learning, and action and accountability. Both a review of the CFG literature and the findings of a multiple case study provide a basis for the analysis presented here. The chapter concludes with a list of questions based on this analysis that leaders or members of learning communities might use as reflective prompts for stimulating their own group's development.

Professional Community

Since creating collaborative professional communities was the intent of the CFG design, it is not surprising that a nearly universal research finding is that participation in CFGs leads to deeper levels of professional community and collaboration. For example, Curry (2003) found that CFG participation interrupted the norms of isolation at the high school she studied, creating collegial ties across departments, promoting a shared awareness of the school's reform philosophy, a more schoolwide orientation towards teaching practice, and greater curricular coherence in the school. Similarly, responses to a professional climate survey indicated that CFG teachers collaborate more with each other than non-CFG teachers by sharing ideas and student work samples, meeting to discuss problems, working to develop materials, and seeking advice about professional issues and problems (Dunne, Nave, & Lewis, 2000). If increased community and collaboration is the norm with the introduction of CFGs, then what sets apart the particularly highly functioning group from the rest?

The two composite CFG descriptions illustrate differences in the level of professional community attained in three respects. The first is trust (Wheelan & Hochberger, 1996; Dunne & Honts, 1998; Little, Gearhart, Curry, & Kafka, 2003). The members of the highly developed CFG community at Deer Woods (Composite 2) are willing to be vulnerable with one another and to share their deepest uncertainties about their teaching practices because they have developed deep bonds of trust as they have worked together over time. Trust also allows them to respectfully challenge each other and to give each other honest feedback. In the Middleburg CFG (Composite 1) relationships are beginning to form as members get to know one another in new ways. However, participation is careful, measured, and tentative because members do not yet know whether the sense of safety will last or what might happen if conflict arises.

A second difference between the two groups is commitment (Wheelan & Hochberger, 1996). For members of the Deer Woods CFG, actual evidence from their own teaching practice bolsters their commitment to continued participation. They have seen firsthand how CFG participation helps them to better meet the needs of their students. Members of the most established CFGs often cannot imagine how they ever functioned without it (Neufeld & Woodworth,

2000). In contrast, members of the Middleburg CFG have not worked together long enough to have solid evidence of the benefits of working collaboratively. Their enthusiasm for CFG work often stems from doing something new and different and from an initial affective response experiencing "a breath of fresh air" at meetings.

New CFG participants often describe their group as a safe space, an oasis from the stresses of the profession, a source of affirmation of teaching practice, a support group, an energizer that boosts morale, and a welcome reprieve from the traditionally isolating nature of the teaching profession (Dunne & Honts, 1998; Neufeld & Woodworth, 2000; Yendol-Silva, 2003). This initial affective response could provide powerful inspiration for collaborative work early on, but it is not sufficient to fuel a lasting commitment to collaborative learning. The challenge for this CFG in order to grow in both trust and commitment is to continually delve deeper in truly meaningful activity, that which will result in powerful learning.

Professional Learning

Research examining professional learning within CFGs and how that learning impacts teaching practice and student learning is less conclusive than it is for a CFG's role in promoting professional community. Some participants have named CFGs one of the most powerful professional development activities in which they have ever participated (Dunne & Honts, 1998), and several studies document specific changes in teaching practice to support improved student learning that have resulted from CFG participation (Bernacchio, Ross, Washburn, Whitney, & Wood, 2007; Nave, 2000). On the other hand, Neufeld and Woodworth (2000) describe groups whose meetings were often consumed by administrative details or frittered away with arguments about how to interpret a rubric with little search for the meaning behind the rubric or the student work. Furthermore, Curry (2003) noted a waning interest in CFG participation as group members sensed their participation led to diminished returns in professional growth over time. The questions that arise are: What makes the difference? What factors lead to significant professional learning that can have a profound impact on teaching and student learning? The literature suggests three important factors: time, use of time, and shared purpose.

First, the amount of time CFG members have available to meet together is an important matter influencing possibilities for professional learning. Several authors assert that an administrator's willingness to provide time and space for groups to meet is critical for CFG success (Dunne & Honts, 1998; Dunne, Nave, & Lewis, 2000). Another study contrasted the rich conversations and learning occurring in groups meeting regularly for 60–75 minutes at a time with the lack of depth in conversations where groups met sporadically for 30 minutes or less (Neufeld & Woodworth, 2000).

Although having time to meet is important, how participants use that time is a second crucial consideration. Dunne, Nave, & Lewis (2000) assert that the amount of time a group spends in the rigorous task of analyzing student work is what correlates most strongly with changes in teachers' thinking and practice. A common pitfall for beginning CFGs is putting too much time and focus on trust building or community building activities (Armstrong, 2003; Whitford & Fisher, 2003). The participants in these groups may not realize that the deepest level of trust develops alongside a deepening sense of purpose and meaning while seeking greater insight into students' understanding and using that insight to analyze and plan for instruction.

Finally, the most obvious difference in possibilities for professional learning between the fictional composites described in this chapter is a shared learning purpose (Wheelan & Hochberger, 1996). As with many beginning groups, participants in the Middleburg CFG are caught up in the process of using protocols to structure their conversations. In fact, a common stumbling block for beginning groups is to focus more on trying out a number of different types of protocols or refining their use of the protocols than on the *purpose* of using the protocols to focus their conversation around important questions about teaching and learning (Wood, 2003; Yendol-Silva, 2003). The members of this group have not yet developed a clear sense of shared purpose.

In contrast, participants in the Deer Woods CFG use their collaborative relationships to pursue ongoing inquiries into teaching and learning and use protocols as tools to support those inquiries. Similarly, the characteristic that seems to truly distinguish the most CFGs in the literature is an ongoing inquiry focus or shared goal for student learning. This might be an inquiry into improving student achievement (Yendol-Silva, 2003), an inquiry focus of improving student writing skills (Nave, 2000), or the implementation of a schoolwide literacy reform effort (Neufeld & Woodworth, 2000). In order to pursue these shared inquiries, participants of the highest functioning learning communities have honed their skills in asking meaningful questions about student work and teaching practice in areas connected to the inquiry, accessing relevant outside resources and expertise in order to understand best practice, collecting relevant data, and using the data to make instructional decisions (McLaughlin & Talbert, 2006; Neufeld & Woodworth, 2000).

Action and Accountability

Having a clear plan for professional learning and the skills it takes to pursue that learning is important, but intentionally monitoring progress toward learning goals is the next challenge. A professional learning community must take on a results orientation, assessing its work "on the basis of *results* rather than *intentions*" (Dufour & Eaker, 1998, p. 29). Pursuing learning is not enough. Taking action based on what is learned by analyzing student work and teaching practice and then monitoring the results of those actions is the important next step for learning communities.

It is likely that only the most highly functioning of all CFGs attend to this facet of the work. Only the most highly functioning groups would have a clear enough shared inquiry and well-coordinated efforts for pursuing that inquiry, so it is likely that these are the only groups able to concretely monitor and document the results of their collaboration. This explains why there is no mention of action or accountability in the description of the Middleburg CFG. For the Deer Woods CFG, however, the process of monitoring and documenting learning provides accountability for applying what members are learning and evidence by which they can determine their success.

There is little emphasis presented within the literature to date on action and accountability in CFG work, but a few studies document the importance of this aspect of an effective learning community. The very first cohorts of CFG participants committed not only to meeting regularly as a group, but they also agreed to form peer coaching partnerships for ongoing feedback and support and to develop a portfolio to document their learning and that of their students over a two-year period (Dunne & Honts, 1998; Dunne, Nave, & Lewis, 2000). In this way, accountability was built into the learning community both for the individual participant and for the group as a whole. Participants knew that they were expected to take action on what they were learning as a community. Peer coaching could provide the support they needed to try new instructional approaches, and the portfolio process required that they monitor their own learning and that of their students over time. The portfolios also served as evidence of success for the CFG as a whole. Nave (2000) and Armstrong (2003) each found that the more faithfully a CFG followed this intended program design, the more likely it was to engage in the kind of meaningful reflection and focused work that leads to changes in teacher practice and improved student learning.

Neufeld & Woodworth (2000) also emphasize action and accountability as setting the most advanced groups apart from the others. In these groups, a norm of "reporting back" provides accountability for trying new strategies or instructional practices based on what participants learn in group discussions. This also leads to new questions for the group to explore. Thus, these CFGs engage in a cycle of inquiry and experimentation, monitoring their growth and continuously seeking to improve.

Monitoring CFG Work through Intentional Group Analysis

A multiple case study (Yin, 2003; Creswell, 1998) examining the experiences of three CFGs as they engaged in a process of group analysis and goal setting offers additional perspective on how highly functioning groups might differ from beginning groups in the area of action and accountability. The three cases included two school-based CFGs comprised primarily of teachers and one CFG in which administrators from several school districts met together at one member's home. The members of each CFG had already been working together for a minimum of one year and for as long as four years in one case. During the process of group analysis members of the Case 1 CFG self-identified most often with descriptors of beginning and developing groups, the members of the Case 2 group self-identified with descriptors of both the beginning and the highly functioning group, and the members of the Case 3 CFG self-identified most with the descriptors of a highly functioning group.

The process of group analysis involved three steps. First, participants used descriptors of the three stages of group development based on literature pertaining to CFGs and small-group development to assess the strengths of their CFG and areas in which they would like to grow, ultimately coming to consensus on specific goals to pursue. At a second meeting, they developed an action plan for achieving their goals. Finally, the CFG members checked back in on their goals several months later to consider what kind of progress they had made and what they needed to work on next. Data collection during this study included observations of the CFG meetings, document analysis, an interview with each CFG coach, and a final survey of all participants.

One of the most striking results of this study was the vast difference in response between the Case 1 CFG (self-identifying as beginning/developing) and the Case 3 CFG (self-identifying as highly functioning). First, participants responded very differently to the process. A number of Case 1 participants were quite critical in their response. About half of the participants questioned the value of spending so much time on group analysis and goal setting since it expended time they could have used to discuss their teaching. In contrast, members of the Case 3 CFG expressed the greatest value for the opportunity to participate in this process. First, reflections on their CFG's development during the first meeting were so rich and meaningful that half of the participants suggested that a longer meeting, perhaps even a full day retreat, could have been useful. They did not view this process as being separate from the real purpose of their group, but as integral to their continuing growth, as one participant commented, "I have to say that I don't see this as not being part of our work as a CFG, so that's what made it for me meaningful. . . . So I don't think it was an aside."

Second, participants differed significantly in their response to the descriptors provided. Participants from Case 1 identified with descriptors of the beginning and developing groups, but struggled to find a vision for the possible in the descriptors of the highly functioning group. Several questioned whether their own definitions of a highly functioning group matched the descriptions provided and whether their CFG's specific context and the time they had available would ever allow them to attain the provided descriptions of a highly functioning CFG. On the other hand, group analysis of the Case 3 CFG's development provided a solid grounding for envisioning new possibilities for growth. At the same time, participants suggested that the descriptions of the highly functioning group were not truly indicative of *most* highly functioning, but that they wanted to reach for a challenge beyond that which was described.

Finally, participants in the two cases differed in their follow-through. When the Case 1 participants met for the third meeting in this process, many did not even recognize the goal they had written seven months earlier. In fact, one asked during the meeting, "Did we make that up?" Another commented on the final survey, "[Setting goals] was good at the time, but I've not thought about it since." This lack of follow-through suggests that the group's analysis did little to actually push their work forward. Conversely, the Case 3 CFG has taken the most concrete actions toward meeting their goals. For example, the agenda for their very next meeting reflected their renewed desire to examine student data and to set more concrete learning goals, while plans for taking a CFG weekend retreat are still well underway a year later.

The contrasting experiences of these two CFGs suggest that members of more highly functioning learning communities are more likely to recognize the value of collaboratively reflecting on their group's progress, are more capable of envisioning possibilities greater than their current work, and have a greater capacity for taking action and monitoring progress toward goals.

Pursuing Intentional Group Development

In spite of the stark contrast in response from the members of the two cases described above, data from all three cases suggest that a process of intentional group analysis and goal setting has clear benefits for helping groups to grow in community and professional learning. First, participants from all three cases reported that their discussions helped them to develop more of a common understanding of their work and purpose as a CFG. In fact, the coaches of one CFG felt that one of the most valuable aspects of this process was that all group members had the opportunity to share their perceptions of the group's development and to have a voice in the direction the group should go next. Coming to a mutual understanding of a CFG's purpose and sharing ownership for the group's future directions are important factors in strengthening a CFG as a professional community.

Second, participants from Cases 2 and 3 perceived that this process helped them to narrow their focus and direction. They commented on how the process disrupted each CFG's routine, providing a new vision for the possible, or a clearer direction for their work. A comment by one participant highlights ideas expressed by many: "We became more aware of where we, as a group, may be off track, the direction we want to go, and how we need to reset our group's path in order to reach our goals and deepen the effectiveness of the work we do and the support we provide one another." Another participant stated: "Yes, this is exactly what we need in order to get us excited about this again—to jumpstart what we're doing for this year so we're not in a rut."

Participants were surprised by how this process also enabled them to come up with concrete steps to take toward their goals so that the plan seemed "doable" compared with many of the big, broad ideas they often come up with during meetings. Developing a clearer focus and a "doable" plan are two factors that are likely to lead a group to more effective collaborative work and professional learning. Although following these groups over time would provide deeper insights into the role that group analysis and goal setting might play in facilitating group development, this study provides provisional evidence that this type of intentional reflection is a worthwhile endeavor.

Therefore it is fitting to conclude the paper with prompts for such reflective analysis. The questions provided after this section draw on this chapter's discussion of common obstacles CFGs face in their development in the areas of professional community, professional learning, and action and accountability. This list of questions may support reflection for a CFG's coach, an individual CFG participant, or for an entire CFG; but they are also general enough that participants in any type of learning community are likely to find them useful. Regardless of who uses these questions as tools for reflection, the lessons from this research study suggest that reflective analysis is just the first step. In order to reap the greatest benefit from the process, the group should also identify the concrete steps needed to work toward developing as a learning community, then consider the forces that might help or hinder them in taking these steps, and finally plan to monitor their progress to ensure follow-through.

Questions for Intentional Reflection on Group Development

PROFESSIONAL COMMUNITY

- To what extent do I, as a group member, feel I can speak honestly about my perspective? To what extent do our norms support safe yet challenging interactions during our meetings?
- What barriers exist between group members? How can we work to overcome those barriers? How do we address conflict when it arises?
- To what extent do I, as a group member, fully participate in the work of the group by sharing my expertise, by bringing my own questions to the group, and by helping to shape the vision for where our group is headed?
- Why am I a part of this group and to what level of commitment?

PROFESSIONAL LEARNING

- What is our purpose as a group? What concrete goals or inquiries are we working toward individually and/or as a group? Why are these pursuits important?
- To what extent does each of our meetings help us to progress toward our goals?
- To what extent does our work depend on actual data, whether student achievement data, work samples, or reading research from the field?
- How do we access and use perspectives and expertise from those outside our group?

ACTION AND ACCOUNTABILITY

- How do we challenge ourselves to meet our goals and purpose?
- How do we hold one another accountable to taking action based on what we learn and discuss as a group, whether within our own individual practice or within our organization as a whole?
- How do we know when we are making progress as a group? How do we measure success?
- What evidence or documentation do we have of our own learning and impact? What improvements can we see in student achievement across all subgroups?

Final Reflections

The content of this chapter outlines a number of features that distinguish the most highly developed CFGs from those just beginning their work together in respect to professional community, professional learning, and action and accountability. It points to evidence that reflective group analysis has potential for facilitating group development, and it provides prompts for groups interested in engaging in such a process. Yet this chapter leaves many questions about group development unanswered. For example, what is the role of the larger context in facilitating or obstructing group development? To what extent is group development dependent on the skills, dispositions, or vision of the CFG coach, or leader, versus its membership as a whole? What factors contribute to a group's "readiness" to intentionally analyze its collaborative work, set challenging goals, and take action based on those goals? Future research should address these questions in order to further illuminate the factors that distinguish the most highly functioning learning communities in order to provide further direction for those seeking to start or strengthen their own learning community.

The current body of literature provides more insights into the challenges that CFGs have faced than into the factors that lead to strong professional communities. For this reason, future researchers should particularly focus on the strongest examples of CFGs available. One avenue for future research is to continue examining the relationships between professional learning within a CFG and student learning in classrooms and what factors influence that relationship. A second important direction for research is to identify multiple effective practices for ensuring action and accountability for CFG members. These practices would help participants to follow through in the busyness of their professional work, translating professional learning into practice. Strategies for monitoring ongoing learning will help participants to document and celebrate successes. These strategies will also help a group monitor its development as a professional community. Focusing on these specifically named directions for future research will provide a strong foundation for CFGs to envision new possibilities for strengthening their collaborative work.

References

Armstrong, K. (2003). Advancing reflective practice and building constructive collegiality: A program's influence on teachers' experiences in urban schools. Ed.D. dissertation, Harvard University, United States—Massachusetts. Retrieved September 7, 2005, from ProQuest Digital Dissertations database. (Publication No. AAT 3086978.)

Bambino, D. (2002). Critical friends. *Educational Leadership, 59*(6), 25–27.

Bernacchio, C., Ross, F., Washburn, K., Whitney, J., & Wood, D. (2007). Faculty collaboration to improve equity, access, and inclusion in higher education. *Equity & Excellence in Education, 40*(1), 56–66.

Creswell, J. (1998). *Qualitative inquiry and research design: Choosing among five traditions.* Thousand Oaks, CA: Sage Publications.

Curry, M. (2003). Critical friends: A case study of teachers' professional community in a reforming high school. Ph.D. dissertation, University of California, Berkeley, United States—California. Retrieved July 10, 2004, from Dissertation Abstracts database. (Publication No. AAT3105191.)

Dufour, R., & Eaker, R. (1998). *Professional learning communities at work: Best practices for enhancing student achievement.* Alexandria, VA: Association for Supervision and Curriculum Development.

Dunne, F., & Honts, F. (1998). *"That group really makes me think!" Critical friends groups and the development of reflective practitioners.* Paper presented at the AERA Annual Meeting, San Diego, CA. ED 412188.

Dunne, F., Nave, B., & Lewis, A. (2000). Critical friends: Teachers helping to improve student learning. *Phi Delta Kappa International Research Bulletin (CEDR), 28.* Retrieved June 5, 2008, from http://www.pdkintl.org/research/rbulletins/resbul28.htm.

Grossman, P., Wineburg, S., & Woolworth, S. (2001). Toward a theory of teacher community. *Teachers College Record, 103*(6), 942–1012. Retrieved January 31, 2005, from ERIC database.

Little, J. (1982). Norms of collegiality and experimentation: Workplace conditions of school success. *American Educational Research Journal, 19*(3), 325–340.

Little, J., Gearhart, M., Curry, M., & Kafka, J. (2003). Looking at student work for teacher learning, teacher community, and school reform. *Phi Delta Kappan, 85*(3), 185–192.

McLaughlin, M., & Talbert, J. (1993, March). *Contexts that matter for teaching and learning: Strategic opportunities for meeting the nation's educational goals.* Stanford University: Center for Research on the Context of Secondary School Teaching.

McLaughlin, M., & Talbert, J. (2006). *Building school-based teacher learning communities: Professional strategies to improve student achievement.* New York: Teachers College Press.

National School Reform Faculty (2007). *First annual NSRF membership report: Restructuring our organization, advancing our mission.* Retrieved June 10, 2008, from http://www.nsrfharmony.org/membership_report.pdf.

Nave, B. (2000). Among critical friends: A study of critical friends groups in three Maine schools. Ed.D. dissertation, Harvard University, United States—Massachusetts. Retrieved September 7, 2005, from ProQuest Digital Dissertations database. (Publication No. AAT 9968318.)

Neufeld, B., & Woodworth, K. (2000). *Taking stock: The status of implementation and the need for further support in the BPE-BAC cohort I and II schools.* Cambridge, MA: Education Matters, Inc. ED 483020.

Olson, L. (1998, May 27). The importance of "critical friends": Reform effort gets teachers talking. *Education Week.* www.edweek.org/ew/ew_printstory.cfm?slug=37 nsrf.h17.

Wheelan, S., & Hochberger, J. (1996). Validation studies of the group development questionnaire. *Small Group Research, 27*, 143–170.

Wheelan, S., & Kesselring, J. (2005). Link between faculty group development and elementary student performance on standardized tests. *The Journal of Educational Research, 98*(6), 323–330, 384. Retrieved April 12, 2007, from ProQuest Psychology Journals database. (Document ID: 864667831.)

Wheelan, S., & Tilin, F. (1999). Faculty group development and school productivity. *Small Group Research, 30*(1), 59–81.

Whitford, B., & Fisher, H. (2003). *Lucent learning communities in Albuquerque.* Retrieved November 15, 2007, from http://www.harmonyschool.org/nsrf/lucentcase studies.pdf.

Wood, D. (2003). *Lancaster learning communities: The challenges of creating an authentic collegial context for change.* Retrieved November 15, 2007, from http://www.harmony school.org/nsrf/lucentcasestudies.pdf.

Yendol-Silva, D. (2003). *In search of the perfect storm: Understanding how learning communities create power within an era of intense accountability.* Retrieved November 15, 2007, from http://www.harmonyschool.org/nsrf/lucentcasestudies.pdf.

Yin, R. (2003). *Case study research: Design and methods* (3rd ed.). Thousand Oaks, CA: Sage Publications.

CHAPTER 4

Commingling Action Research and PLCs

AN ILLUSTRATION OF KEY COMPONENTS

Diane Yendol-Hoppey
West Virginia University

Nancy Fichtman Dana
University of Florida

Diane Yendol-Hoppey, Ph.D., is the director of the Benedum Collaborative and a professor of education at West Virginia University. The Benedum Collaborative is one of the oldest school/university partnerships in the nation. Diane spent the first thirteen years of her career in education teaching in Pennsylvania and Maryland. In her work at Penn State, the University of Florida, and West Virginia University, Diane has focused on job-embedded teacher professional development and the cultivation of teacher leadership. Her research explores how powerful vehicles for teacher professional development including teacher inquiry, PLCs, and coaching/mentoring can support school improvement. She has authored numerous studies that have appeared in such journals as *Teachers College Record* and *Journal of Teacher Education*. She is coauthor (with Nancy Fichtman Dana) of three books, *The Reflective Educator's Guide to Classroom Research*, *The Reflective Educator's Guide to Mentoring*, and *The Reflective Educator's Guide to Professional Development: Coaching Inquiry-Oriented Learning Communities*, all from Corwin Press.

Nancy Fichtman Dana, Ph.D., is a professor of education and director of the Center for School Improvement at the University of Florida. Under her direction, the center promotes and supports practitioner inquiry (action research) as a core mechanism for school improvement in schools throughout the state. She began her career in education as an elementary school teacher in Hannibal Central Schools, New York, and has worked closely with teachers and administrators on action research, building PLCs, and school-university collaborations in Florida and Pennsylvania since 1990. She has authored numerous articles in professional journals focused on teacher inquiry, as well as a best-selling book (with Diane Yendol-Hoppey) from Corwin Press on the action research process—*The Reflective Educator's Guide to Classroom Research*.

ABSTRACT

Although the idea of teachers learning through conversation in small-group situations has existed in the field of education for more than half a century, the traditional orientation to "sit and get" staff development remains prominent. This chapter provides an illustration of how two powerful vehicles of job-embedded professional development, PLCs and action research, can be commingled to create alignment as well as support what Cochran-Smith and Lytle refer to as the construction of knowledge for, in, and of practice. By merging these two vehicles, teachers create inquiry-oriented PLCs built on a shared goal. The chapter concludes by highlighting five key components that facilitate commingling of ideas that allow teachers learning within these communities to document student learning.

In the past fifty years, we have learned a great deal about what powerful professional development does and does not look like. Historically, the most prominent model of professional development has taken the form of workshops delivered during in-service days (Cochran-Smith & Lytle, 1999; Fullan, 1991; Lieberman, 1995; Lieberman & Miller, 1990; Sparks & Hirsh, 1997). In these workshops, sometimes referred to as "sit and get" professional development, teachers often learn about new strategies, approaches, and pedagogy from an outside expert and then are expected to return to their classrooms and independently implement the new knowledge. This type of training emphasizes developing a certain type of knowledge referred to as knowledge *for* practice (Cochran-Smith & Lytle, 1999). Knowledge *for* practice, although important, provides limited support for the integration of that new knowledge into the teacher's practice.

Translating new strategies, approaches, and pedagogy from theory to practice within individual classrooms is a complex task for teachers as dilemmas naturally emerge when implementing an innovation. Given that the knowledge *for* practice model of professional development offers no mechanism to help teachers understand and address these dilemmas during implementation, educators involved with the professional development of teachers have recognized the importance of cultivating knowledge *in* practice. Knowledge *in* practice recognizes the importance of teacher practical knowledge and its role in improving teaching practice. Often this type of knowledge is generated as teachers begin testing out the knowledge *for* practice gained from attending a professional development session. As teachers apply this new knowledge within their classroom and school, they construct knowledge *in* practice. Knowledge *in* practice is strengthened as teachers deliberatively engage in specific teaching episodes, crafting and articulating the tacit knowledge that emerges from their experiences. Knowledge *in* practice is strengthened through collaboration with peers (Cochran-Smith & Lytle, 1999). For example, professional development vehicles including mentoring and peer coaching rely on collaboration and dialogue focused on the teaching and learning activity that can generate reflection as well as make public the new knowledge being created.

A third type of knowledge that is gaining attention from professional developers today is knowledge *of* practice. Knowledge *of* practice stresses that through systematic inquiry "teachers make problematic their own knowledge and practice as well as the knowledge and practice of others" (Cochran-Smith & Lytle, 1999, p. 273). Teachers create this kind of knowledge as they focus on raising questions about and systematically studying their own classroom teaching. Cochran-Smith and Lytle suggest, "what goes on inside the classroom is profoundly altered and ultimately transformed when teachers' frameworks for practice foreground the intellectual, social, and cultural contexts of teaching" (p. 276). What this means is that as teachers engage in this type of knowledge construction, they move beyond the "nuts and bolts" of classroom practice to examine how these "nuts and bolts" might reflect larger issues such as equity that could potentially inhibit student learning. Teachers interested in constructing knowledge *of* practice receive support as they collaboratively inquire with colleagues about how their own teaching practices might inhibit the learning that takes place in their schools and classrooms.

Dissatisfied with the traditional "sit and get" model of professional development, scholars throughout the past several decades have suggested the need for new approaches to professional development that acknowledge all three types of teacher knowledge. By attending to developing knowledge *for*, *in*, and *of* practice, those who support teacher learning can create contexts for real change.

Born out of the dialogue focused on the importance of developing all three types of teacher knowledge and moving away from relying on the traditional "sit and get" professional development model, two emerging professional development vehicles have gained momentum: action research and professional learning communities (PLCs). Action research, also referred to as teacher research, teacher inquiry, or practitioner inquiry, is defined as systematic, intentional study by teachers of their own classroom practice (Cochran-Smith & Lytle, 1993). Action researchers seek out change and reflect on their practice by posing questions or "wonderings," collecting data to gain insights into their wonderings, analyzing the data along with reading relevant literature, making changes in practice based on new understandings developed during inquiry, and sharing findings with others (Dana & Yendol-Hoppey, 2009).

PLCs are groups of six to twelve educators that serve to connect and network groups of professionals allowing them to learn from collaborative dialogue about their practice. PLCs meet on a regular basis, and their time together is often structured by the use of protocols to ensure focused, deliberate dialogue by teachers about student work and student learning (DuFour, 2004; Hord, 1997). The professional dialogue is targeted at changing teaching practice to support student learning.

As vehicles for teacher professional growth, action research and PLCs have a lot in common. Perhaps the most important, core, shared characteristic of action research and PLCs is the foundation upon which each of these professional development vehicles is built. First, both action research and PLCs acknowledge the inherent complexity of teaching and the multiple types of knowledge that teachers must create in order to change their teaching practices in ways that benefit all children (Dana & Yendol-Hoppey, 2009; Dana & Yendol-Hoppey, 2008). Second, both action research and PLCs acknowledge that educators face many problems, issues, tensions, and dilemmas as they teach. Third, teachers who conduct action research or become members of PLCs problematize their practice by deliberately naming them, making them public, examining them, and making a commitment to do something about them. Fourth, through engagement in action research or PLC membership, questioning practice becomes part of the teacher's work and both vehicles can lead to actualizations of an inquiry stance toward teaching that leads to job-embedded teacher knowledge construction (Cochran-Smith & Lytle, 2001).

While teacher research and PLCs rest on a similar conceptual foundation, many times they exist and operate independently of one another. This disconnect limits each vehicle's potential. For example, without the tools of inquiry, PLCs often lack a shared focus and the systematic study that can document changes in practice (Dana & Yendol-Hoppey, 2009). Similarly, when teachers engage in action research their work is often completed in isolation, robbing the teacher of the dialectic or opportunities for socially constructed knowledge that can be created when learning within a community (Dana & Yendol-Hoppey, 2009).

In working with practicing teachers during the past decade, we have identified ways to combine these two professional development vehicles into inquiry-oriented PLCs. Together, these two vehicles can strengthen each other, and therefore, magnify the professional development practices occurring in many schools and districts across the nation. In this chapter, we illustrate an inquiry-oriented professional learning community in action and share the lessons we have learned by studying inquiry-oriented PLCs. Finally, we identify how coupling PLCs and action research cultivates the development of all three types of knowledge: knowledge in, of, and for practice.

Conceptual Illustration: An Inquiry-Oriented PLC Explores Differentiated Math Instruction

This illustration of an inquiry-oriented PLC takes place in an elementary school where Kevin Thomas, the math coach, meets during a shared fourth- and fifth-grade planning period with six elementary teachers each Tuesday for one hour. The planning period began as a team meeting where Kevin and his colleague typically shared and resolved logistical features of their work such as upcoming events and paperwork, functioning more like a committee than a context for professional learning. In order to re-culture the orientation toward professional learning within the school building, the principal and team leaders decided to adjust the schedule to allow a ninety-minute planning period. During this period, grade level teams would commit to spending sixty minutes engaged in collaborative learning each week. In addition to dedicating time to learning, the principal worked with her faculty to redesign their alternative supervision tool to emphasize teachers documenting their professional learning and student learning. These structural shifts set the stage for a culture of professional learning to emerge within the school.

Given that Kevin recognized the importance and potential difficulty of shifting the use of the planning period from logistics to learning, he began by working with his colleagues to help them understand the concept of a professional learning community. To this end, Kevin introduced a reading by DuFour (2004) during their first August meeting, and the group engaged in a text-based discussion using a National School Reform Faculty (NSRF) protocol (http://www.nsrfharmony.org/). The dialogue that emerged as a result of the text-based discussion helped the team envision what the new orientation toward learning could look like.

The following week, the group moved toward defining an area of shared interest they could explore within the learning community. Knowing that students were not doing well on the state math exam, the group had chosen to focus on understanding what the difficulty in mathematics might be. During the first thirty minutes of the gathering, the group examined a variety of student data sources using the NSRF protocol "Looking at Patterns in Student Work" (http://www.nsrfharmony.org/protocol/learning_from_student_work.html). These data indicated the bottom and top quartile students were not making the desired progress entering their classroom. The data conversation revealed a shared concern about the students' progress in mathematics. Although the group had recently engaged in a series of differentiated instruction workshops and implemented a new math curriculum with fidelity, the students seemed to have differentiated success rates. As a result of these concerns, the PLC decided to explore ways of differentiating mathematics instruction to meet all learners' needs. The process of collaboratively examining data allowed the group to identify a shared purpose for working together.

Interestingly, although many of the teachers on the team had participated in traditional differentiated instruction workshops during the previous year, few of the teachers felt confident in their ability to implement differentiated instruction within their classroom. Applying differentiated instruction strategies required them to adjust how they grouped students, how students learn new material, and how students could best present information they had learned (Tomlinson, 2001; Tomlinson et al., 1995). Because this method takes time and practice to master, they believed that collaboration could strengthen teachers' use of differentiation. During the next few weeks, the teachers deepened their collaboration efforts by engaging in at least one peer observation of a colleague's mathematics instruction using the protocols found on the NSRF website (http://www.nsrfharmony.org/protocol/school_visits.html).

As a part of the next meeting, each teacher crafted a sub-question that connected to the overarching, shared inquiry question, "How do we differentiate mathematics instruction to meet all learners' needs?" For example, Mr. Johnson, a fifth-grade classroom teacher, and Mrs. Smith, the Exceptional Student Education (ESE) teacher who spends the entire ninety-minute mathematics block in Mr. Johnson's classroom two days each week, have elected to seek answers to the following questions: "How does co-teaching allow teachers to differentiate math instruction for their students?" and "What happens to student learning as a result of their co-teaching?" Other teachers inquired into individual questions related to differentiation in math such as, "How does differentiating my assessment tools influence student learning?" and "How do I adjust mathematics curriculum content to meet the needs of struggling learners?" Although the sub-questions held by individual teachers within the group differed, the entire PLC was committed to supporting each other's teaching as well as student growth in the area of mathematics.

As October began, Kevin identified a variety of tools that could deepen the group's inquiry work. During the first meeting of the month, he realized that the teachers needed to review what differentiation meant and develop an image of what differentiated instruction looked like in classrooms. Kevin found one of Carol Tomlinson's books on differentiation and began a book study that helped teachers begin to discuss with each other how new knowledge could be applied to their classrooms.

Over the course of the year, Kevin continued the external knowledge thread by bringing in guests who were knowledgeable about differentiated instruction to speak with the group. By building on knowledge introduced at the in-service presentation and bringing in new knowledge from external sources, Kevin acknowledged the importance of knowledge *for* practice while simultaneously realizing that he must make sure there are opportunities at other PLC meetings for teachers to move beyond the processing of disseminated information to engage in real and meaningful change in the classroom.

During the following meeting, Kevin attended to the teachers' needs to engage in real and meaningful change in the classroom. To this end, he created an opportunity for teachers to examine the kind of math work that the students were currently engaged in as well as get a sense of the learning that was and was not occurring. As a result, Kevin introduced the learning community to some protocols created by the NSRF (http://www.nsrfharmony.org/protocol/looking _work.html) that facilitated looking at student work from their own classrooms. By examining their own students' work, the PLC members deepened their knowledge of the students' strengths and weaknesses, the strengths and weaknesses of their curriculum, and their own planning. The teachers' collective focus on student work also helped shift the group toward a culture of professional learning.

At the next PLC meeting, Kevin wanted to move beyond looking at student work to raising questions about their own teaching practices. Kevin asked teachers to bring dilemmas of practice associated with their early attempts at differentiation and the changes they had made as a result of examining the student work. Over the course of the year, Kevin used many protocols created by the NSRF to address dilemmas (http://www.nsrfharmony.org/protocol/learning _dilemmas.html) to facilitate conversations and help the PLC members dialogue about ways to resolve these dilemmas of practice.

During the second and third months of school, Kevin selected inquiry-oriented PLC activities that required teachers to test out new ideas. This testing out of ideas allowed the teachers to begin creating knowledge *in* practice and encouraged dialogue about that activity that has the potential to generate knowledge *of* practice.

Finally, during one of the meetings in October, Kevin turned the group's gaze toward action research. He began the meeting by presenting the action research process and sharing an example of his own action research. Details about the six phases that Kevin followed are presented in Figure 4.1 (Yendol-Hoppey, 2004) that is drawn from the professional learning community work in Broward County, Florida, and heavily influenced by the Lucent Learning Communities work (Whitford & Wood, in press).

Given that the groups had already identified their collective and individual

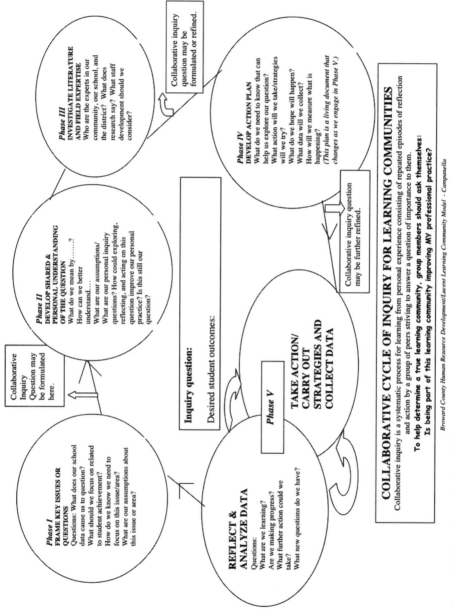

Phase I
FRAME KEY ISSUES OR QUESTIONS
Questions: What does our school data cause us to question? What should we focus on related to student achievement? How do we know we need to focus on this issue/area? What are our assumptions about this issue or area?

Collaborative Inquiry Question may be formulated here.

Phase II
DEVELOP SHARED & PERSONAL UNDERSTANDING OF THE QUESTION
What do we mean by.......? How can we better understand.... What are our assumptions/ What are our personal inquiry questions? How could exploring, reflecting, and acting on this question improve our personal practice? Is this still our question?

Phase III
INVESTIGATE LITERATURE AND FIELD EXPERTISE
Who are the experts in our community, our school, and the district? What does research say? What staff development should we consider?

Collaborative inquiry question may be formulated or refined.

Phase IV
DEVELOP ACTION PLAN
What do we need to know that can help us explore our question? What action will we take/strategies will we try? What do we hope will happen? What data will we collect? How will we measure what is happening? *(This plan is a living document that changes as we engage in Phase V.)*

Collaborative inquiry question may be further refined.

Inquiry question:

Desired student outcomes:

Phase V

TAKE ACTION/ CARRY OUT STRATEGIES AND COLLECT DATA

REFLECT & ANALYZE DATA
Questions:
What are we learning?
Are we making progress?
What further action could we take?
What new questions do we have?

COLLABORATIVE CYCLE OF INQUIRY FOR LEARNING COMMUNITIES

Collaborative inquiry is a systematic process for learning from personal experience consisting of repeated episodes of reflection and action by a group of peers striving to answer a question of importance to them.

To help determine a true learning community, group members should ask themselves:
Is being part of this learning community improving MY professional practice?

Broward County Human Resource Development/Larcen/ Learning Community Model - Campanella

Figure 4.1 Inquiry-oriented PLC cycle.

wonderings (Phase 1) and investigated the literature (Phase 2), during the initial action research meeting the teachers generated an inquiry plan by developing a research plan that contained the purpose of their action research, the stated wondering, how data would be collected and analyzed, and a tentative time line for the project's completion. The knowledge development that the external knowledge and protocols facilitated in the group during the earlier meetings jump-started the teachers' thinking about differentiating instruction in mathematics and provided early data for many of their research studies.

During the first quarter of the year, all teachers developed and received feedback on plans for their individual or shared research around questions that differed somewhat, but all related to the common theme of differentiated mathematics instruction (i.e., "How does co-teaching allow teachers to differentiate math instruction for their students?" or "How does differentiating my assessment tools influence student learning?" or "How do I adjust mathematics curriculum content to meet the needs of struggling learners?").

Later PLC activities supported the other phases of the inquiry process. For example, meetings focused on each member of the PLC sharing, analyzing, and inquiring into the data they collected as a part of the inquiry using activities from *The Reflective Educator's Guide to Professional Development: Coaching Inquiry-Oriented Learning Communities* (2008). The group realized that one of the key attributes of the inquiry process was that they focus on gathering and analyzing data that could serve as evidence of changes in teacher and student learning. The data allowed them to self-analyze whether the changes they were making actually made a difference.

Most of the year was spent moving in and out of the various knowledge for, in, and of practice activities based on the group's articulated needs. For example, some meetings would be dedicated to various components of the action research process while other meetings were used to examine student work, resolve dilemmas, debrief classroom observations, engage in lesson study, and incorporate external knowledge into the group through readings and guest presentations.

By engaging in action research within the inquiry-oriented PLC, observing each other, and using protocols to deepen the analysis of both student work and implementation dilemmas, the educators had the opportunity to create all three types of professional knowledge construction: knowledge *for* practice, knowledge *in* practice, and knowledge *of* practice. Additionally, by the end of the school year, all but one of the teachers in the PLC demonstrated changes in practice and celebrated noteworthy student gains in both their lower and top quartile students. The remaining teacher in the PLC demonstrated changes in practice with modest student gains.

Key Components of Inquiry-Oriented PLCs

In some schools where teachers are engaged in action research, they engage in their research without the sustained, regular support of a PLC. When action research becomes a part of PLC work, individuals' engagement in inquiry is more thoroughly developed and refined at each PLC meeting, deepening the learning and knowledge construction that occurs as well as the quality of the action research process. Furthermore, when action research becomes a part of PLC work, there is a greater likelihood that the learning that occurs from individual teacher inquiries will spill over into collective inquiries conducted by a group of teachers sharing a goal for school improvement.

Conversely, in some schools where teachers are PLC members without engaging in action research, the group's work targets supporting one another in reflecting deeply on practice. At each PLC meeting, rich conversation occurs about the topic of the day (i.e., a teacher's dilemma, looking closely at student work, fine-tuning a lesson plan to be taught the next day), but there is no specific target goal that ties each meeting to the next. The learning of PLC participants engaged in teacher research into their practice are enhanced as meetings are given a focus over time by developing individual or shared wondering(s) for exploration, analyzing data, and making findings public.

The illustration in this chapter provides a glimpse of the ways action research and PLCs can commingle to create an inquiry-oriented professional learning community, and the ways inquiry-oriented PLC work can play out in schools. This model for school-based professional development combines the strengths of action research and PLCs, and in the process, addresses a weakness that has been defined in traditional professional development practices. This hybrid entity is the "inquiry-oriented professional learning community" defined as a group of six to twelve professionals who meet on a regular basis to learn from practice through structured dialogue and engage in continuous cycles through the action research process (Dana & Yendol-Hoppey, 2008).

In each of the activities described in this chapter—the text-based discussions, the student work examination, the dilemma investigation, and the action research—educators shared a question that focused their collaborative work: "How do we differentiate mathematics instruction to meet the needs of all learners?" Providing a shared research question gave focus, content, and meaning to all of the inquiry-oriented PLC activities over the course of the year.

As a result of studying inquiry-oriented PLCs across multiple professional development contexts, we have identified key components that, when attended to, strengthen the collaborative work. First, the members of the PLC took time to create a new image of professional and collaborative learning that differed substantially from business as usual in their school. They did this by engaging in text-based discussions of conceptual and research-based articles outlining PLC work as well as talking to others who have been involved in learning community work. By dialoging about the nature and purpose of PLC work, they were able to distinguish the PLC work from traditional team meetings.

Second, the principal and school faculty took the time to adjust the structural and cultural conditions that would support the PLC work. This included logistical changes in team meeting time and length as well as changes in the supervision criteria used by the principal in the school. The shift toward documenting inquiry as a part of the supervision process encouraged a cultural shift within the school toward cultivating a learning stance toward teaching and learning.

Third, the facilitator purposefully selected protocols and other PLC activities to address the specific needs of the group at a specific time. This selection was based on the type of knowledge (for, in, and of) that needed to be constructed at a particular time.

Fourth, the PLC did not rely solely on insider expertise. Rather, the group invited external knowledge into their dialogue through research-based readings and guest speakers.

Finally, the PLC adopted an inquiry stance and process that laid out its theory of change. This theory of change could be traced through the action research cycle and the result of the cycle was the documentation of teacher and student learning. This component is consistent with Whitford and Wood's (in press) argument that inquiry-oriented PLCs require an explicit and well-understood theory of change that is shaped and owned by the learning community participants.

Inquiry-oriented PLCs create a context in which teacher learning not only translates to student learning but creates a mechanism for both teacher and student learning to become explicit and available for professional scrutiny. Across the nation, district staff development directors are being pressed to capture how their districtwide professional development efforts transfer to teacher and student learning. Teacher research-based PLCs offer an opportunity to make and document the connection between professional development and student learning. The illustration provided in this chapter traces the district's initial efforts to develop teacher knowledge for practice in the area of differentiated instruction and the use of a new mathematics curriculum to efforts to develop teacher knowledge in and of practice through the cultivation of inquiry-oriented PLCs. This alignment allows for all three types of knowledge construction and ties district to school-based professional development efforts. Inquiry-oriented

PLCs cultivate inquiry as a stance that uses inquiry as a tool to facilitate change in teaching and document student learning.

References

Cochran-Smith, M., & Lytle, S. L. (1993). *Inside/Outside: Teacher research and knowledge.* New York: Teachers College Press.

Cochran-Smith, M., & Lytle, S. L. (1999). Relationships of knowledge and practice: Teacher learning in communities. *Review of research in education, 24,* 249–305.

Cochran-Smith, M., & Lytle, S. L. (2001). Beyond certainty: Taking an inquiry stance on practice. In A. Lieberman & L. Miller (Eds.), *Teachers caught in the action: Professional development that matters* (pp. 45–58). New York: Teachers College Press.

Dana, N. F., & Yendol-Hoppey, D. (2008). *The reflective educator's guide to professional development: Coaching inquiry-oriented learning communities.* Thousand Oaks, CA: Corwin Press.

Dana, N. F., & Yendol-Hoppey, D. (2009). *The reflective educator's guide to classroom research: Learning to teach and teaching to learn through practitioner inquiry* (2nd ed.). Thousand Oaks, CA: Corwin Press.

DuFour, R. (2004). What is a "professional learning community?" *Educational Leadership, 61*(8), 6–11.

Fullan, M. G. (1991). *The new meaning of educational change.* New York: Teachers College Press.

Hord, S. M. (1997). *PLCs: Communities of continuous inquiry and improvement.* Austin: Southwest Educational Development Laboratory.

Lieberman, A. (1995). Practices that support teacher development: Transforming conceptions of professional learning. *Phi Delta Kappan, 76*(8), 591–596.

Lieberman, A., & Miller, L. (1990). Teacher development in professional practice schools. *Teachers College Record, 92*(1), 105–122.

Sparks, D., & Hirsh, S. (1997). A new vision for staff development. Alexandria, VA: Association for Supervision and Curriculum Development; Oxford, OH: National Staff Development Council.

Tomlinson, C. A. (2001). *How to differentiate instruction in mixed-ability classrooms.* Alexandria, VA: Association for Supervision and Curriculum Development.

Tomlinson, C. A., Callahan, C. M., Moon, T. R., Tomchin, E. M., Landrum, M., Imbeau, M., et al. (1995). *Preservice teacher preparation in meeting the needs of gifted and other academically diverse learners.* Charlottesville, VA: National Research Center on the Gifted and Talented.

Whitford, B. L., & Wood, D. (in press). *Teachers learning in community: Realities and possibilities.* Albany: State University of New York Press.

Yendol-Hoppey, D. (2004). *Lucent Learning Communities evaluation report.* Gainesville: University of Florida.

CHAPTER 5

Posing Questions
TEACHER RESEARCH GROUPS IN SEARCH OF ANSWERS

Michaelann Kelley
University of Houston

Karen North
Houston Independent School District

Cheryl J. Craig
University of Houston

Michaelann Kelley, M.Ed. and doctoral candidate at the University of Houston, is a teacher at Eisenhower High School, in the Aldine Independent School District, where she teaches art, ceramics, and higher-level studio art in the International Baccalaureate Programme. She works with teachers in developing their knowledge of their practice through collaboration and reflection. As a National School Reform Faculty National Facilitator, she has personally trained more than three hundred teachers to be critical friends group coaches in the regional area.

Karen North, M.Ed., is a technology specialist in the Houston Independent School District. She has taught math, business, computer science, and other technology courses since 1986. She works with teachers developing 21st-century learning practices. As an officer with ISTE Computing Teachers SIG and TCEA Technology Application/Computer Science SIG she has worked to integrate technology into K–12 math. Details on her work, presentations, and publications can be found at http://teachertech.rice.edu/Participants/knorth/.

Cheryl J. Craig, Ph.D., is a professor in the Department of Curriculum and Instruction, College of Education, University of Houston, where she coordinates the Teaching and Teacher Education Program and is the director of elementary education. Her research centers on the influence of school reform on teachers' knowledge developments and their communities of knowing. Her book, *Narrative Inquiries of School Reform* (Information Age Publishing), appeared in 2003.

ABSTRACT

This chapter asserts the primacy of teachers' position with respect to students' learning and the importance of teachers pursuing self- and group-driven inquiries in concert with one another. More specifically, the work offers an insider view of two teacher research groups in action, along with what can be learned from each group's story of experience. The value of cross-group inquiry is additionally examined with emphasis placed on the change agent roles that individual teachers played in their respective school contexts.

> To be honest, it took me a long time to learn a lesson most research-
> ers and school administrators have not yet learned: no research study,
> no brilliant discovery, no book, no seminal article, no journal, no
> program, no policy, no mandate, or no law can change what happens
> to kids in schools. Only teachers can do that. (Goodman, 2000, p. 6)

As teachers in two "teacher as researcher" groups mentored and supported by a university professor (Cheryl J. Craig), we recognize that we are "agents of education" (Schwab, 1954/1978) in ways that a bevy of others—researchers, administrators, and policymakers, for example—do not. We also understand that our work becomes increasingly potent when we reflectively share our inner thinking and deliberate potential actions with peers both within and outside our unique school contexts for the purpose of improving student learning.

In this chapter, we chronicle the work of our two teacher research groups: one is lodged in Eagle High School, which has had a long-term university faculty mentor (Craig), and one situated at West Houston High School, which has two participating members from feeder pattern middle schools. Sponsored by the Houston A+ school reform movement, these two teacher research groups met separately and collectively to share their learning over the 2006–2007 school year. In this chapter, we center on how the two teacher research groups formed their inquiry questions and how those questions shifted during the year of intensive study, creating insights somewhat different than those anticipated. We furthermore pay attention to major understandings that arose as a consequence of the two teacher research groups collaborating and speaking across school and school district boundaries about the broader experience of educating youth in dramatically shifting milieus in Houston, the fourth largest urban center in the United States.

Background

The place and role of teachers in educational planning and in the conduct of educational research is a disputed topic. Some, for example, understand Tyler's (1949/1969) curriculum rationale as positioning teachers as curriculum implementers, enacting reform proposals of those in possession of more power and/ or hierarchical authority. Others (Clandinin & Connelly, 1992; Connelly & Clandinin, 1988) view teachers as curriculum makers, actively developing curriculum in the throes of classroom interactions with their students. In the first scenario, teachers are mere users of knowledge created by others. In the second scenario, teachers hold, use, and produce knowledge. That is, they employ the knowledge made available to them by others and generate knowledge of their own accord. In this way, the curriculum that teachers live in relationship with their students is both individually and collectively—and practically and professionally—informed.

As practitioners, we embrace the teacher as curriculum maker metaphor because it credits us with being "moved by [our] own intelligences" (Dewey, 1908). In other words, the metaphor acknowledges that we "have some smarts of our own," as one of the Eagle group members phrased it. It also enables us to study our own teaching so that we and others can search for a new "epistemology of practice" (Schön, 1995) and create "a new scholarship of teaching," one that restores the fundamental relationship between "the knower and the known" (Dewey & Bentley, 1949; Fenstermacher, 1994). At the same time, we recognize the ongoing messiness (Gudmundsdottir, 1991; Lyons & LaBoskey, 2002; Richert, 2002) surrounding whether we are simply an arm of the public doing society's bidding or more than that: minded professionals who take our individual sensibilities and our personal knowledge of our particular students as well as other demands and proposals into account in our classroom curriculum making with students.

As such, this chapter focuses on the teacher inquiries on which we embarked. The approach to teacher professional development we describe here stands in sharp contrast to the diet of compliance training activities on which we have been raised. Following Schwab, we are cognizant that capacities and incapacities can be developed in teachers as well as students. We furthermore recognize that, on many occasions, our past preparations have made us increasingly reliant on administration and consultants for direction and less confident in the veracity of our personal and shared knowing cultivated over years of individual and collective practice. To increase our capacities as teachers, we are aware that "the experience of moving toward . . . understanding" (Schwab, 1954/1978, p. 107) rather than the ongoing instrumental use of knowledge (routinely meted out to us by others) is necessary. Our desire as experienced professionals with nearly five hundred years of collective experience is to move toward "informed and reflective practice" (Schwab, 1959/1978, p. 170). This chapter maps our journey.

Introduction to the Two Teacher Research Groups

Eagle High School is a comprehensive high school in the northwest area of Houston with a student population of approximately 2,300 students. Over the past fifteen years, the once majority Caucasian country club community school has dramatically changed to a majority minority campus with more than 85 percent of students on free or reduced lunch. The current demographics of the campus are 58 percent African American, 38 percent Hispanic, 3 percent Asian, and 1 percent Caucasian. The enormous shift in school demographics over time has heightened the challenge to meet the needs of every student on the campus, particularly since 68 percent of Eagle students are at risk of academic failure.

Eagle High School's teacher as researcher group has existed since 2004 and is an offshoot of a campus critical friends group (CFG), which had been working together for seven years prior to that. The current group is diverse in numerous ways, with seven teachers emanating from four departments—science, mathematics, fine arts, and career and technology—as well as one member (Craig) from a local university. The Eagle High School group is also diverse in years of experience ranging from two to twenty-nine years of teaching practice. Where the group is less representative is in reflecting the diversity of the school's student population. The group is 29 percent African American, 14 percent Asian and 57 percent Caucasian.

Located in a school district bordering the one to which Eagle belongs and also within Houston's city limits, West Houston High School is a Title I campus serving 3,000 students, 50 percent of whom are low-income and at risk of educational failure. West Houston High School's demographics are 34 percent Caucasian, 29 percent African American, 27 percent Hispanic, and 10 percent Asian.

The teacher research group at West Houston High School consists of mathematics, technology, art, English, and ESL teachers with three to thirty years of experience teaching in middle school, high school, and college contexts. Group members also included two teachers from feeder middle schools where the majority of students are also diverse and economically disadvantaged. Taken together, the racial makeup of West Houston's teacher research group was 50 percent African American, 42 percent Caucasian, and 8 percent Asian, which made it somewhat more diverse than Eagle's teacher research group, but still not a mirror image of its school's student population. As with Eagle High School's group, membership in the West Houston High School teacher research group was voluntary.

An Insider View of Two Teacher Research Groups and Their Inquiries

What follows are two stories capturing the activities of the two teacher as researcher groups. These narratives chronicle our coming together in our respective groups, the perspectives individuals brought to our group deliberations, and the questions individual group members and groups posed. They also document our learning along the way and the manner in which our inquiries and actions shifted over time in response to the conditions in which we were working and the responses we were receiving. We begin with the Eagle High School teacher research story and follow with the West Houston High School teacher research story. After that, we reflect on both narratives, highlighting themes that emerged along the way.

EAGLE HIGH SCHOOL TEACHER RESEARCH STORY

It is 2:45 p.m. and the bell rings. Classroom doors swing open and thousands of students fill the halls. Students run off to their buses, some to their cars and hundreds to their afternoon activities. Mixed in with the students are six teachers and one university professor who are headed toward room 309 for their afternoon of teacher research work. Most of the teachers have been working collaboratively for the past two years investigating their teaching practice. Each teacher has chosen a specific question or topic on which to concentrate over the school year. During the monthly meetings, the group has used CFG protocols to examine their own assumptions and practices to order to create better learning conditions for their students.

The group launched into a discussion of the questions arising in our individual classroom practices. The majority of the stories shared were about "connecting" to either a student or colleague. In short, relationship was the common thread as we reflected back on how we had come to develop trust in one another. At the same time, we acknowledged that it is a challenge to work in the isolation of your classroom in a large comprehensive high school where the teacher is the sole authority and then to turn around and work collaboratively with your colleagues, publicly declaring that you have unresolved questions and are not the authority on all matters relating to teaching and learning.

Over time, each teacher research member has investigated his self-initiated questions and shared the tremendous impact each person has had on the individual stories. Each narrative is written from the perspective of the individual teacher, but other group members have influenced and informed the telling.

One teacher pushing to impact student learning through his practice is Roy, a 28-year veteran of public school teaching and a 10-year member of the group. Roy documents his ongoing teacher transformation. Meanwhile, Prophetess, a new member of the Eagle group, proposes ways to look for moments to build relationship with hard-to-reach students. Chris, the group's second new member, offers new perspectives on inclusion and special education, and Sharon, a longtime group member, ventures into the territory of adult relationships in an educational hierarchy and her struggles with wearing many hats. As for Arthur, he has been a teacher as well as a teacher research group member for two years. He explores changes in his teaching strategies and the locus of control in his classroom, which happens to be a chemistry lab. Finally, as the coach of the group for the past ten years, Betty works to support others while growing her own knowledge as a teacher and as a coach. This year (2006–2007) she has studied the addition of students from the self-contained autistic unit into her regular art classroom.

As can be seen, each group member's investigation, while diverse, reflects only a slice of the work in which each teacher engages on a daily basis. At the same time, the declaration and taking up of the individual questions in the group setting allowed each member to make changes in her or his practice over a period of time. CFG protocols helped to nurture a trusting, supporting, yet challenging space for inquiry. The following are passages extracted from each member's research that speak to the impact of teachers engaging in professional development in a teacher group setting. Roy describes a moment in his work in the group as follows:

> To use a phrase I love, "I had an epiphany" during a critical friends group text-based discussion on the article *Serving African American Learners: Literacy as Access* by Dwight C. Watson. In his article Watson stated, "What is best for African American learners is best for all learners." How simple and how profound and so true. My content will basically stay the same, but my teaching practice must change. There will be juxtaposition from strategies for student success and achievement to strategies for teacher success. My strength and education has been teaching art, and I am not trained as an English teacher; it makes sense that I need strategies to teach and incorporate

literacy in my art program. Some of the strategies that I plan to use will require restructuring of lesson plans to better engage the learner.

Roy's initial research question revolved around African American learners, particularly males, which was a school district priority. However, in the process of conducting his personal inquiry he came upon a statement that spoke to him: "What is best for African American learners is best for all learners." This threw him back into his teaching practice and brought a fresh perspective to bear on his situation. He reevaluated the trajectory of his investigation and made literacy strategies more of his focus.

As for Prophetess, she had been involved in a mentoring group that Betty, the facilitator of the teacher research group, had led. While Prophetess was new to the school, she was not new to teaching. Yet, school district policy expected teachers such as Prophetess to participate in the mentoring group as a way to ease them into district rules and regulations but also to the subtleties of the Eagle High School context. Prophetess and Betty had worked well together in the past and were eager to continue their association in the teacher research group context as well. Prophetess wrote in her reflections:

> Everything must change . . . these are the words to a once popular song of the eighties. For me, it applies to the learning environment first encountered after entering secondary education versus the atmosphere that I find myself in today. [One of my students, Earl,] appeared to be introverted at first. He entered the classroom before the tardy bell rang each day, took his seat, and patiently waited for class to begin. In a short period of time, it was noticeable that he did not "participate" in class discussions even when called upon. Checking for understanding using routine methods was out of the question. I began to feel stressed . . . thinking that I was not able to meet the need of my student. Strangely, there was not a single other student in class that I could not establish relationship with—*this was stressful.* But, where and how soon could I put my hands on it? Would it be in time to make a difference?

Over time and through conversation with her trusted peers, Prophetess was able to bridge the chasm that estranged her from Earl. In fact, she continues to maintain the relationship even though both have moved to different venues. Prophetess continues:

> This incident with Earl made me realize that in spite of being an experienced classroom teacher, there is always more to learn. For me, our teacher research group highlights exciting classroom experiences that invoke compassion, empathy, and even sympathy.

Chris was the second new addition to the Eagle High School teacher research group. Over the past several years, the group has been investigating increasing literacy with special population students in our classrooms. Chris brought new insights to the group because she is a special education teacher in the mathematics department. Below Chris chronicles her challenges with newly mandated inclusion policies:

> Paul is a tenth-grade student who has received math services in a resource room since the third grade. Paul's individual education plan states that he is currently working on the sixth-grade level. However, due to No Child Left Behind, and the state push that all students should be "included," Paul has been placed in a tenth-grade regular education classroom. Paul, in my opinion, is a *victim* of inclusion! Paul is one of many students who is being inappropriately placed in what is unfamiliar territory. Paul sits at the back of the room with two students he knows are "special education" too. The three of them speak only to each other, and when working in groups, make every attempt to work together while getting little to nothing accomplished as a group.

What Chris paints here is a somewhat bleak picture of the state of special education affairs, specifically relating to inclusion. A very poignant question reoccurred in the discussions within our research group for Chris. It was this: "If Paul is a victim, who is the assailant? Is it me, the teacher; the slave to the bureaucratic master?" Within the safety of the Eagle High School teacher research group, Chris resisted the image of teacher understood solely as implementer of others' mandates. She shows the challenges that emerge when policies crafted for hypothetical situations meet face-to-face with the tough realities of the classroom as a microcosm of society.

In contrast to Prophetess and Chris, Sharon was a longtime member of the group, one who has sought to carry forward her knowledge and skills developed in our teacher research group to her work as a department head in the science department. Sharon illuminates how the struggles we face in building productive relationships in classrooms with students are mirrored in the relationships of the adults in our building. Sharon reflects:

> It is an odd position to be in. As a part of the administrative team and district department chair team, I am supposed to be a touchstone for information; a receiver and transmitter of the latest policies and procedures. This communication pathway is meant to keep the right hand informed about the left, to foster a feeling of family and team through knowledge. My position should put me in a pivotal spot of knowing and then using the knowledge to support cohesive and efficient efforts of the teachers. In fact, when I first began, all depart-

ment members knew everything I did. However, I learned quickly that it is not a good idea to broadcast everything you are told. Time and time again, I have communicated prematurely only to have to explain new requirements and actions. Over a period of years, this skewed effort has left me feeling alienated from other teachers and "twice shy" of administration.

In the above passage, Sharon communicates her feelings of alienation and defeat as she finds herself caught in the crux between the other science teachers in her building and school district officials. But in the Eagle High School's teacher research group, guided by CFG protocols, Sharon finds refuge, as she explains below:

I hold to the belief there are vital conversations that generate ideas that can spring to life and inspire questions that are often creatively answered. This actually happens in my life on campus as a member of a teacher research group and as a classroom teacher. In my experiences using CFG and as a classroom teacher, this simple process leads to interesting, thought provoking, and empowering experiences that I share with my peers and students. In fact, what transpires in CFG conversations often directly relates to classroom experience. Hence, my classroom and my teacher research group are places where communication and the information highway are in sync with one another.

In the aforementioned passage, readers witness Sharon experiencing a measure of satisfaction and a partial story of success, one she is attempting to spread from her individual teaching practice to her administrative role.

In contrast to most others in the group, Arthur is a two-year veteran of teaching who came to his position, also as a science teacher, from industry. Arthur brings a fresh analytical voice to the teacher research group and sometimes a successful, but unorthodox, way of learning. Arthur, for example, tells of a blind experiment into practice in which he engaged:

I happened to walk past the classroom of Ms. Green, a friend and colleague who teaches art on my hall and is in my teacher research group. I saw something very curious: students working in groups, quietly, *and* very much on task. Could this be the Holy Grail? I wondered. I needed a way to investigate this classroom, but I had one more problem. In the past when I had requested a session from one of my peers, the experience felt very synthetic and artificial. I needed a way to get into [my peer's] classroom with permission, but be invisible both to students and the teacher. I needed to set up a blind experiment.

Arthur continued:

> One day the opportunity presented itself. A former student gave me
> a work of ceramics that she had made for me in Ms. Green's class. I
> began to ask her about how she had made the project and expressed
> an interest in someday learning how to do ceramics myself. "Why
> don't you just join our class?" This is how I could observe without
> interfering with the outcome of the experiment. I would sit in not as
> a visiting teacher, but as a student.

He went on:

> With Ms. Green's permission, I joined the class, and more impor-
> tantly, a group. I was tutored by my former student and I had to
> prove my competence before I could move on to higher projects. I
> secretly collected subjective data on the students and teacher that
> were successfully implementing what I had always believed to be the
> impossible: a fruitful peer tutorial.

And, in Arthur's words, what did he learn in his blind experiment concerning
his colleague's practice?

> The key was a simple concept of moderation between the strict
> teacher-directed and completely structured environment in my sci-
> ence class and the student-directed chaos of my previous experiences.
> Ms. Green's had, it would seem, grown some additional eyes and
> ears. I was amazed at how she was able to keep track of conversations
> from across the room and to intervene only when necessary. The
> structure was there, but hidden behind the fluidity of the classroom.
> At this point, I realized that I had been using this method all along,
> not in the classroom, but in the laboratory. The conclusion I reached
> after days of research was that I needed to bring my lab work method
> to my classroom.

As can be seen, Arthur positioned himself as a student in order to organically
learn from another teacher so that his learning could be unencumbered by the
teacher's self-modifications of her teaching. His "blind experiment" story stands
as a strong model of a teacher desiring to learn in the years following the confer-
ral of a degree. With Arthur's artificial experiences of observing others' practices
also shaping his knowing, he called forth his knowing of science—particularly
of the laboratory—to leverage self-identified changes in his teaching.

The final member of the Eagle High School teacher research group is Betty,
the group facilitator who is in her fifteenth year of teaching. As part of her
personal investigation this year, Betty recalls experiences where she has struggled
to keep her head above water. These experiences have prompted her to question

her identity as a teacher. She has asked: "Am I a bad teacher and therefore I cannot handle it?" But then she pauses and reflects: "I think it is just the opposite; I am a good teacher and therefore realize that each individual student requires pinpoint laser actions." To make her case, Betty discussed four new students from the autistic unit who have been integrated into her regular art classroom. She centered on how she has adapted her teaching and classroom through personal and shared inquiry:

> The first day the students came was traumatic for the other students; I had to spend more than 80 percent of the class time with the autistic students. It was a very trying day; I found out that having an additional teacher and two aides were only as good as their knowledge of what I was teaching. I was really teaching seven people instead of four. As the week went on, the process got a little easier and the students and adults caught on quickly. Just as I thought it was getting easier the wind changed. The students were very cognizant that I was the teacher in the room, they did not want to receive instructions from their teacher, and to them she no longer possessed the content knowledge authority. The students now perceive her as no more than an aide in my classroom. This created tension in the room; I had to spend an inordinate amount of time with four students, and the majority of the students were [ironically] being Left Behind.

Inevitably, the shift in classroom composition and teacher positioning created tensions between Betty's "new" students and her "regular" students, all of whom were simultaneously experiencing creative challenges as emerging artists. Below Betty captures how David, one of the autistic students, and she developed a productive working relationship in the classroom where none previously existed:

"Ms. Green, Ms. Green, Ms. Green, Ms. Green," David bellows from across the room.

"David, David, David, David," I yell from the other side.

David smiles and realizes the humor. He then says, "I need you over here, now."

"I will be right there. I am finishing up with these students." A quick nod of approval, and I continue working with the table of students.

It takes a little bit before I get to David's table to look at his notebook for grading. While grading, I check out his current sculpture about the food chain. "What animal are you working on, David?"

He replies, "A bird." I look again and see an oval shape with four legs. I question him again, expecting that I did not hear his answer correctly. No, he did say a bird.

I immediately go into "teacher" mode. "David, how many legs does a bird have?" He thinks and then looks at his sculpture longingly, unwilling to part with the piece. "Now David, we all know that birds have two legs. How many do you have?"

He laughs and says four, but quickly states that his other teacher "told me to put four."

We both laughed and talked some more. . . . He then looked and stated matter-of-factly, "If you would have come over the first time I called you and checked my notebook, I would have two legs."

The urgency that David reflects in his learning is the same urgency Betty and her Eagle High School colleagues experience in their teacher research group setting. The individual needs of students must be met in a group setting, just as the needs of individual teachers must be met within a group dynamic. The stories told by the individual members of the Eagle High School teacher research group point to the impact of the collaborative work on individual teachers' thinking, practices, and relationships with students. In the Eagle teachers' shared experience, seven heads appear better than one.

WEST HOUSTON HIGH SCHOOL TEACHER RESEARCH STORY

It is 3:15 p.m. and the bell rings at another Houston area high school where a group of teachers also gather to work collaboratively. The West Houston High School teacher researcher group, unlike the Eagle one, is a relatively new group that has focused on the shared interest of critical thinking skills rather than on individual inquiries that coalesce as a whole.

When West Houston High School's teacher group first began, it centered on the question of how to use programming to increase algebraic computation. However, the original inquiry changed in vivo from researching the effectiveness of programming to finding ways to provide time to allow students to become critical thinkers by incorporating problem solving and design tools. Twelve teachers initially came together over lunch, dinner, and through online conversations. All were struggling to help students think critically. They decided to form a teacher research group and, like the Eagle High School group, use CFG protocols to help organize and focus their thinking. In the process, the teachers revealed not only student needs, but teacher needs as well. It soon became apparent that time sat at the core of everyone's conundrum.

For example, art teacher Brian Kane, a new teacher of only three years who came from the business and creative arts world to the field of education, recognized:

> In the quest for continuous improvement in education, we as teach-
> ers strive to incorporate the best and the brightest research into the
> methods of instruction. The problem arises as shrinking resources
> meet greater burdens; the only remaining asset to be squeezed is
> time. Unfettered, unburdened time for teachers is now the most im-
> portant and most rapidly vanishing resource we face today. . . . With-
> out time . . . we are like a seedling withering in the sun, with only a
> question of how long we will survive, if at all.

Yet, in the throes of this knife's edge dilemma, Brian found the West Houston
teacher research group to be a space where teachers "communicate, debate, revise, improve, and ultimately succeed," despite the less-than-positive forces
shaping their work. The space is one made for, and by teachers, a space that
provides Brian and other teachers with the conditions necessary to investigate a
shared topic of importance.

Fourteen-year veteran ESL (English as a second language) teacher Laurie
James agreed with newcomer Brian's point of view, but from a second language
learning perspective. Laurie shared that she has

> watched students like Maria come into [her] classroom speaking lit-
> tle, if any, English. . . . But Maria is no longer a middle school
> student with four to six years to master the English language. Not
> only is time limited in English classes, but Maria has a small window
> of time to pass necessary courses and tests to receive her diploma.

This has caused Laurie to wonder: "Why does Maria struggle to keep up with
her peers? She ponders, "Is it because [Maria's] parents have no formal education?" which is a commonplace response. However, from where Laurie is situated,

> The real issue for nonnative English speakers dropping out of school
> is that they have not been given a sufficient amount of time to learn
> the language, yet are required to perform at the same level as native
> English speakers on state-mandated tests. We need to press for time
> to make up for lost time for students like Maria since language flu-
> ency and critical thinking go hand-in-hand.

Thus, for Laurie James, the time problem includes many elements that sit below
the surface of generalized assumptions unquestioningly believed to be fair and/
or true for all students.

English teacher Amy Onstadt additionally noted that in her previous teaching assignment at another school she had managed to find time to meet with
each student individually to examine work and build resources to promote critical thinking. But, at West Houston High School, she has not experienced oppor-

tunities due to the increasing specificities of the required high school curriculum and a heightened emphasis on assessment. A thirty-year veteran who has taught English at both the middle and high school levels, Amy noted that if time were available, it "would allow student-centered learners to become actively involved in learning with the teacher acting as manager, coach, and mentor." It also would "empower students with a sense of control over the direction of their work." However, student-directed learning requires time for dialogue and community building in much the same way that teacher researcher groups need sustenance for growth.

Technology teacher Mike Johnson, originally a CFG research team member and a fifteen-year veteran teacher from a feeder pattern middle school, also reflected on the absence of time but from a different angle. He raised issues that challenged others in his teacher research group to comprehensively consider the effects of computers in schools.

> Children are overtaking adults in learning computer technology. . . . But children's health experts have expressed alarm over the time children spend in front of a computer screen. Many are concerned about a child's creative and psychological welfare. Unfortunately, computer technology has been used deceptively as a panacea for educational problems, but time spent on using this computer technology effectively is lacking. . . . It seems educational policymakers recognize the value of integrating technology but not the value of teaching logic through programming and computing.

In Mike's view, schools are beholden to software developers who foist their products on campuses, sometimes without concern for impact on youth. To his way of thinking, the development of genuine research skills has been hampered because students can search the Internet and find hundreds of easy hits. For Mike, the problem with software is whether it accomplishes what it claims to teach. "Is the software really helping to develop critical thinking skills?" Mike rhetorically queries as he brings his personal thinking to bear on the West Houston teacher researcher group's inquiry question.

For Mike, the teacher research group has provided a safe place for him and his colleagues to share their wonders and ponders. In it, he has found a haven where the "conversations with groups of teachers from various subject areas help us to learn how to use technology effectively." In the group's interactions, he and his colleagues have "weigh[ed] alternatives, observe[d] lessons, and determine[d] the impact on our students and their learning time."

Meanwhile, ten-year high school and university computer science veteran teacher Nick Banes has been frustrated with the lack of support for implementing technology time-saving tools. So much so, he moved to a private school in the hope that he might enter into face-to-face discussions with stakeholders. To Nick,

> Computer science is a problem-solving course. My student, Mario, for example, learned that, as it helped him get accepted to M.I.T. to continue his ability to think creatively. Its foundation is mathematics, and all applications of computer science require an understanding of the dependency, correlation, and relationship between variables, all of which require the sharing of ideas with our professional peers, practice, and time to develop.

Like Nick, 29-year high school teacher Steve Nguyen also voiced serious concerns about teaching computer aided drafting and design (CADD) courses, which seek to increase algebraic literacy. Steve shared that

> CADD programs give his students such as Jesse and David a better understanding of how math skills are practically applied in real-world settings and are used to help solve problems in engineering and technology. . . . Focusing on "pure" math and science education is not the only way to improve math and science. Students like Jesse and David gained a greater understanding of why math and science are important and saw firsthand how mathematical and scientific concepts were applied to solve engineering and technology problems in all types of industries.

However, while there is high demand for these courses in the preparation of architectural, civil, piping, mechanical drafting, design technicians, technologists, and engineers, Steve recognizes that the majority of students are not introduced to these program alternatives because of crowded high school timetables, competition with prescribed courses, and an overall lack of time and attention to the contributions such courses make to students' understanding and employment opportunities.

Meanwhile, high school and college math teacher of twenty years Jessica Taylor attempted to use the math problem-solving tools the teacher research group developed in the first two years of their shared study. Like her counterparts, she discovered there was no time available due to the Texas Essential Knowledge and Skills (TEKS) requirements coupled with a lack of availability of a computer lab. Jessica spoke metaphorically of time being held in her hands. Her story unfolded in this way:

> I have never before seen the amount of technology-driven programs available to embrace and categorically use in classrooms. [However,] as the wealth of knowledge is offered in the left hand and my mind extends my right hand to welcome these technology tools, the reality

is that I am faced with unsolicited brake shoes that stop the two hands from meeting. As I constantly push forward seeing the other hand in sight, I am pushed backward by the absence of time. My global outlook tells me it is necessary to embrace this opportunity, my educated mind says it is certainly within possibility, but my experience has taught me that this enormously powerful item, absence of time, is not allowing the goal to be maximized.

For Jessica, as with her teaching colleagues, the sources contributing to her time deficit are many: administrators focused on other priorities, changes not being integrated into existing curriculum documents, and lack of adequate teacher professional development, to name a few.

In contrast to the other West Houston teacher research group members, community college preservice teacher Denise McGregor did manage to use the design tools the group developed to prepare future math teachers. However, Denise questioned whether the tools were used in the classrooms of the future teachers she prepared. She knows that, at West Houston High School, teachers' use of instructional technology has significantly decreased. Given her fifteen years of experience, Denise's concerns are remarkably similar to those of Jessica. To Denise, accountability demands have become the prime concern on the educational landscape and have consumed teachers' time and attention. Overloaded with "auditable paperwork,"

> Teachers cut corners to make sure they meet all the demands that are required of their time. . . . Meanwhile, students suffer when teachers cut corners to spend time filling out auditable documents. The choice as to how to allocate time is made each minute in a classroom. Many students come to the teachers performing below level and, as a result, teachers try to wear multiple hats. Technology was supposed to ease the paper load for teachers, but by the time teachers have learned one type of software, a new advanced one has been placed on the market.

The situation becomes further complicated as Denise continues to explain in her words:

> When teachers ask to go to training to keep abreast of the changes in technology, it is not supported and approved by the principal. The attitude is that teachers need to be in the classroom and take training on their personal time. Yet, during personal time, teachers are still trying to deal with auditable paperwork.

All in all, a "vicious circle" has evolved:

> The students are not getting the needed time with the teachers and teachers are not able to give the time to prepare for students or work

individually with students. The teachers feel there is not enough time and always feel rushed. This results in a deficiency in learning that starts in elementary school and carries over to college. Students need to learn to learn and not learn to memorize to pass the test. They need more time to work on self-directed projects that build critical thinking. Therefore teachers need more time for training, planning, and collaborating to be more proficient in the classroom and with technology.

Middle school math and technology teacher Grace Watson, who has twelve years of teaching experience, forms somewhat of a case in point. She designed and enacted computer science problem-solving resources as a technology teacher the first year of the teacher as researcher grant period. In the second year and third years of West Houston's teacher as researcher grant, she also did not have enough time to implement the resources in her math classes. She extended Denise's aforementioned thinking by noting:

> Students end up being passed through the public school system . . . year after year even though they do not have their basic math foundation securely in place. Time intended to be spent improving critical thinking skills through solving multiple step problems is reduced or traded for time spent reteaching skills that students have in the past memorized for short bursts of time to pass the TAKS test.

In this way, the conundrum faced by members of the West Houston teacher research group takes on new elements of complexity each occasion it appears and reappears.

Finally, 25-year mathematics, computer science, and technology teacher Nikki Lake gained important insight into how to deal with the time problem that she and the members of the teacher research group she facilitates face. As a result of her conversations in her school group and across the district with the Eagle teacher as research group, she, too, made the decision to leave her high school teaching position. In contrast to Nick Banes, she decided to take a job as a technology specialist in an elementary school, a personal choice she explains below:

> The discussions in the teacher research groups gave me an opportunity to step back and see that administrators have their own priorities and their own list of options to improve academic achievement. I realized I must find a home where my solutions fit those of policymakers, and teachers might have the time to implement collaborative solutions.

In a nutshell, Nikki came to this conclusion:

> I need to take my research down to the elementary level to find out what happens at the beginning of a child's mathematical education.

That way I can come back to high school teaching refreshed with more ideas that fit my paradigm of what should happen for each individual child. . . . I want others to find what I am doing is important . . .

Nikki furthermore noted that the examination of her thinking through the telling and writing of her and her group's narratives of experiences provided "a channel to see that I must be patient and not move too fast."

In many ways, Nikki Lake and her colleagues in the West Houston teacher research group collectively came to see that time in and of itself offered its own set of solutions. Increasingly, group members paid attention to an overview of high school curricula, declaring the absolute necessity of a revamping of the 4-by-4 foundation curriculum. As Figures 5.1 and 5.2 suggest, such a revision would position computer science at the hub of inquiry and pursue a humanities approach to the study of English and social studies. Embracing this potential solution, West Houston's educators, like the Eagle teachers before them, came to realize that a dozen heads are better than one, particularly when vexing educational issues such as the one they chose to deliberate are taken up.

REFLECTIONS ON THE TWO TEACHER RESEARCH GROUP STORIES

As can be seen, teachers in the Eagle and West Houston teacher research groups examined their practices in a sustained manner and addressed questions of personal and collective relevance. Whereas the Eagle group centered on teaching and gaps in relationship, the West Houston group focused on technology-en-

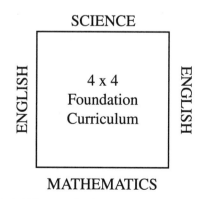

Figure 5.1 4-by-4 foundation curriculum.

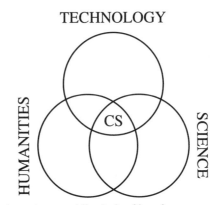

Figure 5.2   Computer science at the hub of inquiry.

hanced curriculum and the gaps between policymakers' dictates and what teachers are able to accomplish within the realities of their classrooms with the diverse learners before them. Despite the decidedly different research bents, both teacher group narratives are filled with examples of teachers attempting to assert their agency. Both also show a multitude of contextual factors constraining teachers' actions and, in some cases, thwarting their efforts. In this way, the messiness of the situations within which both sets of teachers attempted to maneuver in a less-than-supportive policy environment came into public view.

What also stood out was the different ways the two teacher as research groups were configured. The Eagle group had a long history of association and promoted individual teacher inquiry around a shared interest that became personally interpreted. Meanwhile, the West Houston group embraced a common question that "morphed" as individual group members' research and experiences pushed the inquiry in different directions. In short, the two research groups formed two very different models of affiliation. For the Eagle group members, inquiring into a topic of personal significance in a group setting provided the impetus for inquiry. In the West Houston case, teachers experiencing isolation due to the content areas they taught and/or personal research interests committed themselves to a core idea that bound them together in shared investigation and community.

In addition to the messiness of the teachers' situations and the different models lived by the two teacher research groups, the matter of how the teachers responded to the situations in which they found themselves bubbled to the surface. Arthur, in the Eagle narrative, for example, conducted a personal inquiry involving an element of deception to authentically observe a colleague's (Ms. Green's) teaching practice. Meanwhile, Nick Banes and Nikki Lake at

West Houston decided to test the waters of private school and elementary school settings to see if technology would be approached differently in those contexts. Nikki additionally committed herself to researching the place of computer science in teaching and learning across the K–12 continuum with the expressed goal of returning to high school teaching in a more informed manner.

Another closely linked theme was the moral stances of the teachers involved. For example, Chris, in the Eagle High School story, declared that some of her special needs students were "victims" of inclusion policy and posed the critically important question concerning who was the assailant. And Mike Johnson, in the West Houston narrative, spoke truth to power when he named the blatant profiteering taking place in the educational marketplace. He especially discussed the lack of concern for impact, particularly where the cultivation of students' critical thinking skills is concerned.

If teachers' moral stances repeatedly arose in this work, so, too, did their resilience. The way Eagle's Betty Green adjusted to the autistic children placed in her already overcrowded classroom speaks volumes to this quality. Her story of experience clearly demonstrates how her new students became part of her teaching narrative and renegotiated identity. Also, Nick Banes and Nikki Lake, as introduced earlier, deliberately moved to learning environments more closely aligned with their visions for technology. In both cases, the teachers moved forward with fresh hopes for the future as opposed to regrets concerning an unfulfilled past.

THE VALUE OF CROSS-GROUP INQUIRY

The significance of the two teacher research groups meeting and discussing teaching and teacher research issues across school and school district boundaries cannot be underestimated. While the Eagle teacher research group formed a strong model of teachers assuming leadership and plodding on—often in spite of official school leadership, the West Houston group showed how group strength could be built—even without face-to-face member contact. It seems the Eagle High School group encouraged the West Houston group to press on without hierarchal approval. At the same time, the West Houston teacher research group brought forward for public consumption the revamped 4x4 curriculum, which caught the attention of the Eagle teachers who also wrestled with time constraints and accountability demands related to No Child Left Behind.

In both the Eagle and West Houston teacher research group stories, there also was strong evidence of teachers developing voice and honoring one another's voices in spite of the authoritarian views swirling around them, demanding that they think and act in ways contrary to their personal and collective sense-making. The fact that Nikki Lake and Nick Banes did not retire or permanently leave teaching may in part have been attributable to the support provided by the in-school and cross-campus teacher research groups. The same can be said for Roy in the Eagle group. Eligible for early retirement, Roy continued to experience "epiphanies" related to his teaching and his students' learning, which he consistently shared in the Eagle teacher research group and in the cross-group inquiry.

At the same time as the teacher research groups sustained veteran teachers like Nikki, Nick, Roy, and others, they worked in ways that supported teachers new to the profession and new to the particular school sites. They did so by affirming the teachers as knowers of their particular situations. This was especially true of Arthur at Eagle and Brian Kane at West Houston. But it also was the case for Prophetess at Eagle who was taken under Betty Green's wing and invited into the group and cross-group deliberations in which she enthusiastically participated.

Final Word

This chapter depicting teachers' learning in teacher research group settings both within and across school contexts illustrates how absolutely vital teacher inquiry is to student learning and to the breaking down of boundaries between and among teachers representing different subject areas. Rather than teachers acting as cogs in a worn-out piece of educational machinery, they can serve as "agents of education" as this investigation into the activities of two teacher research groups in two metropolitan Houston high schools shows. When observed distantly, it is difficult to ascertain teachers' efforts to reform their schools and practices. Viewed from the inside out, however, the complexities of the change process become palpable in the narratives of experience shared by the individual Eagle and West Houston teachers as well as their respective groups. What Laurie James, Jessica Taylor, and Denise McGregor had to say particularly comes to mind here.

To end, the future of the two groups will be touched on. Because the facilitator of the West Houston group (Nikki Lake) moved to an elementary school and other group members dispersed, the group as previously described no longer exists. However, the online community of teacher learners thrives, despite the cutting off of geographical, school, and economic ties. Meanwhile, the Eagle teacher research group received additional Houston A+ Challenge funding for continuation of its ongoing investigations—a competitive award that other continuing teacher research groups were not awarded due to funding limitations. In a second Houston A+ Challenge grant competition, Eagle High School also received an award to support the preparation of more CFG members and coaches in the school. This move also will serve to grow teacher research in the Eagle High School context. Ever different, the work of the two teacher research groups forges on.

Authors' Note: Eagle High School appreciates the funding it has received from the Houston A+ Challenge (formerly the Houston Annenberg Challenge) since 1997. West Houston High School is also thankful for the Houston A+ Challenge assistance it has received. Cheryl J. Craig personally expresses gratitude for the opportunity to work with the high school teachers with the support of Houston A+ Challenge funds.

References

Clandinin, D. J., & Connelly, F. M. (1992). Teacher as curriculum maker. In P. Jackson (Ed.). *Handbook of curriculum* (pp. 363–461). New York: Macmillan.

Connelly, F. M., & Clandinin, D. J. (1988). *Teachers as curriculum planners: Narratives of experience.* New York: Teachers College Press.

Dewey, J. (1908). The practical character of reality. In J. McDermot (Ed.), *The philosophy of John Dewey.* Chicago: University of Chicago Press.

Dewey, J., & Bentley, A. (1949). *The knower and the known.* Boston: The Beacon Press.

Fenstermacher, G. (1994). The knower and the known: The nature of knowledge in research on teaching. *Review of Research on Teaching, 20,* 3–56.

Goodman, K. S. (2000). I didn't found whole language. In N. D. Padak, T. V. Rasinski, J. K. Peck, B. W. Church, G. Fawdett, J. M. Hendershot, et al. (Eds.), *Distinguished educators on reading: Contributions that have shaped effective literacy instruction* (pp. 6–19). Newark, DE: International Reading Association, Inc.

Gudmundsdottir, S. (1991). Story-maker, story-teller: Narrative structures in curriculum. *Journal of Curriculum Studies, 23*(3), 207–218.

Lyons, N., & LaBoskey, V. K. (Eds.). (2002). *Narrative inquiry in practice: Advancing the knowledge of teaching.* New York: Teachers College Press.

Richert, A. (2002). Narratives that teach: Learning about teaching from the stories teachers tell. In N. Lyons & V. K. LaBoskey (Eds.), *Narrative inquiry in practice: Advancing the knowledge of teaching* (pp. 48–62). New York: Teachers College Press.

Schön, D. (1995, November/December). Knowing-in-action: The new scholarship requires a new epistemology. *Change,* 27–34.

Schwab, J. J. (1954/1978). Eros and education: A discussion of one aspect of discussion. In I. Westbury & N. Wilkof (Eds.), *Science, curriculum and liberal education: Selected essays* (pp. 105–134). Chicago: University of Chicago Press.

Tyler, R. (1949/1969). *Basic principles of curriculum and instruction.* Chicago: University of Chicago Press.

Zeichner, K. (1999). The new scholarship in teacher education. *Educational Researcher, 28*(9), 4–15.

CHAPTER 6

Creating Learning Communities

AN INTERROGATION OF A SUSTAINABLE
PROFESSIONAL DEVELOPMENT MODEL

Anne Rath
University College Cork, Ireland

Anne Rath, Ed.D., is a teacher educator from Ireland. Her main research focus is on how to create the kind of learning environments where people can grow and develop to their full potential. This includes such diverse areas as teaching for social justice, critical reflective learning, development education, and teaching for transformation. She has a doctorate from Harvard University and currently teaches courses at the Ph.D., master's, and postgraduate levels.

ABSTRACT

This chapter reports on a year-long research study with a group of six primary teachers in developing an Action Research project to interrogate situated problems of practice at a time of intense curricular, social, and cultural change in the Republic of Ireland. The author initiated the project in partnership with the professional development unit of the largest teacher's union in Ireland, the Irish National Teachers Organization, which was the main sponsor of the initiative. The Action Research project took as its starting point the idea that the transformation of teaching to constructivist approaches demanded, at a minimum, that teachers themselves experienced such constructivist learning environments (Feiman-Nemser, 2001; Darling-Hammond, 2006). Furthermore, it was premised on the assumption that learning is fundamentally a social process and that the situated and social aspect of teacher knowledge is a major constituent of what is learned (Putnam & Borko, 2000; Lave & Wenger, 1991; Wenger, 1998; Wells, 1999). A sociocultural framework is applied to explore the kind of teacher knowledge and learning that is advanced by this research, the learning processes involved, the social and cultural practices that the Action Research project highlighted and how these impacted on teachers' lived practices with each other and with their students. Two teachers' stories are used to highlight the dominant themes and practices that unfold in teacher learning and how these themes become embedded in new commitments to mentor and support other teachers' development. Key experiences in the Action Research project continue to have meaning eight years after the project ended, suggesting a sustainable professional development model.

Introduction

This chapter reports on a year-long research study with a group of six primary teachers in developing an Action Research (AR) project to interrogate situated problems of practice at a time of intense curricular, social, and cultural change in the Republic of Ireland. The author initiated the project in partnership with the professional development unit of the largest teacher's union in Ireland, the Irish National Teachers Organization (INTO), which sponsored the initiative.

From March 2000 through March 2001, a group of six teacher researchers came together for monthly meetings from diverse parts of Ireland to learn AR and reflective practice. The timing of the AR project was intentionally set to coincide with the publication and rollout of a Revised Primary Curriculum (RPC) by the Irish Department of Education and Science (DES) in 1999, a curriculum package of more than twenty-three separate documents and the cumulative result of a decade-long engagement in curriculum reform and consultation.

The curriculum, which remains in effect, is largely influenced by constructivist learning theories and advocates the creation of learner-centered teaching and learning environments. It conceptualizes learners as active agents in their own learning and advocates strategies that focus on higher-order thinking and problem-solving skills, learning through guided activity and discovery, and social/emotional development. It particularly emphasizes the use of talk and discussion as a central learning strategy in every part of the curriculum (GoI, 1999, p. 15). To support the dissemination of this revised curriculum the DES set up the Primary Curriculum Support Programme (PCSP), which provided subject-based seminar days to all teachers. A Regional Curriculum Support Service (RCSS) was also set up to support the development of teachers who were seconded to become *cuiditheoiri* (Gaelic for helpers) and whose role was to provide school-based support.

It was envisaged that the AR project would provide a useful juncture from which to understand and inform teachers' learning processes at a time of curricular implementation and to support the enactment of new pedagogical under-standings and structures that emanated from the RPC. A baseline assumption for the genesis of the project was that meaningful professional learning that leads to changes in teacher thinking, attitudes, dispositions, and commitment to new practices demands ongoing deliberate attention in a public space supportive of such inquiry (Wells, 1999; Guskey, 2000).

The AR project took as its starting point the idea that the transformation of teaching to constructivist approaches demanded, at a minimum, that teachers themselves experience constructing their own understanding and knowledge about their context and their actions/decisions (Feiman-Nemser, 2001; Darling-Hammond, 2006). Furthermore, it was premised on the assumption that learn-ing is fundamentally a social process and that the situated and social aspect of teacher knowledge is a major constituent of what can be learned (Putnam & Borko, 2000; Lave & Wenger, 1991; Wenger, 1998; Wells, 1999). It acknowl-edged in particular the central role that relationship plays in the negotiation of meaning and value and the need to explicitly teach reflective engagement as a way of being in the world of teaching. In sum, the AR project would mediate and support teachers' reading, understanding, and enactment of the curriculum with the support of a learner-centered professional development model.

A sociocultural framework is applied here to explore the kinds of teacher knowledge that is advanced by this research, the learning processes involved, the impact on teachers' lived practice, and their understanding and reframing of their identities and practice as teachers. The framework identifies dialogical processes as fundamental structures to meaningful professional learning and pos-its that in experiencing these processes in the small learning group, teachers were able to appropriate inquiry and constructivist practices as valued social and professional practices in their classrooms with their students, in future engage-ment with colleagues, and their engagement and commitment to professional development initiatives generally.

The movement from teacher as "knower" to teacher as learner is identified as a key movement and change in participants as they appropriated new identi-ties of teacher, learner, and researcher. Sociocultural perspectives offer a power-ful lens on the interplay between the nested contexts of learners, practices, cultural tools, and social contexts as they shape teaching and learning practice and knowledge generation. In addition, as people take on and practice different roles and identities, new knowledge and perspectives of each nested context are generated and expanded. These nested contexts reflect the often competing and challenging environments and identities that form the habitus of teachers' lived and storied lives in schools, families, and the wider professional community.

It is argued that the active engagement in teaching as inquiry in a commu-nity of inquirers (Wells, 1999) provided a safe and explicit scaffold for the construction and appropriation of new identities and meaning for participants as learners, teachers, and researchers (Lave & Wenger, 1991; Wenger 1998; Wells, 1999). It is also argued that these new emerging identities or "ways of being" in the world of teaching provided cultural tools that are rarely afforded teachers in schools or in teacher education programs generally that can be characterized as coming from a "received knowledge" paradigm (Belenky et al., 1986).

Participants used these cultural tools to reconstruct and reclaim earlier identities and values as beginning teachers and in so doing illuminated the often constraining features of school professional cultures that compromise teacher learning, dialogue, and inquiry. The teacher participants also reflected upon and critiqued traditional forms of professional development that leave little room for dialogue and inquiry. In addition, through participation in a dialogical- and inquiry-oriented culture, the six primary teachers came to new understandings and were able to commit and value the pedagogies espoused by the RPC and DES guidelines because now they had an experiential base of embodied knowing and practice.

The necessity for such embodied knowing in practice is often overlooked in traditional forms of professional development that research demonstrates have little impact on practice (Sugrue, 2002; Hoban, 2002). Teachers' self-efficacy, competence, and confidence are increased in the process of solving problems of consequence to them in their own site.

The study's main goal was to construct a community that provided an authentic learning context for teachers to identify a "problem of practice" from their own lived experience and put this into conversation with the RPC and theoretical knowledge in designing and enacting new teaching/research practices that are evaluated within the context of the group in conversation with theory and RPC guidelines. Developing an intentional community of learners where the distributed knowledge and expertise of members is acknowledged and where relational practices sponsor deeper and more meaningful participation in the community is viewed as a necessary bridge for uncovering the tacit knowledge that is embedded in situated practice problems (Lave & Wenger, 1991; Wenger, 1998).

Wenger (1998) conceptualizes knowing as not just the acquisition of information but as involving active participation in social communities that engage learners in meaningful practices and in "providing access to resources that enhance their participation, of opening their horizons so that they can put themselves in learning trajectories they can identify with, and of involving them in actions, discussions, reflections that make a difference to the communities they value" (p. 10).

Through advancing case studies of two of the six teachers with whom I worked, I will map some of the key themes that emerged from the research project. In particular, I will focus on teacher learning and its impact on teacher identity, lived practices, and pedagogies of engagement. I will argue that attending to the meanings, values, and multiple identities of teachers as learners is a crucial and often missed process in dominant professional development endeavors. Using Wenger's (1998) two key concepts of identity and participation, I will argue that change requires negotiation that is relational, time-consuming, and messy by nature. I maintain that this messy relational field is at the center of teacher learning, and it is here that enough safety and trust are negotiated in order for teachers to transform themselves and be transformed by their participation and engagement. The learning environment then becomes the laboratory to construct, mirror, and reflect back the pedagogical structures that are valued and are made manifest over commitments of time and space.

The commitment to stay with this work is sustained by the quality of the interactions and relations that are afforded in the learning community. The transformations of knowledge, practice, and identity become manifest in the relational field of stories, artifacts, and classroom practices that mediate and sustain the ongoing participation and understanding of teaching and learning. Therefore, the work of community building within this group is viewed as a key part of professional development work, a community where teachers can "learn what they need to learn in order to take actions and make decisions that fully engage their own knowledgeability" (Wenger, 1998, p. 10).

Context of Ireland: Curricular Reform and Disjunctures

The past two decades in Ireland have seen rapid and unprecedented economic, social, demographic, and cultural change, which has spawned an enormous societal reflection and reevaluation (Drudy, 2006). (This includes the following: two White Papers on Education, Education Act 1998, Equal Status Act, 2000, Teaching Council Act, 2001, Special Needs Legislation, Equal Status Act.) This shift has placed enormous pressure on schools and teachers to become responsive, adaptive lifelong learners. Due recognition has been given to the vital link that educational investment has played in economic growth. Alongside this recognition there has been an acknowledgment of an under-resourced bureaucratic educational system, ill-prepared to meet the needs of a dynamic and changing society, which has led to much investment in in-service provision (OECD, 1991).

Despite this major investment there has been a pervasive lack of change in the conceptualization of the teacher as learner (Leonard & Gleeson, 1999; Kellaghan, 1999; Sugrue, 2002). Leonard and Gleeson (1999) in a review of major policy and curricular reform developments in the previous decade identify a pervasive technical interest permeating top-down policies that run counter to new views of teacher learning and that significantly constrain the development of teacher education. Two major national reviews of teacher education, the first of their kind in the history of the state—Primary Teacher Education Review (2002) and the Post-primary Teacher Education Review (2002)—have yet to be endorsed by the DES, leaving a vacuum in terms of direction and setting a vision for change. In addition, there has been no debate nationally either among teacher educators or the media about the content and direction set by these documents and how they might influence or reconceptualize teacher learning (Conway, Rath, & McKeon, 2008). However, the recently established Teaching Council (2006) is charged with leading change in this area.

Sugrue (2002) in a major review of professional development provision has identified a void in coherence and fragmentation in professional learning opportunities and a lack of differentiation that is sensitive to context, need, and career stages of teachers. He also notes the lack of engagement with teacher educators as key partners in providing new structures and views of teacher professional learning. His research on the usefulness of in-service provision generally suggests that pedagogical issues are often not engaged to any great degree. Sugrue (2002) writes:

> Cumulative evidence is beginning to establish a definite, if tentative, pattern, that when it comes to dealing with pedagogical issues, courses are significantly less successful, and this point was reinforced repeatedly by many of the interviewees. (p. 326)

He concludes that the lack of a research culture or a culture of inquiry in the Irish education system continues to perpetuate a "culture of dependency among teachers and that current provision of professional learning opportunities, both in terms of content and process, may actually be contributing to its perpetuation" (p. 335).

In a careful reading of the RPC, it is interesting to note that, largely, the teacher and school are viewed as willing, committed partners in realizing the aspirations of the curriculum in terms of pedagogical orientation, stance, and competence of teachers. The teacher is viewed as someone who will "bring a rich, imaginative and innovative range of strategies and resources to the learning process and be aware of changes and developments in educational theory and practice . . . committed to a process of continuing professional reflection, development, and renewal" (GoI, 1999, pp. 20–21). The working assumption is clearly one that the meanings of the practices espoused in the curriculum are self-explanatory and that these meanings can be supported by a "one size fits all" model of in-service support. It could be argued that the very structure of the professional support afforded teachers through the PCSP, which allocated two seminar days approximately for each subject area in the RPC, reflects a technical rational framework with its focus on content delivery and knowledge acquisition.

The additional provision of *cuiditheoiri* to schools for on-site support was an attempt to provide contextually specific support to schools and teachers in the enactment of the RPC. A recent evaluation of this service has documented that much of the support was focused on curriculum content and planning, with two-thirds of support personnel indicating that they did most of the talking during visits to schools with severe pressure to cover as much material as possible so as not to take up too much time and disturb principals who viewed this work as an unwelcome interruption of schoolwork (Johnston, Murchan, Loxley, Fitzgerald, & Quinn, 2007).

In addition, the tension between providing standardized professional development, on the one hand, which sometimes led to scripted teacher professional development days and which may have pressurized *cuiditheoiri* to have a "curriculum coverage" focus, and the need for highly contextualized engagement was never fully resolved (Loxley, Johnston, Murchan, Fitzgerald, & Quinn, 2007). Furthermore, a recent review of the RPC by the NCCA reported that teachers had limited ownership of child-centered teaching methods and identified the need for "much greater exemplification of methods" (NCCA, 2005). The research reported here emphasizes the highly contextualized nature of teacher learning and the need for teachers to dialogue, inquire, and present practical dilemmas and concerns over time in a community that is committed to such inquiry.

Research in this project highlights the lack of access to educational research and theory and the constraining nature of school cultures that do not have strategies or structures in place to unpack practice-oriented meanings and make productive use of educational theory. This lack of a discourse community is experienced by teachers as highly constraining and stifling. Here is how Nora, a participant with twenty years' teaching experience, speaks to these questions:

> The AR project has equipped me with skills, techniques, and understandings that I had not been exposed to nor had the privilege and opportunity to acquire prior to AR project. Since joining the project I have antennae that pick up associated understandings and knowledge that before I would have missed. Exposure to readings, articles, and reflective tools was very important to me and something I can now live out. I believe that the method in which the course was conducted and the sessions facilitated and promoted self-understanding and personal insight rooted in my perception of myself as teacher

and educator and challenged those perceptions. A knowledge base vis-à-vis reflective practice and action research finely tuned into teacher needs in the context of the revised curriculum is now familiar territory to me. (Nora, Reflection, 2002)

Nora went on to share her affective response:

> I delighted in being introduced to this whole body of work and being assisted in accessing it. I was never made to feel inferior because of my lack of knowledge in the early days. In turn this prompted me to learn as much as I could about the area. . . . Too often courses offered at in-service have lacked that tangible, inspiring, biddable dimension that send you home feeling "I must do that now," stemming from a desire to do it because it will be meaningful and helpful. Often one leaves such in-service resigned to the need to do what was presented because it is required. (Nora, Reflection, 2002)

In fact, Nora, in direct contrast to her previous professional development experiences, shared:

> I sought out the different suggested readings and was heartened to see all these books contain extracts from everyday teachers' journaling, dissecting and reflecting on incidents and processes, methods, and meanings that were engaging them, and communicating these ideas and reflections to other ordinary practitioners for feedback and reflection. I wondered about the absence of such a culture in my own experience of schooling and teaching. I have sought out such sharing of minds in all my professional career, but the received wisdom and the prevailing culture in schools seemed to indicate that to engage in that kind of stuff one should seek out a college course. Classrooms were for working; let that theorizing happen elsewhere. It was as if the "license" were granted to do that in college and then you had to leave all that behind. (Nora, Reflection, 2002)

In Nora's reflective comments, the culture of professional life in schools is highly relevant. Nora experienced the community as providing her with the resources to access a body of literature that she finds liberating and that prompts further research. Thus, in her experience, the project is described as providing her with "tangible, inspiring, and biddable" tools that further her development. She makes a distinction between changing practice because it is required and changing practice because it is meaningful and helpful in context. Research has highlighted the conservative nature of school practices and the reproductive nature of school cultures (Britzman, 2003; Sarason, 1982; Fullan, 1993; Wideen & Lemma, 1999). In addition, the failure of professional development interventions to change instructional practice may be explained in part by the difference between intentions and goals of teachers and policy-makers (Kennedy, 1991).

To construe teachers as having the confidence, resourcefulness, or commitment to change instructional practices without resourcing schools as learning communities seems unwarranted given research evidence to the contrary and given the professional learning conditions that characterize schools as organizations (Craig & Olson, 2002; Fulton, Yoon, & Lee, 2005). In addition, there is now an increasing body of research literature that points to the need to teach and scaffold reflection in a very conscious way since reflection and meaning-making are rarely an integral part of dominant learning patterns (Lyons, 1998, 2002; Rodgers, 2002; Rath, 2002; Kuhn, 2005). In this study the processes through which teachers commit to, engage with, and value instructional change is central as are the processes through which teachers experience and live out their personal agency, values, and identity.

RESEARCH METHODS

A number of research tools were used to inquire into the learning impact and processes of this project forming a large longitudinal and mixed-method compilation. These included document analysis of participant research journals and final action research reports, e-mail communications between participants and the project leader that served as summary reflections on each day during the AR year as well as providing a feedback loop for teachers on "works in progress." In addition, surveys, reflections, and interviews were conducted at key points during the project. Surveys were administered at the beginning, midway, and at the end of the project. Semi-structured interviews were conducted at the conclusion of the project and one year after that as well.

Final presentations of projects were videotaped. Participants were again surveyed and interviewed seven years after the project ended, which generated valuable longitudinal data at a time when the RPC was embedded in school contexts. These later surveys and interviews focused on the meaning of the project for teachers now in relation to their professional learning and practice and to explore if, and to what extent, they continued to enact dialogue, reflection, and inquiry as practices in their professional lives as these were key practices introduced in the project. These data were analyzed around various themes that included shifts in identity, disposition, knowledge, and learning orientation, and shifts in practice orientation. Participants were informed that all data would remain confidential and that all identifying features would be removed to safeguard this confidentiality. This was especially important given the sensitive nature of some of the disclosures.

LEARNING IN CONTEXT: BUILDING A LEARNING COMMUNITY

The six primary teachers who participated in the project were all female and came from diverse geographical contexts in Ireland. Initially twelve members signed up for the AR project, but this group decreased to six by the third meeting. This was due to a number of issues such as time commitment, new job commitments, travel, and various other logistics. Participants had an average of fifteen years' teaching experience, ranging from the youngest member, Deirdre, who had two years of teaching, and the oldest member, Maura, who had twenty-eight years' experience. (Pseudonyms are used for participants.) The nature of the small group enabled members to become consciously aware of the dynamic nature of professional knowledge as they engaged with practice problems, the contextual surround that shaped this knowledge, the constraints they met in their current contexts, their vulnerability as teachers, their values and assumptions, and the dissonance between espoused theories and theories in use.

The author focused on negotiating the structure, pedagogy, and content of research meetings to mirror the kinds of skills and knowledge that are needed for reflective learning communities. Participants were invited to explore, investigate, and analyze a "puzzle of practice" (Dewey, 1933). Activities were driven by "real questions" as a way to advance their own and others' understanding, and in the process new strategies and procedures were adopted in order to effectively inquire into their topic. This included searching out further resources and documents in order to deepen understanding. Action research tools, methods, reflective tasks, and action research exemplars were introduced to members, but the focus was on developing a reflective environment where inquiry was central.

Each day was structured around teachers making a short presentation to the group of their teaching context, their values, research activities, and issues to be addressed as a way of promoting shared understanding, collaboration, and ownership of work. According to Wells (1999), this advances both individual and group modes of knowledge generation. The focus on cultivating an intentional dialogical discourse community was central to developing dispositions of open-mindedness, wholeheartedness, and responsibility, essential components of both the reflective method and practice (Dewey, 1933). In so doing group members were also developing new professional practices of articulating situated knowledge, explaining and justifying actions and observations in light of beliefs and values, teaching and learning principles, and RPC guidelines.

All of these activities focused on getting participants into engaged, substantive, conversations with each other about their particular projects. Participants were encouraged to create a formal "critical friend" structure with each other, a relationship that was committed to sharing and responding to ongoing thinking and writing between meetings. Feedback on projects was constantly sought as well as a formal scaffolding structure at research meetings. There was a clear ethic of viewing research as a "work in progress," and viewing giving and receiving feedback as an essential part of learning. This involved attention to the development of key thinking strategies including learning to withhold judgment, centering on description, seeing thinking as interpretation and partial, and focusing on the asking of generative questions. These activities viewed teaching as inquiry and viewed professionals as knowledge generators.

In order to support this practice, it was intentionally structured into meeting days, communicating its validity as a valued social professional practice. Writing was viewed as a key tool to be used to clarify meanings, describe context, and to demonstrate enactment and evidence of new pedagogical practices in the field. The RPC as a text, along with other key AR exemplars, was constantly used as a backdrop to these discussions. Again these practices were experienced as essential for participants and validated their sense of self-efficacy. Deirdre, for example, had the following to say:

> I think validation is a key word when I think of the AR project. That is not to say the group was a "patting ourselves on the back" session! They were sessions in which I faced a difficulty and where I actually did something constructive with these problems. Instead of going into the classroom and facing the same problems again and again, I felt I was getting time out in a comfortable environment to play around with ideas in my head and to progress forward. There was a great sense at the end of every session of having turned a corner and although not coming to the end of the road, I felt I was facing a clear stretch with some of the journey behind me. Thus, one felt validated—I am doing something, and other people think what I am doing is worthwhile. (Deirdre, Reflection, 2002)

Deirdre went on to say:

> One of the key learnings for me is that it dispelled my hatred of writing. Through training college and secondary school I became very restricted in my writing and found that the criticism I received often made me clam up when having to write. I knew that despite my best efforts I would be criticized for my style and grammar and was never given the opportunities to work through drafts with lecturers/teachers. It was generally an assignment/result process. Practicing free writing and working through the content of ideas and presentations gave me the confidence to look at these areas first and look at writing style later. Using e-mail as a method of keeping in touch was great in terms of ease of contact. (Deirdre, Reflection, 2002)

The relational context that was created in the group allowed members to invest their time, energy, and commitment to the group in the face of political, social, ideological challenges to the sustainability of the group. The AR practices that were engaged in validated teachers' funds of knowledge and the unique contexts in which they were working. Participation in a discourse community to solve "consequential practice problems" that greatly reframed their relationship to themselves as professionals, relationship to each other and the larger knowledge base of teacher research became a new focus (Schön, 1995). Thus, commitment of time and energy became a valued social practice that mentored participants' movement from legitimate peripheral participation in the community of scholarship to central participation (Lave & Wenger, 1991; Wenger, 1998). Participants saw this time as a valuable commodity and time to "explore" their own concerns as teachers.

Initially concerns that had external value such as professional acknowledgment, acquisition of propositional knowledge, and academic accreditation of the project were central concerns for participants, but this shifted as they began to commit to the intrinsic value of the learning process itself. (Teachers who engage in week-long professional summer courses can take three personal holidays during the school year.) These externally motivated learning concerns shifted focus, as the action research group became a community of learners.

The AR project in and of itself had no credibility or visibility within mandated or credentialed professional development structures at the time and followed no historical or cultural footprint in terms of professional development. Thus, the involvement and commitment of members was voluntary. However, the professional development unit of the INTO, which wholeheartedly endorsed and financed the project, was a key variable insofar as basic traveling and subsistence expenses were provided to participants. In addition, it ideologically gave permission for participants to transgress the public stance the trade union took in relation to professional development policies that they were negotiating as part of pay deals and conditions of work with the government. During this time the INTO's stance was that all professional development work should occur during the school day, and teachers should be provided with substitute teachers to allow this work to occur.

INSTITUTIONAL SUPPORT: THE DIFFICULTY OF BREAKING NEW GROUND IN THE ACADEMY

To acknowledge the commitment of time and energy invested in this work and as a value stance, the author attempted to find a route to credentialing this work within the current university M.Ed. structure of the university. However, this was not possible within the then inflexible infrastructure of the university system. Practitioner research as a valued and credible knowledge base and professional development structure was not viewed as a valid structure. Indeed, the author attempted to "buy" time away from other university duties in order to build a meaningful partnership approach with the INTO. However, this "partnership" work was considered peripheral to university obligations.

Although the university and department "espoused" a partnership approach with schools and teachers, there was a lived gap between "espoused theories" and "theories in use" (Argyris & Schön, 1996). Thus, the AR project was done on the periphery of academic work mirroring teachers' participation in this time-consuming professional development as peripheral work. Lack of contextual and institutional support for the AR project meant that I was working without a "community of university peers" to support, challenge, or validate this work. This raises issues of the importance of changing institutional perception of such work and the kind of support institutions are willing to give in supporting innovative pedagogies and partnerships with schools and policy-makers.

ACADEMIC CREDIT AND TEACHER RESOURCES

The AR project did not produce any tangible reward in terms of academic credit or acknowledgment. This ran counter to the "product"-oriented ethos in much of professional learning where graduate work is acknowledged in an additional payment in salaries. This point proved to be an issue throughout the first part of the year for some participants who wanted some sort of credit for the work and created some uncertainty.

The project had been envisaged around teachers having access to libraries, the Internet, and ICT resources, but this proved not to be the case in reality. This situation has substantially improved now with a national well-resourced network of Education Centres and ICT infrastructure throughout Ireland. Early on it became clear that teachers had little access to theoretical readings or readings of a professional nature. In addition, e-mail facilities in schools were limited, and teachers did not routinely check e-mail or respond to e-mail communications.

In addition, family commitments and life stage of members competed with the continuity and learning needs of the group. Not all members could commit equally to the group endeavor, and there were various differences in group members' needs and availability. Setting up a place and time to meet took an inordinate amount of time with initial plans having to be negotiated around other heavy commitments. Initially the project had been envisaged around a "book" emanating from the project, with each teacher writing a chapter on their AR engagement, their learning process, and findings from AR interventions. However, early on it became clear that this would not materialize as negotiating the various venues, times, and agenda took far more time than was envisaged and limited the availability of all concerned.

As a way to promote and disseminate the reflective work and action research skills, I, in partnership with the INTO, attempted to organize a week-long summer course that group members would contribute to and run. Life circumstances also interrupted these goals substantially. In the course of a year, important life transitions were experienced by group members including changing jobs, a pregnancy, illness, and mothering commitments.

STORIES TO LIVE BY: INQUIRY, COMMUNITY, AND BREAKING SILENCE

> There is a profound connection between identity and practice. Developing a practice requires the formation of a community whose members engage with one another and thus acknowledge each other as participants. As a consequence, practice entails the negotiation of ways of being a person in that context. This negotiation may be silent; participants may not necessarily talk directly about that issue. But whether or not they address the question directly, they deal with it through the way they engage in action with one another. Inevitably, our actions deal with the profound issue of how to be a human being. In this sense, the formation of a community of practice is also the negotiation of identities. (Wenger, 1998, p. 149)

Wenger's attention to the connection between identity and practice challenges us to give careful consideration to the context of learning as a major constituent of the learning process. In dominant models of in-service training this is rarely addressed to any significant degree. The negotiation of "ways of being a person in that context" such as the negotiation of learning goals, meaningful activities, and processes rarely are points of discussion or viewed as integral to learning. In this project, however, careful consideration was given to the negotiation and co-construction of the learning environment between the six teacher researchers, the teacher educator, and the INTO. Attention to issues of relationship, power, identity, and safety were paramount in the construction of the learning environment. Two beginning assignments set the stage for the exploration of identity and practice in the project:

• Participants were asked to write a reflection on their own development as teachers and the issues they wished to address in the AR project.

- Participants were asked to select and present an artifact from their professional lives that communicated an important value and practice in their work.

These assignments were greatly influenced by the work of Lyons (1998) and Connelly and Clandinin (1999), whose work on portfolio making and "stories to live by" respectively highlight the importance of meaning-making, dialogue, and relational rich communities in developing generative professional identities of teachers. Lyons (1998) describes the portfolio-making process as the dynamic process of growth through the documentation of work, reflection and evaluation of it, and through the sharing of it in a public space. Furthermore, Clandinin and Connelly's work over two decades of research on the intersection of teacher knowledge, context, and identity coined the term "personal practical knowledge," which they define as the "teacher's past experience, in the teacher's present mind and body, and in the future plans and actions. Personal practical knowledge is found in the teacher's practice" (Connelly & Clandinin, 1999, p. 25). Their research highlights how context shapes and is shaped by a "professional landscape" where:

> Knowledge is composed of a wide variety of components and influenced by a wide variety of people, places, and things. Because we see the professional knowledge landscape as composed of relationships among people, places, and things, we see it as both an intellectual and a moral landscape. (Clandinin & Connelly, 1995, pp. 4–5)

More recently Connelly and Clandinin's (1999) work on teacher identity speaks of identity as "stories to live by":

> The term stories to live by is the intellectual thread that helps us understand how knowledge, context and identity are linked and can be understood narratively. Stories to live by, our term to refer to identity, is given meaning by the narrative understandings of knowledge and context. Stories to live by are shaped by such matters as secret teacher stories, sacred stories of schooling, and teachers' cover stories. (p. 5)

These two assignments then sought to create a context that focused on meanings, context, and values as central signifiers in understanding teacher knowledge. These reflective exercises set the tone for the AR project meetings as a whole and became an important learning context and touchstone experience that participants referred back to again and again as they engaged in the project. It created a safety for members to become connected to themselves and their values and created a space for them to communicate these values and practices to other participants, thereby creating a "community" of participants.

I believe the exercise of asking professionals to select an image or artifact that communicates what they value in their work is a powerful exercise and invites risk-taking around personal meaning-making that ordinarily is not exercised in dominant forms of professional development. The context itself and the participants affect the level of trust and risk-taking afforded and become part of the story that is told. Participants reported on the difficulty they had in selecting something meaningful and significant, and the process of searching back into their past and remembering incidents and events brought them in touch with earlier identities that they had forgotten along the career continuum.

The stories told and presented artifacts were interwoven throughout the project. Thus, the "curriculum and content" of that first day were generated by participants and consciously shifted the locus of knowledge and attention onto participants as knowledge generators. My aim was to create a learning space where dependence on me as the "knower" or deliverer of professional development, a well-honed and familiar role bestowed on university lecturers and professional developers, was contradicted consciously by the task. As the group leader I saw my role as co-participant and facilitator who would balance the fine developmental functions of confirming and challenging perspectives in order to create enough "disequilibrium" to promote growth and development (Kegan, 1982).

This first experience of the project proved to be a profound one for all participants. In particular, they noted that they had never been asked to reflect in this way or to make professional learning personally meaningful. For some, it connected to earlier identities and idealism as beginning teachers. One participant, Maura, a veteran teacher of twenty-eight years, conceptualizes this experience as "hearing what is at the core of ourselves. One could spend years with colleagues before sharing this type of information" (Interview, 2001). The project for her initiated a period of personal inquiry and career change. Two years after the AR project ended, she did a postgraduate course in school counseling and then interviewed successfully to become a member of the School Development Support Service, becoming a teacher educator herself.

At the time of the project, however, Maura was a mid-career professional who was feeling very constrained by her school context and the isolation of classroom teaching. She reflects on her idealism as a beginning teacher and how this idealism is tempered by experience. This is a theme that comes up again and again in teacher interviews and meaning-making around the project. The experience of learning on the project connected them with deep meanings about the very reasons that teaching as a career attracted them initially. They began their teaching careers with high self-efficacy and hopes, but many years later they were questioning this ideal and belief in making a difference. In the passage that follows, Maura talks about how the project affords her the opportunity to "look back" and of the poignancy of this "looking back" when she meets herself as a mid-career professional:

> When asked to reflect on my practice I wrote that Archimedes' quotation "Give me a lever big enough" and this would have epitomized how I felt on the bus journey to my first teaching post, which was in the heart of Dublin. Twenty-eight years onward, life had taught me many lessons, and seeds of self-doubt and feelings of inadequacy had replaced the invincible nature of that lady on the bus. The implications of this self-doubt and feeling of lack of validation were affecting my relationships with my colleagues and the standards of my teaching. Therefore, the opportunity to become involved with this project came at a very poignant time in my professional development. We met in a small room on UCC campus. Within a very short time we discovered that while our research-questions were diverse, because of the safe climate in which we found ourselves, we were able to embark on a voyage of discovery and commit to engaging in a questioning and a searching. (Maura, Interview, 2001)

Here we see a teacher who had vast amounts of energy, passion, and belief in herself as a beginning teacher. Maura's story of learning is a story of connecting back to this and articulating it in a public space with a community of peers. The support of the AR community highlights the lack of collegiality and support in her own context, an inadequacy that was stifling her growth. The feelings of "self-doubt" coming from years of "lack of validation" were having an impact on her sense of herself as a teacher. In the project she was also constructing a new identity as a teacher who "cared" about the social development of her students and "cared" about improving her practice. I continue with Maura's explanation, in her own words:

> The fact that a group of total strangers could come together and almost immediately, feel a sense of empathy, a sense of belonging, a "safe house" to unfold and absorb and grow was in itself amazing! I wrote "Voiceless in the Classroom," a poem, not just about my own frustration and lack of "voice" but, I felt I was giving a voice to those hundreds of committed teachers in the workplace, who were being stifled through the rigidity and bureaucracy used by agencies who feel threatened by questioning and enquiry. (Maura, Interview, 2001)

Maura here describes the AR community as a "safe house to unfold and absorb and grow." In striking contrast, she depicts schools as sites that are bureaucratic, conservative, and oppressive.

Maura's poem "Voiceless in the Classroom" was written in response to an

AR day where she had shared a "critical incident" that she had experienced five years previously and that encapsulated her experience in her school. The experience had greatly impacted her view of herself as a professional. Maura witnessed the principal publicly castigating a group of Traveler children, who had come to school without any uniform, and who had therefore "broken" school rules. (Travelers are recognized as a distinct ethnic group and experience great discrimination in society and the educational system as a whole. The Equality Act specifically addresses this.) The principal sent these children home and told them not to come back unless they obeyed these rules and acted like everyone else in the school.

Although Maura had disagreed with the principal's actions and his actions were a contravention of the school's anti-bullying policy, she remained silent and did not address it in any way in school. She had become "tired" of being the teacher who addressed problematic issues and felt constantly dismissed by her colleagues. This incident had made her question teaching as a way of life that she could continue to be engaged and committed to in the wake of the "double standard" that she experienced in her school around Travelers and around other important social issues. Although the school had an anti-bullying policy, she personally felt that this incident along with others was a form of institutionalized bullying that was tolerated and that her silence was a form of collusion. She also personally had felt bullied into being silenced by powerful dictates around professional loyalty, questioning, authoritarian and hierarchical roles in schools, and a group of people who had exercised their power in inordinate ways and appropriated resources such as status and power accordingly.

Maura's story surfaced as a response to another member's presentation. Claire, the visiting teacher for Travelers, had just presented her attempt to engage Traveler parents in their children's education and had set up focus groups for parents to talk openly about the issues that concerned them, the first time such an attempt was made during a fifteen-year engagement in the role. Listening to Claire's presentation on what she had learned from these focus groups and the prevailing racism that Traveler parents experienced in their engagement with teachers and schools prompted Maura's revelation and prompted a rich discussion on professionalism, bullying, culture and learning, and the silences that surround these issues in Irish schools. Thus, Claire's story gave Maura permission to "break" the silence around this issue.

Breaking this silence was an enormous relief for Maura and sealed the "safety" of the group for her and other members. It also prompted a rich discussion around school cultures with few resources to dialogue around the meaning of cultural diversity at a time when cultural diversity was becoming a "burning issue" in Irish schools. Questions were posed such as: What is professional responsibility in such an incident? What are the implications of such silences in terms of professional learning? What are the kinds of actions one could engage with in this incident to promote a more fair and just outcome? Sharing an incident that she had experienced five years earlier and the ensuing silence that surrounded it allowed Maura to unpack the meaning of it in more complex ways. Other participants shared similar stories. In this way the culture of nested relations that actively resists change *is* unpacked and understood.

The following interview excerpt clearly exemplifies a practice of constructing "stories to live by" and reconnects Maura to her own value structure in seeing teaching as significant and powerful work, a message she now advocates in her work as a professional developer in the School Development Service. It points to the significance of stories to hold significant power and meaning in teacher development work:

> Maura: Remember Joan's story? [Joan had only come to the first two meetings and then a new job commitment as a curriculum support person made her decide to leave the project.] It was on our first meeting together. I tell it all the time when I speak to teachers in schools and when I try to get them to take on board the importance and significance of our work as teachers. Joan's story was so poignant to me and has stayed with me all these years.
>
> Anne: Joan?
>
> Maura: Joan only came to the first and second meeting. She brought in a picture of herself as a child. She told us that as the child of an alcoholic mother, she often went to school dirty and disheveled. She described herself as one of the students who felt invisible to teachers and who felt she didn't matter. But then when she went into fourth class her teacher took her aside and talked to her and told her he expected her to work hard because she was bright. He then set up a meeting with her mother and told her mother how important it was that she make sure her daughter came to school with a clean dress, lunch. . . . He told her it was her job to pay attention to her daughter and the importance of her in helping her with her school work, to make sure that she had it done. For some reason, Joan's mother heard him and listened to him and from then on she made sure Joan's dress was clean and she had her school work in order.
>
> That teacher's action changed the course of Joan's life and motivated her to work hard and become a teacher. She is now a principal of a school. She talked about how that teacher "seeing" her was the first time she felt valued as a person and made her see herself as valuable. She now brings that perspective to her work as a principal. That story so moved me and fired me up. Yes, it reminded me of my own ideals as a beginning teacher and why I went into teaching in the first place. I now want to connect teachers to this again. (Maura, Interview, 2008)

So, eight years later, the experience of being moved by another participant's story still lives on in her practice and is communicated to teachers as a way to "communicate the power we have as teachers." Interestingly, Maura also shared that, as a staff developer, her energy is focused on getting teachers to reflect on their own questions. Furthermore, she promotes the value of keeping a reflective/research journal for teachers. Thus, a key tool that was introduced in the project continues to have a life in her continuing practice as a teacher. Maura is highly attuned to creating a context for teachers to share their own meaning in their work, as she explains in her words below:

> I tell Joan's story as a way of empowering teachers to see their work in a new way. We have to be so careful in what we say, do, and act. We have tremendous power as teachers. (Maura, 2008)

Thus, the project afforded Maura a space to "live the life" she wanted to live as a teacher and to have more congruence between her values and her practice. She cites the project as the reason she had the courage to explore other options and to vigorously pursue professional development in her current role as a school development planning (SDP) support person. When asked to evaluate the project in terms of a professional development model, this is what Maura wrote:

> I have always described the AR project as the beginning of my journey in professional development, a journey that I have pursued vigorously, sometimes to the neglect of other priorities in my life. The enthusiasm and energy generated in the group were infectious. I would come home, having driven for five hours each way, to and from the venue, and the adrenalin would be flowing when I arrived home. The excitement I felt at being listened to, being validated, being challenged, was like an adrenalin rush! This contrasted with the didactic authoritative approach of other in-service providers. I have carried that enthusiasm for my profession and I believe, ignited others through the facilitation of the school development planning in-service model for the past seven years, and I continue to do so. The AR project had a profound effect on me, which I cherish, and endeavor to share with others. (Maura, Survey, 2008)

Another participant, Nora, who was introduced earlier and who has taught for twenty years, framed her experience of this first day as an invitation to be reborn and saw it as the beginning of a powerful professional journey. Below is what Nora had to say:

> I was at a point in my career where I was frustrated. I felt limited and constrained by my work as a teacher and did not believe in its value any more. I was losing hope and had lost a concept of myself

as a learner. I wasn't aware that this kind of learning was available or valuable, and I remember being like that in college where I was constantly asking questions and so open. The discourse we engaged in and the tasks we set really opened up a new vista of learning for me. Learning was made personal, and I had never experienced that in teacher education or in-service before. The keeping of a journal made me aware of my own thinking and learning. I became proactive in defining my work and in asking questions. It reminded me of my beginnings as a teacher and why I had come into teaching in the first place. I wanted to make a difference to students. (Nora, Interview, 2002)

Furthermore, in the survey six years later where she was asked about what skill or practice she continues from the AR project she responded that it is the research journal that was of most significance to her and that it became her "constant companion" in her professional work. Interestingly, both of these teachers left the classroom within two years of the project; both were searching for more enriched contexts for development and professional growth. Additionally, both found teaching contexts too constraining and isolated as mid-career professionals, suggesting that life stage is an important shaping force in the design of professional development. Both teachers express dynamic, passionate, and engaged practice. The lack of engagement in their school contexts with issues that mattered to them personally and professionally proved to be a great demotivator.

TEACHER LEARNING AS NEGOTIATING MEANING IN COMMUNITY

Negotiating meaning involves both interpretation and action. In fact, this perspective does not imply a fundamental distinction between interpreting and acting, doing or thinking, or understanding and responding. All are part of the ongoing process of negotiating meaning. This process always generates new circumstances for further negotiation and further meaning. (Wenger, 1998, p. 54)

In the following vignette I look more closely at the learning process of one participant, Sarah, a learning support teacher whose research project focused on developing a collaborative teaching relationship with mainstream classroom teachers in her school. She identified the practices of presenting her "work in progress" in the group and to her "critical friend" as central to her learning. In this vignette I demonstrate that learning is a process of negotiating meaning in the terms that Wenger above uses. The AR project provides Sarah with a context for inquiring into the meaning of her engagement with colleagues in her school and the meaning of RPC guidelines and learning support guidelines (DES, 2000). Her participation in the project and the experience and expertise that are generated provide her with the cultural tools and practices to transform her practice, and to understand collaborative planning in an embodied way. This generates a critical perspective on in-service models that do not allow for negotiation of learning goals, dialogue, and inquiry. One of the most important capacities that Sarah learns is the power of engagement and reflection.

Sarah's project questions DES's assumptions about teachers' ability to collaborate and plan for learning together in school cultures that do not support such work. As part of her project she designed a protocol for teachers to write their observations and track student literacy learning. At one stage in the project she became very despondent because teachers were not writing much in these protocols. Thus, there was very little "data" being generated for her AR project, and she initially interpreted this as teachers' lack of engagement. During a presentation to the AR group another member suggested she interview teachers rather than expect them to write down their observations as she noted her own resistance to keeping a reflective research journal. This prompted Sarah to go back and set up specific times with teachers to explore what they had observed, what they were learning, and how the collaboration was working for them. She was amazed at the observations and insights that teachers shared, observations that they did not count as "knowledge worth noting."

The learning was immense and caused her to reframe the direction of the project and her engagement with teachers. She now saw her role as providing teachers with a context to explore their thinking and engagement in new literacy and collaborative practices. In addition, she began to ask students for feedback on the new literacy practices and therefore to develop new feedback loops in her teaching. These practices are integral to the RPC. She is amazed at the rich insights gleaned from student feedback and continues this as a valued pedagogical practice eight years later. This is how she talks about the impact of the AR project and its relationship to the RPC.

> As I referred to in my AR project, my personal discoveries through this reflective work made me welcome much of what is advocated in the RPC guidelines and in particular the learning support guidelines. I feel validated in my own beliefs when I see the emphasis put on case conferences for children with special needs. (Sarah, Survey, 2002)

Again the issue of validation and understanding that emanates from her own research is what is left with Sarah. However, she questions the implementation of the RPC and the instrumental nature of its delivery in schools. In particular she questions the devaluing of teacher meaning-making and dialogue:

The manner in which the curriculum is being implemented also calls for much discussion on teaching and learning within school staff-rooms. I would have reservations about our abilities to hold these types of discussions and formulate school policies as a result. We don't have sufficient experience, and I feel that much of the value of these discussions is lost due to the pressure of time constraints. New subjects are being introduced far too quickly, and people are rushing through the formulation of policies on subjects already introduced in order to be able to give attention to the next one. I feel if we don't mirror one of the underlying principles of this curriculum in our approach to it, we are unlikely to truly adopt it in the classroom. It is an emphasis on either process or product. (Sarah, Survey, 2002)

The impact of the AR project on Sarah is that she now understands, values, and is committed to the DES Guidelines. However, this understanding has not come directly from DES in-service but circuitously from her own engagement with this issue through the AR project. She counts this experience as crucial in her engagement. She begins her AR project with the following story, which highlights the lack of attention to process and teachers' meaning-making in more conventional approaches:

In January 2000 we had our first planning day based on the Revised Curriculum. What a nice way to start off Term 2, I thought, eager to meet everyone after the Christmas break. I didn't even have to bother with sandwiches; lunch was being provided. By 11 a.m. I was aware of the fact that something was attacking my sense of joie de vivre. By lunchtime I was feeling quite confused and alone, and by the end of the day I was really disillusioned. All my hopes for a designated day for our staff to spend working collaboratively had been dashed. Throughout the day there had been no emphasis on process. Some people's opinions were not sought at all. There was no opportunity for small-group discussions. In fact the more vocal staff members hogged every discussion and forced conclusions as quickly as possible in order to get the job done. Indeed it was ironic that this was how we conducted our first planning day on a curriculum that is so filled with emphasis on process. The revised curriculum is grounded in a constructivist theory of knowledge. All the cognitive research says that knowledge is socially constructed, in the moment, in the process of teaching and learning. How were we going to achieve this in our classrooms when we had no sense of it ourselves? (AR Report, 2001, p. 1)

It is the experience of participating in a community of inquirers that allows her to engage wholeheartedly with enacting the principles of the curriculum as an ongoing learning project. The AR project gives Sarah tools in negotiating the meaning of new pedagogies and strategies. She acknowledges that a key shift for her came when her critical friend Helen challenged her concept of "team teaching" since she pointed out that Sarah was doing all the planning and teaching. Her so-called partner was not active in the collaboration. She initially framed her study as negotiating with teachers to "team-teach," and coming to a shared understanding and commitment to collaboration became a much larger project than she envisaged. Sarah wrote:

> I would never have understood the implications of this work or stayed with it, without the support of the project. I now know the meaning of building collaborative relationships, and I see it as a process of talking together about our work. . . . When I asked teachers to document their observations they were so scant that I initially saw them as disengaged. I would have given up at this stage and dismissed my colleagues. It was only when I talked to them and asked them about what they observed that they could share what they knew. In these conversations they made important links and observations, but they didn't see these as important enough to write down! What does this say about teachers and our sense of ourselves as knowers? (Sarah, Survey, 2002)

In the above passage, Sarah is beginning to understand the complexity and necessity for engaged and committed conversations in building "collaboration" and a culture of inquiry about the best use of resources, documentation of practice, sharing planning and evaluation, observations of literacy work, and so on. She continues to use the reflective journal as a dialogue tool and working through problems of practice, as she explains below:

> Through the journal, I have now become my own critical friend, able to articulate my own learning needs, my questions, and my thinking. . . . But we need support and expertise on how to work collaboratively and how to use reflections. Without a caring and respectful group, I would have given up my attempts at the first obstacle. (Sarah, Survey, 2002)

At a learning support conference a year after the AR project ended, Sarah reported on the anger, sense of outrage, and cynicism that learning support teachers generally expressed toward the new DES learning support guidelines. While she understands this reaction, she also feels that teachers need to be more proactive in demanding the kind of in-service that scaffolds the kind of professional skills that were being advocated. She also states that the AR project and the skills she learned as part of that learning community have stayed with her and as a result she relates to the DES guidelines in a proactive way. She also begins to question the received wisdom of the DES who send out guidelines to schools without any support or inquiry about how different school cultures interpret, enact, or mediate these guidelines:

> It has been a huge learning for me—a real shift of the boundaries. There just isn't a culture of inquiry and collaboration in schools. Teachers are not making observations and are not monitoring their work as teachers. You have to provide teachers with the tools they need to examine their practice. Teachers' cynicism—you can't dismiss it—there's a lot of sense in that given the structures in schools. . . . But we have to be proactive ourselves rather than being defensive. It is a reasonable request to ask for in-service in this area. When I started team teaching in my school I could not offer any guarantees to teachers, any certainty of where it was going, but the process has taught me a lot about the real meaning of teaching and learning. (Sarah, Interview, 2002)

Later in the interview, Sarah acknowledges some of the tools she has appropriated to clarify her thinking. Reflection and using the reflective journal as a way to articulate her professional knowledge and learning needs are central to this learning.

> Because of our work in the AR group I did not have the same resistance to the guidelines and curriculum (RPC) as others. I believe if we are doing our own work, being our own critical friend, reflecting on our work, we won't have the same chip on our shoulders. The work in the AR project validated me and my values and I arrived at the same point as the Guidelines. Without the work I would have been as critical as other colleagues about the departmental guidelines. Teachers feel that stuff is constantly imposed on us and that we don't have any ideas of our own, but maybe we as teachers overuse this argument. Maybe it is used as an excuse. If we are doing our own reflective journaling, being our own critical friend, we will be able to say more about what our needs are and be able to articulate our needs. We need in-service and expertise about working collaboratively. We need to be reflective on our own practice and develop theories ourselves. (Sarah, Interview, 2002)

The reflective journal becomes a space where she maps her questions and concerns.

> Before I would have said I have nothing worthwhile to say. But the reflective journaling was very useful both as therapeutic tool and as a way of mapping concerns, questions, and as a way of knowing. It is something I would now use on my own. However I needed the support of the group for this in an atmosphere of respect. The process of the AR project was important because I would have seen my in-

ability to communicate with colleagues as my problem. I would be ashamed of letting colleagues down in sharing my problem. It would have been an "ouchy feeling" inside, and I would have written it off. The experience of being listened to and being validated by people's nods and attention in the AR group helped me see that it is part of a whole system rather than my individual problem.

Sarah continued:

> The AR project in encouraging me to continue developing strategies to communicate and look at what I was doing sustained me in keeping with my concern and question. Otherwise the whole thing would have died. It was such a caring and respectful group. We haven't got this with colleagues, and even if you don't know what you are doing you act as if you do know. This way of working isn't part of school timetables. It was reassuring for me to work in such a democratic way; there were no power relations. Everybody was empowered. There was partnership and it was democratic. We had one common goal to improve our practice. This was a different role. During the group we modeled for each other how we could become our own critical friends. Helen's feedback on my team teacher not pulling his weight gave me a space to see my part in the whole thing and helped me see a way out of it. (Sarah, Interview, 2002)

In these lengthy excerpts, Sarah is beginning to name a core part of the project that focused on developing an awareness of the teacher's own learning process, of learning how to sustain such engagement with inquiry in contexts that do not support such wholehearted engagement. The support of an interested other is crucial in such risk-taking and contravenes the dominant professional garb that teachers routinely wear that in actual fact constrains learning and inquiry. The AR process is highlighted as a key part of sustaining such engagement. Like Maura earlier, Sarah's concern shifts to critiquing the "system" that silences teachers, but she is also beginning to question the stance and identity of teachers who do not actively pursue their own learning agendas. Sarah now identifies herself as a reflective practitioner and is committed to the reflective process. She views her experience in the group as being "mentored" into being the kind of professional she always imagined herself to be. She now mentors other newly qualified teachers, a development discussed below:

> As a direct result of becoming a reflective practitioner I became very aware of the NQT (newly qualified teacher) and the ineffectiveness of the current diploma awarding system: put on a show for the day, write copious amounts of notes and be expected to cope effectively with all the perils of being the new kid on the block, get by somehow and once you have that piece of paper you need never write a note

again really until the inspectorate bother you again with a school inspection. This is the attitude because of the top-down approach and, in an effort to do something about this, to change this, to try and provide some support, to walk with and listen to NQT, I am currently involved in the new pilot project on mentoring. (Sarah, Survey, 2008)

Here we see that Sarah now continues to be interested, engaged, and interactive with her professional development and with the professional development of younger colleagues. The mentoring metaphor is also evident in her approach to her classroom teaching. Here, she describes how she empowers students to appraise and evaluate their work and to set goals for further learning. She uses the RPC to justify her teaching approach.

Just as I now take responsibility for my work I urge students to do the same re: editing or evaluating a piece of work and to ask what is the next step in learning. This is a new element that is very much part of the RPC: appraisal of work, evaluation of own work and others. Also the value of building trust in a group, sharing and learning in a supportive environment would be very much evident in my teaching approach and in the environment I create. (Sarah, Survey, 2002)

Sarah continues to bring a critical perspective to "top-down" models:

The AR project gave me the experience of a very respectful and supportive environment. It gave me the feeling of being mentored and it is very similar to what I am now experiencing in the training for mentoring and the role that the mentor plays in the life of the NQT. I suppose I actively sought out this role as a result of AR project. We have to go to the DES in-service days. We are sitting ducks, a captive audience, and are dished out any old thing quite often. Tutors have a very specific brief and have to deliver the same rigmarole every day to every group. This leaves no room for a fresh and appropriate connection with a particular group. There is no room in these days to tease things out, and even in the school development planning days at school level the attitude is not as diligent as it would be if we had chosen to become part of a study or other. (Sarah, Survey, 2008)

For Sarah, the experience of being a "sitting duck and a captive audience" in DES in-service is experienced as an affront to her intelligence, experience, and engagement. Her own commitment to "teasing out ideas" and taking a "fresh" look at issues stands in stark contrast to what she experiences at these in-service days where a "one size fits all" predominates. Here she is echoing the argument of Hargreaves (2003) when he talks of command-and-control centralized frameworks being the antithesis of what is needed in transforming schools into learning systems.

> Government must learn to abandon command and control as the primary means of intervention to achieve progressive social ends for two reasons. First, command and control is simply unsuited to the complex, unpredictable demands of organizational life in the knowledge age. Secondly, command and control systems tend to treat people in instrumental ways in which government priorities and values are used to control others, when in fact their active consent is needed. (p. 72)

Sarah's response to inflexible systems is to seek out another project where she can live out her expertise and values. She now is engaged as a mentor in mentoring NQTs. She has confidence in the "teasing out" process and taking responsibility for her work as a professional. Sarah's embodied knowledge, or what Craig and Olson (2002) call narrative authority, is coming from her interaction and experience of learning in community. She is expressing both the intellectual and social capital that is badly needed if we are to create the kinds of learning environments that are needed for a knowledge-based society.

Conclusion

> Because the narrative version of knowledge construction is transactional, authority comes from experience and is integral as each person both shapes his or her own knowledge and is shaped by the knowledge of others. Thus, narrative knowledge becomes the expression, enactment, and development of a person's narrative knowledge as individuals learn to authorize meaning in community with others. . . . When officially authorized versions of professional knowledge are presented as givens, narrative authority can be thwarted or silenced. Ironically, however, the choices teachers and preservice teachers make and the actions they take necessarily continue to come from their own narrative authority, however unexamined it may be. Unless there are spaces for stories to be brought out into the open and shared with others, they become unreflective bases for professional practice and decision-making. (Craig & Olson, 2002, p. 116)

This chapter has explored the kind of learning that can occur when a community of teacher researchers is created that allows space for both the public and private stories of practice to emerge, be engaged with, questioned, modified, and enlarged. The careful construction of a space that was safe for inquiry, relationship, and the messiness of coming to know in community was crucial as was the questioning of professional knowledge as an unproblematic given. These stories of change, commitment, and enactment are honed and finely tuned to the personal and professional contexts and histories of each teacher researcher as he or she looked back in order to move forward in his or her professional life.

In order to make the intellectual and emotional commitment that such professional engagement requires, a basic trust in real relationships was necessary. One might ask the question at this stage, So what? What was the learning and what was the impact? Can professional development models invest such time and energy? What is the value-added dimension of such an investment? Although this paper has not focused on the classroom practices that teachers engaged with, there is evidence that these six teacher researchers have shifted their relationship to themselves as knowers to practice and to their identity as teachers.

It seems that governments and policy-makers have answered the questions above in their continued investment in professional development models that leave little room for the construction of knowledge and inquiry into what really works in the multifaceted and situated complexity of practice. In the continued rollout of curricula implementation with little thought to teachers' lived and embodied knowledge, there is a stifling of growth and innovation. There is an enormous psychic, emotional, and material cost to stepping over the learning needs of teachers. This cost is borne out in the reproduction of school cultures that continue to be hierarchical, bureaucratic, and places where both teachers and students cannot commit to wholehearted engagement.

Some themes are striking in all the stories of change. The first is that learning has to be personally meaningful. Second, teachers' concerns, questions, embedded knowledge, and experience need to be the "curriculum" of professional development. Listening with care to teachers seems to be a scarce commodity in the press for "curriculum coverage" and the prescribed nature of school work.

Eight years after the AR project all participants continue to be engaged lifelong learners and practitioners suggesting a sustainable learning model. Although we glibly use "lifelong learning" as a goal in our work as teacher educators, we need to deeply question the prevailing learning environments that continue to be "learning about" rather than "learning to be" (Lave & Wenger, 1991; Wenger, 1998). The AR days were days spent learning to be engaged in "productive inquiry" in authentic questions that are at the heart of teaching and learning (Dewey, 1933). The AR became a community of practice where teachers were legitimately engaged in real research that challenged and stretched them to go beyond the call of duty in their professional lives in terms of their engagement in experimentation, documentation of practice, and sharing with colleagues.

There were cultural, social, ideological, and geographical challenges to sustaining the practitioner research group and indeed many limitations. However, these were overcome because of the quality of the relationships between members. The democratic and open environment that was created was an environment in which teachers could flourish and grow. A testament to the generative nature of the group is that key practices continue to be lived out in classrooms and staff development efforts.

Reform is only possible if we can create the kind of cultures that foster critical reflection, inquiry, communication, and multiple feedback loops. Experiencing and participating in a community of practice where real questions and issues were engaged with and listened to with care were the essential building blocks of the community as was the commitment to act, attend to, and be responsible for the impact of actions in the classroom setting. Eight years later Maura, Sarah, and Deirdre continue to be engaged in their work and active in the professional development of themselves and others. A willingness to work through obstacles, resistances, power relations and ambiguities around change is necessary as is the commitment to challenge practices that run counter to democratic participative practice. If learner-centered professional development is to be a valued social practice, policy-makers need to attend to models that can sustain themselves long after the initiative ends or the pilot project finishes.

Author's note: I would like to express my appreciation for the teachers who participated in the project and the INTO professional development unit, especially Edna Jordan and Catherine Byrne.

References

Argyris, C., & Schön, D. A. (1996). *Organizational learning.* New York: Addison Wesley.

Belenky, M. F., Clinchy, B., Goldberger, N. R., and Tarule, J. M. (1986). *Women's ways of knowing.* New York: Basic Books.

Britzman, D. (2003). *Practice makes practice: A critical study of learning to teach* (Rev. ed.). Albany: State University of New York Press.

Clandinin, D. J., & Connelly, F. M. (1995). *Teachers' professional knowledge landscapes.* New York: Teachers College Press.

Cochran-Smith, M., & Lytle, S. (2001). Beyond certainty: Taking an inquiry stance on practice. In A. Lieberman & L. Miller (Eds.), *Teachers caught in action* (pp. 45–58). New York: Teachers College Press.

Connelly, F. M., & Clandinin, D. J. (1999). *Shaping a professional identity: Stories of educational practice.* New York: Teachers College Press.

Conway, P., Rath, A., & McKeon, J. (2008). *Trends and dilemmas in review and reform of primary and post-primary initial teacher education in Ireland.* American Educational Research Association Annual Meeting, New York City.

Craig, C. J., & Olson, M. R. (2002). The development of narrative authority in knowledge communities: A narrative approach to teacher learning. In N. Lyons & V. La-Boskey (Eds.), *Narrative inquiry in practice: Advancing the knowledge of teaching* (pp. 115–129). New York: Teachers College Press.

Darling-Hammond, L. (2006). Assessing teacher education: The usefulness of multiple measures for assessing program outcomes. *Journal of Teacher Education, 57*(2), 120–138.

DES. (2000). *Learning support guidelines.* Government of Ireland, Dublin: Department of Education and Science.

Dewey, J. (1933). *How we think.* Mineola, NY: Dover Publications, Inc.

Drudy, S. (2006). Change and reform in teacher education in Ireland: A case study in the reform of higher education. In P. Tgaga (Ed.), *Modernization of study programmes in teachers' education in international contexts.* Ljubljiana, Slovenia: Pedaggoska Faculteta.

Feiman-Nemser, S. (2001). From preparation to practice: Designing a continuum to strengthen and sustain teaching. *Teachers College Record, 103*(6), 1013–1055.

Fullan, M. (1993). Change forces: Probing the depths of educational reform. New York: Falmer Press.

Fulton, K., Yoon, I., & Lee, C. (2005). *Induction into learning communities.* Prepared for the National Commission on Teaching and America's Future.

Government of Ireland. (1999). *Primary school curriculum.* Dublin: Stationery Office.

Guskey, T. R. (2000). *Evaluating professional development.* Thousand Oaks, CA: Corwin Press.

Hargreaves, A. (2003). *Teaching in a knowledge society: Education in the age of insecurity.* New York: Teachers College Press.

Hoban, G. (2002). *Teacher learning for educational change.* UK: Open University Press.

Johnston, K., Murchan, D., Loxley, A., Fitzgerald, H., & Quinn, M. (2007). The role and impact of the regional curriculum support service in Irish primary education. *Irish Educational Studies, 26*(3), 219–238.

Kegan, R. (1982). *The evolving self.* Boston: Harvard University Press.

Kellaghan, T. (1999). Introduction to Papers. In M. Killeavy (Ed.), *Towards 2010: Teacher education in Ireland over the next decade.* Dublin: IFUT.

Kennedy, M. M. (1991). *An agenda for research on teacher learning.* East Lansing, MI: Michigan State University National Center for Research on Teacher Learning. Special report.

Kuhn, D. (2005). *Education for thinking.* Cambridge, MA: Harvard University Press.

Lave, J., & Wenger, E. (1991). *Situated learning—legitimate peripheral participation.* Cambridge: Cambridge University Press.

Leonard, D., & Gleeson, J. (1999). Context and coherence in initial teacher education in Ireland: The place of reflective inquiry. *Teacher Development, 3*(1), 49–65.

Loxley, A., Johnston, K., Murchan, D., Fitzgerald, H., & Quinn, M. (2007). The role of whole-school contexts in shaping the experiences and outcomes associated with professional development. *Journal of In-Service Education, 33*(3), 265–285.

Lyons, N. (Ed.). (1998). *With portfolio in hand: Validating a new teacher professionalism.* New York: Teachers College Press.

Lyons, N. (2002). The personal self in a public story: The portfolio presentation narrative. In N. Lyons & V. LaBoskey (Eds.), *Narrative inquiry in practice: Advancing the knowledge of teaching.* New York: Teachers College Press.

NCCA. (2005). *The primary curriculum in schools: Insights from the curriculum implementation evaluation and the primary curriculum review.* Dublin: National Council for Curriculum and Assessment.

Organisation for Economic Co-operation and Development. (1991). *Review of national policies for education: Ireland.* Paris: OECD.

Putnam, R., & Borko, H. (2000). What do new views of knowledge and thinking have to say about research on teacher learning? *Educational Researcher, 29*(1), 4–15.

Rath, A. (2002). Interrogating cultural assumptions using a reflective portfolio process. *Irish Educational Studies, 21*(2), 33–46.

Rodgers, C. (2002). Defining reflection: Another look at Dewey and reflective thinking. *Teachers College Record, 104*(4), 842–866.

Sarason, S. (1996). *Revisiting the culture of schools and the problem of change.* New York: Teachers College Press.

Schön, D. (1995). Knowing-in-action: The new scholarship requires a new epistemology. *Change, 27*(6), 27–34.

Sugrue, C. (2002). Irish teachers' experience of professional learning: Implications for policy and practice. *Journal of In-Service Education, 28*(2), 311–338.

Wells, G. (1999). *Dialogic inquiry: Towards a sociocultural practice and theory of education.* Cambridge: Cambridge University Press.

Wenger, E. (1998). *Communities of practice: Learning, meaning, and identity.* New York: Cambridge University Press.

Wideen, M., & Lemma, P. (1999). *Ground level reform in teacher education.* Calgary, Alberta: Detselig Enterprises.

Summary and Implications

Cheryl J. Craig

Louise F. Deretchin

Mary Kooy's chapter on community, collaboration, and professional development matters began with a literature review that not only set the context for her essay, but also for this particular issue of ATE's *Teacher Education Yearbook*. Kooy asserted that teacher development and school reform will not happen until the teacher is recognized as integral—indeed, the deciding factor—in whatever changes are introduced to schools, teaching, and teacher education. Furthermore, those initiating change efforts need to be respectful of the primacy of how the teacher is positioned in the educational enterprise. In a nutshell, desired reform simply will not happen without teachers' willing participation (Tyack & Cuban, 1995).

Because large group efforts at teacher development are not tuned to individual teacher needs or interests and lack sustaining power, Kooy argued for small teacher development groups—in her case, book clubs—as sites for productive teacher inquiry. In these relational places, individual teacher knowledge is nurtured in community. In Kooy's research, teacher growth in small-group settings (book clubs in her case) became seeded within teacher education programs and continued throughout teachers' careers. Kooy proved this point through her ongoing work with both preservice and in-service teachers in Canada.

In Chapter 2, Lily Orland-Barak spoke of the same desire to control teaching through standardization as Kooy did. However, Orland-Barak's research focused intently on the kinds of conversations that took place within small teacher development groups in Israel. In her study, she identified three contrasting cases of how teachers converse with one another: (1) talking "close," (2) talking "open," and (3) talking "close and open." Through these three approaches, teachers grappled, in varying ways, with issues of diversity, identity, and power. From this, Orland-Barak's variations of a theme emerged that suggested professional conversation, regardless of its being "close," "open," or "close and open," was inherently feminist. For Orland-Barak, this was how practicing teachers in Israel learn to negotiate meaning and come to terms with the standardization and accountability agendas setting boundaries on their practices.

Like Lily Orland-Barak's Chapter 2, Ellen Ballock's Chapter 3 reminded readers that not all small teacher research groups interact in the same way. Ballock's chapter focused on CFG groups, which emerged as a teacher development strategy in the context of large-scale school reform in the United States. Through surveying the available literature, Ballock showed how the agendas and learning of teachers in emerging and established CFG groups differ. Her chapter suggested that there is a continuum of how and what teachers learn in CFG groups and that progression along that continuum is anticipated, though certainly not automatic.

Next appeared Yendol-Hoppey and Dana's Chapter 4, which centered on close interactions between a group of elementary teachers and their math coach, Kevin Thomas. Like Ballock's Chapter 3, the teachers, at their coach's urging, used CFG protocols to look at student work and engage in text-based discussions. Overall, the chapter peeled back the rhetoric surrounding professional learning communities and showed how they can work in a particular school setting when commingled with action research—which Yendol-Hoppey and Fichtman Dana likened to teacher research.

In a sense, Kelley, North, and Craig's Chapter 5 built on Ballock's Chapter 3 and Yendol-Hoppey and Fichtman Dana's Chapter 4 and echoed themes present in Kooy's and Orland-Barak's Chapters 1 and 2 as well. The connection with Ballock's and Yendol-Hoppey and Fichtman Dana's work was that the teacher research groups grew out of the CFG work already underway in two U.S. high school contexts—with one group having a shorter history (West Houston High School) and the other group being more established (Eagle High School). The link to Kooy's work was that the teacher researchers openly claim their roles as active curriculum makers (Clandinin & Connelly, 1992), living curriculum alongside their students, rather than serving as mere conduits (Connelly & Clandinin, 1995; Craig & Olson, 2002) implementing others' reform prescriptions. Further to this, the teachers described how they have been under the thumb of others (policymakers, administrators, consultants) and fed a compliance diet, which was not conducive to them producing knowledge of their own accord, which was one of their goals in writing this particular chapter. The resonance between the Kelley, North, and Craig and Orland-Barak work was that the two teacher research groups lived two different stories or "models" of engagement. Yet, both assisted the teachers in grappling with the increasing complexity that arose in the midst of their ongoing work.

The final chapter in Division 1 was Rath's Chapter 6, which resonated well with Yendol-Hoppey and Fichtman Dana's Chapter 4 (action research) and Kelley, North, and Craig's Chapter 5 (teacher research). In it, readers were transported to Ireland and introduced to a research project funded by the largest teachers' union in Ireland, which was not unlike Yendol-Hoppey and Fichtman Dana's professional learning community inquiry in Chapter 4 (Lucent funding) and Kelley, North, and Craig's teacher research group in Chapter 5 (Houston A+ Challenge funding). Rath's close work with five primary teachers, like the work with the mathematics teachers in Chapter 4 and the high school teachers in Chapter 5, assisted the teachers in claiming their narrative authority (Olson, 1995; Olson & Craig, 2001) and in speaking truth to power. In Rath's essay, the teachers returned to the values that attracted them to the teaching profession and pledged to assist colleagues and preservice teachers in developing their practices and refining their knowledge.

In Division 1, the value of teacher learning in small-group settings was both presented and instantiated. Not only that, the context of teaching was conveyed as a backdrop against which the practices of soon-to-be credentialed teacher candidates would unfold. With this essential background in place, Division 2 focuses on the theme of teacher education and explores small-group practices underway in that arena.

References

Clandinin, D. J., & Connelly, F. M. (1992). Teacher as curriculum maker. In P. Jackson (Ed.), *Handbook of curriculum* (pp. 363–461). New York: Macmillan.

Connelly, F. M., & Clandinin, D. J. (1995). *Teachers' professional knowledge landscapes.* New York: Teachers College Press.

Craig, C., & Olson, M. (2002). The development of narrative authority in knowledge communities: A narrative approach to teacher learning. In N. Lyons and V. K. La-Boskey (Eds.), *Narrative inquiry in practice: Advancing the knowledge of teaching* (pp. 115–129). New York: Teachers College Press.

Olson, M. (1995). Conceptualizing narrative authority: Implications for teacher education. *Teaching and Teacher Education, 23*(3), 119–125.

Olson, M., & Craig, C. (2001). Opportunities and challenges in the development of teachers' knowledge: The development of narrative authority through knowledge communities. *Teaching and Teacher Education, 17*(6), 667–684.

Tyack, D., & Cuban, L. (1995). *Tinkering toward utopia.* Cambridge, MA: Harvard University Press.

Division 2

TEACHER EDUCATION

Overview and Framework

Cheryl J. Craig

Louise F. Deretchin

In Division 2, our attention focuses on what is happening in teacher education with respect to teacher learning in small-group settings. As foreshadowed, connections between teaching and teacher education are necessary, anticipated, and totally unavoidable. As readers immerse themselves in the forthcoming eight chapters, themes that emerged in Division 1 (teaching) will resurface, and ideas and approaches will continue to reverberate as readers further explore the "teacher learning in small-group settings" theme.

Chapter 7, written by Anthony Clarke and Gaalen Erickson of the University of British Columbia, begins our "teacher education in small-group settings" discussion. Clarke and Erickson tell of a teacher education cohort they pioneered and the small-group learning situations they have developed within it. In their chapter, they discuss how complexity theory forms the most representative and illuminative construct with which to explain their and their teacher education candidates' journeys as knowers of their own situations over time.

Then, in Chapter 8, we cross the American-Canadian border to Washington State and the essay contributed by Jacque Ensign of Evergreen State College, Olympia, Washington. In her essay, Ensign applauds the value of small-group seminars. Further to this, Ensign illustrates how preservice teachers carry their learning forward, and ideas gleaned in small-group seminars begin to appear—in changed forms, of course—in K–12 classroom discussions with students.

"Preservice Candidates 'Looking at Student Work' in a Professional Development School Setting" is the title of Chapter 9. In it, Kami Patrizio of Towson University centers on the professional development school as a backdrop for teacher candidates' small-group learning experiences. In Patrizio's essay, the preservice teachers use the "looking at student work" protocol, often associated with critical friends group (CFG) work, as the activity through which the teacher candidates advance their knowledge of how they make sense of student work samples in ways that would allow them to move forward in their teaching practices in more informed ways.

Next in our lineup of essays having to do with teacher education is Paulien Meijer and Helma Oolbekkink-Marchand's Chapter 10, "Tracing Learning in Collaborative Reflective Meetings of Student Teachers." In that chapter, the two teacher educators from the Netherlands interrogate what and how student teachers learn in a collaborative research setting and uncover some findings that differ from those of some of their Dutch colleagues.

Returning once more to the United States, Don Halquist and Sue Novinger's Chapter 11, "Cracks in the Mirror: Discovering Teacher Candidates' Strategies for Resisting Reflection," appears next. In it, Halquist and Novinger trouble the content of the reflective letters written by two "reflection resisters" in their early childhood education cohort of twenty teacher candidates. Along the way, the two teacher educators unmask some of their own unexamined suppositions concerning the students believed to be reflection resisters.

In Chapter 12, Nancy Gallavan, from the University of Central Arkansas, addresses the topic of exploring the significance and benefits of group learning for developing cultural competence with teacher candidates. As her chapter unfolds, what is happening in teacher education with respect to cultural competence is linked to what is going on in K–12 classrooms and with ATE Standard 2, Cultural Competence.

"Beginning Teachers' Inquiry in Linguistically Diverse Classrooms: Exploring the Power of Small Learning Communities" is the title of Chapter 13, which is authored by Barbara Merino and Rebecca Ambrose of the University of California at Davis. In their essay, the two teacher educators focus on how a teacher research project assisted Pablo, the beginning teacher participant in their study, to transition from his teacher education program to teaching in a high-needs school peopled by a significant population of English-language learners.

In our final chapter in Division 2: Teacher Education, Chapter 14, we cross the border once again, moving from California on the U.S.'s West Coast to Nova Scotia on Canada's East Coast. And once more, the topic of diversity is taken up in Joanne Tompkins and Jeff Orr's essay, "'It Could Take Forty Minutes; It Could Take Three Days': Authentic Small-Group Learning for Aboriginal Education." In this work, small-group teacher education practices with Canada's First Nations and Dene people are highlighted. So, too, are the transformative possibilities of small groups given credence.

All in all, the eight chapters in Division 2 invite readers to experience a rich palette of activities underway in the field of teacher education. What occurs within cohorts, seminars, professional development schools, and collaborative conversation groups is examined. Furthermore, the value of small group's learning about diversity—that of learning about others in relation to oneself—is stressed.

CHAPTER 7

Cohort Learning and Complexity Thinking
THE CASE OF THE CITE TEACHER EDUCATION PROGRAMME

Anthony Clarke
University of British Columbia

Gaalen Erickson
University of British Columbia

Anthony Clarke, Ph.D., is a teacher educator at the University of British Columbia with an interest in teacher education, student teaching, and advisory practices. Teacher inquiry, self-study, and practitioner research, as they pertain to professional learning communities, is also another area of research interest.

Gaalen Erickson, Ed.D., is a professor at the University of British Columbia whose research interests have focused on the methods and theories used to identify and interpret student and teacher learning. His work also examines models of teacher professional development examining the relationships between research and practice as they are enacted in projects documenting the nature of practitioner inquiry and professional knowledge.

ABSTRACT

In this chapter, we outline a series of theoretical and practical perspectives of an elementary teacher education cohort that was created to address some of the perennial problems of fragmentation in teacher education programs (i.e., Tom, 1996). In particular, we focus much of our discussion and analysis in terms of a perspective on learning emerging from a field known as complexity theory or complexity thinking (Davis & Sumara, 2006; Davis, Sumara, & Luce-Kapler, 2000). In drawing upon this field of complexity thinking, we examine some of the dynamical properties of "interdependent learning systems" and provide an account of the nature of what we are calling "cohort learning" as it relates to the "learning in small groups" theme of this book.

Introduction and Context

For the past eleven years, a small group of teacher educators at the University of British Columbia (UBC) have had the freedom to design an alternative Bachelor of Education elementary program for a cohort of thirty-six preservice elementary teachers in an attempt to address some of the most vexing issues in teacher education. The nature of the challenges that we were attempting to address have been well documented in the teacher education literature (in particular see Tom, 1996). They include the fragmentation between courses, the separation of course work and practicum experiences, the programmatic decisions that are driven more by scheduling than by pedagogical imperatives, thus creating a situation where the preservice teacher is expected to make sense of and integrate himself all the various perspectives and "messages" that he experiences in the program. (While many different terms are used to describe those enrolled in teacher education programs, we shall use the term "preservice teacher" rather than student teacher or prospective teacher.) Our cohort is known as CITE: Community and Inquiry for Teacher Education. Our definition of a cohort is an intact group of individuals (comprised of preservice teachers and campus and school-based educators) who are engaged in a common experience and who (in a teacher education context) take many if not all of their courses together (Mather & Hanley, 1999). The students in CITE are enrolled in a twelve-month post-degree Bachelor of Education elementary program. The CITE cohort is nested within a larger program at UBC that graduates around five hundred beginning elementary teachers each year. Our own work and inquiry within this cohort have allowed us to shape the CITE B.Ed. experience quite differently from the regular program while still fulfilling all the requirements of the program. In this chapter we discuss our analysis and reflections on the challenges identified above in terms of a perspective on learning emerging from a field known as complexity theory or complexity thinking (Davis & Sumara, 2006; Davis, Sumara, & Luce-Kapler, 2000). In particular, we wish to look at some of the dynamical properties of interdependent learning systems and to provide an account of the nature of what we are calling "cohort learning," as it relates to the theme of this book.

OUR CONCEPTION OF COMMUNITY AND INQUIRY

As the name of the cohort suggests, the principles of community and inquiry are central to CITE. While the original team members who articulated the principles and commitments for CITE held a range of theoretical conceptions of community and inquiry, we did agree upon a general, shared set of meanings as to the way in which such a community would function and how it might encourage the CITE students, as well as the instructors, to inquire into their own teaching practices. We articulated these shared principles and commitments in an on-line handbook (see: http://educ.ubc.ca/courses/cite/) that all new participants are expected to read and discuss with the instructional team. These principles are:

- Learning is continual and transformative; it takes place in a variety of contexts and through different means as both an individual and collective activity.
- A learning community is one in which members are committed to ongoing inquiry, critical reflection, and constructive engagement with others.
- Teaching is a moral enterprise, and learning to teach is a matter of developing dispositions as well as gaining content and pedagogical knowledge.
- A reflective and coherent teacher education program fosters meaningful connections between curricular, foundational, and field-based areas.
- A responsive teacher education program is attentive to all the communities it serves.

While we did not claim to draw upon any particular theoretical perspective on learning some twelve years ago, our subsequent analyses of the type of learning environments engendered by these principles and the CITE program as it has evolved over time has strong parallels with our current understanding of complexity theory. Part of the ongoing journey of the CITE instructional team has been to interrogate, interpret, and continue to enact these principles with the end in view of creating a community that is able to inquire, individually and collectively, into the teaching and learning of its participants—the preservice teachers, the university-based instructional team, and our school-based teacher educators. As a community, each of the CITE members is not only responsible for her or his own learning, but is also expected to support the learning of others by participating fully in all activities within the community. To further enhance a sense of community, all students take the majority of their courses together and are typically clustered into groups of four to seven students per school for their practicum experiences. Also, wherever possible, CITE instructors are responsible for two or more instructional components within the program so that the relationship between instructors, students, and the program components is closer and more informed by the activities in each course than in our traditional teacher education program. We believe that the emphasis on collaboration between members of the community is one of the most significant points of departure for our students from their earlier school experiences or from their university coursework where competition amongst their peers was their dominant experience. Over time our conception of community has changed as our work within CITE has evolved. For example, we now realize that the distinctive cohort community that emerges each year cannot be replicated from one year to the next. We recognize that something important happens in the dynamic spaces created by the engagement and interactions between the CITE participants in the various activities that comprise the program. These interactions result in the emergence of new understandings and new practices within and across the community.

In combination with our conception of community, the concept of inquiry has also been critical to our endeavors in the CITE cohort. For us, inquiry is a defining feature of professional practice. When members of the teaching profession cease to be inquisitive about their practice, as when teachers are no longer inquisitive about how students learn or about new approaches and strategies to teaching, then their practice ceases to be professional (Clarke & Erickson, 2004). Without inquiry, one's practice becomes perfunctory and repetitive, duplicative and routinized. This is an important distinction for us, as the concept of inquiry distinguishes teaching as a profession. Similar to our emergent conceptions of community, our concept of inquiry has developed progressively over the years. For example, we have become increasingly open to the idea that, within the constraints of a twelve-month Bachelor of Education program, "less is more." That is, rather than trying to cover as much material as possible in the short time that the students are with us, we are more interested in the quality of the questions they generate as a measure of their readiness to enter the teaching profession. Therefore, inquiry has taken on a more substantive role in our conceptualization of CITE than originally anticipated. For example, one of the continuing practices in the CITE program is that the CITE instructors identify their particular research foci for that year and invite the students to participate in these inquiry projects as well as their own. In the past eleven years, CITE students and their instructors have generated more than sixty publications and conference presentations exploring various aspects of the CITE program.

Cohorts in Teacher Education

Tom (1996), in his book on "redesigning teacher education," outlined a number of "design principles" that he argued would result in better teacher education programs. Among the structural design principles enumerated, he identified the use of a cohort model as an effective way of engaging preservice teachers in both campus and field-based settings. Subsequently, Bullough, Clark, Wentworth, and Hansen (2001) argued that although the cohort concept in teacher education has received a positive reception within the educational community over the past two decades, they note that there have been remarkably few published studies. The literature that does exist generally addresses practical issues related to cohorts (Fenning, 2004; Seifert & Mandzuk, 2004). Bullough et al. note that although cohort organization has great educative potential, "this potential is not realized simply by administratively shuffling students into groups . . . structural changes to teacher education like cohort organization must be complemented by efforts to alter common-sense conceptions of teaching" (p. 109). We agree with Bullough et al. that structural changes in themselves are insufficient to make any significant changes in our teacher education program, but we would submit that the more fundamental issue that requires altering is our common-sense conceptions of learning, which include conceptions of "learning to teach." In this regard we have since the inception of CITE explored a number of perspectives on professional learning, from Schön's (1983) notion of "reflective practice" to Scardamalia and Bereiter's (1992) "knowledge building communities" to Lave and Wenger's (1991) work on "communities of practice." While each of these perspectives captures some important aspects of learning in professional and group settings, they fall short in some important regards in terms of looking at the ways in which the cohort as a group learns and why it is such an effective structure for organizing teacher preparation programs. We currently think that "complexity thinking" offers us the most fruitful perspective on the nature of cohort learning at both the individual and community level in terms of both providing an adequate account of our current practices as teacher educators as well as how our cohort has changed over time.

Why Complexity Thinking?

The notions of complexity and complex systems have been in use in both the popular and the scientific literature for well over fifty years now, but nonetheless they remain difficult to articulate because they are used in so many different disciplinary fields and contexts with a variety of approaches to address many different types of problem areas in those fields. Davis and Sumara (2006), likely the most prolific writers on the subject in the field of education, capture some of this difficulty in the preface to their book on *Complexity and Education*. They state that "complexity theory/science/thinking is young and evolving—and as we develop, it refuses tidy descriptions and unambiguous definitions. Indeed, it is not even clear whether it should be called a field, a domain, a system of interpretation, or even a research attitude" (p. ix). In their attempt to address some of this diversity they cite Richardson and Cilliers's (2001) discussion of three broad schools of thought on the field: *hard or reductionist complexity science* (typically as practiced by physicists attempting to understand the nature of reality), *soft complexity science* (common in biology and the social sciences to describe and interpret living and social systems), and *complexity thinking* (concerned with the philosophical and pragmatic implications of assuming a complex universe, that, as such, represents a *way of thinking and acting*) (p.18). Davis and Sumara seem to prefer to use "complexity thinking" to describe the ways in which educational researchers may draw upon complexity writings, and we are likewise persuaded that the focus on ways of *thinking about* and *acting upon* education phenomena is both an attractive and generative perspective for researching our own practices as teacher educators. Hence we have opted for the use of "complexity thinking" as the term to describe the general perspective and approach that we draw upon in this chapter.

One overarching connection between the incredibly wide variety of phenomena that have drawn upon notions of complexity—in disciplinary fields within both the natural and social sciences—has been the conception of "self-organizing adaptive systems" (Johnson, 2001; Kauffman, 1995; Waldrop, 1992). Davis and Sumara (2006) describe this notion, with particular reference to educational phenomena, as any "sort of system that learns" (p. x). We think the idea of a "learning system" has considerable interpretive and explanatory power. Johnson (2001) uses it to describe a variety of systems including the "connected lives of ants, brains, cities, and software"—the subtitle of his book entitled *Emergence*. Hence we will explore the various qualities of learning systems to articulate our notion of cohort learning within a teacher education program.

QUALITIES OF LEARNING SYSTEMS

We must be necessarily brief in this description, but fortunately we are able to refer the reader to an expanding body of literature on complexity and education. (A good place to begin any search of this literature is the website: http://www .complexityandeducation.ualberta.ca/.) We will draw primarily upon Davis and Sumara's (2006, pp. 5–6) work in summarizing these qualities of learning systems. Complex learning systems are:

Self-organized. They arise as the actions of autonomous agents come to be interlinked and codependent.

Emergent. They manifest properties that exceed the summed traits and capacities of individual agents, and they do not depend upon a central organizer or governing structure.

Nested. They are often composed of other systems that give rise to new patterns of activities.

Short-range. Most of the interactions occur among close neighbors and the coherence of the system then depends upon these interdependences rather than on some centralized control.

Ambiguously bounded. They are *open* in the sense that they interact with their surroundings, and their "edges" are often arbitrarily defined.

Organizationally closed. They are *closed* in that they are inherently stable, and their internal organizational structures endure.

Structurally determined. They can change aspects of their structure in adapting to dynamic contexts—that is, they learn.

In presenting these qualities in synoptic fashion we are also mindful of Davis and Sumara's (2006) cautionary stance that complexity thinking should not be thought of as "a *metadiscourse*—that is, an explanatory system that somehow stands over or exceeds all others" (p. 7). Rather, they, and we, view it as a "notion that draws on and elaborates the irrepressible human tendency to notice similarities among seemingly disparate phenomena. How is an anthill like a human brain? How is a classroom like a stock market? and so forth. These are questions that invoke a poetic sensibility and that rely on analogy, metaphor, and other associative functions of language" (p. 7). Hence the issue that we wish to explore in the remainder of this chapter is whether these qualities of complex systems provide a fruitful approach for describing and understanding our cohort as we have experienced it as participants for the past eleven years. But most importantly, does this analysis provide us with richer understandings of our own practices and inquiries in the CITE program in order to think and act in new and productive ways.

WHAT IS "COHORT LEARNING"?

One of the appealing features of cohorts is that they provide the opportunities to create forms of social and structural stability over time that allow the participants in the cohort to address some of the challenges of the piecemeal and fragmented experiences typically associated with more traditional teacher education programs. As Bullough et al. (2001) have noted, "evidence supports the value of cohorts in teacher education as a means of providing beginning teacher support, enhanced opportunities to learn from other beginning teachers, and the realization that learning to teach is a community responsibility" (p. 101). We have argued that these "enhanced opportunities to learn" have emerged from the variety of community groupings (as we initially called them) that occur throughout the program and in a variety of different social and pedagogical contexts (see Farr Darling, Erickson, & Clarke, 2007). Examined through the lens of "complexity theory," these groupings in essence are really nested learning systems, ranging in scale from the individual preservice teacher as an intact system with his or her unique understandings of the diverse knowledge base associated with learning to teach (Hiebert, Gallimore, & Stigler, 2002), to the whole CITE community in its entirety, which includes all of its constituent members, learning to adapt practices, policies, and procedures in response to the uncertainties and ever-changing circumstances characteristic of all professions and professional development contexts (Schön, 1983). It is this latter learning system that we are calling "cohort learning" and that is the primary focus of this chapter.

So, for us, "cohort learning" at the program level refers to the kind of learning that has occurred over time in terms of the ways that we have changed the structural features and in particular the practices of the CITE program. Some of the changes that we are referring to are more predictable than others. One of the structural features of any cohort model is the inevitable change that occurs in the membership of the cohort over time. In other words, there is a new group of preservice teachers each year, and typically there are some changes in both the campus-based instructional team and in the school advisors (the term used by the UBC teacher education program as a parallel term to "faculty advisor"; other programs use terms such as "cooperating teacher" or "school mentor") working with the preservice teachers in their practicum schools. (While there has remained a core group of faculty and we have worked with some schools in the practicum setting over most of the eleven years of the program, there are inevitably changes that do and must occur in the individual participants constituting the CITE program.) Other less predictable and highly context-dependent structural changes that have necessitated some form of adaptive response by the CITE program have been occasioned by changes in the requirements for teacher certification at the provincial level, and changes in the basic program structure for teacher education at the faculty level.

Examples of these types of changes include the scheduling of the various course components such as courses and practicum experiences, the mode and methods for course delivery and some of the overall program emphases such as curricular integration. Most of these changes have been accompanied by smaller groups of participants engaging in some form of systematic inquiry into the potential consequences and outcomes of these changes. From the outset of the CITE program we have been determined to inquire into our own practices (Clarke & Erickson, 2004) and to document the nature and outcomes of these shifting practices. A number of these changing practices are the subjects of individual book chapters in a recently completed book entitled *Collective Improvisation in a Teacher Education Community* (Farr Darling, Erickson, & Clarke, 2007), celebrating the tenth anniversary of the CITE program. (While ten years is not a long time for established programs, the life span of experimental teacher education programs involving a continuing core group of participants is typically much shorter than this: e.g., Tom, 1996.)

In the next section we examine how a complexity thinking "reading" of our past experiences and practices can illuminate the "irrepressible search for patterns" and whether the qualities of a complex learning system, as described in the literature, will enable us to see new connections and possibilities in our own work as teacher educators, and at the same time provide an invitation to others in the community to share in this endeavor.

COMPLEXITY THINKING AND COHORT LEARNING

How might this sensibility of complexity thinking be used to describe some of our practices in the CITE program with respect to "cohort learning" and provide us with some directions for future actions? One way of proceeding is to consider each of the above listed qualities in light of our experiences in the CITE program.

Self-Organizing and Emergent

Because these two qualities of learning systems are closely connected, we are discussing them together. The notion of "self-organization" is one of the most common attributes associated with complex systems, and it is this quality that results in the "emergence" of capacities and/or actions that cannot be predicted in advance and that exceed the potential of the sum of the individual system members. Examples from the literature (Johnson, 2001) include the way ants self-organize themselves into colonies and humans create social and political entities such as cities or monetary systems. The actions of the group members become interlinked and codependent upon each other and the system does not necessarily have centralized control, but rather this control is distributed among the constituent agents. Nonetheless, the system as a whole maintains a coherent identity.

Over the eleven years that CITE has existed we can offer many examples of emergent ideas and practices that have occurred at the cohort level. While these occurrences of codependent thinking and problem solving occur in a variety of settings, one particular structure developed as part of the program—the scheduling of three distinct types of group meetings, each with its own particular set of purposes—stands out as a particularly fertile source for the emergence of new perspectives and practices. These types of regularly scheduled meetings consist of:

- a regular weekly meeting with the campus-based instructors and three to four representatives from the preservice teacher group to discuss ongoing instructional and program issues and to share aspects of the different course activities with other instructors
- a regular bimonthly meeting with the school coordinators of each of the participating schools with members of the CITE campus-based instructional team to discuss ways of improving communication between the teaching and learning practices occurring on campus and those in the practicum schools
- yearly three-day retreats at the end of the academic term when the campus-based instructional team meets to review, deconstruct, and reflect upon the events and practices of the previous year and to plan activities and orientations for the upcoming year

In each of these quite different settings, with different agendas, we have experienced a form of "collective intelligence" emerging from the group discussions, and we frequently invent new procedural and structural possibilities "on the spot." One of the earliest illustrations of this type of emergence at a weekly meeting occurred early in the term in the second year of the CITE program when several of the preservice teacher representatives asked a question about curricular integration—one of the thematic orientations for the program announced at the beginning of the year. In the discussion that ensued several instructors also expressed some concern that our previous attempts that year at curricular integration had been somewhat superficial and that we needed to give more thought to our curricular goals and different possibilities for integration. This initial discussion then led to further inquiry into different models of integration by the preservice student inquiry groups (that have become a prominent feature of the CITE program) and by several instructors. At the next meeting these models were discussed and a proposal was made to focus our attention in all five of the curriculum methods courses that were being taught that term around a traveling exhibition on "The Life and Contributions of Leonardo da Vinci," which was being held in the provincial capital, Victoria. We decided to organize a field trip to the exhibit. The preservice students took responsibility for organizing the travel plans (which included a ferry trip) and accommodation arrangements. Each of the CITE methods instructors then reorganized parts of their course syllabi and assignments to incorporate relevant aspects of the Leonardo exhibit and engaged in several sessions of team teaching illustrating how one could examine particular aspects of the Leonardo exhibit to integrate important ideas in art, science, mathematics, language arts, and social studies. This event also provided an opportunity to examine the nature and logistics of the use of out-of-school learning environments (such as museums) and to discuss the logistics and responsibilities of teachers in taking children on field trips of this nature.

This decision to engage in such an extended manner with what started out as a rather innocent question was both spontaneous and "emergent." It could neither have occurred in a non-cohort structure nor in a structure that was controlled in a top-down fashion with a set of predetermined procedures and structures. It illustrates the potential of a self-organizing learning system with distributed control. However, even with this degree of flexibility, the considerable expenditure of resources and willingness to alter one's curricular plans requires a strong, shared commitment on the part of all participants in the program. Clearly we all shared a strong belief in the value of both this type of "thematic curricular integration" and in the importance of firsthand experience in a field setting.

We could provide numerous examples of how the deliberations at our three-day retreat meetings at the end of the teaching term have resulted in significant changes in our program structures and practices. While we do not have sufficient space to provide a full account of these "emergent structures," we can simply enumerate them and direct the interested reader to a number of publications that have described and analyzed the impact of these practices. One such cluster of practices came from an early discussion by the instructional group to systematically inquire into how some of the new "learning technologies" may be integrated into the CITE program in a seamless manner that did not include a separate computer or learning technologies course. This commitment to the curricular integration of learning technologies has now been a long-standing one and has led to a number of different inquiries, such as the incorporation of online forums in addition to class discussion and the use of presentational technologies such as "HyperStudio," "PowerPoint," and "Slowmation." Many of the early efforts in this regard were described in a doctoral dissertation by Mitchell (2001) entitled *Computer Technology in Teacher Education: Tool for Communication, Medium for Inquiry, Object of Critique*. Many other accounts of these endeavors can be found on our website (http://educ.ubc.ca/courses/cite/) and in the 2007 book on CITE mentioned above.

Nested

As indicated above, the CITE cohort is comprised itself of several nested learning systems, and the individual preservice teacher can be considered a learning system. (See the argument made by Davis, Sumara, & Luce-Kapler [2000, p.

56]). So also are the various subgroupings of preservice teachers and/or campus-based faculty in the program (i.e., a group of preservice students working collaboratively on particular projects or in smaller subgroups in a school in a practicum setting), the group of school advisors working together with their respective preservice teachers, and a faculty advisor in a particular school setting.

All of these learning systems are engaged with different types of problems, and hence the nature of the learning and the inevitable interaction between each varies accordingly. This last point brings into sharp relief the possibility that the lack of relationships or connections between these nested learning systems is one of the primary sources of program fragmentation. A primary motive for initiating the cohort at the outset some eleven years ago was to address these fragmentation problems, and it remains an overarching concern.

How might a "complexity thinking attitude" (Davis & Sumara, 2006, p. 19) provide some new insights into this persistent issue of program fragmentation? Our current response to this question is that by being aware of the different types and levels of learning systems within the cohort, we need to better understand how each one functions for the purpose of attempting to design optimal learning environments for these learning systems. Perhaps most importantly, from the program fragmentation perspective, we need to promote ways of enabling and fostering interaction between these learning systems. While we have made some efforts in this regard—the most notable of which would be the inclusion of representatives from all of the constituent groups in our regular meeting structures (described above) and the creation and continual updating of a cohort website—we nonetheless recognize the need to more deeply inquire into how these particular structures function to increase communication and increase understanding across the learning systems.

Short-Range

This quality describes an important mechanism for learning systems to adapt and grow in response to changes in the learning environment. It has been described by many commentators looking at changes in complex learning systems in terms of the need for diversity or a variation principle, whereby it is recognized that it is critical to create "structures to allow ideas to bump together [and] is one of the hallmarks of all progressive human institutions, including higher education, research settings, business, and most governments" (Davis et al., 2000, p. 199). Many other commentators theorizing about learning systems have drawn upon this principle of variation, ranging from the evolutionary biologist Stephen Gould (1996) to Ference Marton's "Theory of Variation" (Marton & Booth, 1997). For example, Gould (1996), in his book entitled *Full House: The Spread of Excellence from Plato to Darwin*, argued:

> I think that my approach of studying variation in complete systems
> does provide genuine resolution for two widely discussed issues that
> can only remain confusing and incoherent when studied in the tradi-
> tional, persistently Platonic mode of representing full systems by a
> single essence or exemplar—and then study how this entity moves
> through time. I find both resolutions particularly satisfying because
> they are not so radical that they lie outside easy conceivability.
> Rather, both solutions make eminent good sense and resolve true
> paradoxes of the conventional view, once you imbibe the revised
> perspective based on variation. (pp. 2–3)

The challenge offered by this quality for educators and teacher educators is one
of creating the conditions for learning environments to contain sufficient diversity to support growth, yet maintain some degree of coherence and stability
within the system. This growth or learning depends much more upon the interactions among the system participants rather than some form of external, centralized control, such as the imposition of "standards" or mandated curriculum
(including assessment) structures. We have engaged with just such a situation in
the past two years as the professional body governing teacher certification in
the province of British Columbia—the British Columbia College of Teachers
(2004)—recently introduced a set of "Standards for the Education, Competence,
and Professional Conduct of Educators in British Columbia" (see: http://www
.bcct.ca/documents/edu_stds.pdf for the most recent version). Teacher preparation programs in British Columbia must be able to demonstrate to the College
that its graduating preservice teachers are able to demonstrate competency in
these standards. While the UBC Faculty of Education has decided that each
preservice teacher should create an electronic portfolio that would function to
demonstrate how the teacher education program has prepared him or her to be
competent in each of the eight general standards, the CITE program decided to
take a more collective approach to the task and created a wiki environment
where each of the standards was discussed and critiqued by the whole cohort of
preservice teachers. (The College originally circulated a draft of the Standards
Document that contained thirteen standards and a number of sub-standards.
After two years of consultation and discussion with Faculties of Education in
British Columbia and the British Columbia Teacher's Federation, this list has
been reduced to eight fairly general standards in the most recent version, February 2008.) The rationale and outcomes of our "distributed response" to the
centralized requirements imposed by the Standards are discussed in detail in a
chapter by Phelan, Erickson, Farr Darling, Collins, & Kind (2007).

Ambiguously Bounded

This quality of a learning system points to the notion of nested learning systems,
since boundaries between the various learning systems are often blurred and the

various group members in the CITE program often participate in more than one learning system. For example, some faculty members participate only in the campus-based program and focus primarily on issues related to course design and integration of these courses, whereas other faculty members also participate in the practicum component of the program and hence work closely with school advisors and school administrators in attending to the varied issues associated with practicum experiences. We see this as a strength of our cohort model where the participants are involved in and knowledgeable about several major components of the program. An excellent example of this movement between different roles and learning systems can be found in our experiments to locate some of the program coursework, which is normally done on campus, to a school setting with the school advisors taking a lead role in the instructional component. We have explored this model with both an immersion course in a physical education methods context (Hubball & Clarke, 2002) and with significant components of a social studies methods context (Clouston, Hunter, & Collins, 2007).

The important thing here is that overlap and interaction occur at local borders where shared understandings and system similarities are sufficient (although a distinctiveness still exists) to allow productive engagement and mutual advancement to occur with minimal "threat" to the individual systems themselves—although they will inevitably change as a result of the interaction. Such conditions give rise to new possibilities that are not available within the individual system. For example, in one case cited above, an inquiry arose that resulted in a master's thesis for one of the teachers in the host school (that was not anticipated at the outset), which gave rise to curricular changes in the course in the years that followed. In another instance, a teacher became a vocal proponent within the school district for an employment regulation reform for beginning teachers that led to a districtwide policy change that the university had been concerned about for a number of years. The new policy benefited not only beginning teachers but teachers with a continuing contract as well. Both examples illustrate nested systems interacting at a local level and resulting in within- and across-system change.

Organizationally Closed and Structurally Determined

We are combining the last two qualities as they represent the dynamical aspects of learning systems that highlight their structural integrity on the one hand and their flexibility on the other—enabling higher levels of emergence over time, that is, learning! Clearly, any teacher preparation program exhibits varying degrees of these dynamic properties as it exists in stable institutional and even societal contexts to address particular needs and functions in those contexts. A key to the design of successful teacher preparation programs is to create as flexible and adaptive structures as possible, given the constraints of the institutional and governmental settings. As alluded to earlier, Tom (1996, p. 25) has identified eleven design principles for "redesigning teacher education." Several of these principles directly address this issue of structural and programmatic adaptability. They are:

Principle 5. Policies and processes should be set up for reviewing, examining, and renewing the teacher education program need to be part of the programmatic design.

Principle 9. Instead of staffing programs horizontally (by specialty), they should be staffed vertically (by interdisciplinary teams or another method that helps bridge among areas of specialized knowledge and practice).

Principle 10. Rather than being treated as individuals to be managed bureaucratically, prospective teachers should be grouped into a cohort that moves through a professional program as a unit.

While we were not aware of Tom's work at the time of creating CITE (we were meeting to discuss the philosophical and conceptual framework at about the same time as this article was published in 1996), his principles certainly strike a strong accord with our thinking and our subsequent practices over the past eleven years. Hopefully the reader will see the enactment of these three principles, particularly in the examples we provided earlier in the chapter, and also see how these principles reflect the two qualities of learning systems under discussion.

For example, for our cohort to operate with some success, we needed to be given a degree of autonomy and flexibility that was not evident in the existing program. The most prevailing feature of the existing program was a course-based approach to teacher education. Everything was determined in terms of individual courses (staffing, scheduling, assessment, etc.). This course-based economy created a lockstepped globalized structure that was totally unresponsive to requests from the local level. "Dynamic" would be the last word to describe the program. CITE turned this highly centralized approach to teacher education on its head by arguing for a more distributed and programmatic approach to teaching and learning. Suddenly a very different mind-set was called for: one that still respected the integrity of the enterprise (teacher education) but placed the educative agenda above a system of schooling (Fenstermacher, 1999).

Some Concluding Remarks

We think that this notion of cohort learning has allowed us to reconsider many of the things that we have done over the past eleven years in a new light that shifts the emphasis away from those philosophical knowledge and learning traditions that rely exclusively on rational and structural underpinnings to those that allow for a fuller sense of the simultaneous, emergent, and collective knowing that we believe characterizes our work within CITE. As the title of our recent book signals, we have become much more aware of the need for "improvisation" as we have come to recognize the value in embracing the inherent uncertainty that exists in our own practices as teacher educators, as well as in the teaching practices of the CITE preservice teachers. In short, complexity thinking represents a significant shift away from a model of teacher education programs based on the elusive search for "best practices" (Grant, 1994) or "evidence-based practice" in teacher education (Davies, 1999; Howe, 2005). These dominant models for teacher education have been prominent in a number of government policy initiatives in both the United States and the United Kingdom. For example, the Lighthouse Partnerships for Teacher Preparation was a U.S. federal government program designed to improve teacher education by

> funding a number of partnerships among teacher preparation institutions and school districts in high-poverty urban and rural areas. The proposed program addresse[d] three critical needs in teacher preparation. First, as a nation, we must identify and rigorously evaluate *best practices* in teacher education, especially in preparing teachers to teach in high-poverty schools. Second, when *exemplary teacher education practices* are identified, they should be disseminated to other institutions; otherwise, good programs will remain islands of excellence with little impact on the great majority of prospective teachers. Third, because quality teacher preparation demands strong collaboration with elementary and secondary schools, school districts and teacher preparation institutions must work together in real partnerships to prepare teachers [emphasis ours]. (http://www.ed.gov/up dates/inits98/titlev.html, accessed March 10, 2008)

In the United Kingdom there have also been a number of government policy initiatives based on a notion of "evidence-based practice"—a slogan adopted from the medical profession. There was a lively exchange between Hargreaves (1997) and Hammersley (1997) about the merits of this approach to both research and policy after these policy directives began to emerge from government agencies in the United Kingdom. Our work and perspective on learning to teach has represented a move away from these attempts at creating programs that "get it right" (an approach that resulted in the monolithic program that we rejected ten years ago).

As we have tried to convey in this chapter, we have been much more sympathetic to an approach or sensibility based upon complexity thinking that leads us to continue to inquire into and explore new and innovative approaches, take risks (and explain why we have adopted this approach to the preservice teachers and school advisors), and in general model the very practice that we hope our preservice teachers and school-based educators will take on in their respective professional lives in schools. After a lifetime of working in many diverse teacher education programs, both of us have found the CITE experience over the past eleven years to be one of the most interesting and motivating projects of our careers as educators and researchers. While many of our colleagues have eschewed active involvement in teacher education programs, opting for the greater "prestige" (and we might add lower class sizes) of teaching in graduate programs only, we continue to mess around in the "swamp." See Schön's (1987) discussion of the varied topography of professional practice where he invokes the metaphor of the "swamp" versus the "high hard ground" referring to the nature of the problems to be found in the messy, confusing field of practice versus those relatively unimportant problems that can be addressed "through the application of research-based theory and technique" (p. 187)—the latter being the approach we described earlier as "evidence-based practice."

We do so not only because it is an energizing and generative space of inquiry, but also because we think that these are the contexts where some of the most important work of educators located in the academy is situated. Furthermore, we embrace complexity thinking because we think that it provides an excellent interpretative frame for the kind of learning that occurs in teacher education programs. For us, it has provided not only a fruitful way of thinking about our work, but has also generated a much more interesting and thought-provoking set of questions about our practices than when we started down this path some years ago.

References

British Columbia College of Teachers. (2004). *Standards for the education, competence, and educational conduct of educators in British Columbia.* Vancouver, BC: British Columbia College of Teachers.

Bullough, R., Clark, C., Wentworth, N., & Hansen, J. (2001). Student cohorts, school rhythms and teacher education. *Teacher Education Quarterly, 28*(2), 97–110.

Clarke, A., & Erickson, G. (2004). Self-study: The fifth commonplace. *Australian Journal of Education, 48*(2), 199–211.

Clouston, D., Hunter, L., & Collins, S. (2007). Social studies education in school. In L. Farr Darling, G. Erickson, & A. Clarke (Eds.). *Collective improvisation in a teacher education community.* Dordrecht, Holland: Springer Academic Publishers.

Davies, P. (1999). What is evidence-based education? *British Journal of Educational Studies, 47*(2), 108–121.

Davis, B., & Sumara, D. (2006). *Complexity and education: Inquiries into learning, teaching, and research.* Mahwah, NJ: Lawrence Erlbaum Associates.

Davis, B., Sumara, D. J., & Luce-Kapler, R. (2000). *Engaging minds: Changing teaching in complex times.* (2nd ed.). New York: Routledge.

Farr Darling, L., Erickson, G., & Clarke, A. (Eds.). (2007). *Collective improvisation in a teacher education community.* Dordrecht, Holland: Springer Academic Publishers.

Fenning, K. (2004). Cohort-based learning: Application to learning organizations and student academic success. *College Quarterly, 7*(1), 24–34.

Fenstermacher, G. (1999). Agenda for education in a democracy. In W. F. Smith and G. D. Fenstermacher (Eds.), *Leadership for educational renewal* (pp. 3–28). San Francisco: Jossey-Bass.

Gould, S. (1996*). Full house: The spread of excellence from Plato to Darwin.* New York: Random House.

Grant, C. (1994). Best practices in teacher education for urban schools: Lessons from the multicultural teacher education literature. *Action in Teacher Education, 16*(3), 2–18.

Hammersley, M. (1997). Educational research and teaching: A response to David Hargreaves' TTA lecture. *British Educational Research Journal, 23*(2), 141–162.

Hargreaves, D. (1997). In defence of research for evidence-based teaching: A re-joinder to Martyn Hammersley. *British Educational Research Journal, 23*(4), 405–419.

Hiebert, J., Gallimore, R., & Stigler, J. (2002). A knowledge base for the teaching profession: What would it look like and how can we get one? *Educational Researcher, 31*(5), 3–15.

Howe, K. R. (2005). The education science question: A symposium. *Educational Theory, 55*(3), 235–321.

Hubball, H., & Clarke, A. (2002). Development and evaluation of a Physical Education methods course as an immersion experience for student teachers in an elementary school setting. *Physical and Health Education Journal, 68*(2), 42.

Johnson, S. (2001). *Emergence: The connected lives of ants, brains, cities, and software.* New York: Scribner.

Kauffman, S. (1995). *At home in the universe: The search for the laws of self-organization and complexity.* New York: Oxford University Press.

Lave, J., & Wenger, E. (1991). *Situated learning: Legitimate peripheral participation.* New York: Cambridge University Press.

Marton, F., & Booth, S. (1997). *Learning and awareness.* Mahwah, NJ: Lawrence Erlbaum Associates.

Mather, D., & Hanley, B. (1999). Cohort grouping and preservice teachers' education: Effects on pedagogical development. *Canadian Journal of Education, 24*(3), 235–250.

Mitchell, J. (2001). *Computer technology in teacher education: Tool for communication, medium for inquiry, object of critique.* Unpublished doctoral dissertation. British Columbia, Canada: University of British Columbia.

Phelan, A., Erickson, G., Farr Darling, L., Collins, S., & Kind, S. (2007). "The Filter of Laws": Teacher education and the British Columbia College of Teachers' teaching standards. In L. Farr Darling, G. Erickson, & A. Clarke (Eds.), *Collective improvisation in a teacher education community.* Dordrecht, Holland: Springer Academic Publishers.

Richardson, K., & Cilliers, P. (2001). What is complexity science? A view from different directions. *Emergence, 3*(1), 5–22.

Scardamalia, M., & Bereiter, C. (1992). Collaborative knowledge building. In E. de

Corte, M. C. Linn, H. Mandl, & L. Verschaffel (Eds.), *Computer-based learning environments and problem solving* (pp. 41–66). Berlin: Springer-Verlag.

Schön, D. (1983). *The reflective practitioner: How professionals think in action.* New York: Basic Books.

Schön, D. (1987). *Educating the reflective practitioner.* San Francisco: Jossey-Bass.

Seifert, K., & Mandzuk, D. (2004, February). How helpful are cohorts in teacher education? Paper presented at the 25th Forum on Ethnography in Education, Philadelphia, PA.

Tom, A. (1996). Principles for redesigning teacher education. *Journal of Primary Education, 6*(1 & 2), 19–27.

Waldrop, M. (1992). *Complexity: The emerging science on the edge of order and chaos.* New York: Simon & Schuster.

CHAPTER 8

Seminars as Small-Group Learning Sites in Teacher Preparation

Jacque Ensign
Evergreen State College

Jacque Ensign, Ph.D., wrote this chapter while she was a visiting faculty member at Evergreen State College. Her current areas of interest include culturally relevant teaching, teacher development, and preparing teachers for effectively teaching a diversity of students.

ABSTRACT

Small seminars are settings for learning communities in teacher education programs and help programs align their pedagogy with recommendations for quality teacher education. By actively involving preservice teachers in collaborative learning, teacher educators can promote deeper learning of theory and methods as well as model effective pedagogy for use in K–12 classrooms to meet the needs of a wide diversity of students.

As a former classroom teacher who has successfully used the enthusiasm of K–12 students working together in small groups, I have been searching for ways of forming such learning communities in teacher education. Recently, I have had the privilege of learning new ways for "teaching with your mouth shut," which describes The Evergreen State College's approach to teaching (Finkel, 2000). Through my experience teaching preservice teacher education students in a program that uses seminars instead of lectures for much of the content, I've been able to reflect upon preservice teacher learning that can take place in small groups.

This chapter focuses on the use of seminars as settings for small-group learning communities in teacher preparation, thus fostering engrossed participation and deeper learning as well as building community. As settings for cooperative group work in teacher education, seminars not only foster small-group learning communities within their individual settings, but also help to model pedagogy that can be used in K–12 settings. After describing the context of the teacher education program that used seminars, this chapter will then explain how seminars function, how some of our preservice teachers used seminars in their student teaching, and will conclude with a discussion of the implications of using seminars for small communities of learners in teacher preparation.

Context

This chapter is my reflection as a participant observer in the teacher education program at Evergreen State College. As a visiting faculty member for nearly three years, I was an active participant in two two-year cohort cycles that used seminars as an integral part of their entire programs. As a visitor, I kept field notes and solicited preservice teachers' reflections on their experiences with seminars. Those have informed this reflection on our practice of using small-group seminars in preservice teacher education as well as on some preservice teachers' subsequent use of small-group seminars in their student teaching classrooms.

Evergreen State College in Washington State is well known for its innovative approaches to undergraduate teaching, including its interdisciplinary team-taught programs that use seminars, workshops, and experiential learning. The Master in Teaching program I describe reflects the undergraduate programs by also being an interdisciplinary program taught by a team of professors rather than a collection of single subject courses taught by individual professors.

The aim of the Master in Teaching program is "to develop teachers who can put principles of effective and meaningful classroom teaching into practice, and who can create classrooms that are culturally responsive and inclusive, democratic and learner-centered, developmentally appropriate and active" (Evergreen State College, 2007, Our Program Themes section, para. 1). In the Master in Teaching Program three faculty members teach a cohort of forty-five students for nearly all of the coursework for the two years of the program in which students get their state teaching credential and master's degree. Each cohort includes preservice teachers preparing to teach elementary, middle, or secondary grades, and much of the learning takes place in heterogeneous groups across the K–12 spectrum.

Even though this chapter focuses on the use of seminars in teacher education, variations work well in other settings. I have used many of the underlying guidelines to effectively use seminars at other levels of education, including K–12 classrooms and undergraduate classrooms, as well as in more traditional teacher education courses of up to thirty students, including subject-specific methods courses, at other universities. Indeed, many of the guidelines for seminars in teacher education are adapted from those developed for K–12 classrooms, especially those using small groups (i.e., Cohen, 1994), group-facilitated learning (i.e., Atwell, 1998) and discussions (i.e., Hale & City, 2006; Billings & Roberts, 2006; Great Books Foundation, 2005).

How Seminars Function

Seminars were the foundation of on-campus learning in Evergreen's two teacher education program cycles described in this chapter (note: not all cycles use seminars as extensively as those described in this chapter). Instead of lectures in this full-time graduate interdisciplinary program, students spend two to three three-hour sessions a week in workshops on content and methods, and one to three two-hour sessions a week in seminars on texts in the program. Workshops are for the entire cohort of forty-five students, with small breakout groups working cooperatively on the workshop material, interspersed with whole cohort times in which mini-lectures, guest speakers, or audiovisuals are used. To assure continuity throughout the program at Evergreen, all faculty teaching in a two-year cycle are present for all whole cohort times even though only one faculty member may be facilitating. For seminars, students are purposefully grouped into heterogeneous groups across subject and grade level endorsements. In the Master in Teaching Program, seminars have fifteen graduate students working under the guidance of one faculty member for an entire quarter.

In contrast to hands-on learning that occurs in workshops, seminars are best described as "minds-on" learning. As opposed to workshops in which the teacher decides what key information needs to be considered, seminars allow students' questions about a text by an expert to guide much of what is discussed. The National Paideia Center (2007) describes seminars for K–12 in terms very similar to how I have experienced seminars functioning in teacher education:

> The Paideia Seminar is a formal, intellectual dialogue facilitated with open-ended questions about a text. It is one of the most powerful ways to teach the ideas and values that shape your curriculum, thereby making it both more accessible and more relevant for your students. The Seminar is designed specifically to teach your students to think critically while simultaneously enhancing their conceptual understanding of the curriculum. By engaging in seminar dialogue, students also practice a wide range of fundamental literacy skills: reading and writing in addition to speaking and listening. (Introduction to the Paideia Seminar: K–12 section, para. 1–2)

As opposed to informal freewheeling discussions, seminars require guidelines to be followed in order to function well as a community of inquiry. Students' voices should be those primarily heard, with faculty voice only to guide or redirect the seminar back to a focus on the text, asking for clarifications of what students say or summarizing what has been said before moving on to a new topic or question. As a teacher, I find my most productive seminars include all or almost all voices with none predominating.

I come to the seminar with key questions and topics about the text that I'd like to see the seminar address, but I also expect students to come with their questions and topics. Each student comes to seminar with a written paper of quotes from the text accompanied by responses and questions that can be used in seminar. Ideally, questions I bring are ones for which I'm not sure of an answer, as those provoke more interactions with the text and participants. As Gordon Wells (2000) has said so well, "To be able to wonder aloud about these issues and to take action to understand them better not only provides an excellent model for the students to emulate, it also demonstrates the authenticity of the teacher's commitment to inquiry" (p. 65). We often take the first few minutes of seminar to list our questions and topics on the board so everyone can see them. If there are too many, we choose which are most important to include in this seminar session. Even though our seminars are small, I often begin by breaking the group into much smaller groups to assure everyone is actively involved in speaking as well as listening. Groups of two to five students can pick different key questions to discuss before reporting back to the whole seminar. Sometimes these smaller groups all discuss the same question, which then jumpstarts the whole seminar discussion when we reconvene.

To keep the seminar focused on the text, participants need to have the words in front of them so each person can direct everyone to a text passage as a way to either start or reinforce what they are adding to the dialogue. This helps everyone get a deeper understanding of the text that they have previously read individually. Finkel (2000) aptly describes the process of seminars as one in which "Everything will be submitted to joint discussion and the multiplicity of perspectives such conversation brings. Through these means, their understanding of the book will deepen" (p. 37). By having students reference specific passages in the written word, the focus stays on the text throughout the seminar.

Useful guidance for designing and leading Evergreen-style seminars can be found in Finkel (2000). Hale and City (2006) is an excellent resource that is written for use in K–12 classrooms but is equally useful in undergraduate and graduate seminars. Because our students at Evergreen love seminars but wonder how to incorporate them in their K–12 classrooms, Hale and City (2006) is a valuable book to have preservice teachers use first in their graduate seminars and then in their student teaching. Gilmore (2006) has additional strategies that our

Evergreen program as well as middle and secondary teachers have found helpful in adding variety and action to seminars.

Seminars depend on social interaction of participants, not just on the content. Wenger (1998, p. 272) notes that the social aspect in learning communities is essential for motivation. Beyond the motivation provided by social interaction, Lidz and Gindis (2003) argue that social interaction is key to providing an essential component of learning, quoting Vygotsky (1978) that "learning awakens a variety of developmental processes that are able to operate only when the child is interacting with people in his environment and in collaboration with his peers" (p. 90). Unlike many who insist on a more capable peer or teacher to promote development, Wells (2000) has concluded:

> In tackling a difficult task as a group, although no member has expertise beyond his or her peers, the group as a whole, by working at a problem together, is able to construct a solution that none could have achieved alone. In other words, each is "forced to rise above himself" and, by building on the contributions of the individual members, the group collectively constructs an outcome that no single member envisaged at the outset of the collaboration. (p. 324)

Seminars allow this group expertise to drive deep learning for all the participants. That said, teachers have an important role. Randell (2001) found that "students need to be discovering but not to be totally on their own in seeking the path. . . . Teachers are constantly guiding by knowing the subject matter and providing the framework for the students' efforts" (p. 135). Just as in K–12 education, the role of the teacher is vital in structuring and guiding the group's activities and learning in a teacher preparation program. While students do most of the talking in seminars, the faculty member's role is to steer the seminar discussion to be sure students understand the text and its connections to the rest of the program.

Besides general education courses, methods courses can also use seminars. For example, as part of interdisciplinary studies of literacy at Evergreen that spanned three quarters, in two-hour seminars students discussed *Reading Process and Practice* (Weaver, 2002); *Boy Writers: Reclaiming Their Voices* (Fletcher, 2006); *Literacy with an Attitude: Educating Working-Class Children in Their Own Self-Interest* (Finn, 1999); *Ain't No Makin' It: Aspirations and Attainment in a Low-Income Neighborhood* (MacLeod, 2004); "The acquisition of a child by a learning disability" (McDermott, 1996); *The Inner World of the Immigrant Child* (Igoa, 1995); and *Multicultural and Gender Equity in the Mathematics Classroom: The Gift of Diversity* (Trentacosta, 1997). In-depth small-group seminar discussion of these seminal texts drove much deeper understanding than I have seen lectures or individually completed assignments produce. Reflecting within a small-group seminar on how literacy learning interacts with multicultural factors such as gender, socioeconomic class, race, exceptionality, language, and content studies including mathematics has helped our preservice teachers continually consider how they will foster literacy growth in their students no matter whom and what subjects they are teaching.

Building Communities of Learners

Not only do seminars promote student engagement and depth of learning, they also build community by capitalizing on their small group size. Seminars both depend on a community and also help build community, which is well described by McCartney in a monograph on seminars: "At the heart of effective seminaring is the development of a community of learners, and all the techniques in the world cannot create this heart. However, we have found that attention to the seminaring process can contribute to the desired effect of a community of learning" (Washington Center for Undergraduate Improvement, n.d., p. 12). Research on discussion groups in high schools has shown similar effects of discussions building a community of learners: "This reenvisioning of a class of individuals as a collective, as a learning community, came about *through* discussion" (Miller, 2003, p. 312). Because of this community building aspect, Evergreen carefully structures seminars to have the same members for at least ten weeks, whereas workshop membership, which is less dependent on a community, shifts frequently to allow students to get to know everyone in their cohort.

Since seminar discussions in the Evergreen Master in Teaching Program function best in a contained and safe community, the first four or five seminar sessions require attention to community building as well as to discussion of texts. In the first session, seminar participants are guided by the instructor in writing a community contract that lists habits and rules that will foster a strong community of inquiry. Community is more strongly built with twice weekly seminars instead of only once a week. With twice a week seminars, by the third week the members are usually able to take more risks in seminar, asking questions of their classmates about content they don't understand and disagreeing with classmates in a constructive manner. Revisiting the seminar community contract occasionally and checking in weekly with the seminar participants (either through brief exit surveys or oral debriefs with the whole seminar group) ensures continued support for the learning community.

Seminars in Student Teaching

Besides the immediate pedagogical advantages of small-group seminars for our teacher education program, by using seminars throughout the program, we are also modeling and helping evaluate an effective teaching strategy our future teachers can use in their K–12 teaching. "Pedagogy is a critical and complex aspect of teacher education; it can be thought of as both one element of the *content* of teacher education, as well as the *process* of teacher education. However one thinks of it, though, it must become an explicitly considered aspect of teacher education because . . . pedagogy can have both a powerful and a positive effect on what preservice teachers come to understand about teaching" (Thompson, 2006, p. 204, italics in original). Experiencing seminars in their teacher education encourages preservice teachers to use them later in their own K–12 classrooms. Furthermore, critically evaluating seminars with our preservice teachers helps them consider best uses for seminars in their teaching. Preservice teachers who have experienced seminars and workshops in their teacher education program are more likely to use and be effective in using these strategies in their own teaching.

In the quarter before their student teaching, we used *The Teacher's Guide to Leading Student-Centered Discussions* (Hale & City, 2006) as a text to help our students learn to lead seminars. Using Hale and City as a guide, each student led an hour seminar on the text for that session, including time for debriefing and for written feedback to the facilitator. Students practiced ways to add to a discussion of a topic by referring to previous related comments, to portions of the text, to previous lectures or seminar discussions. They used graphic organizers on the board, quick writes of their ideas during seminar, small-group discussions, and end of seminar notes. Having experienced seminars as participants as well as facilitators in three quarters prior to student teaching, Evergreen preservice teachers were encouraged to use seminars in their K–12 student teaching classrooms.

FOURTH-GRADE SEMINAR

Kellee had enjoyed learning in seminars at Evergreen and wanted to incorporate seminars in her fourth-grade student teaching classroom. In the third week of the school year, she decided it was time to begin using seminars with her students. As the school was near two military bases, Kellee had heard many patriotic comments in her classroom, prompting her to use the United States Pledge of Allegiance as the first text her class would discuss.

After gathering her twenty-two students into a large circle, Kellee distributed a copy of the Pledge of Allegiance to each student. While a student read aloud, everyone followed on his or her copy. Kellee then asked them to quietly read it again and circle one to three words that were very important. Opening the floor to begin the seminar, she reminded students to listen respectfully to each speaker. She suggested that their discussion would be more meaningful if they could tag onto previous speakers' comments by adding to them in agreement or disagreement. One by one, students volunteered a word they had circled with a reason why. Kellee did not comment on students' contributions but rather kept a careful chart of who had spoken and what each had said. This helped her monitor air time and topics so that every student had a chance to participate in the thirty-minute seminar. In the first ten minutes, many students noted that they had circled the word "God" and explained why. When Kellee noticed that some students were having difficulty with some of the vocabulary, she briefly focused on key words by asking for volunteers to define the words. Without any prompting from Kellee, soon the discussion centered on whether allegiance always resulted in justice for everyone. The seminar became very animated as students discussed whether wars are always just and whether the United States has always fought wars that resulted in liberty for everyone. Near the end of the seminar, Kellee asked each student to write one or two important things to remember from the seminar discussion and then gave each student a chance to share in a round-robin wrap-up.

In our debriefing when students had gone to recess, I asked Kellee how she believed the seminar had gone. She had come prepared for vocabulary students might need help understanding so felt that went well. She was prepared to keep the discussion focused on the Pledge but said she had been very nervous about how to allow students to discuss it without directing them in their conclusions. She knew that students might believe very differently from her own beliefs but knew that to be effective, she had to allow students to work out their own interpretations. She found that keeping a written record of the seminar had helped her stay out of the discussion and make sure everyone had a chance to participate. She was amazed how complex their discussion had gotten and how much these students revealed about their knowledge of history. Rather than being a pat "party-line" discussion, students had brought up concerns and conflicting information that resulted in a very complex discussion that had nearly everyone engaged and thinking. Having recorded their contributions, she could later build on concepts or gaps in understanding. Overall Kellee was pleased how well her first seminar had gone with her students and felt emboldened to continue doing seminars each week during student teaching.

SEVENTH-GRADE MATH SEMINAR

Joyce student taught in a seventh-grade math classroom with a diverse student population (32 percent White, 24 percent African American, 16 percent Asian, 12 percent Hispanic, 8 percent Native American, 4 percent Pacific Islander, and of whom approximately 58 percent receive free and reduced lunches). She had first introduced her class of twenty-four students to seminar when the school honored a "Day of Silence" in memory of a gay student who had been murdered because he was openly gay. The class agreed to talk if they could discuss gay rights. Joyce arranged the tables in a large rectangle so everyone could see each other. Joyce recalls:

> This topic was an excellent introduction to seminar. As the discussion developed, many opportunities arose to remind students to be respectful in both what they said and the way they said it. They were instructed that they could disagree with someone's idea without insulting the person. Students were asked not to talk over others, and if more than one person spoke at the same time they were reminded to pause, assess who was trying to speak, and then yield to the person who had spoken the least so far. Students spoke freely, and their ideas were challenged by others. Toward the end of the seminar one student mentioned the "debate," and a new conversation began about how seminar was different than a debate. One student commented, "A debate is when you know where you stand on a subject and you try to win people over to your side. This feels different because we are hearing lots of points of view and we are free to change what we think about it." With this successful introduction to seminar behind us, I felt the students were ready to seminar on a math-related topic.

Joyce had organized groups of four students to learn information on a specific mathematical topic and then teach that topic to the whole class. Most students found this very challenging and resisted the assignment. Many claimed that they could not learn mathematics without being taught directly by a teacher and that this way of learning would take too much effort. When student work had come to a standstill, Joyce decided to have a second seminar, this time on the math assignment.

> For this seminar I wanted the students to address two questions: "Why are you being asked to do this presentation project?" and "Why do you need to learn math?" At first, the responses were many and were very negative. Many of the students shared their views about feeling like I was making them do all the work so I could have a break. I wanted to defend myself and tell them that I had actually done quite a lot of work writing learning expectations for the presentation and for each subject, creating a rubric for the project, deciding which topics would be taught, and finding the appropriate materials to provide instruction. But, I stayed out of the discussion. Some of the students stated that they were never going to be teachers so it was stupid for them to be expected to do this. Soon students were

answering my second question saying they didn't need to know this kind of math and they agreed they would forget it by the time they graduated anyway. One student offered that his parents didn't need this math and he wouldn't either. I just listened. I was very tempted to interject something positive into the discussion or even ask if everyone felt the same way, but I was glad that I did not. It took awhile, but one student finally spoke up in opposition saying that she always learned more when she had to teach it to someone else. She said that when she put more work into something that she usually got more out of it. Her remarks started a positive rally of commentary. Students began defending learning math, saying that math is everywhere, and that you don't know what you will need in the future. Some offered specific ways they could see that they would use math in the future. One student still stubbornly clung to the idea that he would not need mathematics because he was going to play football. Another student challenged him about having a backup plan in case he got hurt. He replied that his backup plan was to go to tech school and take computer classes. Everyone laughed as he admitted that he probably needed to learn math. I felt that he probably would not have made this admission if someone in a position of authority had challenged him.

There was no need for me to interject my thoughts into the seminar. However, I did remind students to take turns speaking, to address the entire seminar, and not to engage in side conversations. Every thought that I wanted to voice was spoken (in most cases in a way that I could not have articulated) and evaluated. Students came to their own conclusions. At the end of seminar I asked students to summarize what had been discussed. The ideas they shared demonstrated student thought and reflection. And in the days to come these ideas were brought up by class members many times. Overall, student work increased and attitudes improved. Furthermore, I gained useful insights into the way my students thought about math and issues they wrestled with that affected their success in mathematics.

SEMINAR IN A JUVENILE-DETENTION
CENTER CLASSROOM

Jennifer student taught in a classroom within a jail, teaching eight to twelve incarcerated youth per class all subjects in 7th–12th grades as well as GED-based basic education. Wanting to use a book that had relevance to her students while also helping them develop vocabulary and comprehension skills, she decided to use a book we had studied in our teacher education program at Evergreen, *The Pact: Three Young Men Make a Promise and Fulfill a Dream*. In order to support all of her students, a few who could not read, the majority who could read at a fifth- to seventh-grade level, and those reading at nearly college level, she structured daily oral reading of the text combined with seminars. Each day the students reviewed what had already been read (which helped those with processing disorders as well as the newcomers who had just entered detention) and then students and teacher took turns voluntarily orally reading the next 12- to 25-page passage in the text. Jennifer describes how she wove seminars into daily reading lessons:

> After reading, it was time to put it all together. I quickly discovered that the key to seminar in detention was flexibility. With students receiving only three hours of instruction a day, and some staying less than a day, there was no time to train the class on the finer points of seminar theory. To a different degree, all students participated in seminar. Some shouted out answers. Others raised their hands. Some answered my daily directive ("name three main parts of the reading today"), others found personal examples to discuss their connections to the text, and still others had their own questions to ask. Suddenly, the mix of ages was no longer a negative as more mature students with higher skills taught the higher concepts (perseverance, strength in unity, disproportionality) in the book to the younger students. Students with higher skills were able to come up with key areas of the reading, allowing the low- and nonreaders to increase their comprehension. The discussion started by higher level and older students did not remain theirs, however, as knowing the key concepts (I wrote them on the board as students brainstormed, students had a handout on which to take notes that provided a three key concept structure) allowed low- and nonreaders to ask their own questions or tell their own stories. *The Pact* discusses parental drug use, divorce, poverty, parental illiteracy, juvenile detention, and other themes that provoked heartwrenching stories from the students, who frequently shared their own tragic stories aloud in our daily seminar. In these stories students often found commonality and compassion amongst each other, and a psychological element, often present in a correctional classroom, surfaced. Students were rarely negative, especially to each other. More participation would have been ideal, particularly from the lower level students, but these students were often completing their notes or listening intently, and may have been too preoccupied with comprehension to jump in verbally. In the future I would like to experiment with short pair discussions before the whole group discussion.

HIGH SCHOOL UNITED STATES LITERATURE CLASS

As part of a unit Lauren was teaching about famous twentieth-century novelists in the tradition of the Harlem Renaissance, students read Richard Wright's *Black Boy*. Previously, as part of a secondary literacy strand in the Evergreen teacher education program, her cohort had used Gilmore's (2006) *Speaking Vol-*

umes: How to Get Students Discussing Books—And Much More. Wanting her students to discuss key themes in the book, she opted for small-group seminars instead of a whole-class seminar. Curious to see if her students would like fishbowl discussions as much as she had, she assigned small groups of three to five students a theme that they would discuss for twenty minutes in a fishbowl seminar while the rest of the class observed. Part of the structure of a fishbowl discussion is that one seat, called the "hot seat," is left open so anyone outside the fishbowl can briefly join the fishbowl discussion. No one on the outside of the fishbowl speaks unless he or she sits in the hot seat. She was surprised how popular the hot seat was, and how it generated deeper small-group seminars while keeping the entire class involved. While she knew *Black Boy* would generate some heated discussion, she heard comments she had not expected, such as, "When he wrote for white people, he wrote kinda smarter." Rather than interrupting the discussion to challenge such comments, she redesigned her following lessons to guide students in analyzing their evidence and assumptions in making those comments.

Implications of Using Seminars for Small-Group Learning in Teacher Preparation

Given the national ramifications of high-stakes testing in which drill is fast replacing interactive learning in public schools, teacher education is faced with the challenge of helping teachers learn strategies that will promote skill development while also promoting critical thinking and life skills for working and learning in communities. In summarizing the research of Howey and Zimpher on exemplary teacher education programs, Zeichner and Conklin (2006) described these programs as having, among other attributes, "high levels of rigor and academic challenge, a good balance between general and pedagogical knowledge, [and] an interdisciplinary curriculum approach" (p. 718). Seminars contain all of these attributes as they can be used effectively to provide depth of learning, a critical understanding of issues in education, and experience using and critiquing teaching strategies that promote learning for all students in all disciplines.

To foster deep learning, nearly a century ago John Dewey (1916/1966) advocated the use of teachers guiding students through active learning rather than through lectures and memorization. Following in Dewey's footsteps, learning communities in which students engage in small-group seminars on texts help preservice teachers not only to learn content but also to experience democratic practices that they can use effectively in their own K–12 classrooms. Using learning communities based on philosophies and strategies of progressive educators can be key for developing meaningful and sustained learning experiences at all levels of education.

In considering whether to use seminars in teacher education programs, similar factors of time and curriculum constraints face teacher educators as face K–12 teachers. As to the time factor, because seminars depend on a small-group community of learners to promote quality learning, they need to be used on a regular basis with a consistent group membership throughout a program, not just a few times. If only used occasionally, students do not have the chance to develop the community that produces high quality, in-depth learning. Program accreditation and teacher certification requirements often force teacher education programs to be crammed with a hodgepodge of individual courses. In using an interdisciplinary approach, a teacher education program can devote the time needed for seminars to function well, while still meeting accreditation and certification requirements, just as some progressive K–12 schools do to promote stronger cross-discipline learning.

Another factor to consider is the level of investment each student has toward learning in the community instead of only as an individual. This is related to the previous factor of how much the community of inquiry has been developed but is also a function of the assessments used. As in K–12 education, if the assessments are not in line with the use of seminars but instead are only based on work that individuals can complete without engaging in seminars, students will not be invested in seminars for their learning. By using performance and portfolio assessment, a teacher education program can keep assessment in line with the seminars that are a predominant feature of the program. Peer and faculty feedback in debriefing at end-of-seminar sessions is a formative assessment that guides students in their learning. Students get summative assessment from faculty in end-of-course evaluations based on their seminar performance, their seminar preparation papers, their notes taken during seminar, their reflections on seminars, and how they have used seminar content in other assignments in the program.

There is power in using small-group learning communities for teacher education. In 1990, Goodlad argued that to be effective, teacher education needs to use pedagogy that is in line with what advances learning in K–12. Being part of a small-group community provides motivation for participants to both participate and to learn since peers see both the participation and the evidences of learning of all the group members.

Learning communities cultivate deeper understanding and learning than transmission models of education because participants' differing views and interpretations provoke more cognitive dissonance. Critical text analysis during seminars and workshops helps develop skills for critically analyzing classroom curricula, experiences, and decisions. Not only do small-group learning communities promote learning during teacher education, they also provide support networks once the members disperse as teachers into different schools and school systems. Unlike students from less community-based programs, Evergreen students have gotten to know each other very well—well enough to be able to be vulnerable with each other, to support each other when faced with daunting challenges in their classrooms, to ask critical questions about a situation and possible solutions, and to critically evaluate materials and approaches with an eye for advocating for a diversity of students' needs.

Time and again, research has described characteristics of exemplary teacher education programs (e.g., Goodlad, 1990; Cochran-Smith & Zeichner, 2006). By using seminars as sites for small communities of learners, teacher education programs can align their pedagogy with recommendations for teacher education programs as well as model effective ways of using small-group learning communities in K–12 classrooms.

Author's note: A special thank-you is extended to those student teachers who shared their experiences using seminars in their student teaching classrooms: Kellee Raines, Joyce Kilner, Jennifer Clement, and Lauren Locke.

References

Atwell, N. (1998). *In the middle: New understanding about writing, reading, and learning.* Portsmouth, NH: Boynton/Cook Heinemann.

Billings, L., & Roberts, T. (2006). Planning, practice, and assessment in the seminar classroom. *The High School Journal, 90*(1), 1–8.

Cochran-Smith, M., & Zeichner, K. (Eds.). (2006). *Studying teacher education: The report of the AERA Panel on Research and Teacher Education.* Washington, DC: American Educational Research Association.

Cohen, E. G. (1994). *Designing groupwork: Strategies for the heterogeneous classroom* (2nd ed.). New York: Teachers College Press.

Davis, S., Jenkins, G., & Hunt, R. (2002). *The pact: Three young men make a promise and fulfill a dream.* Riverhead Books.

Dewey, J. (1916/1966). *Democracy and education.* New York: Free Press.

Evergreen State College. (2007). Evergreen's Master in Teaching (MIT) program. Retrieved July 20, 2007, from http://www.evergreen.edu/mit/.

Finkel, D. (2000). *Teaching with your mouth shut.* Portsmouth, NH: Heinemann Boynton/Cook Publishers.

Finn, P. (1999). *Literacy with an attitude: Educating working-class children in their own self-interest.* Albany, NY: SUNY Press.

Fletcher, R. (2006). *Boy writers: Reclaiming their voices.* Portland, ME: Stenhouse Publishers.

Gilmore, B. (2006). *Speaking volumes: How to get students discussing books—and much more.* Portsmouth, NH: Heinemann.

Goodlad, J. (1990). *Teachers for our nation's schools.* San Francisco: Jossey-Bass.

Great Books Foundation. (2005). *Getting started with Great Books in the classroom: A tutorial for K–12 educators.* Retrieved July 21, 2007, from http://www.greatbooks.org/tutorial/index.html.

Hale, M., & City, E. (2006). *The teacher's guide to leading student-centered discussions: Talking about texts in the classroom.* Thousand Oaks, CA: Corwin Press.

Igoa, C. (1995). *The inner world of the immigrant child.* Mahwah, NJ: Erlbaum.

Lidz, C. S., & Gindis, B. (2003). Dynamic assessment of the evolving cognitive functions in children. In A. Kozulin, B. Gindis, V. Ageyev, & S. Miller (Eds.), *Vygotsky's educational theory in cultural context* (pp. 99–118). New York: Cambridge University Press.

McDermott, R. P. (1996). The acquisition of a child by a learning disability. In S. Chaiklin & J. Lave (Eds.), *Understanding practice: Perspectives on activity and context* (pp. 269–305). New York: Cambridge University Press.

MacLeod, J. (2004). *Ain't no makin' it: Aspirations and attainment in a low-income neighborhood* (2nd rev. ed.). Boulder, CO: Westview.

Miller, S. (2003). How literature discussion shapes thinking. In A. Kozulin, B. Gindis, V. Ageyev, & S. Miller (Eds.), *Vygotsky's educational theory in cultural context* (pp. 289–316). New York: Cambridge University Press.

National Paideia Center. (2007). *Introduction to the Paideia seminar: K–12.* Retrieved July 20, 2007, from http://www.paideia.org/content.php/profdev/introsem.htm.

Randell, C. (2001). Teaching by learning from children. In B. Rogoff, C. G. Turkanis, & L. Bartlett (Eds.), *Learning together: Children and adults in a school community* (pp. 133–135). New York: Oxford University Press.

Thompson, C. S. (2006). Powerful pedagogy: Learning from and about teaching in an elementary literacy course. *Teaching and Teacher Education, 22,* 194–204.

Trentacosta, J. (Ed.). (1997). *Multicultural and gender equity in the mathematics classroom: The gift of diversity (1997 Yearbook).* Reston, VA: National Council of Teachers of Mathematics.

Vygotsky, L. S. (1978). In M. Cole, V. John-Steiner, S. Scribner, & E. Souberman (Eds.) *Mind in society: The development of higher psychological processes.* Cambridge, MA: Harvard University Press.

Washington Center for Undergraduate Improvement. (nd). *Seminars: A collection of materials on seminar approaches and evaluation strategies.* Retrieved July 28, 2007, from http://www.evergreen.edu/washcenter/natlc/pdf/seminars.pdf.

Weaver, C. (2002). *Reading process and practice* (3rd ed.). Portsmouth, NH: Heinemann.

Wells, G. (2000). Dialogic inquiry in education: Building on the legacy of Vygotsky. In C. Lee & P. Smagorinsky (Eds.), *Vygotskian perspectives on literacy research: Constructing meaning through collaborative inquiry* (pp. 51–85). New York: Cambridge University Press.

Wenger, E. (1998). *Communities of practice: Learning, meaning, and identity.* New York: Cambridge University Press.

Wright, R. (1945). *Black boy.* New York: Harper & Brothers.

Zeichner, K., & Conklin, H. (2006). Teacher education programs. In M. Cochran-Smith & K. Zeichner (Eds.), *Studying teacher education: The report of the AERA Panel on Research and Teacher Education* (pp. 645–736). Washington, DC: American Educational Research Association.

CHAPTER 9

Preservice Candidates "Looking at Student Work" in a Professional Development School Setting

Kami M. Patrizio
Towson University

Kami M. Patrizio, Ed.D., is an assistant professor of instructional leadership and professional development at Towson University. Her research interests are mentoring, professional development, and school renewal. Her work has been published in *Teaching and Learning: The Journal for Natural Inquiry and Reflective Practice* and *School University Partnerships.*

ABSTRACT

Incorporating small-group professional development activities into preservice learning experiences is an essential consideration for teacher educators that holds value for preservice coursework design. This chapter describes the redesign of a field-based, graduate level licensure portfolio-development capstone course in a professional development school using the small-group professional development practice of "looking at student work" (LASW). Examination of this intervention was driven by two questions: How can we structure a portfolio development process that satisfies licensure standards and facilitates inquiry? How do we know when it is doing so? Findings that surfaced using a typology of reflective practice (van Manen, 1977) and grounded theory (Glaser & Strauss, 1967) show that the LASW intervention increased participants' levels of reflection, their understanding of assessment, their disposition toward collaboration, and their capacity to engage in inquiry.

It is five o'clock on a Friday afternoon and three university graduate students and their instructor have gathered in a coffee shop near the local high school. With books spread about the table, the four women read intently from stacks of photocopied papers. As they read, they make marks on the papers, underlining, circling, writing comments, and posing questions in the margins. Every now and then an exclamation of surprise or thoughtful wonder breaks the busy silence, but the women continue to read; they will not stop to discuss the line that has made them laugh, nor to ask the questions the work raises for them. Another patron of the coffee shop, watching the focused study going on at the next table, might assume that these women are deeply involved with a business project, proofreading important articles, or studying for some vital exam. Yet, if one were to peer over a shoulder to catch a glimpse of the papers under examination at the table, she might be puzzled to notice the messy cursive and sketchy drawings of a twelve-year-old child. The questions and comments begin to flow and a rich dialogue about the writing ensues. "I noticed that the story emphasized chronology . . ."; "The piece was in the first person, then switched to the third . . ."; "All of the stories contain examples of figurative language . . ."; "I wonder if this aspect was a requirement in the writing prompt . . ."

It is through this process that the stories this student's work has to tell begin to unfold (all names in this chapter are pseudonyms):

> "How do we avoid imposing our own assumptions on student work, how do we know what students intended in their work, and how much does this matter? How can this much attention be possibly paid to each piece of work when seventy-five students are handing in work? How do we account for the context within which the work was done, how much effort was put into it, etc.?"
>
> After fifteen minutes of devoted attention to the copies of this child's work, one of the women calls everyone to look up from their reading. They begin to discuss the notes they have made and the questions they have jotted down. The discussion may start broadly, but inevitably narrows down to the finest details of the writing. (Candide, preservice teacher, reflective journal entry)

Professional development practices that result in meaningful learning are an imperative for improving school renewal and student achievement. The introductory narrative, written by a member of an interdisciplinary, secondary level graduate cohort in a northeastern professional development school (PDS), qualifies how preservice teacher education programs might invest "in the knowledge and skill necessary" (Elmore, 2002, p. 5) so that those working in schools might "learn to do their work differently and to rebuild the organization of schooling around a different way of doing the work" (p. 5). The writer's description of her experience with the professional development practice of LASW in a capstone practicum course suggests that it is possible for preservice teacher education programs "to develop the capacity of those in the organization to learn what to do, and to create settings in which people who know what to do teach those who don't" (p. 26) by providing preservice candidates with small-group, inquiry-based learning experiences such as LASW.

The Need for Professional Development Activities in Teacher Education Programs

Addressing the question of how to meaningfully prepare teachers to participate in a culture of inquiry is both a mandate and a challenge to teacher educators. The situation in education is not that different from what it was more than a decade ago when Fullan, Hill, Crevola, and Elmore (2006) lamented the fact that "in school education, there is no built-in mechanism that leads to ongoing improvement in classroom instruction" (p. 42). Program accreditation, teacher certification requirements, and the cultures of practicum sites add layers of contextual, process, and content-related opportunities and challenges for teacher educators. The question that emerges is how to provide preservice learning opportunities that are clearly focused on improving student learning.

The PDS model of teacher education, as the moniker suggests, is one venue that holds such promise. It relies heavily on processes that Goodlad, Mantle-Bromley, and Goodlad (2004) refer to as the *cycle of inquiry* (evidence-based dialogue, decision making, action, and evaluation or *DDAE*) and *simultaneous renewal* of school and university partner programs. Theoretically, participants take an inquiry-based approach to improving student learning as they learn together about themselves, their practices, and their students. Ideally, this process of simultaneous renewal renders the PDS a *center of pedagogy*, a place where university and field-based educators "collaborate in the work of building curriculum, field experiences and the structures that produce good teachers" (p. 116).

Best professional development practices, such as LASW, support all of these processes and theoretical ideals. They engage teachers in data-based inquiry and analysis of their own work and practice, simultaneously promote inquiry and reflection, and are deeply rooted in action-oriented exploration of professional practice (Easton, 2004; NSDC, 2007). LASW, lauded for its "potential for bringing students more consistently and explicitly into deliberations among teachers" (Little, Gearhart, Curry, & Kafka, 2003, p. 192), involves the use of student work samples and protocols to engage teachers in professional development in just such a fashion. At the heart of the work is the cycle of inquiry. As a result, participants learn to ask questions with the intent of taking immediate action in their own practice.

MOVING FROM GROUNDED THEORY TO GROUNDED ACTION

The PDS had been the site of a larger case study for two years prior to the LASW capstone course intervention. Table 9.1 contains a chart outlining the methodology of the study. Grounded theory (Glaser & Strauss, 1967) that emerged from analysis pointed to the need for rethinking the capstone class. This grounded action, "the application and extension of grounded theory for the purpose of designing and implementing practical actions" (Simmons & Gregory, 2003), was based on two findings. These included 1) a deeper understanding of reflective practice and how to operationalize it within the PDS and 2) data pointing to the need for the university to make changes to its coursework that emerged from the experience of the school-based participants.

The Role of Reflective Practice

The term reflective practice took on new dimensions that altered PDS participants' understanding during the course of the initial case study. They began to

Table 9.1 The Larger Case-Study Context

Method	Sample
Standardized, open-ended interviews (Patton, 2002)	11 mentor teachers 3 PK–12 instructional leaders 2 higher-education faculty members
Document review (Merriam, 1998)	6 sets of minutes/observations from PDS steering committee meetings 4 sets of minutes from university PDS meeting University program guidelines 4 semesters of university course syllabi 4 semesters of University and PDS evaluations and instructor reflections 4 quantitative climate surveys conducted by internal/external evaluating bodies
Reflexivity journal (Patton, 2002)	10 observations of PDS-related events Reflections on interviews and transcription process Connections to relevant literature

consider the idea of reflection as happening on three levels: technical reflection, practical, and critical (van Manen, 1977). The lowest level, technical reflection, deals with matters of efficiency and efficacy in curriculum design, particularly as these matters pertain to specific learning outcomes for students. Practical reflection involves unpacking personal assumptions and biases. Teaching and learning are seen as processes of "analyzing and clarifying individual and cultural experiences, meanings, perceptions, assumptions, prejudgments and presuppositions, for the purpose of orienting practical action" (p. 226). At the highest level, critical reflection, the process of educating involves considering the extent to which the ideals of "justice, equality, and freedom" (p. 227) are accounted for in the learning environment.

This reconsideration of the term reflective practice had three outcomes that were germane to the redesign of the capstone course. First, it informed participants' understanding of how to better identify and support the development of reflective depth in new teachers. Second, it led to the design of an assessment tool that connected the theoretical typology to the practical school environment (Table 9.2). This tool prompted faculty at the PDS to reevaluate their own standards for the quality of reflective practice they expected to see from preservice interns. The reconsideration and questions of quality ultimately illuminated a gap between theory and practice that demanded programmatic attention.

Simultaneous Renewal Can Mean Not Leaving Well Enough Alone

The university could have left its coursework in its pre-intervention format. There was some evidence suggesting that the work interns were doing in their practicum licensure portfolio was highly acceptable during the two years of the larger case study. The university had a 100 percent pass rate on its portfolios for the two years of the case study. Faculty felt that the quality of the portfolios had improved with the inclusion of more student work samples and better organization within the portfolio.

Data generated from the school context in the larger case study, however, suggested an occasion for simultaneous renewal. Findings suggested that the nine-credit capstone practicum course, whose primary summative assessment was the licensure portfolio, was an organizational endeavor akin to the practice of "teaching to the test" in a pre-K–12 classroom. The class, which occurred in the second and final semester of the interns' program, was viewed primarily as a technical exercise in efficiency and efficacy that did not live up to its potential to help interns connect pedagogy and practice. Figure 9.1 demonstrates the linear organization of the course. Each class focused on one aspect of the state's Portfolio Assessment Rubric (PAR). These included lesson structure and planning, learning over time, accommodating special needs, collegiality and reflec-

Table 9.2 The Reflective Taxonomy: Assessment Tool Connecting Theoretical Typology and Practical School Environment (van Manen, 1977)

Technical Reflection: Efficiency and Efficacy	Practical Reflection	Critical Reflection: Morality and Social Justice
"Application of educational knowledge and of basic curriculum principles for the purpose of attaining a given end" (p. 226)	"Analyzing and clarifying individual and cultural experiences, meaning, perceptions, assumptions, prejudgments and presuppositions, for the purpose of orienting practical action" (p. 227)	"How social factors influence teaching and learning and the extent to which the ideals of justice, quality, and freedom" (p. 227) are accounted for in the learning environment
What are the types of curriculum that I might use to support student achievement?	What do I believe about teaching and learning? Why? How?	What structures exist at the school/district/ state/federal level to support and challenge my beliefs?
What are the options for designing, implementing, and assessing student learning experiences that will support student achievement?	How do my past and present experiences impact my feelings about teaching and learning? Why?	How do these structures affect my beliefs about teaching and learning? Does this matter? Why? How?

tion. While some of these classes involved small-group work, they usually involved one of two whole-group activities: discussions about portfolio content and organization according to the PAR language, or nonstructured dialogue about practicum experiences. There were two job skills workshops included during the course for participants as well.

Research data from the larger case study also suggested that, overall, the interns' reflective journals differed substantially between the first and second semesters of their year-long cohort's placement at the site. During the first semester, when interns were taking nine credits at the university and spending three days a week in a support role at the site, the interns engaged in far more critical reflections. When interns stepped into greater responsibilities for their solo teaching experience during the practicum semester, their reflective journals came to resemble laundry lists that dealt with issues of efficiency and occasionally the efficacy of their classroom-based experiences. Findings suggested that

Table 9.2 (Continued)

Technical Reflection: Efficiency and Efficacy	Practical Reflection	Critical Reflection: Morality and Social Justice
What does the research say about how effective and efficient these options are? In what ways do these options relate to each other?	Am I creating a learning environment that is respectful of differences? Why? How? How do I approach working with other people at my school to improve student learning? Why? Is it important to get to know my students both inside and outside of the classroom? Why? Do I favor certain learning styles or forms of intelligences in my choices of curriculum, instruction, and assessment? Why? Do gender, socioeconomic status, ethnicity, or sexual orientation affect my choices about curriculum, instruction, and assessment? How do they affect the ways that I work with others, including my students? Why?	What do I believe to be true of the ways that my colleagues approach their work in the school? Why? How do I teach my students to value each other? What are my beliefs about the rights and learning abilities of my students, my colleagues, and myself? Why?

the capstone component of the PDS experience was not only underused as a formative learning tool for the interns, but that it took valuable time away from interns' work in their practicum setting. The course might be used more effectively as a formative assessment tool to help interns understand their own solo teaching experiences, from which the class was perceived as being almost entirely disparate. There was an occasion for simultaneous renewal between the school and university partners. A question emerged about the PDS course de-

Whole cohort, some small-group activities embedded ⟶

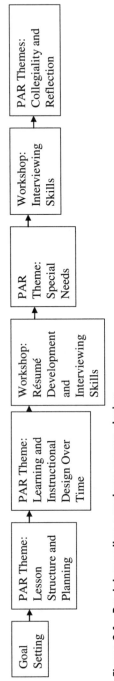

Figure 9.1 Pre-intervention capstone course design.

sign: Can the portfolio development process better satisfy licensure standards and support sustained inquiry about classroom-based processes of teaching and learning? And if so, how is this demonstrated by licensure candidates?

THE COURSE REDESIGN: CHANGING THE PROCESS AND FOCUS

Figure 9.1 provides a visual of the capstone course prior to the LASW intervention. The year-long, field-based cohort of graduate interns, ranging from 9 to 12 interventions over the course of the data collection, met as a whole group roughly seven times a semester. Most of the whole-group meeting sessions addressed one of the themes of the PAR: lesson planning, learning and instructional design over time, accommodating special needs, collegiality and reflection. Interns were asked to consider and reflect on evidence from each of the PAR's six domains. Some of these sessions included small-group activities based on this evidence or on the PAR language. The semester also included two skills-based workshops to assist students in preparing for their job search.

Data from the larger case study suggested the linear structure of the course was problematic for three reasons specific to the school program: 1) PAR themes did not align with interns' practicum activities, 2) scheduling meeting times inevitably caused either site-based or university class conflict for interns, and 3) the linear and separated nature of the PAR domains did not reflect the dynamic interactions of the teaching and learning and learning to teach processes. All of this made it difficult to use the PAR as a formative assessment tool that helped interns to connect theory and practice.

Figure 9.2 provides a graphic of the course redesign that incorporated the professional development activity of LASW. The course differed in both structure and focus. First, it relied on whole cohort and small-group meetings. The cohort's entrée into portfolio development began with a whole-class exploration of an extensive collection of longitudinally collected work samples from a university archive. These work samples had come from a small, alternative school for students aged four to twelve years. After working with the archives, the class split into two smaller groups. Each group set its own schedule, met with the course instructor, and used LASW protocols to collaboratively examine their own students' work. Interns relied on two protocols: the "tuning protocol" and the "collaborative assessment conference" (Allen, 1998), to generate their own questions about student work samples and facilitate inquiry amongst themselves based on the work and protocol.

The first method, the tuning protocol, worked best for using student work to promote consideration of curriculum design. The second method, the collaborative assessment conference, served as a way for the group to examine student

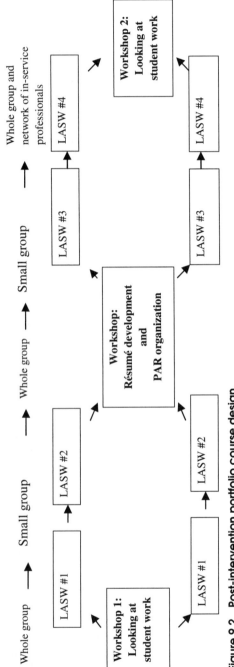

Figure 9.2 Post-intervention portfolio course design.

work to learn more about specific students. Unlike the tuning protocol, which addressed the curriculum and the *teacher's* actions by looking at student work, the collaborative assessment conference focused the group's inquiry on the strengths and needs of particular students and how to adjust and modify practices accordingly. While a number of protocols exist for looking together at student work, using these two allowed participants more in-depth experience with the protocols' utility and execution.

At the end of the semester, the cohort attended a regional workshop hosted by a national professional development organization. This workshop brought practitioners together to explore a third way of looking at student work, the descriptive review (Himley, 2002). This process is designed to elicit a deep understanding of an individual student's development through thematic analysis of student work collected over time. The joining of these course members into a community of educators outside of the PDS functioned as a professional scaffold at the end of their preservice experience.

Data Collection and Analysis

Assessing the impact of the course redesign included work samples from seven graduate course participants, six structured observations of interns looking at student work sessions (Patton, 2002), document analysis of program assessments (Merriam, 1998), two structured observations of day-long LASW workshops (Patton, 2002), both course- and program-related PDS-designed evaluation assessments, and a structured reflexivity journal maintained by the researcher. The data were analyzed using Spradley's domain analysis (Lincoln & Guba, 1985) and a typology of reflective practice (van Manen, 1977).

Outcomes of the LASW Intervention

The LASW redesign intervention improved interns' capacity to develop as reflection practitioners and better meet the needs of their students. It did so by creating a collaborative venue that suspended evaluative lenses, thereby allowing student voice to surface from work samples. Engaging in this activity increased interns' ability to make substantial changes to their practice and changed their beliefs and assumptions dispositions toward collaborative work in the school setting.

THE LASW BRIDGE BETWEEN THEORY AND APPLIED PRACTICE

Pre-assessments suggested that prior to the course, interns demonstrated theoretical understanding that curriculum, instruction, and assessment are connected.

Curriculum in theory and practice were perceived as matters involving the teacher–student dyad. Teachers were responsible for presenting content in a way that met students' needs; student work demonstrated whether or not they understood the content. Assessment was a critical bridge that allowed teachers to make judgments about the efficacy of their teaching. One intern, Barney, articulated this understanding:

> By examining student work closely, a teacher can see what is going well and what isn't with curriculum, instruction, and assessment. I believe that the difficulty is determining . . . which of the pieces the one causing difficulty is. For example, it may be that a student doesn't understand a concept because of instructional reasons, or it may be that he or she has difficulty answering essay questions.

Articulating the "looks like, sounds like, feels like" of these beliefs, or how interns made the leap from student work to curricular modification and back again in the course of their day-to-day practices was difficult prior to the course, even when participants were prompted to do so.

Interns also came to the LASW intervention with the ability to critically reflect on the value of having a more holistic view of students as learners "for the purpose of orienting practical action" (van Manen, p. 226). Sam put it this way:

> If student work were a painting, it would be Gustav Klimt's "The Three Ages of Woman." As teachers, we are concerned with the education of a complete person, the child in our class today, and the adult she will become.

Responses on the pre-assessment also suggested that interns believed student work helped them to develop relationships with students as people, what they perceived as essential to engaging students in content. To put this in terms of their reflective practices, participants entered with the assumption that there was importance in educating the whole child because it would have lasting effects on that student as a human being.

Central to this assumption was their sense that multiple forms of student work, including summative and formative assessments and randomly collected anecdotal data, were all necessary evidence for teachers to consider. Those few participants whose pre-assessments connected secondary learners to their own instructional context did so by generally describing teaching processes and vaguely speaking about classroom trends. They attributed these trends to students' learning styles. Kristen described noticing

> how differently each individual student interprets and processes knowledge. This became apparent to me immediately, as the first

> batch of assignments I graded was a summary of a reading that included the concepts students had learned about in class. One might think that there are only so many ways to summarize an article, but the number of approaches surprised me a great deal. Some students chose to write a brief summary first and then separately define key terms by using examples from the text; others incorporated the two. The range of success was drastic.

Similarly, another remarked:

> Students are much less likely to think, and more likely to blindly copy definitions or descriptions (or become frustrated and give up) when they are either disinterested in the subject or when they find the content extremely difficult. We recently began a unit, and though the introductory activity was relatively simple, students had a very difficult time understanding the assigned reading, which was laden with complicated technical jargon. Therefore, rather than proceeding with the simple activity, they all bombarded me at once with questions about what they were supposed to do, instead of asking me to help them understand the reading.

Both of these examples illustrate that interns were aware of the importance of listening to students. Their interpretations of the student work were more informed by what they believed students should be able to do instead of how the students' prior knowledge or their own instructional design equipped them to actually do it. These two interns evaluated the reasons behind students' actions without engaging in description or evidence-based inference about the work. The first describes the wide range of ways that students interpreted the assignment's call for summary, and then skips to evaluation of their performance before exploring what the varied student outputs demonstrated about their content knowledge or how it was elicited by the instructional situation. The second references activities as "relatively simple" even though admitting that the assignment was "laden with complicated technical jargon." There is an absence of consideration of how the activity was informed by students' prior knowledge, specific student voices, the assessment criteria, or how the intern instructionally addressed the situation.

THE VALUE OF COLLABORATIVE INQUIRY

Prior to the activity of LASW, the implicit assumption of almost all interns was, "when you assess, you assess alone." Some interns articulated that mentor teachers used student work to check for student understanding and to grade. There was no mention of use of student work in departmental or content area teams, and participants were unable to concretely articulate, even when specifically prompted, the ways in which student work might be able to improve the quality of classroom instruction. Indeed, any references to how student work was approached by others in the school were substantiated with generalized stories of interns' *own* interactions with student work products as opposed to details of other people's approaches.

During the course of the LASW intervention, the assumption that when "you assess, you assess alone" evolved into a belief in the value of collaborative, evidence-based inquiry. Lucy described it as follows:

> Our experience with looking at student work that took place in this graduate course has emphasized to us the importance of communication amongst educators. These protocols didn't attempt to limit the time that we spent looking at student work alone; they articulated ideas and strategies that we could use so that our time was spent in a productive, focused way. It helped us to learn and to learn *how* to learn—both from each other and from our students. We have come to understand that it is these perspectives that will help strengthen our practices and improve student learning on the roads that lie ahead of us.

Interns realized that other eyes could see other stories in their students' work samples, and that these stories could have powerful and immediate effects in their classroom. Julie described one such experience with the collaborative assessment conference:

> As we wrapped up solo-teaching requirements at our respective secondary schools, many of us shared examples that illustrated the ways in which the process had helped us to provide students with better, more individualized instruction. One intern recounted how looking closely at the writing of a struggling student in her class helped her to see that he actually was understanding more of the larger concepts than she had initially believed. Although this student's writing was riddled with spelling and mechanical errors and often appeared to be incomplete or rushed, a close examination of the writing revealed that there was in actuality a great depth of understanding hidden within the hurriedly constructed sentences . . . this student's issue was not that he didn't understand key concepts, but that he needed additional support in developing his ability to communicate these understandings in his writing. After tutoring the student one-on-one, this belief was confirmed. Verbally, the student expressed not only a full grasp of the major concepts associated with the content and its application to the reading that he had done, but also a passionate interest in the subject. LASW helped her gain vital information about this particular student's ability, and she was then able to use

this information to focus her teaching in the area where he most needed her.

LASW revealed the value of collaborative inquiry to interns, who perceived the experience as being of immediate worth because it translated directly back to their lived experiences in classrooms.

Discussion

These outcomes of the capstone intervention illustrate how considering the levels of reflective practice and incorporating the small-group professional learning activity of LASW increased the capacity of the course to better meet preservice teachers' needs. The typology of reflective practice surfaced a gap in the ecology of the intern cohort's reflective practices. Interns had yet to practically or critically reflect on the implications of applied curricular design. The questions of "How do I approach working with students at my school to improve learning?" and "Do I favor certain learning styles or forms of intelligences in my instructional choices and why?" had remained unexplored. Discrepancies between interns' expectations were attributed to student dispositions or ability (motivation or effort) instead of instructional design, the participants' own choice of how to implement the curriculum, or the participants' beliefs about teaching and learning.

Absent before the activity of LASW were any *questions* from interns about curriculum, instruction, and assessment. Interns described specific lessons and activities and students' reactions to them at the technical level of reflection: "The students did x, then they did y, then they did z. They didn't seem to like it." They had yet to think about the relationship between lesson design and student responses, or the specific qualities of student work samples that let them know that students, as one participant suggested, "Didn't seem to like it." Incorporating LASW into the course design provided a structure for collaborative inquiry in which they could question and make meaning of the intersection of theory and practice.

After looking together at student work, interns demonstrated a more sophisticated understanding of how individual student work samples could be used to improve the quality of their instruction. Using protocols, clearly articulated focusing questions, samples of their own students' work and their own assignments helped them to better understand the relationship between curriculum, instruction, assessment, and student learning. As one intern queried early on in the process, "How do I know whose meaning matters the most? Mine or the student's?" Another wondered, "How do I avoid imposing our assumptions on student work? How do we know what students intended in their work, and how much does this matter?" Their assumptions about teaching practice emerged as fodder for important inquiry. Unlike the experiences outlined above, wherein challenges were seen as related to students' motivation or efforts, interns' role in the process of teaching and learning presented as one that required intense reflective vigilance on their part.

One can infer from these findings that while interns' beliefs and assumptions about curriculum in theory and applied practice increased in depth and breadth, they also developed practical skills of curriculum design and how to look at student work. Much of the learning that emerged from interactions with student work came from activities that required description and evidence-based inference making about student work samples. Previously, interns had rarely engaged in evaluation of the student work samples. Doing so collaboratively added new depth to their understanding. Student voices surfaced when evaluative lenses were suspended, and interns' ability to metacognitively reflect on their practices increased.

Conclusion

> Improving instructional practice requires a change in beliefs, norms and values about what it is possible to achieve as well as in the actual practices that are designed to bring achievement. In other words, improvement requires a theory of individual learning. (Elmore, 2002, p. 18)

Identifying individual reflective practices within a clearly articulated framework, such as the typology used in this research, provides essential evidence that can inform the design of preservice teacher experiences. Incorporating the process of LASW into coursework expands the depth and breadth of individual reflective practices in preservice teachers by facilitating an evidence-based cycle of inquiry. LASW is an organic way of using classroom-generated data to focus preservice teacher learning. It facilitates connection between theory and practice in a meaningful way that has immediate implications for improving instructional design and student learning.

Author note: I would like to thank Sarah Hall and Molly Tonino for their help with this chapter.

References

Allen, D. (Ed.). (1998). *Assessing student learning: From grading to understanding.* New York: Teachers College Press.

Easton, L. B. (2004). Forward. In L. B. Easton (Ed.), *Powerful designs for professional learning*. Oxford, OH: National Staff Development Council.

Elmore, R. F. (2002). *Bridging the gap between standards and achievement: The imperative for professional development in education*. Retrieved on March 15, 2007, from http://www.shankerinstitute.org/education.html.

Fullan, M., Hill, P., Crevola, C., & Elmore, R. (2006). *Breakthrough*. Thousand Oaks, CA: Corwin Press.

Glaser, B. G., & Strauss, A. L. (1967). *The discovery of grounded theory*. Mill Valley, CA: Sociology Press.

Goodlad, J. I., Mantle-Bromley, C., & Goodlad, S. J. (2004). *Education for everyone: Agenda for education in a democracy*. San Francisco: Jossey-Bass.

Himley, M. R. (Ed.). (2002). *Prospect's descriptive processes, the child, the art of teaching, and the classroom and school*. North Bennington, VT: The Prospect Center.

Lincoln, Y., & Guba, E. G. (1985). *Naturalistic inquiry*. Beverly Hills, CA: Sage Publications.

Little, J. W., Gearhart, M., Curry, M., & Kafka, J. (2003, November). Looking at student work for teacher learning, teacher community, and school reform. *Phi Delta Kappan, 85*(3), 184–192.

Merriam, S. B. (1998). *Qualitative research and case study applications in education: Revised and expanded from case study research in education*. San Francisco: Jossey-Bass.

National Staff Development Council (NSDC). *Standards for staff development*. Retrieved on May 15, 2007, from http://www.nsdc.org/standards/index.cfm.

Patton, M. Q. (2002). *Qualitative research and evaluation methods*. Thousand Oaks, CA: Sage Publications.

Simmons, O. E., & Gregory, T. A. (2003). Grounded action: Achieving optimal and sustainable change. Retrieved on March 5, 2006, from http://www.qualitative-research.net/fqs-texte/3-03/3-03simmonsgregory-ehtm.

van Manen, M. (1977). Linking ways of knowing with ways of being practical. *Curriculum Inquiry, 6*(3), 205–228.

CHAPTER 10

Tracing Learning in Collaborative Reflection Meetings of Student Teachers

Paulien C. Meijer
Utrecht University

Helma Oolbekkink-Marchand
Radboud University Nijmegen

Paulien Meijer, Ph.D., is an associate professor and teacher educator at IVLOS Institute of Education, Utrecht University, in the Netherlands. Her research focuses on teacher learning and teachers' knowledge development. She works with beginning as well as experienced teachers, mainly in secondary education.

Helma Oolbekkink-Marchand, Ph.D., works as a teacher educator and researcher at Radboud University in Nijmegen, the Netherlands. She completed her doctorate (2007) focusing on teachers' beliefs in both secondary and university education. Her research now focuses mainly on teachers' professional development.

ABSTRACT

Although teachers indicate that working with other teachers provides valuable learning opportunities, research on such learning is impeded by the complexity of the phenomenon. In this small-scale study, we attempt to investigate just what and how student teachers learn in a collaborative reflection setting. How do the content and nature of the interactions that occur during collaborative reflection meetings relate to the learning of student teachers? Data from audiotaped meetings were combined with data from questionnaires that probed perceived learning. Analysis of the meetings showed the student teachers spend most of their time together searching for solutions to practical teaching problems. In the questionnaires, however, they indicated that they learned most from discussion of fundamental themes together. The themes addressed the boundaries of one's task as a teacher and ideas related to "deep" learning, which goes beyond "knowing how to" to the perspective of "being someone who." In discussions about such themes, the student teachers spent more time discussing the essence of a problem or situation than finding—for example—solutions. These results indicate that student teachers' learning can be stimulated when they focus more on the "being someone who" perspective. This asks for more sophisticated models for enhancing collaborative reflection, such as collaborative self-study.

Meetings as a Setting for Learning

Among the most essential moments for teachers working and learning together is when they meet either formally in discussion groups, for example, or informally during a coffee break, for example. When teachers must start working together due to a decision on the part of the school administration, such meetings may be essential and are often scheduled for the teachers. When teachers start working voluntarily together, the planning of such meetings often constitutes the first step and may even occur without the support of the school administration. And when teachers want to not only work together but also learn from each other, such meetings may be even more important (e.g., Little, 2002). However, just what and how teachers learn from such formal and informal meetings is unknown. Wilson and Berne (1999) described several projects in which teachers worked and learned together but found little systematic investigation of what and how the teachers learned. Teachers nevertheless reported collaborative learning and reflection to be very useful for their teaching.

THE CONTENT OF COLLABORATIVE
LEARNING MEETINGS

In collaborative learning meetings, student teachers can reflect upon their experiences and thereby better understand their teaching practices and identify places for improvement. During such meetings, student teachers can also train their reflection and communication skills, which can further promote their professional development. Essential for such collaborative reflection are (a) equality of the participants and (b) discussion of freely chosen issues. Collaborative reflection therefore fits into a concerns-based approach to teacher education (e.g., Anderson, Smith, & Peasley, 2000).

The concerns of beginning teachers have been studied for a long time. Fuller (1969) and Veenman (1984) identified self-, task-, and other-oriented concerns, for example. Many studies recently expanded this list to include concerns about the curriculum, management, and parents—among others (see Table 10.1).

Table 10.1   Concerns of Beginning Teachers

Author	Method	Identified Concerns
Adams & Krockover, 1997	Interviews with 12 student teachers: "Thinking back about your first year of teaching, what did you learn about schools, students, and teaching?" "What advice would you give to new teachers for the next year?"	Job assignments Teaching responsibilities Curriculum development The art and craft of teaching Time management Discipline/classroom management Presentation of content
Ghaith & Shaaban, 1999*	Questionnaire among 122 beginning teachers (with up to 5 years of classroom experience)	Self-survival Task Impact
Conway & Clark, 2003* **	Interviews with 6 intern teachers over a 6-month period about hopes and fears	Self-as-teacher Children Curriculum and instruction University expectations Self-as-teacher/classroom management Relationship with collaborating teacher Parents Professionalism
Haritos, 2004	Written question to 47 elementary and 47 secondary school teacher candidates. "What do you believe are the challenge(s) of teaching?"	Pupils (6 sub-concerns) Teaching situation (5 sub-concerns) Survival (15 sub-concerns)

* Based on Veenman (1984) and Fuller (1969).
** Based on Fuller's analysis of teachers' concerns (1969).

INTERACTIONS DURING COLLABORATIVE
LEARNING MEETINGS

The formation of teacher groups for learning purposes can lead to investigative groups, study groups, so-called intervision or collaborative reflection groups, and/or discussion groups. The members of such groups all share the same intention, namely to discuss and improve their teaching in one way or the other. The activities of the groups can lead to discussions of research papers, cases, and specific problems. Depending on the purpose of the group, the organization of the group, and the activities of the group, moreover, the way in which the members of the group communicate and react to each other can also vary (van Eekelen, 2005). Several scholars described the interactions of such groups, from very different perspectives. For example, Fischer, Bruhn, Gräsel, and Mandl (2002) studied the nature of the conversational processes that occurred during the discussions of learning groups in order to find indications of collaborative knowledge construction. Korthagen, Kessels, Koster, Lagerwerf, and Wubbels (2001) outlined a four-phase model of collaborative reflection for use in a teacher education setting. And Konig (1995) has described a continuum of individual interaction skills that may be relevant for describing interaction in more detail.

LEARNING FROM COLLABORATIVE MEETINGS

Teachers can learn in different ways. According to van Eekelen (2005), four different learning strategies can be employed: learning by doing, learning in interaction, learning by reading, and learning by thinking. Van Eekelen further distinguishes three categories of learning in interaction: (a) learning in interaction with students, (b) learning in an informal, unplanned interaction with a colleague, and (c) learning by participating in a formal or planned meeting with several colleagues or external experts. And according to van Eekelen, participation in meetings with colleagues constitutes a very powerful learning mechanism.

Little (2002) has also emphasized the importance of conversations between colleagues for teacher learning but noted that it is very difficult to know how teachers actually deal with the content of such conversations. How can you actually "see" that people have learned something from a meeting? Analysis of a single conversation or group discussion does not establish what teachers have learned from working together. "To move from speculation about what might be learned to claims about what (apparently) has been learned requires evidence spanning a longer trajectory of time and space" (Little, 2000; p. 932).

RESEARCH QUESTIONS

The study presented here was based on the above insights regarding the content, interactions, and learning related to collaborative reflection in particular, just what and how student teachers learn from collaborative reflection meetings. Our main question was "How do the content and nature of the interactions that occur during collaborative reflection meetings relate to the learning of student teachers?"

In order to capture the essence of such learning, the data stemming from two sources were combined: the data from group meetings and the data provided by the participants in response to a questionnaire. In order to answer the main question, the following three subsidiary questions were also posed:

1. What was the content of the collaborative reflection meetings?
2. What was the nature of the interactions of the student teachers during the collaborative reflection meetings?
3. What did the student teachers appear to learn from the collaborative reflection meetings?

Method

SETTING

Eight student teachers participated in the present study. Each of the student teachers entered a one-year postgraduate teacher education program after completing a degree in business. One component of the teacher education program was participation in regular collaborative reflection meetings, where a group of student teachers discussed topics related to their own teaching experiences. The main purpose of the meetings was to help the teachers better understand their own teaching for improvement purposes, and for learning of reflective skills.

The participating student teachers were all teaching secondary school (12- to 18-year-old students); their average age was 31.9 years (SD = 8.3, range of 23 to 43); and their average amount of teaching experience was 2.1 years (SD = 2.7, range of 0 to 8). Four of the student teachers were male; four were female. Two groups of four teachers were formed with two males and two females in each group. The supervisor, who was not present at the meetings, prepared the student teachers on such reflection techniques as conversational skills, asking different types of questions, and providing feedback.

Each collaborative reflection meeting started with a list of the problems encountered by the student teachers. One or two problems were then selected for further discussion in keeping with the model of Korthagen et al. (2001), which suggests four sequential steps for the discussion of problems: recall/describe the situation, formulate the essential aspects, develop alternatives, and choose a solution. In step one, the student teacher recalls a teaching experience he or she wants to analyze, responds to questions from the other student teachers, and describes (factually, without interpretation) what actually happened. In step two, the student teacher focuses on essential aspects: What is the real issue behind the teaching experience? In step three, the student teacher formulates possible alternatives in dealing with the experience just analyzed. Finally, the student teacher selects an alternative for future implementation.

PROCEDURE FOR DATA COLLECTION

The two student teacher groups met several times during a period of three months. Three of the meetings for each group were audiotaped. Prior to the first meeting, the student teachers completed a questionnaire about the expected learning outcomes and their expectations for the meetings in general. After each meeting, the student teachers also completed a questionnaire about the meeting process and their learning results with regard to (a) practical hints, (b) support, (c) understanding of what happens during their lessons, (d) understanding of theoretical notions, and (e) understanding of their own learning processes.

DEVELOPMENT OF CATEGORIES AND ANALYSIS
OF THE DATA

A four-step procedure was followed to answer our research questions. First, the concerns of the student teachers (i.e., the *content* of the meetings) were analyzed. The topics of the discussions that occurred during the meetings were grouped and labeled using the specific categories identified in the studies described in Table 10.1. The specific categories, which were adapted to our data, are presented in Table 10.2. The exact description of the coding of these categories is provided in the first part of the Appendix.

The category "boundaries on teaching responsibilities" can be related to concerns about "job assignments: teaching responsibilities" and "tasks" that

Table 10.2   Concerns of Student Teachers Expressed during Regular Meetings for Collaborative Reflection

Concerns	Labels
Student who hardly ever comes to class Dishonest student Student walking away after being reprimanded for the sending of sms-messages All students distract each other None of the students are motivated	Students
Teaching after class was taught by ''bad teaching'' colleague Motivation in badly scheduled hour after long break Lack of testing moments in Montessori school Appointed mentor in one-way administrative decision	Context
Responsibility for student who does not show up Consider individual student's private problems when student does not hand in assignments Responsibility for unmotivated student	Boundaries on teaching responsibilities

Adams and Krockover (1997) reported in their study. In our study, the student teachers sometimes specifically discussed the boundaries on their responsibilities regarding specific aspects of teaching. These aspects might be "students" or "school context"—categories we also identified—but we made specific differentiations in our discussion of these aspects, and of the boundaries of these aspects. We did so, because it appeared that student teachers indicated they learned a lot more when explicitly discussing these boundaries. We will further elaborate on this in the next section.

In the second step of the analysis, the interactions of the student teachers during the meetings were analyzed. Given that the focus of the study was on collaborative reflection and the learning of student teachers, only those parts of the discussions that related to the potential learning and kinds of interactions that can lead to learning on the part of student teachers were analyzed.

Based on Fischer et al. (2002), Korthagen et al. (2001), Konig (1995), and the data from a small pilot study, it was decided that a two-tiered system of categories suited our data best. The utterances were therefore first categorized according to the four steps for the discussion of problems: recall/describe the situation, phrase essential aspects, develop alternatives, and choose a solution (see Korthagen et al., 2001). Thereafter, the utterances were further categorized on the basis of the distinctions made by Fischer et al. (2002) and Konig (1995). With regard to the recall or description of a situation, for example, it is possible to pose a follow-up question, clarify the situation, interpret the situation, or evaluate the situation. With regard to the formulation of the essential aspects of the situation, one can explain, summarize, concretize, interpret, guide/direct, or provide information. A list with the remainder of the relevant distinctions can be found in Table 10.3. The details of the entire categorization system are presented in the Appendix.

In the third step of the analyses, the frequencies of the expected learning outcomes and perceived learning results were calculated for the student teachers. The differences between the two collaborative reflection groups were then tested in an ANOVA after taking the expected learning outcomes into account.

In the fourth and final step of the analyses, the concerns of the student teachers were linked to their perceived learning results and the characteristics of the collaborative reflection process. In order to create an overview of the collabo-

Table 10.3 Categories of Interaction Used in the Present Study, Frequencies, and Percentages

Steps in discussion of problems (Korthagen et al., 2001) (F; %)	Utterance type (developed using Fischer et al., 2002; and Konig, 1995)	Freq.	%
	Introductory statement	21	3.0
Recall/Describe situation (327; 146.2%)	Follow-up question	116	16.4
	Clarify situation	117	16.5
	Interpret situation	74	10.5
	Evaluate a situation	20	2.8
Formulate essential aspects (191; 31.7%)	Explain	73	10.3
	Summarize	20	2.8
	Concretize	13	1.8
	Interpret	35	10.5
	Guide/direct	32	4.5
	Provide information	18	2.5
Develop alternatives (111; 15.7%)	Request an alternative	12	1.7
	Propose an alternative	30	4.2
	React to an alternative (neg./pos.)	33	4.7
	Explore an alternative	23	3.3
	Advise	13	1.8
Choose a solution (22; 3.4%)	Select/agree on a solution	4	0.6
	Evaluate solution	18	2.8

rative reflection process during a discussion, a schematic map was made of each discussion. The different maps were then grouped according to the topic of the discussion and linked to the perceived learning results for the student teachers.

Results

CONTENT OF THE MEETINGS AND FREQUENCIES OF DIFFERENT STEPS IN THE DISCUSSION OF PROBLEMS

The student teachers talked about three topics: students, school context, and/or boundaries on their teaching responsibilities (see Table 10.2). It is striking that the student teachers did not talk about subject matter or student learning, among other topics.

From Table 10.3, it can be seen that the student teachers devoted most of their attention to the recall/description of the possibly problematic situation (46.2 percent of all utterances). The formulation of essential aspects involved 31.7 percent of all the utterances while the development of alternatives involved only 15.7 percent of all the utterances. Finally, the student teachers paid very little attention to the selection of a solution (3.4 percent of all utterances).

PERCEIVED LEARNING RESULTS

The results outlined in Table 10.4 show that the student teachers report the meetings resulted most in practical hints and support. Understanding of theoretical notions was reported least on average. The relatively high standard deviations nevertheless show the student teachers clearly differ in how they rated their collaborative learning results. The student teachers found the meetings to be a little less time-consuming and less useful than they had expected. They also reported gaining a little less insight into what happens during their lessons than expected and less of an understanding of theoretical notions than expected.

ANOVA was undertaken to test for statistically significant differences between the expected learning outcomes and perceived learning results, but no significant differences were found ($p < .05$). Neither were there significant differences when student teachers' perceptions of their own contributions during the meetings, years of experience, age, gender, or collaborative reflection group were entered as covariates. This means that the initial expectations of the student teachers did not differ significantly from their later perceptions of the collaborative reflection meetings.

Table 10.4   Expected Learning Outcomes Versus Perceived Learning Results for Collaborative Reflection of Student Teachers

	Expected outcomes		Perceived results	
	SD	Mean	SD	Mean
I expect our meetings will be . . . /In general, our meetings resulted in . . . (1 = agree; 2 = sometimes; 3 = no)				
Useful	1.5	0.5	2.0	0.6
Time-consuming	1.9	0.8	2.5	0.8
Fun	1.5	0.5	1.2	0.4
I expect our meetings will result in . . . /In general, our meetings resulted in . . . (1 = agree; 2 = sometimes; 3 = disagree)				
Practical hints	1.5*	0.8	1.7	0.5
Support	2.1	0.6	1.7	0.8
Insight into what happens during my lessons	1.9	0.6	2.3	0.5
Understanding of theoretical notions	2.1	0.8	2.8	0.4
I had a large contribution during the meetings	1.8		0.8	

* Significant difference ($p < .05$) between males (M = 2.0) and females (M = 1.0)

WHAT WAS TALKED ABOUT AND *HOW* AND *WHAT* STUDENT TEACHERS LEARNED FROM IT

When the schematic maps of the collaborative reflection meetings were examined, what struck us first was that the discussions showed no pattern of moving sequentially from one step to the next (i.e., from step one to step two and so forth). The pattern of transitions appeared to be random, but closer analysis of the sequences showed them to be less random than initially suspected.

In all of the meetings, considerable attention was initially paid to the recall and description of the situation, as might be expected. Thereafter, the courses of the meetings diverged, and we found a link between the topic of the discussion (i.e., content/concern), the manner in which the discussion proceeded (i.e., what steps were undertaken in the discussion), and what student teachers reported to learn. The pattern we detected is outlined in Table 10.5 and can be illustrated with the presentation of two examples.

Table 10.5   Relation between Concerns, Steps Taken in the Discussion of Concerns, and Perceived Learning Results

Concerns expressed during meeting (Table 10.2)	Steps in discussion and predominant utterance type (Table 10.3)	Perceived learning results (Table 10.4)
All concerns	Step 1: Recall/describe situation	Support (understand own learning process)
Boundaries on teaching responsibilities	Step 2: Formulate essential aspects	Insight/understanding
Students (school context)	Step 3: Develop alternatives	Practical hints
School context (students)	Step 4: Choose a solution	No link found

The first example involves discussion of the boundaries on teaching responsibilities. In this instance, the student teachers were found to pay relatively a great amount of attention on the phrasing of essential aspects (step two) and much less attention to the development of alternatives or selection of solution (steps three and four). In fact, the student teachers often explicitly indicated during such a discussion that it made them think about their perceptions of the teaching task. In response to the follow-up questionnaires, they also frequently indicated that they had gained more insight into what happens during their lessons and sometimes a better understanding of theoretical notions, which on average was less than they had expected (see Table 10.4). The sequence of the various steps in the aforementioned discussion is shown in Figure 10.1. With the exception of a few diversions in the discussion to consider possible alternatives (step three) or identify a possible solution (step four), it can be seen that the discussion was devoted predominantly to the phrasing of the essential aspects of the situation (step two) as initially described (step one). Theo, whose problem was discussed during this session, concluded: "This really makes sense to me. It's not a problem that needs to be solved, it's a given fact and I have to learn how to deal with it . . . finding my own position on it, that's it . . ."

In the second example, the discussion concerns both the students and the school context. As can be seen in Figure 10.2, the student teachers paid a relatively great amount of attention to the development of alternatives (step three), which resulted in a number of hints or tips for dealing with student behavior. They also paid attention to the selection of a solution (step four), specifically when the school context was the topic of the discussion (see Table 10.5), but

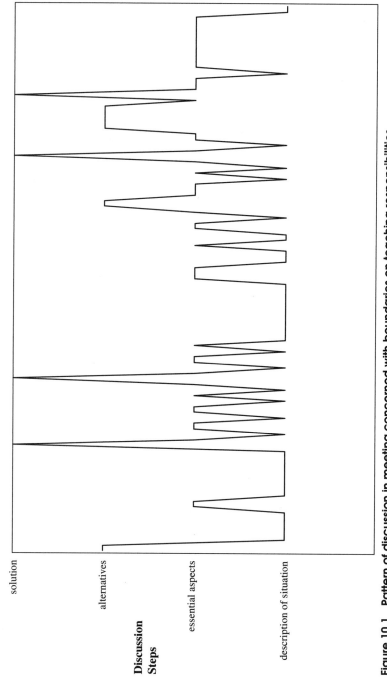

Figure 10.1 Pattern of discussion in meeting concerned with boundaries on teaching responsibilities.

Group 2, Meeting No.2

solution

alternatives

essential aspects

description of situation

Discussion steps

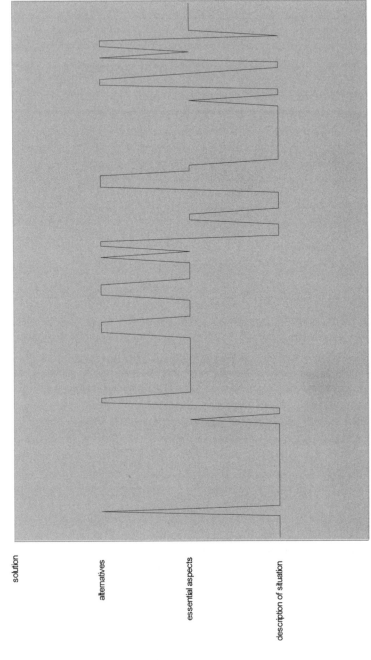

Figure 10.2   Pattern of discussion in meeting concerned with students and school context.

the development of alternatives (step three) predominated. At the end of the session, her fellow student teachers ask Judith, whose problem had been discussed: "Were we of any help to you?" Judith answers: "Well, yeah, thanks for your suggestions. I hope I'll find the energy to do something with them."

In sum, we did not find the four-step discussion sequence that Korthagen et al. (2001) have presented to characterize the collaborative reflection meetings of the student teachers here. In each meeting/discussion, rather, emphasis was placed on *one* of the discussion steps, which related to the topic of the meeting/discussion (i.e., concern) and also influenced the type of learning result.

Discussion

CONCLUSIONS

Regarding the content of the collaborative reflection meetings undertaken by the student teachers in this study (question 1), we concluded that the teachers mostly discussed problems related to individual students, the school context, and the boundaries on teaching responsibilities. The student teachers seemed less concerned about or encountered fewer problems with subject matter and student learning. Stated differently, only a few of the concerns listed in Table 10.1 were mentioned in the collaborative reflection meetings. Concerns about "job assignments: teaching responsibilities" and "tasks" have also been reported by Adams and Krockover (1997) and Ghaith and Shaaban (1999), respectively. Similarly, "pupils" and "children" have been reported by Haritos (2004) and Conway and Clark (2003), respectively. Concerns about the school context have not been identified in other studies. These findings suggest that the problems encountered by student teachers are typical "beginning-teacher problems" and relate to finding their way in the school organization and knowing the boundaries on their responsibilities as a teacher. More than experienced teachers, student teachers are dealing with what it means to be a teacher in terms of the students and the school organization.

With respect to the course of the collaborative reflection meetings and the nature of the interaction during the meetings (question 2), we concluded that the sequence of discussion steps described by Korthagen et al. (2001) did not characterize the meetings. In all of the meetings, the student teachers spent a lot of time describing the—usually problematic—situation (step one of Korthagen et al.'s model). Attention to other steps varied. The findings with regard to the perceived learning results also fluctuated greatly (question 3). The perceived learning outcomes also did not relate to such background variables as collaborative reflection group or gender.

When the content of the meetings (i.e., concerns of the student teachers) was related to the discussion sequences and perceived learning results (main question), clear patterns of interaction became apparent. The content of the meeting influenced the course of the discussion, which influenced the perceived learning in turn, as illustrated in Table 10.5. Interestingly, when the student teachers talked about the boundaries on their teaching responsibilities, they did not pursue all of the logical steps for the discussion of a problem. Nonetheless, they indicated gaining a greater understanding of teaching in general, which is typically considered "deeper" learning than the learning of practical tips. For example, van Boxtel (2000) found that learning in groups is most profound when the members of the group explicitly try to understand underlying concepts together. Similarly, Kelchtermans and Hamilton (2004) argue that reflection needs to go beyond "knowing how" and focus on "being someone who" to learning to be a teacher rather than just learning how to teach. Discussions on "boundaries on teaching responsibilities" show a focus on learning to be a teacher and, according to Kelchtermans and Hamilton, this kind of reflection can lead to "deep" knowledge that "does justice to the full complexity and richness of being a teacher" and goes "beyond the level of surface action to the level of underlying beliefs, ideas, knowledge and goals" (p. 801).

Kelchtermans and Hamilton suggest that self-study may be very useful to answer such questions as "Who am I as a teacher?". And the results of the present study suggest that collaborative reflection may also be very useful. Collaborative reflection appears to cause student teachers to ask each other questions they normally would not ask of themselves. This relates to the findings of Tigelaar et al. (2008), who found that teachers who reflect on teaching experiences collaboratively appear to discuss their experiences within a wider context, not just their technical dimension, but would also include the moral, ethical, and political dimensions. We found a few examples of such questions in our data: "Why would such an approach work for these specific students, why do you think so?" or "Do other teachers have the same experiences with those students?" or "Are those situations similar to those in your other classes?" or "Is it not just typical behavior for children of this age?".

IMPLICATIONS

The present findings suggest that learning as a result of collaborative reflection and the course of such learning should not be studied independent of the initial concerns (i.e., content of the collaborative reflection meetings). That is, student teachers learn different things about different subjects in different ways.

The present findings also have implications for the use of collaborative reflection in teacher education. Meetings for collaborative reflection should not, for example, be restricted to a sequential model. One should not assume that following a fixed sequence of steps or completion of all the steps in the sequence will always lead to better learning that a focus on just one step. In fact, the present findings show pursuit of all the steps outlined by Korthagen et al. to lead to the collection of tricks and practical hints while a focus on step two alone (i.e., essential aspects) leads to a more general understanding of teaching. Kelchtermans and Hamilton (2004) describe such sequential models as promoting technical reflection and thereby the reflective skills of student teachers.

However, teaching and becoming a teacher imply more than just technical skills. One can consider the moral dimension of teaching (see also Fenstermacher, 1990) and ask "To what extent am I doing justice to the students who are entrusted to my responsibility and care as a teacher?". The answers to such a question are very personal, which makes the teacher's choices very complex and the teacher very vulnerable. The discussions of the boundaries on teaching responsibilities in the present study show the student teachers indeed to be searching for the answers to such questions and to also appreciate the discussions. It is not far-fetched to state that such discussions relate more to "becoming a teacher" than "learning how to teach." In addition to training reflective skills following a sequential model such as Korthagen's four-step model, teacher educators should therefore address questions that go beyond a technical perspective, and include the emotional, moral, and political aspects of teaching as well (e.g., Kelchtermans & Hamilton, 2004).

We believe that collaborative reflection and self-study can be fruitfully combined to integrate many aspects of teaching and becoming a teacher. Collaborative reflection can prompt student teachers to ask questions that are sometimes otherwise difficult to ask oneself. Such *collaborative* self-study can also provide critical feedback and thereby help student teachers avoid falling into a trap associated with self-study: namely, self-sufficient navel-gazing (e.g., Kelchtermans & Hamilton, 2004).

SOME METHODOLOGICAL CONSIDERATIONS

The conclusions drawn in this chapter are based on the results of a small study conducted in a single teacher education institution. The observed patterns need to be replicated in other contexts, which may reveal relations between individual contributions and individual learning within a collaborative context as well. One can expect a discussion with a specific teacher's problem as a topic and a focus on the development of alternatives to produce different learning results for the different teachers involved in the discussion, for example. When the focus of the discussion is on the identification of essential aspects of the problem or situation, however, the learning of the student teachers may be more uniform.

The use of multiple sources of data and the examination of the data from different perspectives (i.e., the content and the process) provided significant insight into the learning of student teachers in collaborative reflection meetings. Analyses of collaborative reflection meetings were combined with information from the participants themselves on the meaningfulness of the meetings. In such a manner, it was possible to discern what happens during the collaborative reflection meetings from which student teachers report learning. Not all collaborative reflection meetings and not all parts of such a meeting create learning opportunities.

Given that student teachers appear to learn different things about different subjects in different ways, the complexity of studying the learning of student teachers within a collaborative reflection context is evident. With the inclusion of information on the essential learning experiences according to the student teachers (i.e., what the essential learning experiences are and how they are talked about), one can avoid the danger of using only the meetings themselves as the data source and thus drawing only non-crucial, nonmeaningful conclusions about the learning of student teachers during collaborative reflection meetings (e.g., Little, 2002).

In closing, some methodological implications of the present findings for future research on the learning of student teachers as a result of collaborative reflection are offered: First, one should study both the content and the course of collaborative reflection meetings in order to do justice to the complexity of the learning taking place; second, one should be sure to include the learning perceptions of the participants and thereby avoid speculation about what may have been learned; third, one should strive to combine the results of others' studies with a more bottom-up approach in order to take into consideration the specific context in which the learning has occurred. These implications will be of specific importance in studies that focus more on the complicated learning within the "being someone who" perspective.

References

Adams, P. E., & Krockover, G. H. (1997). Concerns and perceptions of beginning secondary science and mathematics teachers. *Science Education, 81*(1), 29–50.

Anderson, L. M., Smith, D. C., & Peasley, K. (2000). Integrating learner and learning concerns: Prospective elementary science teachers' paths and progress. *Teaching and Teacher Education, 16*(5–6), 547–574.

Conway, P. F., & Clark, C. M. (2003). The journey inward and outward: A re-examination of Fuller's concerns-based model of teacher development. *Teaching and Teacher Education, 19*(5), 465–482.

Fenstermacher, G. (1990). Some moral considerations on teaching as a profession. In J. Goodlad, R. Soder, & K. Sirotnik (Eds.), *The moral dimensions of teaching* (pp. 130–151). San Francisco: Jossey-Bass.

Fischer, F., Bruhn, J., Gräsel, C., & Mandl, H. (2002). Fostering collaborative knowledge construction with visualization tools. *Learning and Instruction, 12*(2), 213–232.

Fuller, F. (1969). Concerns of teachers: A developmental conceptualization. *American Educational Research Journal, 6*, 207–226.

Ghaith, G., & Shaaban, K. (1999). The relationship between perceptions of teaching concerns, teacher efficacy, and selected teacher characteristics. *Teaching and Teacher Education, 15*(5), 487–496.

Haritos, C. (2004). Understanding teaching through the minds of teacher candidates: A curious blend of realism and idealism. *Teaching and Teacher Education, 20*(6), 637–654.

Henson, R. K. (2001). The effects of participation in teacher research on teacher efficacy. *Teaching and Teacher Education, 17*(7), 819–836.

Kelchtermans, G., & Hamilton, M. L. (2004). The dialectics of passion and theory: Exploring the relationship between self-study and emotion. In J. J. Loughran, M. L. Hamilton, V. Kubler LaBoskey, & T. Russell (Eds.), *International Handbook of Self-Study of Teaching and Teacher Education Practices* (pp. 785–810). Dordrecht, the Netherlands: Kluwer Academic Publishers.

Konig, A. (1995). *In gesprek met de leerling [Talking to students]*. Houten, NL: Educatieve Partners/KPC.

Korthagen, F. A. J., Kessels, J., Koster, B., Lagerwerf, B., & Wubbels, T. (2001). *Linking practice and theory: The pedagogy of realistic teacher education*. Mahwah, NJ: Lawrence Erlbaum.

Kwakman, K. (1999). *Leren van docenten tijdens de beroepsloopbaan [Teacher learning during their careers]*. Doctoral dissertation. Nijmegen, the Netherlands: Nijmegen University.

Kwakman, K. (2003). Factors affecting teachers' participation in professional learning activities. *Teaching and Teacher Education, 19*(1), 149–170.

Little, J. W. (2002). Locating learning in teachers' communities of practice: Opening up problems of analysis in records of everyday work. *Teaching and Teacher Education, 18*(5), 917–946.

Tigelaar, D. E. H., Dolmans, D. H. J. M., Meijer, P. C., de Grave, W. S., & van der Vleuten, C. P. M. (2008). Teachers' interactions and their collaborative reflection processes during peer meetings. *Advances in Health Sciences Education, 13*(3), 289–308.

van Boxtel, C. A. M. (2000). *Collaborative concept learning*. Doctoral dissertation. Utrecht, the Netherlands: Utrecht University.

van Eekelen, I. M. (2005). *Teachers' will and way to learn. Studies on how teachers learn and their willingness to do so*. Doctoral dissertation. Maastricht, the Netherlands: Universiteit Maastricht.

Veenman, S. A. M. (1984). Perceived problems of beginning teachers. *Review of Educational Research, 54*, 143–178.

Wilson, S. M., & Berne, J. (1999). Teacher learning and the acquisition of professional knowledge: An examination of research on contemporary professional development. In A. Iran-Nejad & P. D. Pearson (Eds.), *Review of Research in Education* (vol. 24, pp. 173–209). Washington, DC: AERA.

APPENDIX

Description of various coding categories

CONTENT

Students

Topic of conversation is individual student or group of students (e.g., behavior, characteristics).

School Context

Topic of conversation is the school organization (e.g., consequences of the way things are organized at the specific school for the student teacher, or school-specific rules for dealing with students).

Boundaries of Teaching Responsibilities

Topic of conversation is the exact tasks or responsibilities of the teacher, exploration of the boundaries on such, and/or discussion of how to deal with such boundaries

STEPS IN THE DISCUSSION OF PROBLEMS

Recall/Describe Situation

Phase in which the situation, event, and so forth is recalled and described.

Formulate Essential Aspects

Phase in which essential aspects of the situation or events described in the recall phase are formulated (e.g., problems, issues).

Develop Alternatives

Phase in which possible solutions, ways of dealing with the situation, or ways of handling people are contemplated (e.g., brainstorming, debate).

Choose a Solution

Phase in which a solution is selected for further experimentation, for example.

UTTERANCE TYPES

Preparation

Make an introductory statement. Initial description of the situation and/ or discussion of the potentially problematic character of the situation.

Recall/Describe Situation

Ask a follow-up question. Request for further description of certain aspects of the situation or information on other aspects of the situation.

Clarify situation. Additional details and/or clarification of the situation.

Interpret situation. Description of the significance of the situation for one or more of the individuals involved and/or the consequences of the situation.

Judge a situation. Statement of opinion about a situation (but *not* about one's behavior in that situation).

Formulate Essential Aspects

Explain. Provision of reasons for a situation to be problematic or arguments for a particular approach.

Summarize. Briefly recalling aspects of the situation and/or briefly recalling conversation or part of the conversation.

Concretize. Elaboration of the situation or certain aspects of the situation by giving examples.

Interpret. Interpretation of the significance of the situation or aspects of the situation.

Guide/direct. The posing of questions or remarks aimed to guide the discussion in a specific direction, prompt a specific line of thinking, or elicit a specific solution.

Provide information. The provision of factual information.

Develop Alternatives

Request an alternative. A request for an alternative approach or alternative way of working.

Propose an alternative. The proposal or description of an alternative approach to the situation or alternative manner of working within the situation.

React to an alternative (pos./neg.). The provision of a reaction to an approach or manner of working (positive or negative).

Explore an alternative. Description or elaboration of the content or consequences of an alternative.

Advise. Provision of advice with regard to manners of working, behavior, position within school, and so forth.

Choose a Solution

Select/agree on a solution. Select a solution from available alternatives and agree on the best way to deal with the situation.

Evaluate solution. Appraisal of an alternative or its consequences.

CHAPTER 11

Cracks in the Mirror

DISCOVERING TEACHER CANDIDATES' STRATEGIES FOR RESISTING REFLECTION

Don Halquist
The College at Brockport, State University of New York

Sue Novinger
The College at Brockport, State University of New York

Don Halquist, Ph.D., is an assistant professor in the department of Education and Human Development at the College at Brockport State University of New York, where he teaches courses in literacy, diversity, early childhood, and qualitative research methods. His current research interests focus on preservice teacher identity development and the use of critical incidents as means to explore lived experience.

Sue Novinger, Ph.D., is an associate professor in the department of Education and Human Development at the College at Brockport State University of New York. She teaches courses in teacher inquiry, literacy, and early childhood. Her current research interests include examination of preservice teachers' construction of teaching identities, and the politics of early literacy pedagogy and assessment under No Child Left Behind and Reading First.

ABSTRACT

As teacher candidates engage in critical reflection, they construct narratives that give meaning to their experiences, and through those narratives engage in ongoing construction and reconstruction of fluid, multifaceted teaching identities. In this study, letter writing served as a curricular invitation to teacher candidates to reflect on their experiences and engage in identity work. However, while all of our students wrote letters, a number of students explicitly resisted engaging in reflection. In the two case studies presented here, we analyze the letters of "reflection resisters," as we examine the nature of the narratives (and current and imagined identities) they construct, paying particular attention to the compliance and resistance strategies they use.

Like many teacher educators (e.g., Alsup, 2006; Danielewicz, 2001; Flores & Day, 2006; Zembylas, 2005), we are convinced of the importance of engaging teacher candidates in the messy work of identity development, and of the power of critical reflection for supporting students in the ongoing construction and reconstruction of fluid, multifaceted teaching identities. To that end, we designed an assignment that invited our undergraduate early childhood education cohort of twenty students to write a series of reflective letters during two consecutive courses. We saw the letters as a supportive space for students to craft narratives wherein they might reflect on their experiences and engage in identity work. Our previous analyses (Halquist & Novinger, 2006) demonstrated that the reflective letters did, indeed, offer a medium for dialogic construction of identity by engaging students in both internal and social dialogues of critical reflection.

Still, we knew that some of our students seemed to resist our invitations to reflect. These students still wrote the letters, but their narratives did not demonstrate characteristics of thoughtful reflection, nor did they demonstrate shifts in students' identities over time. Our purpose in this chapter, then, is to look carefully and critically at the narratives constructed by the students we thought of, at least initially, as "not good reflectors." In our analyses we seek to explore the nature of these students' reflections, examine the discourses on which they drew, and uncover the resistance and compliance strategies they used. Moreover, we seek to understand what their narratives might reveal about their efforts to construct teaching identities for themselves.

Conceptual Framework

Our framework is informed by several theoretical perspectives: *postmodern perspectives on teacher identity development, critical reflection, story and narrative inquiry,* and *writing as identity work.*

Rather than unitary and consistent across contexts, identities are understood "to be dynamic and multiple, and always positioned in relation to particular discourses and the practices produced by the discourses. Postmodern perspectives argue for the acceptance of multiple and contradictory identities" (Grieshaber & Canella, 2001, p. 13). Identities are produced through the interplay of "internal and external discursive processes" (Danielewicz, 2001, p. 11), and are thus both individual and social. Immersed in multiple, overlapping, and often contradictory discourses about teaching, teacher candidates are confronted by markedly different images of what counts as a "good teacher." To become a teacher, then, requires that students must deconstruct and make sense of these discourses as they continually construct and reconstruct their teaching identities (Alsup, 2006; Britzman, 1991; Danielewicz, 2001; Johnson, 2004; Marsh, 2003).

Engaging in critical reflection supports students in this ongoing process of identity construction (Alsup, 2006; Florio-Ruane, 2001; Starko et al., 2003; Zeichner, 1996). Reflection, however, means different things to different people in different contexts (e.g., Fendler, 2003; Zeichner & Liston, 1996). By critical reflection we have in mind what Alsup (2006) names "borderland discourse," wherein students bring competing discourses into dialogue in order to explore their own shifting, evolving identities. Alongside this notion of borderland discourse, we find Hatton and Smith's (1995) definition of "reflection" most relevant for our work. The authors characterize reflection as deliberate thinking about action with a view to its improvement. This definition takes into account notions of problem posing and problem solving, integral elements in our reflective process.

As students engage in critical reflection, or borderland discourse, they construct narratives that give meaning to their experiences (Connelly & Clandinin, 1990, 1994). And, as Bruner (2002) reminds us, it is "through narrative that we create and re-create selfhood . . . self is a product of our telling" (p. 85). Alsup (2006) asserts, "personal narratives don't simply reflect identities, they *are* people's identities" (p. 53). This process is at the same time intensely personal and intensely social. Indeed, Dyson and Genishi (1994) argue that "the storytelling self is a social self, who declares and shapes important relationship through the mediated power of words" (p. 5).

Researchers such as Cappello (2006), Elbaz-Luwisch (2002), and Lensmire and Satanovsky (1998) have highlighted the valuable role of writing for critical reflection and identity construction. Engaging in critical reflection through letter writing pushes students to make their lived experiences objects of reflection and to explore multiple identities (Danielewicz, 2001). This process has the potential to move them away from the stance of passive receivers of expert knowledge to individuals who actively construct knowledge while valuing their own understandings and experiences (Brookfield, 1987, 1990; Zeichner, 1996).

Students, however, may passively and/or actively resist engaging in critical reflection. Francis and Ingram-Starrs (2005) posit that such resistance might be related to issues of classroom power and other contexts in which students are situated. Admiraal and Wubbels (2005) argue that students might lack the knowledge and skills to critically reflect, and require support within shifting zones of proximal development. Alsup (2006) and Gay and Kirkland (2003) found that many students avoid the discomfort and fear inherent in the tensions and contradictions that are part of sustained, challenging, critical reflection, and instead develop resistance and coping strategies in order to fulfill assignments that call on them to reflect. It is two of our own students—Michelle and Cassie—whose resistance to meaningful reflection that are the subject of our inquiry.

Method

PARTICIPANTS AND CONTEXT OF THE STUDY

During the fall of 2004, Michelle was enrolled in our course, EDI 483, that is the second of two six-credit integrated early childhood curriculum courses in the early childhood program at The College at Brockport, State University of New York. Cassie was enrolled in the same course during the fall of 2005, and during the spring of 2005, she was a student in EDI 482, the first six-credit integrated early childhood curriculum course.

Sociocultural constructivism, critical pedagogy, and inquiry and reflection form the foundation of the early childhood program's philosophy and conceptual framework. Course assignments, activities, and experiences in EDI 482 and EDI 483 provide overlapping opportunities for members of the cohort to create integrated, inquiry-based, antibias curricula and learning environments; understand children's mathematical, scientific, social, and artistic thinking and development; develop strategies for assessment; and create opportunities for meaningful integration of technology across the curriculum. An integral part of both courses is an extensive field experience (forty-five hours) with children in kindergarten and/or first or second grades.

The early childhood program prepares a prospective teacher candidate for initial certification as a teacher from birth to second grade. Eligibility for the program is based on current enrollment as an undergraduate at Brockport in an approved academic major, which range from earth science to interdisciplinary arts for children. Early childhood teacher candidates sequence through four phases, typically over a series of four semesters. The program is based on a cohort model with approximately twenty students progressing through the second and third phases of their coursework together each year. Coursework during the second and third phases includes courses in language and literacy and integrated early childhood curriculum as well as courses in working with diversity. Each phase of the program has a field experience component in preparation for the Phase IV student teaching practicum. Teacher candidates complete a minimum of forty-five hours of field experience during both the second and third phases of the program.

DATA SOURCES AND DATA COLLECTION

The reflective letters that Michelle and Cassie each wrote during their tenure in the early childhood program serve as our primary data source, three for Michelle and five for Cassie. Data collection was embedded in multiple sections of two team-taught, undergraduate consecutive early childhood education courses. Prompts for the letters invited students to write about why they want to become teachers, their strengths, and challenges they face as students and prospective teachers. Students were also invited to reflect on their learning experiences related to course goals and their own goals, what they were noticing about themselves as learners and teachers, and their goals for the following semester (see the Appendix for prompts of each letter).

DATA ANALYSIS

For the initial phase of analysis we used constant comparison methodology (Glaser & Strauss, 1967). We independently read students' letters identifying initial themes. We looked for similarities and differences in the initial themes, and reconciled differences through discussion. We identified three categories of student letters: *personal, professional,* and *personal-professional* stories. Our previous work (Halquist & Novinger, 2006) focused on close analyses of two of these categories: *personal* and *personal-professional* stories.

For the current analysis, we turned our attention to a thread that emerged across both the *personal* and the *personal-professional* stories categories, a thread we call *resisting reflection*. We developed the following questions to frame this round of analysis:

- How do students position themselves as learners? As teachers? Teaching as a profession? In relation to knowledge construction and professional expertise?
- On what experiences and texts do they draw?
- What discourses do students seem to appropriate? To reject?
- What is the nature of the narratives that students construct?
- In what ways do students resist reflection? What compliance strategies (Francis & Ingram-Starrs, 2005) and resistance strategies do they use?

We selected the collected letters of Michelle and Cassie, two students whose work exemplified two different ways of resisting reflection that emerged through our analyses, as the focus for the case studies. Case study methodology is appropriate because case studies are descriptive in nature, and phenomena are studied in sociocultural contexts, allowing analysis and interpretation to be rooted in the reality of participants' experiences (Merriam, 1998).

We reread the letters comprising each case, coding in terms of the questions described above. We identified similarities and differences in coding and interpretation, and resolved differences through discussion. The letter excerpts used in the cases were edited for clarity only. In the representation of both cases, we made every attempt to represent the candidates' voices accurately, fairly, and clearly.

Our analyses revealed similarities and differences across the two cases. Both students constructed narratives that conveyed their current identities and provided glimpses of their imagined, ideal teacher identities, albeit quite different current and ideal identities. The nature and range of experiences, the texts and contexts, and the discourses students drew on in their reflections varied quite dramatically. Additionally, both engaged in what Zeichner and Liston (1996) call technical reflection. Both resisted engaging in critical reflection, but used markedly different strategies to do so, and as a result, told quite different stories about the identities they were constructing for themselves as students and teachers. Neither student's story demonstrated discernable shifts in their identities as teachers.

Looking across these two cases pushed us to reconsider our previous analyses of our students' reflective letters (Halquist & Novinger, 2006). In that work, we demonstrated the affordances of the letters as pedagogical tools that support students' reflections. Our current analyses demonstrate, however, that the letters were not supportive tools for all students. Rather, the letters became contested sites, wherein at least some of our students struggled with and against critical reflection. Our analyses uncovered five different resistance strategies used by Michelle and Cassie: mirroring expert voices, repetition, privileging the practical, avoiding responsibility, and oversimplifying.

Case Studies

CASE ONE: MICHELLE'S STORY

Michelle, whose letters we examine first, is a white woman, and at the time of the study was in her early twenties. A psychology major, Michelle grew up in the upstate New York community where our college is located. In her very first letter, she told us that she "always admired" her teachers and that she "modeled" herself on her own past teachers, and hoped to "be a good role model" for her own students.

During the time Michelle was in our class, we were dazzled by the reflection we thought we saw in her letters. On the surface, she seemed to respond to our prompts in thoughtful ways. It was not until we looked more closely, beyond the surface reflection, that we saw something very different at work in her letters—sustained, subtle resistance to our invitation to reflect on her learning and developing teacher identities. In particular, our analyses uncovered two strategies that Michelle employed, to great effect, to resist critical reflection: *mirroring expert voices* and *repetition*. We now turn to an examination of how she enacted these strategies.

But First . . . A Brief Word about Expectations

One of the prompts for the semester's introductory letter asked candidates to write about what they thought would be their biggest challenges as new teachers. Michelle responded:

> I know I am going to be stressed until I feel comfortable with the material I am supposed to introduce to the students. I will also be stressed until I know what is expected of me in the school that I work in. I guess I am afraid I will not be prepared to teach because I do not know what to expect.

What did Michelle reveal when she wrote that she did not know what would be expected of her and that she didn't know what to expect? That she felt vulnerable? That teaching is a technical activity, simply a matter of knowing what one is expected to do, and then doing it? That good teachers (and good girls) do what is expected of them? That teachers have little voice or real choice in an increasingly standardized, NCLB world? That competing discourses proffer different images, and thus different expectations of "good" teachers?

It is interesting that although she had "dreamed of becoming a teacher" since she was a young girl, Michelle did not know what to expect or what would be expected from her. As the student in a series of classrooms, it may be that Michelle was dazzled, too, by the surface image of what teachers do, and that surface image served to mystify possible teacher identities.

One possibility, of course, when we do not know what is expected, is to turn to an expert—someone we trust and/or someone in a position of authority, who can tell us *what* is expected, and *how* to meet those expectations. We see this in the first resistance strategy we uncovered in Michelle's letters, *mirroring expert voices*.

Mirroring Expert Voices

In the second letter of the semester, written at midterm, Michelle and her peers in the cohort were invited to reflect on what they had learned, what their learning might mean for their own teaching, and to consider what they were noticing about themselves as learners and teachers. The following excerpts from her letter demonstrate Michelle's strategy of *mirroring expert voices.*

> From reading Chaillé [and Britain] (2003) and engaging in class activities, I have taken away many ideas that are important to help children explore and investigate science and nature. . . . I need to model respect for nature and a genuine [interest] in science to better help my students to acquire these traits. . . . I can do this by asking my own questions during inquiry and bringing nature into the classroom. . . . From reading Seefeldt (2005) and engaging in class discussions, I have taken away many ideas that are important to help children take part in a democratic classroom. . . . Teachers should share control and allow children to take part in decision making. . . . I could invite children to help develop classroom rules. I believe [in] making sure children understand what is expected of them.

Here, and elsewhere in her letter, Michelle repeatedly used a rather striking patterned response. First, she wrote about what she has "taken away" from reading expert texts and class discussions in terms of teaching science and social studies. Then, she gave an example or two of how to enact the concept in the classroom. What we find particularly interesting is how Michelle appears to use the term "taken away." Rather than bringing her own lived experiences into dialogue with expert texts, she parrots the pronouncements made by those texts.

Why might Michelle have chosen to enact this resistance strategy? One possibility is that she (and we) were so immersed in expert discourse (Foucault, 1980) that this way of taking up expert knowledge was normalized, taken for granted (Novinger, O'Brien, & Sweigman, 2005). Within such a discourse, teacher candidates are positioned as passive recipients of expert knowledge. As teachers, they will be expected to enact what the experts have told them is right and good. One set of experts, her professors, chose texts by other experts. Michelle's job, as she possibly saw it, was to appropriate this expert knowledge and apply it—in the ways outlined by the experts—in her work as a teacher candidate and future teacher.

Bakhtin's (1981) concept of authoritative discourses helps us think about Michelle's strategy of reproducing expert voices. Bakhtin wrote that authoritative discourse is inextricably "fused with its authority" (pp. 342–343) and that it must be accepted without question (Novinger et al., 2005). Michelle's entries above would certainly seem to fit with this notion. But, what happens when authoritative discourses collide? When one set of expert voices challenges the truths of another? Michelle's next entry shows us one possibility.

> This semester I have enjoyed working with my [mentor teacher]. . . .
> I believe my [mentor teacher's] main instructional strategy is direct instruction. Therefore, I did not see very many connections between class topics and my field placement at the beginning of the semester. However, I have shared my lesson requirements and ideas with my [mentor teacher] and she is eager to explore new ideas and support my lesson designs.

And in a subsequent paragraph:

> I have noticed that I am unsure about myself in the classroom. I am willing to give things a try, but I feel uncertain and afraid I will do something wrong.

In these excerpts, Michelle brought two contrasting expert discourses face-to-face—university sanctioned experts and school experts—but then stopped before bringing these voices into dialogue with each other, or with her own experiences and perspectives. She was faced, it seems, with a real dilemma: how to mirror competing expert voices. Mirroring *our* expertise was the way to be the good student, and to present to us how she was thinking about becoming the good teacher. Mirroring her mentor's expertise was the way to be a good teacher in her lived experiences in her field placement, and most likely, in the real world of schools. She could not do both, so instead held them separate but equal, writing that she was "unable to see very many connections." It is no wonder that she is "afraid" that she "will do something wrong." Situated between competing and seemingly incompatible expert voices, Michelle finds herself in a no-win situation.

Michelle's strategy, in one way, seems to separate her experiences, compartmentalizing her teacher education coursework and her field placement experiences. Britzman (1991) calls this the fragmenting of experience, and writes,

> It is experience that is less than it could be, because fragmented experience cannot be extended or transformed. This form of fragmentation separates knowledge from experience and experience from the knower. Here, knowledge concerns all the ideas, discourses, and possibilities that enable one to reflect upon the meanings of experience. Yet in academic life, knowledge and experience are typically fragmented by tradition and design. There is a disjunction between the authoritative discourse required by the academy and the internally persuasive discourse that can extend the understandings and meanings one already possesses. The fragmentation of knowledge from

experience is so pervasive that we come to expect personal exclusion. Its roots are in the arrangements of academic knowledge, the dualism of content and pedagogy, the selection and politics of knowledge, and the tension between theory and practice. (p. 35)

Immersed in authoritative, expert discourses, Michelle seemed to be paralyzed, unable to mediate between disparate truths, or to reflect on her own experiences in ways that might allow her to construct and enact an integrated teacher identity. As Alsup (2006, p. 131) notes, "denying or suppressing any ideological tensions" can seem safer and far less difficult than engaging in borderland discourse.

We now turn to the second resistance strategy we uncovered in Michelle's reflective letters: *repetition*.

Repetition

At the end of a busy semester, we read Michelle's final letter to us as a competent and thoughtful summary of her learning and implications for her student teaching experience the following semester. When we began our data analysis, though, we were stunned when we realized that her final letter was little more than a rearranged version of her second letter, written about seven weeks earlier. This final letter is comprised of six paragraphs, four of which are lifted from her previous letter: one is verbatim, two are excerpts from longer paragraphs (original typographical errors included), and one includes a new addition to a lifted paragraph.

Why might Michelle have used this strategy? Our first read was that she figured out what the experts (us) wanted to read (she got a favorable response from us to her second letter), and simply gave it to us again. In essence, she was simply doing what she thought we expected her to do. It seems particularly interesting, though, to look closely at how Michelle arranged the paragraphs in this final letter. Instead of leading with what she learned from expert texts as she did in her previous letter, she opened by repeating the paragraph we highlighted above, naming the disparities between the expert discourses of our college classroom and the expert discourses of her field placement site. Her choice to lead with this paragraph seems significant, in that she foregrounded the disparities between the expert discourses in which she is immersed (even though she followed by repeating the paragraphs that parroted textbook authors).

In retrospect, it seems to us that Michelle was highlighting the relevance of the conflict among competing discourses for her developing practice and professional identity. In so doing, she was engaging in what Freire (1972) called problem posing, an important dimension of critical reflection. Indeed, one of our goals is to support our students as problem posers as well as problem solvers—but we did not interpret her entry as evidence of problem posing until this analysis, much after the fact. That may be because once Michelle named the problem, she moved on without trying either to unpack or grapple with the problem. Problematizing *our* expert knowledge was likely a daunting task for Michelle, given the ways that she and we were positioned in power-knowledge relationships. In naming the problem in a letter to us, she was talking back to expert knowledge and beginning to position herself differently within expert discourse.

Michelle also reprised her earlier text about being uncertain and afraid of doing something wrong, but then she extended and elaborated on these ideas by returning to the notion of *expectations*. (Extension is in brackets.)

> I have noticed that I am unsure about myself in the classroom. I am willing to give things a try, but I feel uncertain and afraid I will do something wrong. . . . [However, I am sure I will develop more confidence with practice. As a teacher, I have discovered that planning and really thinking about learning experiences is important in order for things to run smoothly. And even then you'll never know how children will respond to your plans. Therefore, it is important to also expect the unexpected and think about the different ways children can think of a topic.]

In our initial analysis, we read this excerpt as surface level reflection, as Michelle's continued resistance to grappling with the tensions among competing discourses. But now, we see a glimpse of Michelle tentatively crossing into borderland discourse. The importance of thoughtfully considering how young children might engage in a learning experience is an idea that was emphasized in the texts we assigned for the class (e.g., Cadwell, 1997; Chaillé & Britain, 2003) and in our class discussions. In this excerpt, Michelle used that notion as a lens for reflecting on her experiences in her placement classroom. She noted, for instance, that thinking about learning experiences will help "things . . . run smoothly." And, she returned to her deepest concern, not knowing what to expect—writing that thinking about the experiences she will teach makes it possible for her to "expect the unexpected." And although it would seem that Michelle still resisted making her own reflections visible in her narrative, she did indicate that thinking about her experiences had had an impact on her practice.

Summary

A close look at Michelle's letters uncovered two resistance strategies, *mirroring expert voices* and *repetition*. These strategies seem to provide a way for her to comply with the course requirement and to reflect on her learning without bringing conflicting discourses into dialogue. Rather, through her use of mirroring and repetition she appears to keep a safe distance between experts who do not agree.

Britzman (1991) and Danielewicz (2001) both contrast the ongoing, dialogic process of identity construction with taking on and playing a role that has been scripted by expert others. Michelle seems to envision becoming a teacher as learning to play a role—thus her concern with learning "what is expected." As we noted earlier, both she and we were immersed in expert discourses that position preservice teachers as passive recipients of expert knowledge, of how to play the teacher role.

An even closer look at Michelle's letters, though, reminds us that what we initially read as resistance might well be tentative steps into borderland discourse. Might the act of juxtaposing competing expert discourses be the first step toward stepping out of a scripted role, a step toward grappling with the complexities of becoming a teacher?

CASE TWO: CASSIE'S STORY

Cassie, the author of the second set of letters, is a white woman, and at the time of the study was in her early twenties. She grew up in a small town in southwestern New York and was majoring in sociology while in college.

Cassie wrote in her first letter that she has wanted to be a teacher ever since she was a little girl. She recalls reading stories aloud to her imaginary students in her imaginary classroom, a ritual that made her family laugh. Cassie remembers, "I knew back then I wanted to teach. I have always enjoyed working with children, specifically younger kids, kindergarten aged or younger." In elementary school, Cassie had several teachers whose passion for teaching and use of humor made a significant impression upon her; she in turn "would like to have an impact on children the way that many of [her] teachers had on [her]."

Through Cassie's five letters we get a glimpse into how one early childhood teacher candidate offers a descriptive, yet surface-level, reflection of her experiences. We also see how a teacher candidate focuses exclusively on her work in the classroom, never questioning her taken-for-granted assumptions of practice (Loughran, 2002). Taken together, Cassie's letters reveal the strategies of *privileging the practical, avoiding responsibility,* and *oversimplifying various course topics and concepts,* which she used to resist engaging in critical reflection. We examine each strategy below.

Privileging the Practical

In her first letter, Cassie indicated that she is a visual learner who learns best through small-group work, demonstrations, and activities. She also indicated that the act of reading offers her little benefit. In Cassie's words,

> I learn little to nothing when I have to sit down and read a boring article and discover for myself what I am supposed to get out of the reading, although reading guides are useful tools to help with this.

This practice of devaluing the reading process reappears in Cassie's second letter where she wrote:

> I learn much more easily through demonstration, examples, and small-group work than attempting to read something out of a book. This is something that I have come to realize throughout many years, but in this course in particular, I feel it is important because I can read in a book how different forms of assessment are not as effective as others, but until it can actually be seen in results it is somewhat hard to grasp and understand.

Cassie dismissed articles, chapters, and entire books as not helpful or realistic, and instead privileged her experience in her mentor teacher's classroom. The excerpt below offers a second example:

> A book cannot tell you a surefire way on how children will behave; therefore being in a classroom seems the most beneficial . . . teaching these very different, unique children is also impossible to grasp from a textbook.

Over the course of two semesters we used twelve different texts and numerous articles and case studies with our teacher candidates. The readings included a range of topics related to the overarching themes of the courses—social constructivism, inquiry, diversity, and critical literacy, among others. No reading presented positivistic, "surefire ways" for pedagogy, content area instruction, classroom management, or assessment techniques, nor do we believe we worked from an absolute, authoritarian level of instruction. In our written response to Cassie's statement above, one of us (Don) shared: "We encourage you to consider how you might take ideas, concepts, or strategies from the various texts and see what connections you can make to your mentor teacher's classroom and vice versa."

In retrospect, Cassie's beliefs and attitudes toward reading and the reading process may have limited her ability to use the texts as resources and to value, or even acknowledge, what the authors had to say. Given this perspective, we were not surprised that unlike Michelle, Cassie never drew on expert voices or texts in her letters. Instead, Cassie crafted a narrative in which all useful learning took place in the context of her placement classrooms as she worked with mentor teachers and children. We call this resistance strategy *privileging the practical*. Interestingly enough, two of the texts we used—Vasquez (2004) and Cadwell (1997)—were written by classroom teachers-researchers. Through a series of engaging and powerful vignettes, each teacher details her process of working with her students, families, and colleagues. Yet, as Cassie highlights below, her preference is for the practical:

> I feel that being in the classroom has been the most beneficial to me. Actually being in the class gives me opportunities to see different situations and scenarios and how others react and how I myself react. I feel that experience is the best way to understand how to work with children, especially in that every child is different.

Many teacher candidates express how beneficial they find the experiences of working with children with a variety of abilities and in a variety of settings. So in this sense, Cassie is not atypical. What is problematic is the way Cassie values this experience above all others. For her, field experience became the lens through which practice was defined and where learning took place. Cassie ends her second letter directly and simply by stating, "I hope to learn much more in the rest of the semester, especially from my placement."

Similarly, Cassie characterized the lesson planning procedure we asked candidates to use as "too detailed," requiring much more work and thought than teachers did in the "real world." In her words:

> Based on what we are learning in class, we have to spend hours working on a lesson plan and writing it out in great detail, but in a classroom I have never actually seen this done. Each classroom that I have been in the teacher, of course, has lesson plans made up, but they are much more brief—basic outlines. I understand that coming up with lesson plans becomes easier over time, but I don't understand the necessity to write them out in the way that we do. Maybe it is just the format that we are told to use in class that I find to be the problem. Not that it is difficult, just long, tedious, and repetitious to use.

The lesson design framework was often a topic of conversation in our college classroom. The teacher candidates expressed concern that what we were requiring them to use did not match what they were seeing their mentor teachers use and do. We found ourselves reminding our students of the value of thinking carefully about possibilities for inquiry while planning, and the value of generating possible questions to ask students. We encouraged them to value the planning process and to recognize that their mentor teachers had years of experience from which to draw, a resource not available to beginning teachers.

Cassie's desire for a shorter, outline-type of plan, the kind she saw her mentor teacher using, reveals her thinking that what she sees her mentor teacher doing is what is appropriate, realistic, and manageable, and ultimately what she should be doing. We begin to see in this excerpt a bit of Cassie's naiveté in terms of her understanding of the process of lesson planning, and perhaps more importantly, her failure to recognize *and* value the process of becoming knowledgeable and skilled. How does a teacher reach the level of being able to write a lesson plan in the form of an outline? What is involved in this process? Exploring ways of how her mentor teacher developed the knowledge and skills to be able to create a shorter version of a lesson plan would involve a more thorough analysis than what Cassie pursued in her letter.

This excerpt also reveals the tension Cassie was experiencing between the competing discourses related to lesson planning. Yet she stops short of bringing these competing discourses into dialogue with one another; she stops short of acknowledging the value in the planning process, whether it be a long or short format, stops short of the borderland (Alsup, 2006).

During the second semester of our work with the teacher candidates, we explored a variety of approaches and strategies for teaching the curricular areas of math, science, and social studies. We engaged the candidates in a series of inquiries into mathematics, the natural world, physics, and local history. In her fifth and final letter, Cassie does not reflect or highlight any specific pedagogical approaches she explored with us; instead she states:

> I am also eager to learn new strategies and ideas of how to teach science, math, and social studies in the classroom. Each area has so many possibilities, and I look forward to getting feedback from my new mentor teacher about new and different ideas.

It is exciting to read Cassie's realization that the curricular areas hold "many possibilities." But here, too, we see a privileging of the practical through the recognition that the mentor teacher will offer ideas that are new and different, more authentic and sensible. We wonder if Cassie was aware of how actively she was rejecting our repeated attempts to model sound pedagogical ideas and methodologies through the course readings and the multiple experiences we created for the candidates in our college classroom. We recognize the significance that teacher candidates place on field experience. And we certainly value experiential learning, but not at the exclusion or expense of all other types of learning.

Dewey (1933) identified three attributes of reflective individuals: open-mindedness, wholeheartedness, and responsibility. Open-mindedness refers to the ability to refrain from prejudice, bias, and other such habits that close the mind, making it unwilling to entertain new ideas or consider new problems. Cassie's strategy of privileging the practical becomes her bias and her mantra. The result is that Cassie seems to have constructed an identity of teacher as a technician who privileges what works in practice.

Avoiding Responsibility

At times, Cassie used her lack of experience, her negative evaluations of situations and individuals, and her position as "not a real teacher" as ways to define or explain problems she was experiencing in her placement and in our college classroom. We call this second strategy *avoiding responsibility*. Cassie's second letter provides our first example:

> I find that right now in the placement that I am in since I am still a student, the other students [children] find it difficult to think of me as a teacher. It could possibly be the kids who I am working with, but I feel that they are now just warming up to me and looking at me as another teacher in the classroom. I feel it is easier for this to happen if there is more consistent time spent in the classroom, but since they only see me once a week I am still like a stranger to them.

When this letter was written, Cassie had spent approximately twenty-two hours in her mentor teacher's classroom. We were puzzled why Cassie might still position herself in this way given the amount of time she had spent in the classroom. What might she have done to feel less like a stranger? Considering possible alternatives or strategies might have helped both Cassie and the children move into a different type of relationship. Later, in the same letter, Cassie shared:

> It is hard to follow along with the flow of the class when my mentor teacher seems to go in one direction while the aide seems to go in another. They have different styles and ways of handling the children, which makes me question how I should, since I have no power in the classroom.

In this excerpt, Cassie is critiquing the actions of both her mentor teacher and the paraprofessional, and essentially asking, how am I supposed to know what to do if the two adults in the room cannot agree? Here we see an example of problem posing (Freire, 1972). However, by limiting her reflection to a critique of other individuals' actions, Cassie's restricts her ability to consider how she might begin to take a more active role in the classroom, how she might deconstruct the various approaches she sees being used, or perhaps more importantly, how she might problem solve this situation.

Cassie's notion of power is also intriguing. What does it mean to have power in a field placement classroom? Returning to the first excerpt in this section, perhaps she believes that if she has power, the children in the classroom would perceive her differently. What might this look like? This theme of critiquing others resurfaced in Cassie's third letter when she wrote:

> In my last letter, both of you noted that you felt that I had a negative tone and I will explain that. On behalf of the class, we were all extremely stressed out. The time that the second letter was due was right after you had been intense in the way you spoke with us in class. We left class and everyone was overwhelmed and felt we should say something. No one did, but in the end things worked out and we've all made it through the semester!! I felt that you were both negative to us in the class that day and it left me with a negative feeling, which is why my letter appeared that way because I wrote it right after class.

Here, Cassie acknowledges her attitude, but places the reason for and the responsibility for her actions on us, her instructors: You were both negative to us, so I was negative to you. She avoids taking responsibility by rationalizing her actions rather than contemplating possible reasons of how or why she perceived our actions as negative or discussing her own negative feelings in further detail.

Dewey's (1933) notion of responsibility implies the desire to actively search for truth and apply information gained to problem situations. Avoiding responsibility or shifting the responsibility becomes a form of rationalization (Loughran, 2002), rather than a way for Cassie to examine the contexts of her situations. This orientation offers a self that is disengaged or distanced from the situation and from change (Ward & McCotter, 2004). Simply put: I am not responsible, so I do not need to acknowledge the problem, nor do I need to change my behavior.

Oversimplifying

Cassie employed a third and related strategy we call *oversimplifying*. In this strategy, she offered a definitive, pat, and generalized analysis of a situation or concept. Earlier we highlighted Cassie's desire to use an abbreviated version of a lesson plan, like that of her mentor teacher. Perhaps to Cassie, the outline eliminated the complex and messy planning, thinking, and writing processes. However, Cassie's notion that the outline is enough, at this point in her development, suggests to us that her understanding of what is involved in the planning process fails to consider the complexities and the nuances. Further, focusing on and attending to the finished product truncates much of the potential for teaching and learning.

Cassie offers another example of oversimplification in her fifth and final letter where she wrote:

> I have really begun to understand ideas behind critical pedagogy. This phrase seemed scary at first, but it's a rather simple idea. It's simply questioning different things and going about making changes and/or learning from them. People do this without even thinking about it, which is why once I learned more about it, it seemed so easy to understand and see it happening.

Here, Cassie does not discuss how or when she has seen critical pedagogy happening or how she might begin to enact this approach with children. Her notion that people engage in critical pedagogy "without even thinking about" is overtly simple and particularly troubling given our in-depth and extended exploration of the concept. Vasquez (2004) reminds us that "retracing thinking involves theorizing" (p. 3). Cassie's oversimplification of concepts and processes sidesteps the need for theorizing and as a result, the act of retracing, the act of reflection.

Summary

When we focus on the content of her letters, we see ways in which Cassie's methods of reflecting were to privilege the practical, avoid responsibility, and oversimplify concepts. The strategies of privileging the practical and the oversimplification of concepts avoid the messy and complicated work of borderland discourse, and instead position one method over another, and ultimately confine reflection to a superficial level, which we see above in Cassie's definition of critical pedagogy. Further, the three strategies lack any attempt on Cassie's part to engage in a questioning of her taken-for-granted assumptions of her practice (Loughran, 2002), an integral element of critical reflection.

Chak (2006) asserts that reflection is assumed to be a rational process, where the information is critically examined with less attention paid to how one's subjective defenses may affect the interpretation of information. But according to Hamachek (as cited in Chak, 2006), defense mechanisms, such as denial, rationalization, and projection, may hinder the acceptance of the reality or biased interpretation. As we have shown, Cassie's letters reveal aspects of these various defense mechanisms.

Cassie constructed meaning from certain aspects of her own life experiences (Leshem & Trafford, 2006). However, she resisted reflection by privileging certain approaches over others and failed to bring competing discourses into dialogue. Further, she resisted reflection by avoiding taking responsibility for her behaviors or her actions. Most importantly, she resisted reflection by avoiding taking ownership and becoming the subject of her own reflection (Loughran, 2002).

LOOKING AND LOOKING AGAIN

The more we thought and talked about our analyses, the more troubled we became. We felt confident that the resistance strategies that we uncovered in our analyses were well-grounded in the data. We had theorized multiple possibilities about why Michelle and Cassie might have resisted reflection and used these particular strategies. But, we wondered, were we simply engaging in student bashing by framing them as resisting reflection, and further, what might *we* be resisting? We decided that we needed to venture further into our own border-lands, to more deeply trouble the ways in which we and our students are positioned within expert, authoritative discourses (Novinger et al., 2005).

For instance, rather than seeing Michelle and Cassie as "not good reflectors" (as we originally did), we might ask ourselves if our pedagogy actually supported them in learning how to reflect. Like a number of teacher educators (e.g., Admiraal & Wubbels, 2005; Grushka, Hinde-McLeod, & Reynolds, 2005; Leshem & Trafford, 2006; Russell, 2005), we came to realize that we asked our students to reflect, but may well not have provided them with clear definitions and examples of what "counts" as reflection or how to begin to engage in meaningful reflection. Yost, Sentner, and Forlenza-Bailey (2000) believe "teacher educators must find ways to imbue preservice teachers with the intellectual and professional experiences necessary to enable them to reflect on critical levels" (p. 40). We agree, and note that the challenge becomes imagining and enacting conditions that support our students' abilities to reflect (Hoffman-Kipp, Artiles, & López-Torres, 2003).

A logical place to begin is by interrogating what *we* mean when we ask students to reflect. We agree with Fendler (2003), who highlights multiple discursive constructions of reflection, such as instrumental vs. critical reflection, or reflection as expert knowledge vs. reflection as anti-expert knowledge. It is imperative, then, that we clarify for ourselves what we mean when we invite students to reflect, make those meanings explicit and visible for our students, and provide a range of interactive demonstrations. We value problem posing in students' reflections, and realize that we need to engage in joint problem posing with students, support them in doing this on their own, and be clear that this is one process that is a valued and valuable component of reflection, even explicitly naming it. The letters were just one of many ways we encouraged our students to engage in reflection; other engagements included large- and small-group class discussions, their electronic dialogue journal entries and responses, and analyses of their teaching experiences in their mentor teacher's classrooms. Through these endeavors, we engaged our students in shared, ongoing reflections on their experiences. Providing our candidates with more concrete scaffolds through which to internalize strategies for critical reflection might facilitate their process and abilities in a variety of contexts and assignments.

Ultimately, though, we think that we need to consider our *desires*. Mainstream teacher education discourses value reflective practice because of the opportunities created for students to construct deep understandings. More to the point, though, what we, as experts, often desire is for our students to develop understandings of *our* expert knowledge. "What we desire is continuity— continuity of the knowledges that we value and continuity of our positionings as experts" (Novinger et al., 2005, pp. 232–233). Could it be that we read Michelle and Cassie's letters through the lens of our own desires for them to reproduce our own expert knowledge, to become teachers like us? How might acknowledging this stance and looking again from a different vantage point allow us to see their reflections in a new light?

We might, for instance, consider what Michelle and Cassie might have been trying to accomplish through their written reflections. Were they *really* resisting reflection, or did they have different intentions? Was Cassie *really* rejecting expert knowledge, or pushing back against the particular kinds of expert knowledge we valued? Was Michelle *really* unable to grapple with competing discourses, or savvy enough to give us back what we desired? What might they have been trying to communicate that wasn't visible on the surface of their reflections? What strategies did they use to be able to safely talk back to expert knowledge? In short, we need to push ourselves to recognize—and value—the struggles that are real and meaningful for our students, and the myriad ways that they might approach borderland discourse. In so doing, we can create the possibility of meeting them in those borderlands in ways that honor and extend the reflective work that *they* find personally meaningful.

In the process, we enter into interesting and challenging borderlands ourselves. We believe that letters hold the potential for what Russell (2005) describes as "a new way of listening to future teachers" (p. 203). At the same time, we believe that we need to engage in our own problem posing and problem solving around how we and our students use those letters. How might we grapple with the tensions between our vision of the transformative intellectuals our teacher candidates might become and their own desires and choices as they construct their teaching identities? How might we scaffold and challenge our students in this process, without using the letters and other reflective engagements as a kind of disciplinary technology, through which we surveil and regulate students' subjectivities?

This work is messy and unsettling—but will, we think, make us better able to support our students' journeys within their own borderlands.

References

Admiraal, W., & Wubbels, T. (2005). Multiple voices, multiple realities, what truth? Student teachers' learning to reflect in different paradigms. *Teachers and Teaching: Theory and Practice, 11*(3), 315–320.

Alsup, J. (2006). *Teacher identity discourses: Negotiating personal and professional spaces.* Mahwah, NJ: Lawrence Erlbaum Associates.

Bakhtin, M. M. (1981). Discourse in the novel. In M. Holquist, C. Emerson, & M. Holquist (Eds.), *The dialogic imagination: Four essays by M. M. Bakhtin* (pp. 259–422). Austin, TX: University of Texas Press.

Britzman, D. (1991). *Practice makes practice: A critical study of learning to teach.* Albany, NY: SUNY Press.

Brookfield, S. D. (1987). *Developing critical thinkers.* San Francisco: Jossey-Bass.

Brookfield, S. D. (1990). *The skillful teacher: On technique, trust, and responsiveness in the classroom.* San Francisco: Jossey-Bass.

Bruner, J. (2002). *Making stories: Law, literature, life.* New York: Farrar, Straus & Giroux.

Cadwell, L. B. (1997). *Bringing Reggio Emilia home: An innovative approach to early childhood education.* New York: Teachers College Press.

Cappello, M. (2006). Under construction: Voice and identity development in writing workshop. *Language Arts, 83*(6), 482–491.

Chaillé, C., & Britain, L. (2003). *The young child as scientist: A constructivist approach to early childhood science education,* 3rd ed. Boston, MA: Allyn & Bacon.

Chak, A. (2006). Reflecting on the self: An experience in a preschool. *Reflective Practice, 7*(1), 31–41.

Connelly, F. M., & Clandinin, D. J. (1990). Stories of experience and narrative inquiry. *Educational Researcher, 19*(5), 2–14.

Connelly, F. M., & Clandinin, D. J. (1994). Telling teaching stories. *Teacher Education Quarterly, 21*(1), 145–158.

Danielewicz, J. (2001). *Teaching selves: Identity, pedagogy, and teacher education.* Albany, NY: SUNY Press.

Dewey, J. (1933). *How we think: A re-statement of the relation of reflective thinking to the educative process.* Boston: D. C. Heath & Co.

Dyson, A. H., & Genishi, C. (1994). *The need for story: Cultural diversity in classroom and community.* Urbana, IL: NCTE.

Elbaz-Luwisch, F. (2002). Writing as inquiry: Storying the teaching self in writing workshops. *Curriculum Inquiry, 32*(4), 403–428.

Fendler, L. (2003). Teacher reflection in a hall of mirrors: Historical influences and political reverberations. *Educational Researcher, 32*(3), 16–25.

Flores, M. A., & Day, C. (2006). Contexts which shape and reshape new teachers' identities: A multi-perspective study. *Teaching and Teacher Education, 22*, 219–232.

Florio-Ruane, S. (2001). *Teacher education and the cultural imagination*. Mahwah, NJ: Lawrence Erlbaum Associates.

Foucault, M. (1980). *Power-knowledge: Selected interviews and other writings, 1972–1977*. Brighton, UK: Harvester Press.

Francis, D., & Ingram-Starrs, L. (2005). The labour of learning to reflect. *Teachers and Teaching: Theory and Practice, 11*(6), 541–553.

Freire, P. (1972). *Pedagogy of the oppressed*. New York: The Continuum Publishing Co.

Gay, G., & Kirkland, K. (2003). Developing cultural critical consciousness and self-reflection in preservice teacher education. *Theory into Practice, 42*(3), 181–187.

Glaser, B. G., & Strauss, A. L. (1967). *The discovery of grounded theory: Strategies for qualitative research*. New York: Aldine.

Grieshaber, S., & Cannella, G. (2001). From identity to identities: Increasing possibilities in early childhood education. In S. Grieshaber and G. Cannella (Eds.), *Embracing identities in early childhood education: Diversity and possibilities* (pp. 3–22). New York: Teachers College Press.

Grushka, K., Hinde-McLeod, J., & Reynolds, R. (2005). Reflecting upon reflection: Theory and practice in one Australian university teacher education program. *Reflective Practice, 6*(2), 39–246.

Halquist, D., & Novinger, S. (2006). *Reliving the past, replicating the present, re-envisioning the future: Stories of identity(ies) of two early childhood teacher candidates*. Paper presented at the Annual Meeting of the American Educational Research Association, San Francisco, CA.

Hatton, N., & Smith, D. (1995). Reflection in teacher education—towards definition and implementation. *Teaching and Teacher Education, 11*(1), 33–49.

Hoffman-Kipp, P., Artiles, A. J., & Lopez-Torres, L. (2003). Beyond reflection: Teacher learning as praxis. *Theory into Practice, 42*(3), 248–254.

Johnson, A. S. (2004). Recruiting and recognizing multiple socially situated identities: Consonance and contradiction in the pedagogy of a male preservice early educator. *Contemporary Issues in Early Childhood, 5*(1), 19–34.

Lensmire, T., & Satanovsky, L. (1998). Defense of the romantic poet? Writing workshop and voice. *Theory into Practice, 37*, 280–288.

Leshem, S., & Trafford, V. N. (2006). Stories as mirrors: Reflective practice in teaching and learning. *Reflective Practice, 7*(1), 9–27.

Loughran, J. J. (2002). Effective reflective practice: In search of meaning in learning about teaching. *Journal of Teacher Education, 53*(1), 33–43.

Marsh, M. M. (2003). *The social fashioning of teacher identities*. New York: Peter Lang.

Merriam, S. (1998). *Qualitative research and case study applications in education*. San Francisco, CA: Jossey-Bass.

Novinger, S., O'Brien, L., & Sweigman, L. (2005). Challenging the culture of expertise: Moving beyond training the always, already failing early childhood educator. In S. Ryan and S. Grieshaber (Eds.), *Practical transformations and transformational practices: Globalization, postmodernism, and early childhood education* (pp. 217–241). Amsterdam: Elsevier.

Russell, T. (2005). Can reflective practice be taught? *Reflective Practice, 6*(2), 199–204.

Seefeldt, C. (2005*). Social studies for the preschool/primary child*, 7th ed. Upper Saddle River, NJ: Pearson Merrill Prentice Hall.

Starko, A., Sparks-Langer, G., Pasch, M., Frankes, L., Gardner, T., & Moody, C. (2003). *Teaching as decision making: Successful practices for the elementary teacher.* Upper Saddle River, NJ: Merrill Prentice Hall.

Vasquez, V. M. (2004). *Negotiating critical literacies with young children.* Mahwah, NJ: Lawrence Erlbaum Associates.

Ward, J. R., & McCotter, S. S. (2004). Reflection as a visible outcome for preservice teachers. *Teaching and Teacher Education, 20,* 243–257.

Yost, D. S., Sentner, S. M., & Forlenza-Bailey, A. (2000). An examination of the construct of critical reflection: Implications for teacher education programming in the 21st century. *Journal of Teacher Education, 51*(1), 39–49.

Zeichner, K. (1996). Teachers as reflective practitioners and the democratization of school reform. In K. Zeichner, S. Melinick, and M. L. Gomez (Eds.), *Currents of reform in preservice teacher education* (pp. 199–214). New York: Teachers College Press.

Zeichner, K., & Liston, D. (1996). *Reflective teaching: An introduction.* Mahwah, NJ: Lawrence Erlbaum Associates.

Zembylas, M. (2005). Discursive practices, genealogies, and emotional rules: A poststructuralist view on emotion and identity in teaching. *Teaching and Teacher Education, 21,* 935–948.

APPENDIX

GUIDING QUESTIONS AND PROMPTS FOR LETTER ONE

- Why do you want to be a teacher?
- What are your academic strengths?
- Please describe how you learn best (e.g., Do you like to work on your own or in groups? Are you a visual learner, learn through demonstration? Do you learn best through listening to lectures?).
- How are you smart or what are your multiple intelligences?
- What do you think your biggest challenges will be as a teacher?
- If you were to identify one academic/teaching skill you needed to work on what would it be? (e.g., researching curriculum, reading and synthesizing large quantities of reading material quickly, writing papers, speaking publicly, listening to others before you speak)
- Given the course objectives and topics, which areas do you see as a focus for yourself this semester? Please describe why.
- Please share anything else you feel is relevant or important for us to know.

GUIDING QUESTIONS AND PROMPTS FOR LETTER TWO

For this reflection, we would like you to focus on your experiences thus far in the semester. In order to facilitate your reflection, you may find it helpful to revisit the areas outlined below as well as any other areas that you feel are relevant.

- Children's thinking
- Lesson planning
- Inquiry process
- Field experience
- Classroom management
- Concepts and strategies from readings, class notes, and handouts
- Teaching strategies related to: science, social studies, technology, mathematics, and problem solving

In addition, please address the question: What are you noticing about yourself as a learner and as a teacher?

GUIDING QUESTIONS AND PROMPTS FOR LETTER THREE

Congratulations, you are about to finish the semester and the second phase of the early childhood program. For this reflection, we would like you to focus on your experiences from throughout the semester as well as your work throughout the program. In order to facilitate your reflection, you may find it helpful to revisit the areas outlined below as well as any other areas that you feel are relevant.

- Critical pedagogy
- Lesson planning
- Antibias, multicultural education
- Field experience
- Assessment
- Art making
- Environment
- Classroom management
- Concepts and strategies from readings, class notes, and handouts
- Teaching strategies related to: the arts, health, safety and nutrition, and guidance

In addition, please address the questions: What are you noticing about yourself as a learner and as a teacher? What are your goals for next semester?

GUIDING QUESTIONS AND PROMPTS FOR LETTER FOUR

Note: We asked the teacher candidates to write a letter to their mentor teacher. No data excerpts from either Michelle or Cassie's letters were used in the case studies.

GUIDING QUESTIONS AND PROMPTS FOR LETTER FIVE

Congratulations, you are about to finish the semester and the third phase of the early childhood program. For this reflection, we would like you to focus on your experiences from throughout the semester as well as your work throughout the program. In order to facilitate your reflection, you may find it helpful to revisit the areas outlined below as well as any other areas that you feel are relevant.

- Children's thinking
- Lesson planning

- Inquiry process
- Field experience
- Classroom management
- Concepts and strategies from readings, class notes, and handouts
- Teaching strategies related to: science, social studies, the arts, technology, mathematics, and problem solving

In addition, please address the questions: What are you noticing about yourself as a learner and as a teacher? What are your goals for student teaching?

CHAPTER 12

Exploring Significance and Benefits of Group Learning for Developing Cultural Competence with Teacher Candidates

Nancy P. Gallavan
University of Central Arkansas

Nancy P. Gallavan, Ph.D., professor at the University of Central Arkansas, specializes in social studies, multicultural education, and performance-based assessments. Active in ATE, NCSS, and NAME, Nancy has more than 60 publications, including the books *Developing Performance-Based Assessments, Grades K–5* and *Performance-Based Assessments, Grades 6–12*, and two books with Ellen Kottler: *Secrets to Success for Beginning Elementary School Teachers* and *Secrets to Success for Social Studies Teachers*.

ABSTRACT

Frequently, pre-K–12th-grade teachers organize group learning experiences within safe and controlled learning community contexts for learners to interact respectfully, cooperatively, and productively. These goals contribute positively to developing cultural competence: the processes of valuing diversity naturally, authentically, and holistically while ensuring educational equity and excellence for all learners. Developing cultural competence through effective group learning experiences enhances future successes in higher education, lifelong careers, family life, civic associations, and social responsibilities. Through surveys, teaching interns described benefits of group learning, eliciting significance for developing cultural competence in classrooms, especially to compensate for the "generational perpetuation of practice" that candidates experience with mentor teachers.

> Interns' offer constructive benefits for pre-K–12th-grade learners, classroom teachers, teacher candidates, and teacher educators.

Frequently, pre-K–12th grade teachers facilitate classroom instruction for their learners to participate in group learning experiences to achieve many different academic and social outcomes. Concomitantly, teachers are developing cultural competence. Cultural competence encompasses the processes of acquiring, applying, and appreciating requisite knowledge, skills, and dispositions for valuing diversity in ways that are natural, authentic, and holistic.

Cultural competence includes the abilities to understand the complexity of one's cultural components and to interact with individuals and groups in ways that are culturally responsive (Gay, 2002) and responsible. Berry, Poortinga, Segall, and Dasen (1992) identify their six cultural components as (1) descriptive characterizations—one's nature; (2) genetic origins—one's biology; (3) historical traditions—one's background; (4) structural organizations—one's systems; (5) normative expectations—one's traditions; and (6) psychological problem-solving theories—one's outlooks.

In schools and classrooms, teachers must ensure educational access, equity, and excellence for all learners—three essential aspects of cultural competence (Gallavan, 2007). All learners are entitled to the same quality of education and educational services that all other learners receive; all learners deserve the privilege of being prepared for future schooling, working, and living so everyone can enjoy life to the maximum. Likewise, all learners need and want to learn about all other people; everyone is curious about themselves and one another. These beliefs resonate with teachers too. Lynch and Hanson (2004) stress the interest and need for all educators and other professionals to continually increase their awareness, expand their understanding, and improve their cultural competence in themselves, their schools, and their classrooms.

Supporting Standards Established by the Association of Teacher Educators

Developing cultural competence is supported by the Association of Teacher Educators. ATE Standard 2, Cultural Competence (ATE, 2007), charges teacher educators with the responsibility for preparing teachers to connect and communicate with diverse learners by knowing their own cultures, learning the cultures of their learners' families and communities, selecting inclusive curriculum, and practicing infusive instruction.

The standard emphasizes using a range of assessments to reach all learners and modeling prejudice reduction with pre-K–12th-grade learners, learners' families, teacher candidates, teacher interns, and colleagues at all times to advocate cultural competence. Professional educators must be able to think, feel, and interact in ways that acknowledge, respect, and build upon their own cultures and heritages in order to learn more about the diverse cultural components of the learners, families, and communities with whom they work, and to apply knowledge, skills, and dispositions necessary for working effectively with all learners.

Developing Cultural Competence through Group Learning in Schools and Classrooms

Teachers often facilitate effective group learning experiences for everyone to learn more about themselves, one another, and the world around them. Group learning experiences must be introduced mindfully. They must seamlessly align developmentally appropriate content, interactively challenging processes, and collaboratively constructed products that result in both short-term and long-term outcomes. Short-term outcomes include text connections, class meetings, and team activities; long-term outcomes include project preparations, class demonstrations, and report presentations. Group learning highlighting various outcomes can occur within one classroom during one period or across several locations and periods (e.g., project-based learning), or as schoolwide events within or beyond the school (e.g., service learning).

Group learning experiences are advantageous for learners when teachers (1) establish well-defined learning community contexts in their classrooms to ensure full participation (Johnson & Johnson, 1989; Slavin, 1992); (2) provide clear purposes for the group process and the usefulness of the products (Bassett, McWhirter, & Kitzmiller, 1999; Webb, Troper, & Fall, 1995); and (3) encourage expressive contributions and reciprocated interactions (King, 2002; Palinscar & Brown, 1984). Teachers help (4) advance in-depth understanding and personalized connections to increase achievement and enhance creativity (Johnson, Johnson, & Smith, 1998; Lord, 2001); and (5) debrief the facilitation of the process and reflection on the success of the task to promote critical thinking (Cleland & Pearse, 1995; McBride, 1999). Group learning also contributes significantly to learners' academic proficiencies by enriching (1) immediate recognition of new information, focusing on narrower succinct objectives; (2) essential concepts, integrating and applying academic expectations holistically across the curriculum; and (3) unending understanding, supporting broader goals intricate to lifelong learning and living (Wiggins & McTighe, 2005, p. 71).

Functioning in effective group learning experiences shifts increased responsibilities as well as the ownership or social agency (Bandura, 1989) associated with the processes for the learning from the teacher to the learners, both as members of one cohesive group and as individual members operating within a group. Learners begin to master requisite knowledge, skills, and dispositions to learn the content and skills through the application of the group processes to the resulting outcomes (Baer, 2003).

The overarching aims of group learning focus on the opportunities for learners to acknowledge and experience the efficacy of group learning while refining their dependence, independence, and interdependence in ways that are cooperative, collaborative, and transformative (Cranton, 1996; Gallavan & Juliano, 2007). Ultimately, learners become more motivated, creative, and successful—academically, socially, and emotionally (Turner & Patrick, 2004). As learners hone their abilities and appreciation to operate effectively within assorted group learning experiences, learners are more likely to demonstrate greater understanding of new knowledge coupled with faster application of prior knowledge to different contexts as they perfect their prowess to negotiate with one another and navigate in society.

Relating Group Learning to Employment and Communities

Group learning in schools extends well beyond academic settings. Employers strive for the same types of qualities and outcomes from their employees just as community leaders desire them among their citizenry. When employees interact respectfully, cooperatively, and productively, they learn to both capitalize upon their strengths and nurture their weaker areas. Employees also begin looking forward to their work, the workplace, their colleagues, and their clients or customers. Employees not only gain a sense of self-worth, they realize that the workplace offers them unique opportunities to learn and grow in a valued context (Huitt, 1999).

Such results are not minor expectations for businesses and industries. The turnover rate and replacement costs associated with new employees greatly inhibit companies and agencies from operating at premium levels (National Technical Information Service, 1992). Additionally, individuals reap both intrinsic and extrinsic rewards as they grow personally and professionally through shared activities and teaming (West, 1996). These types of synergy propel businesses and industries to become a shared workplace and, in turn, offer the workforce additional benefits as employees commit more energy to their tasks, advancing both the workforce and the workplace.

Similar events occur within communities and families related to civic associations and social responsibilities. When citizens and family members interact respectfully, cooperatively, and productively, then communication, decision-making, and problem-solving become a shared responsibility (Summers, Beretvas, & Gorin, 2005). Most adults look forward to and like working in groups (Imel & Tisdell, 1996). With an increased sense of social agency (Houston, 2002), concerns and challenges are approached more optimistically as opportunities to express individual and shared viewpoints, experience different perspectives, and resolve conflict constructively.

In workplaces, communities, and families, people face problems together rather than antagonize one another. Less time, money, and energy are dedicated to helping people learn to work together, stay focused, and reap reward. Through effective group learning skills acquired in pre-K–12th-grade classrooms, everyone gets along more congenially, and challenges can be conquered more easily. Thus, workplaces, communities, and families become centers that satisfy, prosper, and grow.

Connecting Cultural Competence and Group Learning with Teaching Interns

Through assorted group learning experiences, teaching interns experience unique opportunities to express and exchange ideas through collaboration in producing an outcome. During these opportunities, interns examine their cultural competence related to the six components in a safe and controlled learning community context. Specifically, interns engage in cross-cultural relationships, find their own voices, discover multiple perspectives, and begin to reconcile similarities and differences between themselves and the world around them. With proper facilitation, interns adeptly uncover and analyze personal, institutional, and systemic factors (Solomon, 2000) that impact the concepts and practices of teaching, learning, and schooling.

These types of connections encompass powerful insights for most interns to transfer to their own future classrooms. In many pre-K–12th-grade classrooms across the United States, there exists a dissonance between the cultures of the learners and the cultures of the teachers. In most educational contexts, there also exist the myths of homogeneity within cultural groups reflected by both the teachers and the learners, educational options for meeting all learners' needs, and equality for and among all learners (Craig, Hull, Haggart, & Perez-Selles, 2000). A review of literature reveals that interns grow significantly from opportunities to participate in well-facilitated and effective group learning experiences to develop their knowledge, skills, and dispositions associated with cultural competence.

Reviewing the Methodology

The study presented in this chapter was organized to explore the benefits of group learning for developing cultural competence as reported by fifty-four teacher interns during the semester they enrolled in their internships while placed in various pre-K–12th-grade classrooms and academic subject areas. A written survey was administered to the interns when they attend a biweekly seminar held on a university campus and required approximately fifteen minutes to complete. Interns were asked to respond to items 1 through 4 by reflecting on their own roles as both a learner and as a teacher in any grade level or subject area. Responses could be written in sentences or short phrases to describe events that interns had experienced, used, seen, or read about in the professional literature. Interns completed and left the surveys before the end of the evening seminar. Following is the survey:

Survey Exploring Group Learning for Developing Cultural Competence

Group learning experiences offer benefits for developing cultural competence—the processes of acquiring, accepting, and applying knowledge, skills, and dispositions for valuing cultural diversity and ensuring educational access, equity, and excellence naturally, authentically, and holistically for all learners.

In this survey, you will share your professional expertise and educational practices. Please follow the directions in each of the two sections. This survey will take you less than fifteen minutes to complete. All identifying information will be removed before the researcher reads your responses. *Thank you in advance for participating in this survey. Your insights will improve teacher education!*

Section I

Respond by writing a few phrases or sentences for items 1–4. Your responses can reflect your roles as a learner, a teacher candidate, an intern, or a teacher in any grade level(s) and any subject area(s). You are welcome to describe a teaching strategy that you have used, seen, experienced, or have read in the literature.

1. Describe one academic purpose for using group learning in classrooms, for example, *Learners can complete a large task.*
2. Describe one social purpose for using group learning in classrooms, for example, *Learners get to know other learners.*
3. Describe one teaching strategy for using group learning in classrooms for developing cultural competence, for example, *As a teacher, I guide learners in making self-portraits with all colors of construction paper and mirrors asking group members to help one another.*
4. Describe one benefit for using group learning in classrooms specifically for developing cultural competence (different from your response to numbers 1–3), for example, *Learners exchange different or conflicting ideas.*

Section II

Write a response for number 5. Mark a large X for the appropriate choices in numbers 6–12, and write a response to number 12.

5. Grade level(s) and subject area(s) that you currently teach. Write "all" if teaching elementary school.
6. Your gender: female ☐   or male ☐
7. Your race/ethnicity: African American/Black ☐, Asian American ☐, Caucasian/White American ☐, Hispanic/Latino/a American ☐, Native American Indian ☐, or other (please identify):
8. Your age group: 18–24 ☐, 25–29 ☐, 30–39 ☐, 40–49 ☐, 50–59 ☐, 60–69 ☐, 70 + ☐
9. Do you like to learn by participating in group learning experiences? yes ☐   or no ☐
10. Do you like to teach using group learning experiences? yes ☐   or no ☐
11. Does the school or classroom where you are placed use group learning regularly? yes ☐   or no ☐
12. Does the school or classroom where you are placed promote developing cultural competence? yes ☐   or no ☐ How?

The 54 interns included 36 women and 18 men; 87 percent of the interns were 21–25 years of age. Approximately 42 percent were assigned to elementary schools; 19 percent were assigned to middle levels (grades 4–8); and 39 percent were assigned to high school. All of the interns had completed the majority of their teacher education courses at the same university where they were completing their internships. These data equip teacher educators and classroom mentors with insights they can use to revise the program to reinforce the necessity for using group learning to develop cultural competence.

The interns' responses were clustered according to the emerging benefits of group learning for developing cultural competence expressed by the interns. Each emerging benefit was given a unifying title that described its purpose. Then, data in each cluster were divided into two categories according to the response (e.g., relating to learners or relating to teachers).

ANALYZING THE FINDINGS

Although the interns provided a wide range of responses, an analysis of the data revealed twelve emerging benefits exhibiting patterns of continuity and consistency. All twelve emerging benefits also supported the three significant spheres of cultural competence: self, others, and society. Cultural competence for educators relating to self both in and out of classrooms can be classified as *personal growth and development*. Personal growth and development connects with individual backgrounds, heritages, experiences, assumptions, values, beliefs, and so forth. People obtain personal guidance and insights from their families, friends, and miscellaneous interactions. Many teaching interns are undergoing changes between young adulthood and adulthood. As they define who they are personally, their discoveries influence how they operate in their classrooms.

Cultural competence related to others especially within the classroom can be classified as *professional growth and development*. Professional growth and development occurs during experiences as learners, teaching interns, and teachers. Becoming educated involves lifelong processes during which people decide what they see and what people want to know along with what people want to learn and use. Interns are bridging the changes between their accustomed role of learner and the new role of teacher. Interns start to define who they are professionally and how these discoveries will influence their own young learners.

Cultural competence related to society within classrooms can be classified as *pedagogical growth and development*. Now interns find effective strategies to help their learners pose inquiries, conduct investigations, make discoveries, and apply the learning to their personal lives and integrate it into educational contexts. Pedagogical growth and development requires the intern to meet the needs and interests of each learner to ensure educational equity and excellence. From learning about self and others, interns make critical pedagogical decisions related to their classroom curriculum, instruction, assessments, and learning communities that can greatly impact their learners' learning and living.

IDENTIFYING TWELVE BENEFITS OF GROUP LEARNING FOR DEVELOPING CULTURAL COMPETENCE

Learning in groups offers the best strategy for pre-K–12th-grade learners to discover keen insights about themselves that might not be revealed working independently or participating in a whole-class discussion. When operating as a group, learners must listen carefully to one another; learners express multiple perspectives and personal viewpoints that may contradict the teacher, the textbook, or other learners in the group and class. Group members are provided the unique opportunity to express their own thoughts and contribute to the group project interacting more with their peers than with the teacher. These types of learning experiences allow individuals to compare and contrast themselves with other people who, at that moment, are most like them.

Learners become more attuned to cultural characteristics that are both similar to and different from other members of their group. During small-group conversations, learners can delve into subjects of their own choice substantiated by individual observations and opinions. Learners can ask questions to examine perspectives in more detail. These conversations require learners to reflect upon their own beliefs and share honestly in ways that the learners may have kept reserved in whole-class discussions.

Data from the interns reveal twelve distinct benefits of group learning for developing cultural competence (see Table 12.1). Each benefit is presented here supported by two illustrative comments. The first comment relates to learning; the second comment relates to teaching.

SUMMARIZING THE IMPLICATIONS

Developing cultural competence encompasses a natural, authentic, and holistic process yielding understanding, commitment, effort, and time. Years of research and practice from the health field reveal that cultural competence requires scholarship, sensibility, and sensitivity (Doyle, Beatty, & Shaw, 1999). During group learning, participants undergo transformations that cause learners to encounter all the stages of change and concern (Fuller, 1969) that define our character academically and socially.

Table 12.1   Twelve Benefits of Group Learning for Developing Cultural Competence from Teaching Interns

Description	Related to Learning	Related to Teaching
1.1. Honestly reflecting on oneself		
For individuals to tell other people about themselves in a personal, academic, professional, civil, or social context, they need to know themselves clearly and what knowledge, skills, and dispositions they possess and what to share.	Learners think a lot about how other people see them and what they believe about themselves and each other.	I ask learners to connect activities to their lives so they will talk about them from different viewpoints.
1.2. Attentively listening to others		
To engage people in a meaningful conversation, people must pay careful attention to everything that is being said as well as how the words are shared physically, emotionally, and socially and the corresponding nonverbal behaviors.	Learners pay more attention to each other than to the teacher.	I use the game of ``gossip'' with my learners so they can check and improve their listening skills.
1.3. Carefully watching others		
To increase their own awareness skills, people must closely observe the interactions of others and their interaction with others.	Learners watch each other all the time; how they treat one another usually tells more about them than what they actually say. Teachers can weave these examples into the context of learning.	I ask one learner in each group to show the other learners in the group how to behave when we begin a new situation with other groups of learners, such as presenting projects or with their families, such as making introductions.

Table 12.1   (Continued)

Description	Related to Learning	Related to Teaching
1.4. Strategically asking insightful questions		
To gain new information and understanding about themselves, others, and society in general, people must learn how to ask perceptive questions that lead to more questions, increased awareness, greater understanding, and stronger connections.	If learners feel safe in their groups, they will ask questions that they've always wanted to know about all kinds of things.	We role-play asking and answering questions. Sometimes I give the learners some challenging questions that I have written on note cards to use during their role playing to jump-start their thinking.
1.5. Skillfully comparing and contrasting infinite similarities and differences		
To categorize and distinguish how people, events, and things are both the same and different, one must be attuned to every detail, intention, and inference.	Working in groups, most learners begin to realize how they are alike and different.	On the first day of school I hand out a picture of a person made of basic shapes. The learners write words that describe them in each shape and share their pictures with their group so we can see how we're alike and different.
1.6. Astutely recognizing the multitude of cultural characteristics among people		
To understand people (ourselves and all others in various places and throughout time), one must be alert, discerning, and realistic.	As learners get older, they start making more distinctions between their own families and other people. Although they want to be like (and liked by) their friends, they begin to realize how different (and still liked) they are.	I add culture into almost everything that is taught so learners learn as much about people as the curriculum.

Table 12.1   (Continued)

Description	Related to Learning	Related to Teaching
1.7. Openly acknowledging that a variety of cultural backgrounds, behaviors, and beliefs exist among people near and far		
To develop cultural competence, people must realize the diversity that defines who we are and who we are becoming as individuals and a society.	When we work in cooperative learning groups, learners have preferences based on their strengths, so I make sure that everyone has a turn at each group role. Sometimes they discover new strengths or interests.	When one of the learners refers to a doctor or government leaders as a man, I add that these people are also women.
1.8. Genuinely appreciating multiple perspectives and ways of expressing oneself		
To grow and change over time, people must be exposed to differing ideas, opinions, and ways of communicating beliefs and behaviors.	Learners will hear ideas from other learners that they have never heard. The new ideas come from books too. We talk about how being different is acceptable.	I try to connect the learning with each of the multiple intelligences to show the different ways that people learn best.
1.9. Actively reconciling various approaches and attitudes about learning and living		
To understand and appreciate that we are people who thrive on differences, one must be guided in learning how to reconcile or resolve differences and be comfortable with compromise and consensus within themselves individually and as members of a group.	When learners have to make a group decision, it can be hard for them when there are learners who overpower the rest of the group and everyone wants to be everybody's friend.	I ask my learners to tell me or show me another way to solve a problem, especially in reading and math. They know I like to see multiple approaches to get the same answer.

Table 12.1   (Continued)

Description	Related to Learning	Related to Teaching
1.10. Successfully gaining information, access, and opportunities for oneself and granting each one of them to others		
All people need to be in the know, be able to go, and have the chance to do what everyone else gets to know, go, and do.	When learners talk to each other, they begin to share how to understand and conquer a situation or system.	I keep careful records of all the times I pick learners to do special things so I am as fair as possible.
1.11. Conscientiously taking ownership of one's prejudices, biases, and stereotypes		
To develop cultural competence, everyone must be cognizant of their words and interactions.	I model for my learners how to say ``ouch'' if one hurts their feelings, to avoid getting into fights. Later we talk about what makes us say ``ouch.'' The learners learn more about themselves and how to set boundaries.	I read a way for learners to share their feelings using food that I will use in my classroom.
1.12. Wholly accepting responsibility for one's own personal growth, professional development, and pedagogical selections		
To become a teacher who truly ensures human rights, democratic principles, and social justice, teachers must see themselves as part of the solution and initiate appropriate actions with themselves and their learners.	The student council at our middle school organizes a canned food drive during the holidays. I asked my learners to discuss this project in groups and then share their thoughts in class.	My school does not do much about cultural competence. I want to find a school where it is important so I can do this in my own classroom. I probably will anyway.

Realizing the power of group learning for developing cultural competence advances individuals' self-understanding and equips them for interacting professionally with others, especially classroom interns preparing for their careers in teaching. In this research, it was noted that most of the interns dislike learning in groups and most of the interns are not using groups in the classrooms where they are placed. These two conditions weaken the likelihood that they will incorporate group learning into their future classrooms. These interns will have to overcome the "generational perpetuation of practice" (Gallavan, 2007) that, unfortunately, interns too often emulate after observing their classroom mentor teachers not modeling the most effective strategies.

Interns must be prepared for the diverse learners, schools, and society that make up the twenty-first century (Ford & Gilman, 2007). All learners must be provided an equal chance to achieve and learn. Not using group learning will become a missed opportunity for all learners to know more about themselves, one another, and the world. Facilitating effective group learning experiences with interns helps them to develop cultural competence in themselves and models an approach for them to use in their future classrooms (Ming & Dukes, 2006; Zawojeski, Lesh, & English, 2003). Thus, a revised generational perpetuation of practice will arise equipping pre-K–12th-grade learners with knowledge, skills, and dispositions beneficial for developing cultural competence as they become adults (*and teachers*) of the future.

References

Association of Teacher Educators (ATE). (2007). *Standards for teacher educators*. Retrieved June 13, 2007, from www.ate1.org.

Baer, J. (2003). Grouping and achievement in cooperative learning. *College Teaching, 51*(4), 169–174.

Bandura, A. (1989). Human agency in social cognitive theory. *American Psychologist, 44*, 1175–1184.

Bassett, C., McWhirter, J. J., & Kitzmiller, K. (1999). Teacher implementation of cooperative learning groups. *Contemporary Education, 71*(1), 46–50.

Berry, J. W., Poortinga, Y. H., Segall, M. H., & Dasen, P. R. (1992). *Cross-cultural psychology: Research and application*. New York: Cambridge University Press.

Cleland, F., & Pearse, C. (1995). Critical thinking in elementary physical education: Reflections on a year long study. *Journal of Physical Education, Recreation and Dance, 66*(6), 31–38.

Craig, S., Hull, K., Haggart, A. G., & Perez-Selles, M. (2000). Promoting cultural competence through teacher assistance teams. *Teaching Exceptional Children, 32*(6), 6–12.

Cranton, P. (1996). Types of group learning. *New Directions for Adult and Continuing Education, 1996*(71), 25–32.

Doyle, E. I., Beatty, C. F., & Shaw, M. W. (1999). Using cooperative learning groups to develop health-related cultural awareness. *The Journal of School Health, 69*(2), 73–76.

Ford, D. Y., & Gilman, W. W. (2007). Another perspective on cultural competence: Preparing learners for an increasing diversity society. *Gifted Child Today, 30*(2), 52–55.

Fuller, F. (1969). Concerns of teachers: A developmental conceptualization. *American Educational Research Journal, 6*(2), 207–226.

Gallavan, N. P. (2007). Seven perceptions that influence novice teachers' efficacy and cultural competence. *Praxis, 1*(2), 6–22.

Gallavan, N. P., & Juliano, C. (2007). Collaborating to create future societies with young learners. *Social Studies & the Young Learner, 19*(4), 13–16.

Gay, G. (2002). Preparing for culturally responsive teaching. *Journal of Teacher Education, 53*(2), 106–116.

Houston, B. (2002). Taking responsibility. *Philosophy of Education Yearbook,* 2000, 1–13.

Huitt, W. (1999). *The SCANS report revisited.* Paper delivered at the Fifth Annual Gulf South Business and Vocational Education Conference, Valdosta State University, Valdosta, GA, April 18, 1997. Retrieved June 13, 2007, from http://chiron.valdosta.edu/whuitt/col/learner/scanspap.html.

Imel, S., & Tisdell, E. J. (1996). The relationship between theories about groups and adult learning groups. *New Directions for Adult and Continuing Education, 1996*(71), 15–24.

Johnson, D., & Johnson, R. (1989). *Cooperation and competition: Theory and research.* Edina, MN: Interaction.

Johnson, D. W., Johnson R. T., & Smith, K. A. (1998). Maximizing instruction through cooperative learning. *ASEE Prism, 7,* 24–29.

King, A. (2002). Structuring peer interaction to promote high-level cognitive processing. *Theory into Practice, 41*(1), 33–39.

Lord, T. R. (2001). 101 reasons for using cooperating learning in biology teaching. *The American Biology Teacher, 63*(1), 30–38.

Lynch, E. W., & Hanson, M. J. (2004). *Developing cross-cultural competence: A guide for working with children and their families,* 3rd ed. Baltimore: Brookes.

McBride, R. (1999). If you structure it, they will learn . . . critical thinking in physical education classes. *The Clearing House, 72*(4), 217–220.

Ming, K., & Dukes, C. (2006). Fostering cultural competence through school-based routines. *Multicultural Education, 14*(1), 42–48.

National Technical Information Service. (1992). What work requires of schools: A SCANS [Secretary's Commission on Achieving Necessary Skills] report for America 2000. Retrieved June 13, 2007, from http://wdr.doleta.gov/SCANS/.

Palinscar, A. S., & Brown, A. L. (1984). Reciprocal teaching of comprehension-fostering and comprehension-monitoring activities. *Cognition and Instruction, 1*(2), 117–175.

Slavin, R. E. (1992). *Cooperative learning: Theory, research, and practice.* Englewood, NJ: Prentice Hall.

Solomon, R. P. (2000). Exploring cross-race dyad partnerships in learning to teach. *Teachers College Record, 102*(6), 953–979.

Summers, J. J., Beretvas, S. N., & Gorin, J. S. (2005). Evaluating collaborative learning and community. *The Journal of Experimental Education, 73*(3), 165–188.

Turner, J. C., & Patrick, H. (2004). Motivational influences on learner participation in classroom learning activities. *Teachers College Record, 106*(9), 1759–1785.

Webb, N. M., Troper, J. D., & Fall, R. (1995). Constructive activity and learning in collaborative small groups. *Journal of Educational Psychology, 87*(3), 406–423.

West, W. W. (1996). Group learning in the workplace. *New Directions for Adult and Continuing Education, 1996*(71), 51–60.

Wiggins, G., & McTighe, J. (2005). *Understanding by design*, 2nd ed. Alexandria, VA: Association for Supervision and Curriculum Development.

Zawojeski, J. S., Lesh, R., & English, L. (2003). A models and modeling perspective on the role of small group learning activities. In R. Lesh & H. M. Doerr (Eds.), *Beyond constructivism* (pp. 337–358). Mahwah, NJ: Lawrence Erlbaum.

CHAPTER 13

Beginning Teachers' Inquiry in Linguistically Diverse Classrooms

EXPLORING THE POWER OF SMALL LEARNING COMMUNITIES

Barbara J. Merino
University of California, Davis

Rebecca C. Ambrose
University of California, Davis

Barbara Merino, Ph.D., a former second-language teacher with a doctorate in educational linguistics from Stanford University, specializes in second-language acquisition, instruction, and assessment in children and adults. As director of teacher education at UC Davis, she led the design and implementation of a credential/MA targeting teacher inquiry on the impact of instruction on student learning in the first year of teaching. She has worked with beginning teachers on their inquiry projects in literacy, math, and science for the past fifteen years.

Rebecca Ambrose, Ph.D., holds a doctorate in mathematics education from the University of Wisconsin, Madison, and is currently on faculty at the University of California, Davis. She works extensively with preservice and in-service teachers to analyze children's mathematical thinking. She researches how this inquiry process transforms teachers' thinking about mathematics instruction. She has worked with beginning teachers on their inquiry projects in literacy and mathematics for the past three years and has previously taught in middle schools.

ABSTRACT

In this chapter, we describe how one promising beginning teacher, enrolled in a credential/MA, negotiated the challenge of working in high-poverty schools with a concentration of English learners and how engaging in a teacher research project helped him navigate this terrain and remain true to his commitment to act as an advocate for educational equity. We furthermore show how key program features supported this teacher and his cohort as they engaged in inquiry in a small learning community. We also analyze and discuss how these communities functioned and how these teachers accessed expertise within and outside the group as their inquiry evolved. For this study, we used teacher research artifacts as our primary data sources and e-mails, surveys, interviews, documents, and artifacts collected over four years as our secondary sources.

Problem Description

The first year of teaching is daunting even for the brightest, best-prepared individuals working in ideal conditions. It can be overwhelming for teachers working in the challenging conditions of high-poverty schools with an abundance of English-language learners (Feiman-Nemser, 2001). Indeed recent studies report that close to half of new teachers leave the profession within five years of beginning their careers (Ingersoll, 2004). Moreover, under the challenging conditions beginning teachers face, many abandon the ambitious pedagogies that they encountered in their teacher preparation program in favor of safer, more traditional practices, according to Feiman-Nemser (2001). She argues that optional induction programs should extend and enrich initial teacher preparation by addressing specific contents of beginning teachers' school environments. As novice teachers learn to use their practice as a site for inquiry by "turning conclusions into questions, trying something out and studying the effects, and framing new questions to extend one's understanding" (p. 1030), they are able to enact ambitious teaching practices in their challenging contexts. Feiman-Nemser suggests that this type of work is best accomplished in the company of others, but few programs for beginning teachers provide such opportunities.

In this study we describe a program that extends and enriches initial teacher preparation through teacher research in small teacher-learning communities. We analyze the case of one beginning teacher while he worked at a low-performing school. Our main research question targets how beginning teachers engage in inquiry and use it to transform and inform their practice. First, we address the explicit and implicit program features that fostered these teacher-learning communities. Next, through an analysis of case data, we explore how the teacher developed his teacher research project and how he accessed expertise within and outside the community. Finally, we discuss how these findings can inform our understanding of the role of inquiry in transforming the professional practice of teachers. We highlight challenges, opportunities, lessons learned, and pathways for future research.

Theoretical Frameworks and Review of the Literature

In a recent review of research on professional development, Dall'Alba and Sandberg (2006) critique dominant models representing this development as "progressively accumulating a set of knowledge and skills" (p. 384). They affirm McDermott's (1993) critique separating content from practice. Dall'Alba and Sandberg argue that this stage model perspective assumes that professional skill is a set of attributes, attitudes, skills, and knowledge, which can be described in a "decontextualized manner separate from the practice to which they refer" (p. 384). They critique stage models because they veil what is being acquired by directing attention away from the professional skills being acquired "of and in practice." They propose "embodied understanding of practice" as an alternative theory for describing professional growth; "embodied" to capture how being in particular contexts shapes practice and "understanding" to portray that individuals' perception about the nature of their role shapes the ways they interpret situations (Borko et al., 1997).

While this theory resembles others that emphasize the importance of beliefs in shaping practice (Wideen, Mayer-Smith, & Moon, 1998), it avoids the mind-practice dualism by suggesting that teachers act out and shape their understanding of practice as they participate in various contexts. Thus, for example, when professional practice for teachers is understood as the transfer of knowledge, professional development efforts might emphasize teachers' presentation of content. Under the restrictive policies found in some low performing schools, beginning teachers sometimes find their professional choices for agency in the classroom limited and their embodied understanding of practice challenged in ways that contribute to dissatisfaction with the profession (Ruiz & Morales-Ellis, 2005).

Teacher education programs vary in significant ways in preparing new teachers to face the challenges of teaching in American schools (Good et al., 2006). Engaging beginning teachers in authentic inquiry about their students' learning both during the credential year and the first year of teaching in small learning communities offers one pathway for mentored professional development, particularly in challenging contexts (Au, 2002; Schulz & Mandzuk, 2005). We share Grossman, Wineburg, and Woolworth's (2001) caution in using the term "community" to describe a group of people and use their characterization of a learning community as being one where knowledge is distributed among individuals who bring different kinds of expertise to the group. Among the benefits of such communities is that they give teachers a safe place to ask questions and to explore the uncertainty inherent in teaching (Snow-Gerono, 2005).

Yet these teacher communities are not always successful as a catalyst for meaningful changes in instructional practices that are genuinely responsive to the learners and their context, particularly when the teacher community operates within a hierarchical structure in a school district resistant to change (Wood, 2007). A challenge for teacher educators in setting up such communities is to orient the participants toward work worth pursuing as pedagogically sound and responsive to learners' needs, while nurturing engagement, competence, and autonomy. Among the requirements of a productive teacher learning community are common ground and a focus on substantive content (Clark, 2001). Without a focus on substantive content, teacher communities can disintegrate into venting sessions where teachers complain about students and administrators. The common ground depends on the teachers viewing one another as having similar levels of competence and commitment (Little, 1990).

Case studies of teacher communities in teacher education have generally documented professional development among experienced teachers. For example, one such study investigated how teachers made instructional shifts when engaging in a new instructional approach, "strategic content learning" (Butler, Lauscher, Jarvis-Selinger, & Beckingham, 2004). In describing her approach to developing communities of practice, Au (2002) drew on Wegner's argument that the type of learning individuals find most transformative occurs in communities of practice where individuals show engagement through active participation in a joint process of negotiating meaning while making sense of the world through a joint enterprise toward a broader good informed by deep knowledge of community needs. This type of model targets the broader community in which schools are situated as the target of inquiry in both contemporary and historical terms and draws heavily on anthropological perspectives.

Some teacher communities have focused on developing subject matter expertise and pedagogical content knowledge by having reading groups (Grossman, Wineburg, & Woolworth, 2001). Some have targeted inquiry about student learning and relied on technology as the main vehicle for promoting inquiry about practice after teachers graduate. Davis and Resta (2002) found that using e-mail in the form of weekly prompts organized around a routine protocol was successful in engaging nine out of twelve graduates in inquiry about some aspect of classroom instruction that they wanted to improve as part of a novice teacher support program. Access to a computer and finding the time to respond were among the most prominent challenges these students faced. Schulz and Mandzuk (2005), in their three-year study of inquiry within their preservice program, found that the open-endedness of the process of inquiry and the way in which a commitment to inquiry can challenge school culture were among the main challenges seventeen graduates of their program reported in focus groups. Clearly paying attention to how inquiry is operationalized in teacher communities is a critical consideration if we hope to understand and address the challenges and opportunities they offer.

There is a wide spectrum of activity that has been labeled teacher research, but, as Cochran-Smith and Lytle (1999) pointed out, all share a focus on teachers posing questions and interrogating their own practices in their classrooms by collecting data of the "daily life" of school with an emphasis on empowering teachers to be knowledge creators rather than knowledge consumers. Scholars disagree about the degree to which teacher research should adhere to formal research methodology (Richardson, 1994) and whether a critique of power relations needs to be at its core (Noffke, 1997), but most endorse the idea that teacher research has the potential to (1) empower teachers to be agents of change and (2) "assuage the isolation of teaching" (Cochran-Smith & Lytle, 1999, p. 22) by promoting social engagement among colleagues about issues of practice. In this study, we will explore the degree to which our teacher research program realized these potentials.

Methods/ Modes of Inquiry

Case study methodology (Yin, 2003) informs the design of our inquiry. We chose our case based on the following criteria: The beginning teacher (1) worked in a program improvement school serving high numbers of English learners; (2) had a high level of engagement with authentic inquiry about student learning; (3) actively collaborated with peers and faculty in contributing to the community; and (4) demonstrated evidence of being committed to being an advocate for equity. We targeted an "instrumental case" (Stake, 1995), a teacher who was above average but not atypical and who offered the opportunity to study the phenomenon of teacher inquiry within a small teacher community.

This case study is nested within a case of a teacher education program, serving between 225 and 300 students a year, which has a long-standing commitment to using the tools of inquiry about teaching and learning as a pathway for advocacy (Athanazes & Martin, 2006). The advent of a new postbaccalaureate credential/MA program served as an opportunity to enhance student engagement with inquiry in their first year of teaching. This teacher case is drawn from one of four cohorts that have completed the new program. We have taken several steps to reduce the potential biases of working as participant/researchers. Each of us mentored a different section of beginning teacher researchers. Relevant data sources were identified jointly, and analytical approaches and preliminary findings have been cross-validated through repeated encounters designed to monitor triangulated trails of evidence in our own inquiry, with each of us taking on the role of critical reader.

Context

The site for this study is a fifteen-month teacher education program within a large research university in California. Students received their credential in the first year and participated in a four-course university-based sequence in which they conducted two teacher research projects, a case study while student teaching, and a more elaborate study while in their first year of teaching. The program mission is organized around four key teaching roles: (1) reflective practitioner; (2) teacher researcher; (3) collaborative professional working in communities of practice; and (4) advocate for equity in learning for their students. A key program mission is to prepare teachers to work with English learners and build strong home–school connections.

During the credential year, student teachers worked in small cohorts in several key courses structured as small learning communities of practice. Specifically, students were assigned to supervisors who worked within a common school setting in linguistically and culturally diverse classrooms, accumulating approximately six hundred hours of student teaching in their field placement. At the elementary level, students were assigned to a long- and short-term placement to maximize exposure at two different grade levels. In the long-term placement, students engaged in two inquiry assignments: a teaching performance assessment, the Performance Assessment for California Teachers (PACT), and an inquiry project designed to enhance the learning of a struggling learner (Merino & Holmes, 2006). PACT was mentored through the supervisor at the field placement. The inquiry project was mentored by a faculty member who also worked with student teachers. Group size in these cohorts was between ten and sixteen students.

In year 2, students worked as full-time teachers and attended classes on a part-time basis over a six-month period. During this period, cohort size for the teacher research classes ranged between eight and sixteen students. Each author taught one cohort of teachers during the teacher research courses. The case study student came from the first author's cohort that included twelve beginning teachers (BTs). Five participated online part of the time, and six had obtained bilingual certification. Five of the BTs were former English learners and six were from an immigrant background. (See Table 13.1.)

The teacher in the study worked at a low-performing K–3 school, Alamo, in a rapidly changing rural/suburban community. The school was 77 percent Hispanic; 62 percent of the students were English-language learners (ELL); and 73 percent received free/reduced lunch. The teachers were under heavy pressure to bring up test scores. During our participant's first year of teaching at the school, the principal left at Christmastime as did other district administrators.

Data Sources

We used two primary data sources for the study: teacher research assignments including final projects with faculty feedback, and interviews conducted with the teacher-participant in his second year of teaching. These were analyzed using the constant comparative method. Secondary sources included students' application essays, formal supervisor evaluations of student teaching, major projects conducted during the credential year, e-mails, and notes of class and individual meetings. (See Table 13.2.) Two major types of assignments were the field notes, labeled Writing about Research Progress (WARPS), and the benchmarks. There were four lead WARPS each organized around a single theme: studying the context, gathering preliminary data, exploring the literature and local expertise, and baseline data collection. Typically each was scheduled every two weeks and each was organized around a set of tasks, with focused questions and supportive materials designed to scaffold the writing of the tasks. These were not graded. The benchmarks targeted key milestones—the proposal for the study was benchmark 1, for example. These were graded, and some required committee approval of two other faculty.

Program Model for Teacher Research

We define teacher research as systematic investigation of how teaching influences student learning over time in a single classroom or learning community. It is

Table 13.1 Comparison of Case to Section Cohort

Variable	Pablo	Cohort – N = 12
Undergraduate GPA	At median	Median = 3.21
EL history	Yes	N = 6/12 EL history
Language(s) proficiency	Spanish	Spanish = 7; Farsi = 1
Program improvement status: grade	Yes; 1st grade	N = 8/12; Kg–6th

Table 13.2   Data Sources

Data source title	Description	When collected
Application mini-essays	7 short Q&A essays targeting experiences, interests, and qualities related to teaching	Fall/winter prior to entering the program
Interview data pre-program	TE faculty and teachers use structured protocol targeting experience, diversity, and communication skills	Winter/early spring prior to entering the program
Philosophy statement	Short essay articulating philosophy	Fall credential year
Inquiry project case study	Single case intervention	Winter credential year
Performance assessment for California teachers	Standardized assessment targeting planning, assessment, instruction, reflection, and academic language	Winter/spring credential year
Writing about research progress: WARP 1–3 context, preliminary data; literature/expert review	Structured field notes organized around short tasks, prompted through Qs	Fall: year 1 of teaching
Benchmark 1	Proposal for study; IRB proposal abstract	Late fall to November: year 1
WARP 4	Baseline data	November to January: year 1
Benchmark 2	Draft of study to baseline	Late fall to December: year 1
Benchmark 3	Comparison of baseline to outcome data	Late January to February: year 1
WARP 5/benchmark 4	Draft/final project report	Late February to mid-March: year 1
WARP 6	Reflection on inquiry	Late March: year 1
Post-program interview data	Structured protocol; joint conversations	Spring/summer after year 2

inquiry that is intentional, contextual, ethical, and, above all, responsive to the learners' strengths and challenges. We draw from three principal traditions to inform our model of teacher research: (1) action research, (2) the case study approach, and (3) instructional interventions.

As mentioned above, the teacher researchers work in a cohort of students who meet on a biweekly basis with a faculty member for two quarters. The teacher research takes place in three phases: (a) the development of a question or focus that addresses students' learning needs culminating in a proposal for an intervention and the study of that intervention; (b) the implementation of the intervention in the classroom along with data collection of the intervention; and (c) analysis and write-up of the study.

The MA/credential teacher researchers (TRs) begin their inquiry by first systematically collecting data about their students, their learning, and their context. Based on preliminary analyses of the data they have gathered, TRs justify an area of inquiry or question they want to pursue to respond to their students' needs. TRs then explore the literature to identify promising instructional strategies and procedures for implementation, data collection, and analysis. Next, TRs propose a study that includes an intervention plan and a data collections plan. Once their proposal is approved, TRs design an instructional cycle of lessons/instructional strategies; collect baseline, process, and outcome data; analyze their data; and report their findings in a written report. The report or thesis is developed over time through an intensive process of discussion, short writing assignments, and group and individual feedback. As a capstone activity, TRs present their inquiry at a symposium to faculty and their peers at the end of winter quarter.

A lead faculty member mentors each student's inquiry process in small cohorts. Each faculty member works with two other faculty in a committee structure, drawing on the committee members' expertise at key points of the inquiry. Faculty mentor the inquiry process through the integration of "scaffolds" or strategies designed to support students' inquiry. These supports include (1) a cohort-based structure designed to promote collaboration and provide support in a community of practice; (2) the design of the inquiry as a series of tasks to report on through WARP assignments; (3) the use of structured feedback throughout the process in a systematic sequence every two weeks, provided by both peers and faculty, via e-mail, and in person conferencing; (4) the use of models from a variety of genres of the research literature; (5) and the use of structured mini-lessons designed to expand students' tools of inquiry and explore teaching and learning, focusing especially on critical skills for gathering, analyzing, and representing data. Faculty mentors are all experienced researchers and experienced teachers who can offer support in both domains.

Results

In this section, we provide an overview of the case, and a few details from the TR's first year of teaching to provide a sense of the teacher's embodied understanding of practice and approach. We focus here on the evolution of the inquiry, how it was negotiated and constructed, and how the teacher researcher accessed expertise within and outside of the community. We identify influences, both from personal history and the context, which helped shape teaching and inquiry practices. All data were organized into electronic files for the case teacher. His faculty mentor also kept electronic files of agendas, feedback to all members of the cohort for each WARP, as well as copies of e-mail communication.

PABLO

Pablo came to teaching with a clear commitment to work with English learners, motivated in part by his family history. He had limited experience working in classrooms and at entry saw one of his roles as a teacher as "diminishing the stigma of being an ESL speaker" (application file). A design major, Pablo took a constructivist stance on teaching and learning as he reflected on his own history, "I learn by doing rather than by watching others" (WARP 1, teacher as learner and educator: task 7). His philosophy statement from the credential year also reflected his commitment to the autonomy of the learner. "Learning does not begin or end with me but is continuous and endless. Students are empowered to learn by incorporating their personal experience." Elements of this perspective can be seen in his approach to working with students early on, in his first year of teaching as he figured out the instructional approach, particularly showing a great willingness to consider numerous possible research questions and various instructional approaches.

Pablo's embodied understanding of practice was articulated within a constructivist stance. "It is important to consider the whole learner and address the needs of learners with different modalities. Therefore, I feel that the students in class learn by creating rather than by doing what has been already created for them."

Influence of the Context: Field Placement and Inquiry in the Credential Year

While enrolled in the bilingual credential program, Pablo student-taught at Alamo and saw the bilingual program eliminated midyear. This raised his awareness of the importance of local policy makers. He reported in class about how poor data management at the district level combined with rapidly changing demographics influenced the decision to cut the bilingual program.

His student teaching inquiry project, a case study targeting an ELL first grader who was significantly behind peers in learning phonics rules in English, focused on teaching the student to read and spell short vowels through the use of manipulatives constructed by the student. For the PACT assessment, Pablo developed a lesson cycle that also engaged students in constructing their own materials as a way of developing meaningful connections with two stories about animals and to scaffold students' retelling of their stories. In both of these assignments, Pablo monitored his students' learning carefully while seeking to engage them in authentic ways in their own learning. He demonstrated as well a scholarly willingness to learn from his mistakes, noting that his plan was too ambitious and showing how he would revise it in the future.

Context and Inquiry in First Year of Teaching

Pablo taught first grade again at the same school and district, a class of nineteen largely Hispanic students with thirteen ELLs. An enthusiastic teacher, Pablo willingly extended himself in his first year in ways not generally seen in first-year teachers. He communicated in Spanish with parents about assignments and ways of supporting their children and discussed concerns about assessment and instructional policies at staff meetings. Initially, through the first three WARPs on context, analysis of preliminary student data, and the literature, Pablo generated twenty-seven possible research questions for his teacher research project. He moved from a broad concern to catch up his students in English vocabulary, to learning high frequency words, to targeting the development of descriptive words in students' writing, a first-grade standard. Finally, he came to the conclusion that developing descriptive skills required providing authentic opportunities for writing descriptive texts and that letter writing offered the best path. This genre was targeted for second grade in the State Standards rather than the first grade, so he had to do some maneuvering at his school site to pull off his project. We will discuss his approach to this maneuvering further below.

A cohort activity analyzing the construct underlying the desired learning outcome of each TR's intervention and making this construct meaningful and authentic to students was an important influence in shaping the direction of Pablo's inquiry project. When the group discussed Pablo's project, the faculty advisor asked the group to think about when adults and children use descriptive words. The group noted that descriptive words often are used to communicate specific ideas about objects that need to be differentiated in some way. So then Pablo came up with the idea of having his students describe Christmas wishes.

The faculty advisor described a teacher research project from a prior cohort in which an RT used letters as a way to engage children in authentic written communication. Pablo began to consider using letters in his classroom.

Data Analysis as Catalyst for Inquiry

A key event in finalizing the focus of Pablo's study emerged as he completed WARP 2, an examination of student achievement data. Pablo used his school district's first-grade fall writing assessment as his achievement data. One of the foci of the district rubric was descriptive words. In discussing both the prompt and the rubric with his faculty advisor, Pablo came to realize that the writing prompt was leading his students to use fewer rather than more descriptive words. He also came to realize that the rubric was not providing him with useful information about his students' writing abilities. He decided to reanalyze the data using his own rubric to gain deeper insight into his students' writing strengths and challenges.

This data analysis led to Pablo's study of how different prompts for writing letters to different audiences combined with explicit instruction on writing descriptively affected his first graders' writing over time. The writing prompts that Pablo developed included writing a letter to Santa requesting a gift with a detailed description of the gift; a letter to Rudolph with a description of their house; and writing a description of a penguin to a friend in another class, for a total of eight different prompts. These prompts were scaffolded—"Dear Santa, This is what I would like for Christmas . . ."—and engaged students creatively, while targeting a specific audience.

The Literature and its Role as an Influence in Pablo's Study

In the WARP 3 assignment, the TRs were required to present annotated citations of professional literature relevant to their area of inquiry. The program faculty provided two textbooks on teacher research, used both years in the inquiry classes (Hubbard & Power, 1999; Murray, 2005). Pablo did not make much use of these sources on his own although he participated actively in class activities that targeted sections, particularly on the issue of drawing up research questions. The program asks TRs to tap into multiple genres of scholarship, teacher research, methods books, case studies, quasi-experimental and intervention research. Initially, Pablo relied on resources from the credential program that had been used in either the language arts methods class (Calkins, 1994) or in the inquiry class targeting a case study among bilingual learners. His faculty mentor suggested Pablo consult a teacher research project from a previous cohort at UC Davis, targeting letter writing in a bilingual program (Wood, 2005). This became an important influence.

Later, as the study progressed, Pablo adapted the rubric that Monica Wood (2005) used to analyze her students' letters as an analytic tool. Pablo also received specific suggestions from the faculty advisor to consider using children's literature to model letter writing, using, for example, *The Jolly Postman* books (Ahlberg & Alhlberg, 2001). It should be said that while the program provided training on searching the literature in courses throughout the program, the challenge of time to search and retrieve materials affected everyone in the cohort. Faculty vary in the degree to which they will offer concrete suggestions on relevant literature, and both authors prefer TRs find their own sources, since we would like the TRs to "own" their inquiry as much as possible. Pablo adopted a very utilitarian approach, targeting few sources, relying on what he knew well from previous classes, and using faculty suggestions to good effect.

Peer Influences on the Inquiry

The program provides multiple mechanisms for peer support including most prominently peer feedback on targeted aspects of the inquiry every two weeks, both in person and online. TRs are asked to request feedback on any issue that they are wondering about and to use checklists and graphic organizers as supports for directing the feedback in productive ways. One especially useful exercise was designed to help students focus their research question, reviewing it through research question "therapy," and targeting the central thrust of the instructional approach and the lead learning outcome they seek to influence.

Students begin this process by reviewing research questions from the research of others, testing out different frames for their own research questions and analyzing these questions using key criteria that target doability within the time frame, validity in terms of responsiveness to learner needs, and research/expert opinion support for the intervention itself. Pablo moved from framing critical questions trying to understand why his students were reluctant to write, for example, "Why is it that when I give my students a certain prompt to write on, such as *Seasons*, they don't write much at all?" (WARP 3) to questions that targeted both an instructional feature and the learning outcome, such as "How does learning to write letters for a specific audience . . . improve ability to write effectively?" (WARP 4). Further refinement led to greater specification of what aspect of writing he would target: writing descriptions.

Feedback is especially important in the data analyses phase, when TRs bring data collection and analysis protocols as well as data sets for consultation from peers and faculty. Faculty typically offered mini-lessons on key areas using the TRs' data as the focus of the lesson. One of the lessons that was pertinent to

Pablo was an activity sorting student work into three categories in order to explicate the attributes of above-average, average, and below-average work, taking one element at a time. Checking in with peers and justifying judgments of quality was a useful process in describing the attributes to develop a rubric. Based on a faculty vignette of how letters were analyzed in one of her research projects, Pablo focused on the social-linguistics rules of letter writing at the level that he expected first graders to perform.

Pablo and two other teachers in his cohort were working in the same school district, and several had done their student teaching there. Consultations about how to negotiate with teachers and administrators was frequently a topic of conversation as Pablo began honing in on his topic and started thinking that he wanted to address a first-grade standard, expanding descriptive vocabulary via a second-grade genre, letter writing. This intervention plan required him to get the support of his colleagues because it was outside of the expectations for first grade.

In sessions facilitated by the faculty, Pablo and his fellow TRs discussed how he could use his data to garner the support of his colleagues. TRs from his district shared their knowledge of district priorities and structures for considering changes. Eventually, Pablo came up with a strategy to implement his proposal at his site. This involved talking to all the grade-level teachers at his school and sharing his analysis of his students' writing samples. Pablo's data analysis along with support from the professional literature smoothed the way for the proposed intervention at the school. Pablo's discussions with his fellow teacher researchers helped him to have the confidence that his plan was pedagogically sound and developmentally appropriate, so he was able to "sell" it to his principal and grade-level team.

Pablo began the program with a strong sense of advocacy and a teaching perspective grounded in his own learning. While learning to teach in a school community in turmoil, he rose to the challenge and engaged with the collaborative teacher community of his school and with his fellow teacher researchers. Most importantly, Pablo continued with the habits of inquiry in his second year of teaching when he was no longer in the MA/credential program. He designed curriculum around having his students act out stories to build comprehension skills, another innovation that engaged his students in "creating" while meeting mandated standards. Pablo talked of the MA experience as giving him the "tools to leverage" his autonomy and respond to his students' needs (interview data).

Significance and Implications

This case demonstrates that even at the outset of his career, a new teacher can demonstrate "expert" performance in assessment and instructional design if provided with appropriate tools and support. This case challenges traditional models of professional development that suggest beginning teachers are so caught up in surviving day to day that they have to focus on class management before they turn their attention to student learning (Dall'Alba & Sandberg, 2006).

Pablo emphasized the importance of his faculty advisor's guidance throughout the process. He noted that she asked him critical questions at critical times to help him see his data in new ways. By having all of the students examine the fundamental constructs of their studies, she helped Pablo think about the purposes of writing and about how he could promote authentic writing activity in his students. The faculty advisor also provided expertise in data collection and analysis approaches, which helped Pablo to be systematic and thorough in his analysis of his students' work (interview data).

We argue that the teacher learning community was critical to Pablo's successful inquiry process. The TRs had the common ground required of such groups because they were all new teachers from the same credential program who were bringing all they had learned in their credential year to the challenging environments of their underperforming schools. Having a shared history, all respected one another's competence and commitment (Little, 1990). The content of community discussions focused the TRs on their students' learning as they tried to make sense of their data. Because the group met outside of the TRs' schools, they were freer to question the practices of their schools and to develop alternative perspectives toward their students' work. Pablo would probably not have reexamined his students' writing samples without having the outside influence of the group challenging him to reconsider the validity of the district rubric.

Having fellow TRs at his school site also supported Pablo in juggling all of the demands of beginning teaching and teacher research. These colleagues provided Pablo with emotional support at his school and at the university. They helped him to consider how much he could expect his colleagues to alter the writing program to accommodate his project. They commiserated with him as he tried to make sense of the rapidly changing personnel in the school and district administration.

Pablo showed sustained engagement with inquiry in exemplary ways. He took data analyses seriously as an important opportunity to understand student needs and to investigate the influence of his practice. The other TRs in his section also engaged in sustained data analysis and ambitious pedagogy. Seven conducted elaborate new analyses from item analyses to establish item difficulty changes after an intervention to charting degree of progress toward the class and grade level median. Ten developed original classroom assessments designed to come closer to the underlying construct tapped in high-stakes assessments.

Conclusions

The three elements that we consider critical to the success of our approach are 1) a data-driven process leading to an instructional intervention that requires TRs to closely examine their students' learning and to consider the effectiveness of their teaching, 2) a faculty advisor with expertise in research who can support the BTs in collecting appropriate data and analyzing it systematically, and 3) a community of learners with a shared learning history that provides TRs with the collegial support to revisit concepts they learned in their teacher education program and to inquire about their practice. We stress the importance of all three elements because there are programs for beginning teachers that have some but not all of them.

Some teacher research programs focus more on narrative history in which teachers write extensively about their feelings toward their work (Hubbard & Power, 1999). We worry that this perpetuates a focus on self rather than a focus on students and their learning and actions a teacher can take to improve the learning environment. Some programs depend on teachers within the schools to guide the inquiry process. We worry that in this model there may not be an individual who challenges taken-for-granted assumptions about students and instructional practices. Without access to expertise in data collection and analysis, beginning teachers may gloss over important details in their students' work (Wood, 2007).

Finally, most programs for beginning teachers include teachers from various credentialing institutions. In these situations, the beginning teachers have no way of knowing to what kinds of pedagogy and theories their colleagues have been exposed. Conversations about teaching methods have to start from scratch with the beginning teachers trying to independently recall what they remember from their credential year.

Our beginning teachers depended on one another to collectively recollect concepts from their credential year and bring these concepts to their work in the classroom. In this way the academic content of the credential program was kept fresh in the beginning teachers' minds and they were able to apply it to the context of their school environments. We hope that this helps the beginning teachers make connections between their teacher preparation and their work as teachers-of-record, a connection that has proven to be tenuous at best in most situations (Good et al., 2006). In these ways the teacher research emphasis in the MA program provided an extension of the teacher preparation year building on the prior learning that the beginning teachers had done in developing teaching strategies responsive to English learner needs.

The teacher research project provided the beginning teachers with a venue to "embody" their understanding of practice. Pablo felt empowered by teacher research and discussed how it was critical to his learning how to negotiate the challenging terrain of working in a high-accountability environment. Consequently, he had data to justify trying a different approach and data to establish the effectiveness of this approach. This strategic use of data is especially important in this era when "research-based" and "data-driven" practices are the coin of the realm. Pablo was not forced to abandon his desires to develop experiences where his English Language Learners could creatively express themselves. We posit that his letter writing intervention constituted what Feiman-Nemser called "ambitious teaching" because it was responsive to his students in meaningful ways. Pablo made an autonomous teaching decision showing his willingness to take risks and extend his understanding. We are hopeful that since he has figured out how to effectively use data from his classroom to justify his pedagogical decisions and to elicit the support of his colleagues, he will be sustained as a teacher and will persist even after he no longer has the support of the university program. We plan to keep in touch with Pablo to see if this is the case.

Update: Pablo is still at his school site teaching first grade and has assumed the leadership role of English-language learner site coordinator. His inquiry project continues to inspire us and new generations of teacher researchers. We are grateful to him for sharing his experiences.

References

Ahlberg, A., & Ahlberg, J. (2001). *The jolly Christmas postman.* London: William Heineman.

Athanazes, S., & Martin, K. (2006). Teaching and learning advocacy in a teacher education program. *Teaching and Teacher Education, 22,* 627–646.

Au, K. H. (2002). Communities of practice: Engagement, imagination and alignment in research on teacher education. *Journal of Teacher Education, 53,* 222–227.

Borko, H., Mayfield, V., Marion, S., Flexer, R., & Cumbo, K. B. (1997). Teachers' developing ideas and practices about mathematics performance assessment: Successes, stumbling blocks, and implications for professional development. *Teaching and Teacher Education, 13,* 259–278.

Butler, D., Lauscher, H. N., Jarvis-Selinger, S., & Beckingham, B. (2004). Collaboration and self-regulation in teachers' professional development. *Teaching and Teacher Education, 20,* 435–455.

Calkins, L. (1994). *The art of teaching writing.* Portsmouth, NH: Heineman.

Clark, C. (2001). *Talking shop: Authentic conversation and teacher learning.* New York: Teachers College Press.

Cochran-Smith, M., & Lytle, S. (1999). The teacher research movement: A decade later. *Educational Researcher, 28,* 15–25.

Dall'Alba, G., & Sandberg, J. (2006). Unveiling professional development: A critical review of stage models. *Review of Educational Research, 76,* 383–412.

Darling-Hammond, L., & Youngs, P. (2002). Defining "highly qualified teachers"; What does "scientifically-based research" actually tell us? *Educational Researcher, 31,* 13–25.

Davis, B., & Resta, V. (2002). Online collaboration: Supporting novice teachers as researchers. *Journal of Technology and Teacher Education, 10,* 101–117.

Feiman-Nemser, S. (2001). From preparation to practice: Designing a continuum to sustain teaching. *Teachers' College Record, 103,* 1013–1055.

Good, T., McCaslin, M., Tsang, H., Zhang, J., Wiley, C., Bozack, A., & Hester, W. (2006). How well do first-year teachers teach: Does type of preparation make a difference? *Journal of Teacher Education, 57,* 410–430.

Grossman, P., Wineburg, S., & Woolworth, S. (2001). Toward a theory of teacher community. *Teachers College Record, 103*(6), 942–1012.

Hubbard, R. S., & Power, B. M. (1999). *Living the questions: A guide for teacher researchers.* York, ME: Stenhouse.

Ingersoll, R. M. (2004). Four myths about America's teacher quality problem. In M. Smylie & D. Miretzky (Eds.), *Developing the teacher workforce.* (pp. 1–33). Chicago, IL: University of Chicago Press.

Lankford, H., Loeb, S., & Wyckoff, J. (2002). Teacher sorting and the plight of urban schools: A descriptive analysis. *Educational Evaluation and Policy Analysis, 24,* 38–62.

Little, J. (1990). The persistence of privacy: Autonomy and initiative in teachers' professional relations. *Teachers College Record, 91*(4), 509–536.

McDermott, R. P. (1993). The acquisition of a child by a learning disability. In S. Chaiklin & J. Lave (Eds.), *Understanding practice: Perspectives on activity and context* (pp. 269–305). Cambridge, UK: Cambridge University Press.

Merino, B. J., & Holmes, P. (2006). Student teacher inquiry as an "Entry Point" to advocacy. *Teacher Education Quarterly, 33,* 79–96.

Murray, T. R. (2005). *Teachers doing research: An introductory guidebook.* Boston: Pearson and Allyn & Bacon.

Noffke, S. E. (1997). Professional, personal, and political dimensions of action research. *Review of Research in Education, 22,* 305–343.

Richardson, V. (1994). Conducting research on practice. *Educational Researcher, 23*(5), 5–10.

Ruiz, N. T., & Morales-Ellis, L. (2005). "Thank you but I'll be looking for another job": A first-year teacher resists high-stakes curriculum. In Altwerger, B. (Ed.), *Reading for Profit* (pp. 199–215). Portsmouth, NH: Heinemann.

Schulz, R., & Mandzuk, D. (2005). Learning to teach, learning to inquire: A three year study of candidates' experiences. *Teaching and Teacher Education, 21,* 315–331.

Snow-Gerono, J. (2005). Naming inquiry: PDS teacher's perceptions of teacher research and living an inquiry stance toward teaching. *Teacher Education Quarterly, 32*(4), 79–95.

Stake, R. E. (1995). *The art of case study research.* Thousand Oaks, CA: Sage Publications.

Wideen, M., Mayer-Smith, J., & Moon, B. (1998). A critical analysis of the research on learning to teach: Making the case for an ecological perspective on inquiry. *Review of Educational Research, 68,* 130–178.

Wood, D. (2007). Teachers' learning communities; Catalyst for change or a new infrastructure for the status quo? *Teachers College Record, 109,* 699–739.

Wood, M. (2005). *Querida senora Wood: Improving second language communication skills through letter writing.* Unpublished teacher research report. Davis, CA: University of California.

Yin, R. K. (2003). *Case study research: Design and methods.* Thousand Oaks, CA: Sage.

CHAPTER 14

"It Could Take Forty Minutes; It Could Take Three Days"

AUTHENTIC SMALL-GROUP LEARNING FOR ABORIGINAL EDUCATION

Joanne Tompkins
St. Francis Xavier University

Jeff Orr
St. Francis Xavier University

Joanne Tompkins, Ed.D., teaches in the education faculty at St. Francis Xavier University, Antigonish, Nova Scotia. Her experience working in Inuit education as a teacher, principal (*Teaching in a Cold and Windy Place*, 1998), consultant in inclusive education and teacher educator in the Qikiqtani Region of Nunavut have laid a strong foundation and interest in transformative teaching and leadership. Her teaching and research interests lie in the areas of diversity, decolonizing educational practices, and critical leadership.

Jeff Orr, Ph.D., has been working in First Nations education for the past twenty-five years as a teacher, administrator, teacher educator, and university administrator. He is currently director of the School of Education at St. Francis Xavier University, where he teaches courses in sociology of education, curriculum, leadership, and research. His research interests include First Nations program evaluation, leadership, and pedagogy, and social studies education.

ABSTRACT

In this chapter, two teacher educators who have spent their public school and teacher education careers working in Aboriginal contexts throughout Canada examine the powerful potential of small-group learning settings to decolonize teacher education for preservice and in-service Aboriginal teachers. Drawing on their lived experiences working together in teacher education classrooms, the authors weave research findings into the essay about the transformative potential of small-group learning settings to impact on teacher practice.

Introduction

In this chapter, we combine research-based knowledge concerning how Aboriginal teacher learning takes place in small-group settings with our own experiences as teacher educators working with Aboriginal and non-Aboriginal students. We explore how preservice and in-service Aboriginal teachers' knowledges develop in small-group settings and how these instructional settings bring Aboriginal epistemology and ontology more fully into mainstream teacher education centers. Believing as Smith (1999) does that decolonizing work should make a difference for Aboriginal peoples, we conclude by examining the influence of Aboriginal educators' learning in group situations on their professional practice.

What Brings Us to This Place?

Together, but in separate places, we have spent all of our public school careers working in Aboriginal contexts. Jeff worked for many years as a teacher and administrator in schools serving Dene children in Northern Saskatchewan. Joanne was a teacher, system level consultant, and administrator in schools serving Inuit students in Nunavut. We both served as teacher union activists in Northern contexts and worked in teacher education programs (TEP) preparing Dene and Inuit teachers to assume classroom leadership in First Nations and Inuit schools.

We have been privileged to work alongside Cree, Dene, Metis, Mi'kmaw, and Inuit peoples in their struggles for self-determination in education. In the mid-1990s, we both found ourselves at St. Francis Xavier University in Antigonish, Nova Scotia, Canada, preparing Mi'kmaw preservice and in-service teachers to teach in both public and band-operated schools throughout the nation. (In the past decade, seventy Mi'Kmaw teachers have been graduated with a Bachelor of Education from St. Francis Xavier University and thirty Mi'Kmaw teachers have gone on to do graduate work.) Our research interests overlap in Aboriginal and Inuit education in the areas of bilingual education, leadership, school change, and policy. Working closely over the past ten years, we have co-planned and co-taught several preservice and graduate courses. Most of our teaching is done in mixed settings where Aboriginal and non-Aboriginal preservice teachers and graduate students are learning together in the same space, but we also teach in contexts where all learners are Aboriginal.

In this chapter, we reflect upon our learnings about how small-group learning settings influence Aboriginal teacher learning. Research-based knowledge will be woven throughout to show how our findings are supported by other scholarly work.

Small-Group Learning Settings

Like Cummins (2001) we believe that "human relationships are at the heart of teaching" (p. 1). Along with other critical educators (Apple & Beane, 1999; Dei, 1996, 2002; Delpit, 1995; Freire, 1970; Lee, 1998; McIntosh, 1990; Nieto, 1996) and Indigenous scholars (Ah Nee-Benham & Cooper, 1998; Battiste, 1999; Graveline, 1998; Smith, 1999) we recognize that factors such as race, ethnicity, gender, class, ability, sexual orientation, age, and religion intersect to profoundly shape the way we experience the world. These intersecting factors and issues of difference and power in classrooms (Orr, Paul, & Paul, 2002; Tompkins, 2002) frame our use of small-group learning in teacher education.

In all of our classes we see a range of diversities. Aboriginal students, whose lives have been profoundly shaped by the historical and contemporary forces of colonization, are sitting next to students who are part of the colonizer group and who, for the most part, understand little of the historical imbalances that those processes have caused (Battiste, 1999, 2005; Binda & Calliou, 2001; Smith, 1999). This colonized consciousness, like ours, has been "bombarded by the Eurocentric philosophies that are necessary to support industrial capitalism" (Graveline, 1998, p. 8).

Male and female students often experience our classrooms and the schools in which they will teach in dramatically different ways. Students in their early twenties, who recently finished an undergraduate degree, could be sitting alongside students in their forties who entered the university after raising a family or as a career change. Other differences are not so visible. Some of our students are parents and grandparents, while others are without family responsibilities. Social class and economic considerations greatly shape our students' lives; these factors dictate where they live, whether they work to support their studies or whether they have money for food or university supplies. Students' religious beliefs, sexual orientation, family prominence, and dialect impact how they experience the world and how they view teacher education. Within any group that we teach, there is a tremendous range of diversity and as a consequence of that, varying degrees of power and privilege.

In teaching exclusively with Aboriginal educators, we have learned that issues of power and privilege are also at work. Differences in power are often based on whether one is a speaker of an Indigenous language and one's level of bilingual fluency. Age, kin connections, the particular First Nations community to which one belongs, type of work, work experience, family obligations, experience in the formal education system, and religious affiliation are additional factors that impact classroom dynamics. The concept of intersectionality (Kerr, 2004; Symington, 2004) is reinforced time and again as we realize there can be as much diversity within the group that we call Mi'kmaw or Inuit as there is between the grouping of Aboriginal and non-Aboriginal peoples.

Each layer of a person's identity is given meaning by our society and can serve to elevate or diminish an individual's power and privilege. Colonial, patriarchal, capitalist society has constructed meaning and given more value to being of the Settler group (Smith, 1999) or being male than being Aboriginal or female. Using Lee's (1985) "Flower of Self," we work with our students to show graphically that within our classroom there are some people sitting with a great deal more power and privilege than others. We have learned that if we open up the large-group classroom setting without prior work on differences and power or without careful rules of protocol, we are most likely to hear only the most privileged and confident voices. Some voices will be rarely heard. Without an acknowledgment of power and privilege, and protocol to ensure democratic spaces are created, the same oppressive tendency of those with more personal power to dominate those with less will occur, even in small-group settings.

The Importance of Aboriginal Epistemology

In David Suzuki's (1997) *The Sacred Balance*, Thomas Berry observed that stories are essential metaphors to guide people and that the challenge for contemporary peoples is finding stories that make sense of and challenge current realities. Our experience has convinced us as teacher educators that unless we act with critical consciousness, prevailing mainstream Eurocentric epistemology and ontology will be centered in the classroom and the hegemonizing effect of public schooling on diverse communities will remain unchallenged. Dei (2002) sees the introduction of Indigenous knowledges into the academy as one way "to rupture the sense of comfort and complacency in conventional approaches to knowledge production, interrogation, validation and dissemination" (p. 3). Aboriginal knowledges can serve to decolonize the academy by challenging the primacy of the Eurocentric canon (Banks, 1999; Battiste, 2004; Dei, 2002;

Smith, 1999). Dei and Banks both argue that students can experience a kind of cultural encapsulation when they only know one knowledge system. Different knowledge systems, both Indigenous and Western, can counter the inability of scientific knowledge to account for the complete histories of ideas and events that have shaped and continue to shape human growth and development.

Making space for Aboriginal knowledges through the use of First Voice (Graveline, 1998) in small-group settings allows counter stories to be heard that challenge the persistent accounts of the underachievement of Aboriginal peoples. Small-group learning settings can create spaces that open up new possibilities. Kirkness and Barnhardt (1991) maintain that for Aboriginal postsecondary students, "respect is the most compelling problem that students face when they go to university. They want a dialogue with the 'producers of knowledge'" (p. 199). When that dialogue can occur, it is a moment of great learning for both Aboriginal and non-Aborginal teachers.

Our Approach to Small-Group Learning Settings

We have two goals in creating equitable small-group learning settings. The first is to model the importance of relationality in our classroom. The second is to amplify the voices of those of our students who have been marginalized and to diminish the voices of those with more power and privilege so as to rebalance relationships that have been skewed by the forces of colonization, racism, sexism, ableism, and classism. More than thirty years ago, in her work with Alaskan Aboriginal students, Kleinfeld (1975) observed, "You've got to be personal. . . . What you have to do is shed the barrier of formality that you put between you and the class. Approach them like people you know. . . . The classroom should be like family" (p. 318). Although challenging, rebalancing historically unbalanced relationships is part of the task of decolonizing work.

Children's literature can serve as a way to gently introduce what is often harshly received by learners who are introduced to basic concepts of colonization, oppression, marginalization, and coercion in schools. Picture books such as *Chrysanthemum* (Henkes, 1991), *Through the Cracks* (Sollman, Emmons, & Paolini, 1994), *Mama Zooms* (Cowen-Fletcher, 1993), *Dear Mr. Blueberry* (James, 1996), and *Encounter* (Yolen, 1996) allow us to talk about ways schools claim authority over children's lives. In the relatively safe space of children's books, discussing these topics opens doors to future discussions about social justice in schools. For most Aboriginal preservice teachers and graduate students these concepts are not new. Their experience in the formal education system has generally been one of assimilation (Battiste, 1999, 2002, 2005; Castellano, Davis, & Lahache, 2000; Lipka, Mohatt, & the Ciulistet Group, 1998; Nicholas, 2001; Ryan, 1996; Smith, 1999). Other students who have experienced marginalization and oppression in schools based perhaps on sexual orientation, gender, social class, or ability difference also see themselves in these texts. Students with considerable privilege usually have not experienced exclusion firsthand, and these books serve to awaken them to the idea that schools do not equally serve the interests of all learners.

As facilitators, with considerable power and privilege as members of the colonizing group, and as university academics, we take time to deconstruct the multiple layers of our own unearned power. We open the space for small-group dialogue to challenge the myth of meritocracy by showing that a great deal of our ability to achieve our station in life was largely due to our sociocultural, sociohistorical, and sociopolitical positioning and not necessarily through our individual efforts. By using our own stories as models, we make ourselves vulnerable and give permission for each person in our classes to create the potential space for exploring his own power and privilege.

We seek to help our students recognize that although there is no denying their power, it is not helpful to languish in guilt. We help our students consider what to do once they know they possess a great deal of unearned power. We counsel our students on how they might act as allies (Bishop, 1994) to diminish the effects of oppression for others. McIntosh (1990) provides an important way for us, Joanne and Jeff, as white educators, to talk about the ways power and privilege remain unnamed and consequently unexamined in our lives. We talk openly about the ways that we work to "interrupt" (Fine, Anand, Hancock, Jordan, & Sherman, 1993) the hegemony of schooling and the times when we have been unable to do so. We talk about how none of us is totally without power nor do any of us have complete power. Talking in small groups about intersectionality helps our students see that a broad category such as "women" does not account for how gender is shaped by race and class. In turn, they see how the category of "Aboriginal" does not consider the influence of geography, social class, access to formal education, and kinship upon such a designation.

Our teaching attempts to help our students and ourselves be more thoughtful about context and location in small-group discussions. We introduce classroom protocol for working across difference that reminds us of the challenges in intersectional dialogue. Phrases such as "our own experience is valid but not necessarily universal" or "expressions like 'those people' or 'they' create stereotypes of a group" or "let us attempt to understand what is being said rather than judge what is being said" serve as guiding principles for our subsequent small-group discussions. We carefully stress the importance of "patience listening" (Morrissette, McKenzie, & Morrissette, 1993) in which our students are encouraged to listen so that they can understand the world through the speaker's eyes. People of privilege often have to work more consciously at active listening.

It is through these pedagogical principles of patient listening, acknowledging power and privilege, and decolonizing knowledge systems that we learn together in small-group settings. Arriving at this point may take between three and five hours of class time. Making the small-group setting an educative rather than miseducative space takes careful and intentional preparatory and ongoing work. This softening of the groundwork is not time taken away from our curriculum; it is our curriculum. If done well, it can open up great potential for Aboriginal teacher learning and provide modeling for our teachers. If done poorly, it will reinforce the tyranny of Eurocentric, colonizing ways of knowing, being, and doing. The small-group pedagogies we use involve base groups and circle pedagogies.

Small-Group Learning Formats

We set up base groups with three people in them, believing that two works best for intimate discussions and that communication becomes more complex when four or five people are in a group. Based on our observations of the large group garnered in the first few days of class and based on having had students share personal knowledge individually about themselves, we try to establish triads where power, privilege, and intersectionality difference are represented as much as possible. We place Aboriginal students with non-Aboriginal students, elementary students with secondary students, males with females, and older students with younger students. We do so believing that we learn more about our own location, power, and privilege from people who are different from us than we do from people who are like us.

James (2001) asserts that most of us manage to live our lives interacting with people mostly like us and that rarely are we, particularly as people of the dominant group, provided the opportunity to encounter and learn from "others." Mi'kmaw students, by virtue of having been colonized, are continuously forced to enter into the colonizer's world. However white people may spend an entire career in public school and postsecondary educational institutions and never enter into real dialogue or relationships with an Aboriginal person. Their only knowing of Aboriginal people may come through the often racist stereotypes portrayed in the mainstream media or through erroneous conceptions garnered from elementary social studies lessons where Indigenous peoples are portrayed as "living only in the past" (Moore, 1999). We use triads for small-group discussion and reflections on readings and films. Triads stay together for the duration of the term so they can develop supportive relationships with each other. We continually reflect on group processing in these triads and model explicit communication employing cross-cultural strategies that enhance dialogue.

Another small-group setting we use frequently is circles. Ah Nee-Benham and Cooper (2000) employed circles in their collaborative research with Aboriginal leaders as a way to create space so that sharing and talking could freely flow. The circle "becomes both a physical and spiritual necessity as it fostered facilitation of discussion and reminded everyone of the important places that circles and ceremony must have in the educational processes" (p. 9). We use several different types of circles (community circles, red stockings, webs, sharing circles, fishbowls). It is the talking circle, a format that provides a democratic structure for hearing all of the voices in the room, that we use most often.

Our variation of the talking circle is guided by sacred Aboriginal traditions. It begins with participants sitting in a circle as one person holds a sacred object. The person who holds the object has the right to speak and may speak as long as the object is held. All other circle members become listeners. When the person has finished she passes the object in a clockwise fashion to the person next to her. As a result, that person has the right to talk. Talking circles allow for each member of the circle to speak, although members have the right to pass. The circle continues until the need to talk is exhausted. Traditionally, the circle would be used to sort out issues and it would continue until the issue had been resolved.

The nonlinearity of the talking circle can pose some difficulty for programs ruled by clocks and time tables. Several years ago a Mi'kmaw graduate student was introducing the talking circle in her graduate class. The non-Mi'kmaw instructor asked how long the activity might take. She replied, "It could take forty minutes; it could take three days!" Hart (2002), who researched the use of circles in social work to challenge ontological imperialism, states "usually there is no time pressure for participants to contribute since they are allowed to speak freely without interruption, and they are aware that the circle may take an extended period of time to be completed" (p. 90). One can see how Aboriginal ontology is closely linked to epistemology. Therefore, if you want to bring Aboriginal knowledges into the classroom, you need to do it in a way that honors Aboriginal ways of being.

Small-Group Learning Settings and Aboriginal Teacher Knowledge

Aboriginal teachers come to teacher education with their individual knowledge. This knowledge is then manifested in their practical actions as they go about the work of educating their own students to become more mindful and valuing of Aboriginal values, relationships, and knowledge systems (Orr, Paul, & Paul, 2002). Most of their Aboriginal knowledge comes from experiences in their family, community, and the larger Aboriginal community. Dei (2002) describes Indigenous knowledge and modes of thought as "expressive and narrative." Indigenous knowledges view communalism as a mode of thought, "emphasizing the sense of belongingness with a people and the land they share. It is grounded in a people and place" (p. 5). Bringing Aboriginal epistemology into teacher education requires that we pay attention to relationality. For this reason, small groups and circles lend pedagogical congruence to the learning setting.

The very act of being able to speak their knowledge and values out loud in this small-group relational space helps Aboriginal students clarify their own thinking, articulate their thoughts, and come to know them more deeply. It is an axiom of cooperative learning that when students have to teach each other, they learn better. Stating their beliefs and experiences out loud builds intellectual competence and confidence in Aboriginal teachers.

When Aboriginal knowledge is made public in small-group settings, it allows Aboriginal knowledge and values to be discussed, affirmed, contested, constructed, and co-constructed. Curriculum pressures in education tempt us to give "received" knowledge to our teacher education candidates, rather than allowing them to actively construct their own learning. Bringing Aboriginal knowledges to this shared place of small-group talk allows for deeper and more robust intellectual understanding of pedagogy because it is now informed by Aboriginal knowledges that acknowledge "the personal, internal nature of knowledge (love)" (Hodgson-Smith, 2000, p. 157).

By allowing our pedagogy to be informed by Aboriginal knowledge, Aboriginal educators come to understand that their knowledge is valued in teacher education. Their cultural framework gives them much that they draw on in teaching. They come to see that "pedagogy is not merely styles, methods and strategies. It is also the epistemological/philosophical framework from which one approaches instruction" (Hodgson-Smith, p. 158). Our circle pedagogies and small-group settings bring Aboriginal knowledge in from the margins, validating them as deep, intellectually robust understandings that have a rightful place alongside Western knowledge.

Creating small-group learning settings where Aboriginal knowledge can be shared also opens the door for dialogue with other oppressed groups. The process of colonization for Mi'kmaw people resonates for many African Nova Scotian preservice teachers in our program, highlighting the unchallenged position of the Eurocentric curriculum that tells stories from the point of view of the colonizers. Marginalized groups see little of their own experience reflected back to them, nor do they see the experiences of others who faced similar injustices and exclusions. Sharing Aboriginal knowledge allows for critical analysis that helps marginalized peoples "connect the dots" and see how their own struggles are connected to the struggles of others (Zinn, 1980).

The Impact of Small Groups on Aboriginal Educators

Small-group learning settings governed by careful and intentional protocol can be decolonizing spaces for Aboriginal teachers. We aim to have our classroom setting challenge Eurocentric epistemology and ontology and, at the same time, unsettle the pedagogical optics of what students see happening in the traditional classroom. Shor and Freire (1987), applying Paulo Freire's work on transformative teaching to university teaching, tell a story entitled "Teaching from Siberia." For each class the teacher moves his physical location in the classroom, always decentering himself as the teacher and therefore interrupting the usual social hierarchies in the class. In this way, he and the students are challenging their assumptions about who they are as learners. This story resonates with our experiences in using small-group settings with Aboriginal students.

Enid Lee (2004) also seeks to unsettle the usual power relations through her teaching and activism. She says sometimes teachers fall into the trap of thinking they have to change everything all at once. She believes that introducing one or two elements into a classroom may in fact disrupt things in surprising ways. Lee declares that too often we struggle in polarities in equity work and that by introducing new ways of being into the classroom, we alter the optics of how the room gets read.

When we use base groups or circles in small-group settings, we as teachers decenter the classroom and make space for Aboriginal voices that challenge the usual power dynamics in the classroom. When Aboriginal students speak and are respectfully listened to, they are affirmed and they are valued. Sometimes, this is the first time in a formal education setting with their non-Mi'kmaw colleagues. In the absence of hearing their voices, the only basis upon which to make judgments about a person are assumptions based on social constructions of class, race, gender as informed by mainstream media. When we make space for preservice teachers to authentically engage with each other intellectually, we open the doors for authentic cross-cultural dialogue to occur. Ultimately in the small-group setting, of either circle or triad, we are presenting alternatives to the hierarchy. As one facilitator described to Hart (2002),

> You know, here we have a hierarchical system which to me comes
> from the Europeans that clashed with tribes and their philosophies

that are in a cyclical system. Now if you look at it in terms of the circle . . . well, it creates an atmosphere of cooperation. It creates an atmosphere of equality. Look at just the symbol itself. You put people in a circle, everybody's the same. Now when you come from a hierarchical system where someone is at the front and someone is at the back, or at the top or the bottom, what does that induce? It creates competition. It creates this atmosphere of someone who is better than or someone who's less than. So there's the difference. . . . Everybody in that circle is on the same plane. You know, there's no hierarchy in the sharing circle. Everybody is the same. Even the facilitator should blend into that. (p. 84)

When Aboriginal students are able to take their individual knowledge and bring it to the public arena where it can be articulated, contested, and validated, their opinions of and confidence in themselves is heightened and a profoundly decolonizing experience occurs. Three examples from our teaching illustrate this point.

COMMUNITY CIRCLES DEBRIEF

In a class on First Nation and Inuit education, we used community circles to debrief the presentations graduate students had shared. A Mi'kmaw elementary schoolteacher had given a very moving presentation on conversations she had with her mother, a residential school survivor. In her debriefing, she was able to articulate for herself and to others the increased empathy and pride she felt speaking for the first time publicly about this topic, which for so long had remained in the shadows. Bringing individual knowledge to a more public space heightened its meaning for her.

SHARING STORIES

In a graduate class two Mi'kmaw educators were sharing in small groups and later in talking circles their experiences in provincial schools. These provincial school experiences, for the most part, did not honor who they were as learners. These two educators spoke about the not-so-subtle ways that low expectations were communicated to them in public school. Perhaps more importantly, they spoke about the subtle ways that colonization, racism, and discrimination continued to be lived out in their careers as teachers and even within our graduate program. Even though they were only two voices in the room, through the small-group sharing and a subsequent talking circle, they were able to impart very important knowledge to the group. Narayan (1988), in her work on oppression, states that insiders, those who experience oppression, have "epistemic privilege" that allows them to know more deeply the multiple and subtle ways that oppression is lived out. Outsiders would do well, she argues, to listen carefully to these conversations.

In spite of the rhetoric about the increasing diversity in North America, we live in a society that manages to keep us quite stratified in our groupings (James, 2001). Though only two voices in a room of sixty, these two Mi'kmaw educators brought Aboriginal epistemic expertise into the room that day. Because of the previous work we had done discussing power, privilege, and the humbling that members of the dominant culture need to embrace if they are to become allies in decolonizing work (Tompkins, 2002, 2006), these two graduate students were able to be listened to with the deep level of respect and honor they deserved. In that classroom, they felt a sense of belonging because of the space created for them. Sharing their stories let them deal with some of the pain they had carried for some time. This was the first time that either of them had articulated these stories outside the family, and they never had done so with non-Native people. During this sharing, our non-Native students were able to carefully listen, which helped them understand from a point of view of the disadvantaged. Mi'kmaw students regularly tell us how difficult it is to share cultural pain, yet how our classroom was safe for them. They tell us they can be open because they know they will not be judged. They realize that few non-Native people have ever heard these experiences.

FISHBOWL STRATEGY

The third story involves the use of a fishbowl strategy. In a preservice teacher education course on diversity, we were discussing the experience that Aboriginal peoples had with residential schooling. The class consisted of Mi'kmaw and non-Mi'kmaw students. The residential school experience represents one of the most assimilationist acts forced upon Aboriginal peoples because of its impact upon language and its cultural destruction. It is a pedagogical challenge to examine this issue in a way that honors the sensitive and painful nature of the experience for those whose families endured it and yet to also educate the dominant culture (Grant, 2004).

In this class we invited five Mi'kmaw students to sit in a small circle facing each other while the rest of the class was outside the circle as observers. The Mi'kmaw preservice teacher candidates shared stories, tears, insights, and moments of silence with each other. As outsiders we were permitted the opportunity to witness and listen but not to interrupt the fishbowl. Later, the Mi'kmaw students commented on how sharing in the small circle with people who had lived the experience gave them a great deal of strength, comfort, and support. They felt they would not have felt the same had they been asked to present this complex and painful topic to a group of outsiders. Their voices were heard in a manner that honored their way of being.

OUTCOMES

In each of these examples, the small-group learning setting allowed Aboriginal teachers to be affirmed and validated in ways that are usually rare in dominant cultural institutions. Graveline (1998) highlights the important links between such settings where Aboriginal learners are given space to find their voice and the deeper pedagogical act of decolonization:

> Decolonization requires and allows reclamation of voice. Traditional-ists believe in the power of expression through voice—words are be-lieved to be sacred. Spoken words/sounds are one way of expressing our relatedness to each other. . . . What we know, what we have learned from our lived experiences is embodied in our voices. When spoken and heard, Aboriginal voices pose a challenge to the domi-nant order of who speaks and who listens in Western society. . . . Through voice we speak/write our acts of resistance, the healing and empowering values of our Traditions and the role of the European colonizers in the destruction of our communities. Through voice we are gaining our own sense of conscious reality and providing another lens through which Eurocentric educators may view themselves. (p. 441)

Galda (1998) maintains that, as children read, they should sometimes see their experiences, their lives, and their realities reflected back to them (mirrors). Like-wise, that reading should also open our world to other people's realities and experiences (windows). Aboriginal students, such as in our cases above, have often suffered from having no mirrors in public school classroom and as such feel an erasure of their identity. In contrast, students with privilege often are surrounded by mirrors but are presented with few opportunities to look into other windows. Students with privilege often develop an overexaggerated sense of their importance in the world, a kind of cultural arrogance (Tompkins, 2006) and have a monocultural rather than multicultural perspective (Lee, 1998).

Opening small-group learning spaces for Aboriginal teachers creates mirrors to articulate, share, and listen to other Aboriginal students to see their lives being reflected back to them as they develop a deeper analysis of the systemic nature of oppression. They also see ways other Aboriginal students have learned to resist and move forward. Their identity, rather than being excluded from academic work, starts to become a source of strength. Mi'kmaw students tell us, when they create mirrors for themselves and augment their confidence, their stories provide important windows for dominant culture students whose Eurocentric arrogance begins to diminish. The role of our classroom becomes "resistance to the dominance of Eurocentric knowledge as the only valid way of knowing" (Dei, 2002, p. 16).

The Impact on Teacher Practice

Aboriginal cultural practical knowledge can decolonize Aboriginal education if it is unearthed, named, and affirmed (Orr, Paul, & Paul, 2002). Kleinfeld (1975) found that many Aboriginal teachers educated in programs based exclusively on Western knowledge feel a conflict between their formal professional learning and the "personalism they say 'worked' in the classroom" (p. 305). Learning in small-group settings in ways that we are researching strengthens Aboriginal teachers' knowledge of their practice.

Our research in Mi'kmaw language immersion classrooms shows how Mi'kmaw teachers are applying Aboriginal epistemology and ontology in their classrooms. Mi'kmaw immersion teachers speak about ways they use circles to build community in their classroom. "We always have them in a circle. And they have to know who they are, it's the first thing that we teach them. . . . So we always use the talking stick so they're used to talking right out loud and we're using that to help each other, and to respect each other" (field notes, 2006). Mi'kmaw immersion teachers also talk about the deep caring of their students that is central to their pedagogy. "We all know each other, we all love each other and I don't think I want to part with them now" (field notes, 2006). These teachers describe how they intentionally attempt to create a homelike feeling in their classrooms. "I went and bought cushions so when it's carpet time, they can have them. . . . I've got five cushions on the floor and they just sit there comfortably reading, that's my reading center. We do baking, we have lunch and we sit together" (field notes, 2006).

Conclusion

Making spaces for Aboriginal voices in small groups has been, in our experience, transformative for all learners. Small-group learning settings provide a way of teaching that helps our students release their words into a public, rather than individual space. In so doing, they allow their teacher knowledge to be contested as it is constructed and co-constructed. Teaching in this way has challenged us as teacher educators to venture into pedagogical relationships with our students that are simultaneously ambiguous, complex, contradictory, and evolving. Kawagley (1995) asserts that teachers who are successful in cross-cultural and minority education settings possess a high degree of tolerance for ambiguity and complexity. We continue to be excited and amazed by the learning that happens through such spaces that we make for teacher knowledge to be constructed and reconstructed in small-group settings.

Authors' Note: We would like to thank the many Aboriginal teachers whose words, lives, and practices have helped shape our understandings.

References

Ah Nee-Benham, M., & Cooper, J. (1998). *Let my spirit soar! Narratives of diverse in school leadership.* Thousand Oaks, CA: Corwin Press.

Ah Nee-Benham, M., & Cooper, J. (2000). *Indigenous educational models for contemporary practice.* Mahwah, NJ: Lawrence Erlbaum Associates.

Apple, M., & Beane, J. (1999). *Democratic schools: Lessons from the chalk face.* Birmingham, UK: Open Press.

Banks, J. (1999). *An introduction to multicultural education.* Needham Heights, MA: Allyn & Bacon.

Battiste, M. (1999). Enabling the autumn seed: Toward a decolonized approach to Aboriginal knowledge, language and education. *Canadian Journal of Native Education, 22*(1), 16–27.

Battiste, M. (2002). *Indigenous knowledge and pedagogy in First Nations Education; A literature review with recommendations.* Saskatoon, SK: Apamuwek Institute.

Battiste, M. (2004, May). *Animating sites of postcolonial education: Indigenous knowledge and the humanities.* Keynote address presented at the annual meeting of the Canadian Society for the Study of Education (CSSE), Winnipeg, MB.

Battiste, M. (2005). *State of aboriginal learning.* Background paper for the "National Dialogue on Aboriginal Learning" Conference. Saskatoon, SK: Canadian Council on Learning (CCL).

Binda, K. P., & Calliou, S. (2001). *Aboriginal education in Canada: A study in decolonization.* Mississauga, ON: Canadian Educators' Press.

Bishop, A. (1994). *Becoming an ally: Breaking the cycle of oppression.* Halifax, NS: Fernwood Press.

Castellano, M., Davis, L., & Lahache, L. (2000). *Aboriginal education; Fulfilling the promise.* Vancouver, BC: University of British Columbia Press.

Cowen-Fletcher, J. (1993). *Mama zooms.* New York: Scholastic Books.

Cummins, J. (1996/2001). *Negotiating identities: Education for empowerment in a diverse society.* Ontario, CA: California Association for Bilingual Education (CABE).

Dei, G. (1996). *Anti-racism education: Theory and practice.* Halifax, NS: Fernwood Press.

Dei, G. S. (2002). *Rethinking the role of Indigenous knowledges in the academy.* Ottawa, ON: NALL Working Paper #58.

Delpit, L. (1995). *Other peoples' children.* San Francisco, CA: Jossey-Bass.

Fine, M., Anand, B., Hancock, M., Jordan, C., & Sherman, D. (1993). *Off track: Classroom privilege for all.* New York: Teachers College Press.

Freire, P. (1970/2000). *Pedagogy of the oppressed.* New York: Herder & Herder.

Galda, L. (1998). Mirrors and windows. Reading as transformation. In T. Raphael & K. Au (Eds.), *Literature-based instruction: Reshaping the curriculum* (XX). Norwood, MA: Christopher-Gordon Publishers, Inc.

Grant, A. (2004). *Finding my talk: How fourteen Native women reclaimed their lives after Residential School.* Calgary, AB: Fifth House Ltd.

Graveline, F. J. (1998). *Circle Works—Transforming Eurocentric consciousness.* Halifax, NS: Fernwood Publishing.

Hart, M. A. (2002). *Seeking Mino-Pimatisiwin; An Aboriginal approach to healing.* Halifax, NS: Fernwood Publishing.

Henkes, K. (1991). *Chrysanthemum.* New York: Greenwillow Books.

Hodgson-Smith, K. (2000). Issues of pedagogy in Aboriginal education. In M. Castellano, L. Davis, & L. Lahache (Eds.), *Aboriginal education; Fulfilling the promise.* Vancouver, BC: University of British Columbia Press.

James, C. (2001). *Experiencing difference.* Halifax, NS: Fernwood Press.

James, S. (1996). *Dear Mr. Blueberry.* New York: Aladdin Paperbacks.

Kawagley, O. (1995). *A Yupiaq worldview: A pathway to an ecology and spirit.* Prospect Heights, IL: Waveland Press, Inc.

Kerr, J. (2004). From "opposing" to "proposing": Finding proactive global strategies for feminist futures. In J. Kerr, E. Sprenger, & A. Symington (Eds.), *The future of women's rights: Global visions and strategies.* London, UK: Zed Books.

Kirkness, V. J., & Barnhardt, R. (1991). First Nations and higher education: The four Rs—respect, relevance, reciprocity, and responsibility. *Journal of American Indian Education, 30*(3), 1–15.

Kleinfeld, J. (1975). Effective teachers of Eskimo and Indian students. *School Review, XX*(XX), (February), 301–344.

Krenshaw, K. (2002). *The intersectionality of race and gender discrimination.* Paper presented for the Expert Group Meeting on Gender and Race Discrimination, Zagreb, Croatia.

Lee, E. (1985). *Letters to Marcia: A teacher's guide to anti-racist education.* Toronto, ON: Cross Cultural Communication Center.

Lee, E. (1998). Anti-racist education: Pulling together to close the gaps. In E. Lee, D. Menkart, & M. Okazawa-Rey (Eds.), *Beyond heroes and holidays* (pp. 26–34). Washington, DC: Network of Educators on the Americas.

Lee, E. (2004, September 24). *Putting race on the table.* Workshop presented to the Equity Advisory Committee at St. Francis Xavier University, Antigonish, Nova Scotia.

Lipka, J., Mohatt, G., & the Ciulistet Group. (1998). *Transforming the culture of schools: Yup'ik Eskimo examples.* Mahwah, NJ: Lawrence Erlbaum Associates.

McIntosh, P. (1990). White privilege: Unpacking the invisible knapsack. In E. Lee, D. Menkart, & M. Okazawa-Rey (Eds.), *Beyond heroes and holidays* (pp. 79–82). Washington, DC: Network of Educators on the Americas.

Moore, D. (CSM). (1999). Personal communication.

Morrissette, V., McKenzie, B., & Morrissette, L. (1993). Towards an Aboriginal model of social work practice: Cultural knowledge and traditional practices. *Canadian Social Work Review, 10*(XX), 91–108.

Narayan, U. (1988). Working together across difference: Some considerations on emotions and political practice. *Hypatia, 3*(2), 31–42.

Nicholas, A. (2001). Canada's colonial mission: The great white bird. In K. P. Binda & S. Calliou (Eds.), *Aboriginal education in Canada: A study in decolonization* (pp. 9–33). Mississauga, ON: Canadian Educators' Press.

Nieto, S. (1996). *Affirming diversity: The sociopolitical context of multicultural education.* White Plains, NY: Longman Publishers USA.

Orr, J., Paul, J. J., & Paul, S. (2002). Decolonizing Mi'kmaw education through cultural practical knowledge. *McGill Journal of Education, 37*(3), 331–354.

Ryan, J. (1996). Restructuring First Nations' Education: Trust, respect and governance. *Journal of Canadian Studies, 31*(2), 115–131.

Shor, I., & Freire, P. (1987). *A pedagogy for liberation; Dialogues on transforming education.* New York: Bergin & Garvey.

Smith, L. (1999). *Decolonizing methodologies: Research and Indigenous peoples.* London, UK: Zed Books Ltd.

Sollman, C., Emmons, B., & Paolini, J. (1994). *Through the cracks.* Worcester, MA: Davis Publications.

Suzuki, D. (1997). *The sacred balance.* Vancouver: Greystone Books.

Symington, A. (2004). *Intersectionality: A tool for gender and economic justice.* Women's Rights and Economic Change, no. 9.

Tompkins, J. (2002). Learning to see what they can't: Decolonizing perspectives on Indigenous education in the racial context of rural Nova Scotia. *McGill Journal of Education, 32*(3), 405–422.

Tompkins, J. (2006). *Critical and shared: Conceptions of Inuit educational leadership.* Unpublished doctoral thesis, OISE/University of Toronto, Toronto, ON, Canada.

Yolen, J. (1996). *Encounter.* San Diego, CA: Voyager Books.

Zinn, H. (1980). *The peoples' history of the United States.* New York: Harper Perennial.

Summary and Implications

Cheryl J. Craig

Louise F. Deretchin

In Division 2, the collection of eight chapters formed a rich array of small-group practices in teacher education contexts. In Chapter 7, Anthony Clarke and Gaalen Erickson told of how cohorts addressed a myriad of difficulties that detracted from the coherency of teacher education programs and the experiences of students enrolled in them. The CITE program they developed that has evolved over a period of twelve years incorporates perspectives on learning that are emerging from a field known as complexity theory or complexity thinking. The theory helps explain the dynamic aspect of small-group learning that precludes expectation of replication of the small-group experience from one group to another. To make their case, they told of how they and their teacher education colleagues took advantage of a traveling exhibition at a local museum and shaped learning activities across the disciplines from it. In addition to this, cohort learning arose in the teacher research projects in which the University of British Columbia preservice teachers engaged alongside their cohort instructors. As can be seen, the cohort, understood through the complexity theory lens, was so much more than an organizational structure. For Clarke and Erickson, it was an "energizing and generative space for inquiry," which the authors maintain is "the defining feature in a professional practice."

In the small-seminar chapter that followed (Chapter 8), Jacque Ensign offered readers a bird's-eye view of the way seminars were used as sites of small-group learning in a teacher education program in Washington State. Here, too, inquiry was cultivated. In Ensign's case, however, the teacher candidates learned to engage in close readings of texts in order to take on perplexing issues that exist in schools and the world today. These discussions eventually occurred with and without the presence of instructors, which suggested that the inquiry stance became habitual. As readers, we learned of how particular teacher candidates developed their knowledge. But we also came to know what transpired in these teacher candidates' classrooms as a direct consequence of their small-seminar experiences.

Next came Chapter 9, Kami Patrizio's essay on preservice candidates looking at student work in a professional development context. Once again, inquiry was the coin of the realm. This time, however, the focus was on attending to student work as evidence of their learning through using the "looking at student work" (LASW) protocol, which is sometimes used in teacher professional development sessions. In this chapter as well, readers got a sense of preservice candidates developing an approach in a small-group setting that was directly linked to the academic development of the students they served, which concurrently advanced the professional development of the soon-to-be credentialed teachers.

In Chapter 10, we moved on to the discussion of teacher learning in collaborative reflection meetings, the essay contributed by Paulien Meijer and Helma Oolbekkink-Marchand of the Netherlands. Their study involved eight secondary educators subdivided into two meeting groups, each of which set about discussing two problems of practice. Contrary to prior research findings of their Dutch peers, the teacher educators found the preservice teachers not progressing through four identifiable phases of development. Rather, they eventually moved beyond more technical understandings of reflection to take on the larger issue of "To what extent am I doing justice to the students entrusted to my responsibility and case as a teacher?". Furthermore, because the teacher candidates posed questions of their peers in the meetings that they has not asked of themselves, Meijer and Oolbekkink-Marchand suggested that preservice teachers engage in self-studies of their teacher practice while simultaneously participating in collaborative reflective meetings. This way teacher candidates' knowledge would be deepened and extended, as their study showed.

Chapter 11 returned us to the cohort as a small-group learning site. Within the cohort, the aperture of the lens narrowed as Don Halquist and Sue Novinger focused on two reflection resisters, early childhood teacher candidates Michelle and Cassie, and what the reflective letters they wrote suggested to their instructors. In the essay, Halquist and Novinger entered in reflective conversations with various passages in Michelle's and Cassie's letters and ferreted out instances where their two female students resisted reflection by narrowing expert voices, engaging in repetition, privileging the practical, and oversimplifying. Then, the authors reflectively turned on the letter writing assignment with fresh eyes. They discovered that what was a supportive pedagogical tool for some was a contested site for identity construction for others (like Michelle and Cassie). Halquist and Novinger additionally interrogated their own pedagogical practices and recognized the extent to which teacher candidates shaped their responses in ways that conformed to what their teacher educators expected to hear. This unsettling revelation raised issues for the teacher educators and enriched their understanding as their work with preservice candidates in a cohort of twenty students continued.

In Chapter 12, we were introduced to Nancy Gallavan's work, which addressed the significance and benefits of small groups as vehicles for cultivating cultural competence. In that essay, we learned of "the generational perpetuation of practice" that teacher candidates experience with their mentor teachers during their internships. But we also learned that the fifty-four teacher candidates in Gallavan's study understood twelve constructive benefits of small groups as sites of learning. This finding bodes particularly well for cultural competence as it relates to self, others, and society. First, cultural competence for educators relating to self both in and out of the classroom constitutes personal growth and development. Second, relating to others in a culturally competent way within the classroom represents a form of professional growth and development. Third, cultural competence related to society within the classrooms is associated with pedagogical growth and development.

In Chapters 13 and 14, readers were afforded a fine-grained account of small-group activity concerning different kinds of diversity. First, in Chapter 13, Barbara Merino and Rebecca Ambrose bridged the gap between teaching and teacher education through a long-term teacher research project undertaken in a small learning community. Merino and Ambrose shared an overview of their work with Pablo, a beginning K–3 teacher who became employed in a culturally diverse school with a high concentration of English learners. Whereas the principal of Pablo's school and the administration of the district vacated their positions under intense accountability pressures, Pablo soldiered on. In short, he sustained his unfolding teacher research project, maintained his commitment to students and quality learning while meeting school and curricular demands, nurtured his relationships with his peers in his small learning community, and benefited from the ongoing support of his faculty advisor. To Merino and Ambrose, three elements contributed to the success of the project: a data-driven approach that emphasized both teaching and learning, a faculty advisor with necessary background on systematic inquiry, and a community of learners with a shared history that was willing to help cultivate and scaffold Pablo's learning.

Division 2 concluded with our second granular look at diversity in small groups, most specifically, Aboriginal education. In Chapter 14, Joanne Tompkins and Jeff Orr shared their narrative histories of working in the field as Inuit and First Nations educators. In their experiences and through their shared commitments to critical pedagogy, Tompkins and Orr came to know Aboriginal ontology and epistemology, which, in turn, aided them in understanding the profundity of the circle and the essence of the small talking group in Aboriginal education. This led the authors to unpack how they used small groups in preservice and in-service education to give voice and recognition of power to Aboriginal students by interrogating the roots of power and privilege and balancing the over-heard voice of the "privileged" with the under-expressed voice of the Aboriginals. In the final analysis, transformation was experienced by all group members (white and nonwhite) as everyone became more awake and sensitive to the experiences of Aboriginal teachers and students.

Combined, the eight chapters in Division 2 provided important insights into the various ways small groups have been employed as sites of inquiry in teacher education, especially where diversity education is concerned. While there is no blanket guarantee that small-group activity is the elixir for all sorts of pedagogical and social problems, it also can be said that small groups, across this set of teacher education essays, created professional venues in which teachers' creative, intellectual capacities were challenged and respected, and provided a safe place for dialogue and response concerning particularly sensitive matters, ranging from what preservice teacher candidates learn from their mentor teachers to how they might better serve the diverse student population entrusted to their care.

Division 3

HIGHER EDUCATION

Overview and Framework

Cheryl J. Craig

Louise F. Deretchin

Having surveyed teacher learning in small-group settings in teaching (Division 1) and teacher education (Division 2), *Teacher Education Yearbook XVII* concludes with what is happening in small groups in higher education (Division 3). Chapter 15, "The Somehow of Teaching: Small Groups, Collaboration, and Self-Study of Teacher Education Practices," written by Mary Lynn Hamilton, reveals how the self-study of teaching and teacher education can be used not only by individuals but by small groups of professionals to improve a teacher education program while simultaneously advancing a research agenda. In Hamilton's view, the approach develops and refines the knowledge held and expressed by teacher educators, while concurrently enhancing the quality of instruction and the role modeling made available to teacher candidates.

Next, in Chapter 16, a collaborative group of Canadian-based teacher educators discuss "The Research Issues Table: A Place of Possibilities for the Education of Teacher Educators." At the research issues table, Anne Murray Orr, Bosire Monari Mwebi, Debbie Pushor, Carla Nelson, Janice Huber, D. Jean Clandinin, Ji-Sook Yeom, Pam Steeves, Florence Glanfield, and M. Shaun Murphy show how they have intimately lived a plotline of how teacher educators could be prepared differently.

Then, in Chapter 17, we move from Canada to the United Kingdom to sample an action research project undertaken with supervisors of dissertation students. The authors, Helen Burchell and Janet Dyson, together with Rosemary Allen, Pat Gidley, Mary Rees, and Marian Woolhouse, also illustrate—this time through artistic metaphor—how a reflective space was created. In that space, professors' tacit knowledge of dissertation research supervision surfaced in ways that both informed and deepened understanding of the instructors and ultimately the students with whom they interact.

Finally, Chapter 18, "The Faculty Academy: A Place for Grounding and Growth," returns readers to the United States to learn about a higher education reform initiative that brought a group of university professors together to grow their scholarship and their relationships with local schools and educators. The multi-author team of Lillian Benavente-McEnery, Blake Bickham, Christa A. Boske, Andrea Foster, Michele Kahn, Carrie Markello, Susan McCormack, Denise McDonald, Heidi Mullins, Angela López Pedrana, Joy C. Phillips, Rita P. Poimbeauf, Chris Witschonke, and Cheryl Craig employ the rhizome metaphor to illuminate the understandings they came to in their shared reflective space. Along the way, challenges experienced by members of the group are candidly discussed.

When combined, the four essays in Division 3 provide a rich cross-section of how international groups of teacher educators are researching their programs and their practices, developing their stances and identities, working rigorously in relationship with one another and the educational community at large, and transcending institutional and subject matter boundaries, all for the purpose of enhancing student learning.

CHAPTER 15

The Somehow of Teaching

SMALL GROUPS, COLLABORATION, AND THE SELF-STUDY OF TEACHER EDUCATION PRACTICES

Mary Lynn Hamilton
University of Kansas

> Mary Lynn Hamilton, Ph.D., is a professor of curriculum and teaching at the University of Kansas. She is a coeditor of *The International Handbook of Self-Study of Teaching and Teacher Education Practices* (2004) and the North American editor for *Teaching and Teacher Education.* Her research interests combine teachers' professional knowledge, issues of social justice, and the self-study of teaching practices.

ABSTRACT

The self-study of teacher education practices encourages work in small groups as a way to study practice and unite teacher educators' interests in practice and theory. In this chapter I offer a definition of the self-study of teacher education practices, suggest strategies with which to undertake self-study, provide examples of collaboration and small-group work, and finally, address the value of self-study as a way to contribute to and empower the work of teacher educators.

Most teacher educators enjoy probing their practice. With improvement as a focal point, these investigations can be private and internal or public among colleagues and friends. How to best convey ideas or to help students develop lines of inquiry serve as core issues as these teacher educators consider ways in which to develop their professional knowledge. While teaching itself can often be described as a solitary act, the development of professional practice and professional knowledge often occurs in relation to others. Individual, private monologues benefit all teacher educators, yet work with others can move them more deeply and more quickly into professional learning.

Better ways to foster the exploration of practice have long been sought and examined. Questions such as, "In what ways might we better support teacher learning and teacher research?" and "In what ways can we foster this learning process?" have been asked. Sometimes the response has come—learning in small groups and among community members may enhance the social construction of teaching knowledge. In fact, proponents of learning in small-group situations have existed in the field of education for some time (e.g., Clift, Veal, Holland, Johnson, & McCarthy, 1995) but the idea has not always been valued. Has there been work done that might inspire another look at the study of teaching practice in small groups? And how might work in small groups fit within the expectations for many American teacher educators to publish their work?

In this chapter I explore the value of self-study in the work of teacher educators with particular attention to small-group involvement as one way to unite teacher educators' interests in practice and theory. To do this, I define self-study of teacher education practices, suggest strategies with which to undertake self-study, provide examples of collaboration and small-group work, and finally, address how engaging in self-study can contribute to and empower the work of teacher educators. The community of teacher educators involved in this work believes that engaging in self-study can contribute to productive change in the ways we approach the preparation of teachers and the development of teacher educators' professional knowledge.

The Self-Study of Teaching and Teacher Education Practices

The self-study of teacher education practices has become one way to engage in the improvement of teaching as it emerges in relation to a growing interest in the roles of teacher educators (Korthagen, Loughran, & Lunenberg, 2005), their pedagogical understandings (Loughran, 2006), and the ways they develop their professional knowledge (Swennen & van der Klink, 2008). While many teacher educators may study their own teaching practices, consider their own actions, the actions of their students, and the ways that they enact their beliefs in their classrooms, the systematic examination of personal practice in their own classrooms has been somewhat disregarded because of pressures within institutions to publish more traditional research (Cole & Knowles, 2004). Recently, however, with the recognition of the self-study of teaching practices as a genre of research in teacher education (Borko, Liston, & Whitcomb, 2007), work of self-study by teacher educators has become more readily accepted in higher education (Loughran, 2007; Zeichner, 2007).

Self-study—the thoughtful, systematic, critical exploration of the complexity of one's own learning and teaching practice (Dinkelman, 2003; Samaras & Freese, 2006)—can be seen as a way to develop knowledge within particular practice settings, mesh with teacher educators' interests in deepening their knowledge of specific teaching contexts, and provide a way to examine more fully the practice of teacher educators (Loughran, 2004). Autobiographical and bound in the personal history, culture, and politics (Hamilton & Pinnegar, 1998), teacher educators bring their personal practical knowledge (e.g., Elbaz, 1983; Connelly & Clandinin, 1985), their personal stories and voices (Goodson & Walker, 1991) to self-study. In self-study, the self has a part in this work, but the focus is on the spaces where self, practice, and context (Bullough & Pinnegar, 2004) intertwine, serving to diminish the gap between theory and practice (Bullough, 1997; Hamilton, 2004).

Teacher educators (for the most part) thoughtfully consider their practice and understand that taking a static approach to teaching and practice confounds the uncertainties of classroom and context. However, the teacher educators' situation becomes more confounded amidst the pressures and demands of the academic environment. There are few times when teacher educators are *only* researchers or *only* practitioners. Recognizing the space between these identities as "working the dialectic," Cochran-Smith and Lytle (2004) describe the tension of "generating local knowledge of practice while making that knowledge accessible and usable in other contexts and thus helping to transform it into public knowledge" (p. 635). This is where those engaged in self-study often find themselves. Simultaneously they juggle many tasks and roles where they value both scholarship and practice and blur the distinctions made by others about professional practice and research in teacher education (Cochran-Smith, 2005).

Self-study serves as a tool to navigate these uncertainties of teaching and academia as teacher educators develop their teaching and understanding (Hamilton, Loughran, & Marcondes, 2008). This work can be attractive for its individual focus, yet it is its use in groups where the learning potential can be maximized. For those who do this work, self-study "holds invaluable promise for developing new understandings and producing new knowledge about teaching and learning" (Hamilton & Pinnegar, 1998, p. 243).

One way to consider self-study as a tool can be as the *somehow* of teaching (Clarke & Erickson, 2004a, 2004b). In his work on practical perspectives to curriculum, Schwab (1978) established four commonplaces within any curriculum as teachers, students, contents, and contexts (milieu). As Clarke and Erickson (2004b) explain, "for teaching to occur, someone (a teacher) must be teaching someone (a student) about something (a curriculum) at some place and some time (a [context] milieu)" (p. 209). Yet, they found that something needs to be added to underscore the importance of the development of professional practice—a fifth commonplace. They claim that for "teaching to occur, there must be a 'somehow,' a way for an educator to know, recognize, explore, and act upon his or her practice" (p. 209). That *somehow* is self-study. Examining the *somehow* of teaching through self-study can strengthen professional learning and understandings and our thinking about teacher education. While there are critiques of self-study:

- It is risky (Pinnegar & Russell, 1995; Bullough, 1997).
- It lacks generalizability (Grossman, 2005).
- It reveals short-comings (Louie, Drevdahl, Purdy, & Stackman, 2003).
- It seems self-praising rather than critical and entails circular ways of thinking (Fendler, 2003).
- It lacks a traditional research approach (Hamilton, 2004).
- It can be seen as a trend away from a modernist approach to research and toward a broadening of what counts as research (Bullough & Pinnegar, 2001).

There are many ways to engage in the work of self-study—individually, in groups with on-site colleagues, in groups with distant colleagues, and in groups with students. How best to engage in the *somehow* of teaching, a teacher educator might ask. How can I engage in a self-study in my classroom? Must I work with my colleagues? In the next few paragraphs I look at the elements of self-study for individuals and groups.

The Methodology of Self-Study

Before I present examples of self-studies to consider, let me outline briefly some critical points regarding the methodology of the *somehow* of teaching. Although this chapter has a focus on small groups and I emphasize that, I want to suggest that individual self-studies can be considered collaborative work, just not in a traditional sense. According to many dictionaries, collaboration defines work done with others in a joint venture. While this definition most often refers to identified others in close proximity, it is possible to use texts, ideas, and experiences as collaborators in the exploration of practice. I also believe that collaboration can occur across distances. Whether undertaken individually or in a group when doing self-study, teacher educators want to ensure good research practice by acting with integrity and demonstrating trustworthiness. Moreover, the depth of analysis needed to do this work can be done whether or not colleagues are readily available.

How do you do self-study? In the work of self-study, the *self* may be important, but contextual elements and theoretical perspectives also remain central as teacher educators generate knowledge about teaching and learning (Hamilton, Smith, & Worthington, 2008). LaBoskey offers five elements of self-study: it is self-initiated and focused; it is improvement-aimed; it is interactive; it includes multiple, mainly qualitative methods; and it defines validity as a process based on trustworthiness (LaBoskey, 2004, pp. 842–853). Even with these elements as a guide, self-study methodology can be difficult to outline because it is the stance of the teacher educator and the depth of the focus that drive the work. That is, the teacher educator must recognize the value of situating self within the context of a social constructed world, yet not be limited by his or her view. Moreover, the teacher educator must bring to bear the influence, or lack of influence, of the theoretical and experiential worlds.

In a self-study endeavor, teacher educators identify a problem or interest and move it from reflection on practice to research to be shared with other practitioners. To do this, they gather documentation from multiple sources to provide clear evidence as they move along in their inquiry. These sources provide clues necessary to analyze the work. Holding a focus on self, others are involved in the process with questions, sharing of their work, and so on. In practice, the professional identity and knowledge of teacher educators emerge as they interact with others. Each step of the way those involved in self-study act with integrity and trustworthiness, knowing they will share their work publicly to probe professional learning and the development of the professional knowledge base.

Whether engaged in self-study as an individual or a group, issues of integrity and trustworthiness (Hamilton & Pinnegar, 2000) must be addressed. To do this, the strategies used in studies must be explicit and the ways that beliefs and actions mesh—or not—must be clear. Honest engagement with students is expected. Working individually, teacher educators bring into the study voices from the texts they read or with whom they exchange ideas. Teacher educators engaged in collaborative work engage actively with colleagues in the endeavor (Kelchtermans & Hamilton, 2004). The critical steps for establishing the *somehow* of teaching include:

- explicit documentation of experiences as they occur
- connection to literature from the broader research base in teacher education to set the context
- details about the aspects of the relevant practices/issues
- written analysis of data collected for the study
- exchange of ideas in public forums with colleagues and interested others beyond the study group

Improving practice, enhancing learning, and contributing to knowledge about teaching (Hamilton, Loughran, & Marcondes, 2008) are three critical elements of the self-study of teacher education practices, and doing this requires a balance "between the way in which private experience can provide insight and solution for public issues and troubles and the way in which public theory can provide insight and solution for private trial" (Bullough & Pinnegar, 2001, p. 15).

One aspect of the interaction in self-study is dialogue. Dialogue can be an essential tool in small-group and collaborative settings. Discussed in detail elsewhere (Arizona Group, 2004, 2006), suffice it to say that dialogue is more than talk. In dialogue empathy, care, commitment to trustworthiness, and integrity play a part. Moreover, there exists a willingness to push beyond boundaries to foster crucial thinking about issues. While some groups doing self-study have a long history of mutual support and relationships, developing a dialogic relationship should be a requirement for all interested groups. For successful dialogue a "shared commitment must exist to respect each others' growth and allow for disagreement where uncomfortable ideas or opinions could be expressed and pursued" (Arizona Group, 2004, p. 1140).

THE TENUOUS NATURE OF CRITICAL FRIENDS

Dialogue in groups will hit moments of tensions as well as moments of feigned niceness. Hopefully the commitment to the study will help to refocus perspectives and the examination of practice. The role of critical friend or colleague requires commitment to the work, and walking this commitment requires particular attention to integrity and trustworthiness when the power differential is not balanced. When working with a department chair or a dean or any perceived authority, walking the line and being honest may take a toll on interactions. When working with students, the power differential can be great. If invited to participate but grades are involved, student definitions of "collaboration" may differ from those teaching. In these situations, teacher educators must work against the possibility of silencing and/or controlling the people with whom they want to work. Vigilance is required.

LOOKING AT SMALL-GROUP SELF-STUDY

Thus far, I have suggested self-study methodology as a way to engage in the study of practice and I have described elements and steps to consider as a part of that methodology, but what does self-study look like?

When doing self-study in small groups, collaboration would occur. In conversation, collaboration provides "spaces for teachers to become aware of and name what is learned and how it is learned" (Zembylas & Barker, 2002, p.

332). In these spaces teachers observe and consider their work (Hug & Möller, 2005) and engage in the "shared adventure" (Loughran & Northfield, 1998, p. 16) of exploring knowledge and practice. Collaborative self-study facilitates a synergistic experience where those involved address teaching in ways that "are rooted in a shared context [and] characterized by common experiences stemming from participation in a mutually constructed set of teacher education activities" (Dinkelman, 2003, p. 14). In fact, Barnes (1998) recognizes collaboration as critical to the work of self-study. Loughran and Northfield (1998) state that the "value of the involvement of others becomes evident in practice and is well demonstrated when interpretations, conclusions or situations resonate with others" (p. 12). The public nature of the work encourages teacher educators to consider and, if necessary, to reframe their knowledge and understandings (Barnes, 1998). What does that look like?

Long-Distance Small-Group Collaboration: The Arizona Group

The Arizona Group (Guilfoyle, Hamilton, Pinnegar, & Placier, 1994, 1995, 1996, 1997, 1998) has engaged in individual and collaborative self-studies that describe development of their professional knowledge and identities. From their entry into academe, these teacher educators discussed their experiences via journals, e-mail communiqués, and other qualitative strategies. Exploring experiences in their classrooms and their departments at their various universities, they juxtapose desires to improve their practice with the pressures to navigate the world of higher education. Initially this group came together because of perceived absences of sympathetic colleagues at their own institutions. Eventually they remained a collaborative group because of the power of the dialogue and relationship.

In an example of individual self-study fitting with the Group's work, Placier (1995) describes her embarrassing experiences of learning to teach at the university level. In her study she asks whether the research of others can understand her own experiences. As she details her grading dilemmas using notes from conversations with students, she talks about hearing "I have to have an A." She listens but does not really understand as their transmission models of teaching confront her transformative notions of teaching. On advice, she attempts to distance herself, but that contradicts her beliefs. She describes fiascos of the experience. In the end, she has the students answer the question about the grade they deserve and why. Still she struggled to come to terms with the chasm between her students and herself. She writes, "In retrospect and as a researcher, I am embarrassed by the ad hoc, individualistic qualities of my development as a college teacher" (p. 60) and wishes that she and her students could "resolve the grading dilemma together" (p. 61). For Placier, self-study provided her a tool to explore the intimacies of failure in a way that allowed her to pull apart the painful moments. The Group served as a listening, engaged critical friend during her experience. As you read her text you understand the commitment she has to her students, and see yourself in that experience.

In a collaborative piece, the Arizona Group used e-mail communiqués to explore issues and invite the readers to engage in the interpretation of their text. In "Obligations to Unseen Children" (Arizona Group, 1997) the Group addresses their struggles to learn to "walk the talk" or align belief with action in their practice. They struggle with a desire to engage students in dialogue and their students' resistance. They explore whether or not they can change students. In this work you can read the struggles they have and experience. The dialogue they share demonstrates how they both respect and push each other's thinking.

In both cases the teacher educators are at the heart of the story. More than once they assert their felt obligations to unseen children as their guide for choices made for teaching and their own learning. More than once they detail pedagogical moments that question and contribute to their professional learning. Individually and collaboratively, these teacher educators, like others who do this work, critically examine their ideas and experiences in the intimacy of a collegial group and in the public arena through writings and presentations. They use each other to confront blind spots and hold a light in the dark tunnel to expand their understandings of professional knowledge.

Examples of this sort of work include Bodone, Guðjónsdóttir, and Dalmau (2004), Freese, Kosnik, and LaBoskey (2000), and LaBoskey, Davies-Samway, and Garcia (1998).

Working with On-Site Colleagues

Another approach to self-study can be the creation of groups around a teaching-focused purpose with on-site colleagues. As an example, a group of colleagues at the University of Missouri (Placier, Cockrell, Burgoyne, Welch, Neville, & Eferakorho, 2005) came together to explore the design and enactment of a particular pedagogical method. These teacher educators (five faculty researchers and six graduate assistants) used student journals, observation, their own reflections, and e-mail memos to document and explore their teaching process. They sought a more meaningful way to address issues of diversity and social justice in their classrooms. Over the course of a semester they designed, presented, collaborated, and reflected together. Personally and pedagogically, it was not a smooth ride. Yet, their systematic study of their experience clearly documented the growth of their thinking and the responses of their students.

The teacher educators in this group were reminded to build trust and attend to potential differences. For the students, initial resistance dissolved slowly into some understanding of diversity, and the experiential nature of the method useful for pushing ideas emerged. Loughran and Northfield (1998) called attention to the importance of a critical "Other." For them, this "Other" is a colleague who helps in the reflective process by pushing on issues and examining ideas to develop perspective beyond the personal. In the participants' descriptions of the tensions as they emerged, we can read the hard moments faced and consider how that fits with our own experience.

Regarding collaborative self-study, examples of this work include Clift, Brady, Mora, Choi, and Stegemoller (2006), Lomax, Evans, and Parker (1998), and Samaras, Kayler, Rigsby, Weller, and Wilcox (2006). Please note that although I offer examples of groups of three or more, there are many self-studies that have been done in groups of two as cited throughout this chapter.

Working with Our Students

Another possibility for self-study comes in work done with preservice students. In one particular study Freese (2006) worked with a small group (eight) of students who used a broad selection of their writings and journal of experiences over a two-year period to explore their learning-to-teach process. Freese and her students turned this work into text that her future preservice students will use.

Another element of this work is that Freese used the work of her students to nudge forward her thinking about her own teaching. Freese and her students detailed experiences with classroom management, uncertainty, and preparation, as well as the move from self-focus to student-focus in their classrooms. As Freese wrote about her students, she also found that she gained insight into herself and the ways that she organized and presented theories and concepts to her students. Freese found that the students' self-studies "were invaluable sources of information about learning to teach, because these preservice teachers articulated and made public the personal knowledge, background and philosophies that influences their beliefs about teaching and their practice" (p. 77).

When working with students, the development of self-understanding and recognition is important (Korthagen, Kessels, Koster, Lagerwerf, & Wubbels, 2001). This self-understanding prepares the student for a potentially successful teaching career by framing the professional knowledge they have and will need to develop. Usually the teacher educator models self-study by engaging in her or his own study alongside the students. While engaging in an extended self-study may not be possible so early in the learning-to-teach process, this preliminary work in university classes can set the foundation for their work when they reach their own classrooms. Freese saw this self-study work as a step in this direction.

Studying a Program

Another small-group possibility involved the self-study of a teacher education program. At the University of British Columbia, teacher educators established a self-described alternative teacher education program based on the concepts of community and inquiry (Clarke, Erickson, Collins, & Phelan, 2005). With a firm commitment to preparing the best teachers possible, they found that the development of community and a strong practice of inquiry would best serve their students. Better described in detail elsewhere (Farr Darling, Erickson, & Clarke, 2007), suffice it to say that they developed community among those that serve the preparation of teachers—the teachers in school, the students, the supervisors, and the instructors. They assert that their view of teaching "is that it consists of a complex set of actions structured around sets of relationship and communicative practices that enable others to learn different forms of knowledge and ways of knowing" (p. 188). In fact, they see themselves creating a "community of memory" where the teacher educators, the teachers, and the students can look both forward and backward in time to facilitate the learning of professional knowledge. They came to see their self-study work as "a recursive process of doing, thinking about what was done, making adjustments, and doing again" (Clarke, Erickson, Collins, & Phelan, 2005, p. 175) and advocate that those engaged in self-study "strive to provide convincing and rigorous evidence" (p. 175) to present for consideration to the larger community of teacher educators.

Self-studies can also be done within programs (e.g., Freidus, 2005; McVarish & Rust, 2006), from virtual contexts (e.g., Ham & Davey, 2006; Johnston, Anderson, & DeMeulle, 1998), and among the arts (Weber & Mitchell, 2002).

INDIVIDUAL SELF-STUDY

As mentioned earlier, individuals can engage in a form of collaboration. While they may individually develop ideas, they engage in a hermeneutical frame where they read, critique, and reflect on text as well as the voices of colleagues that both support and help reframe ideas within the study (Kelchtermans & Hamilton, 2004). Bodone, Guðjónsdóttir, and Dalmau (2004) suggest "self-study research transcends the individual through collaborative, questioning, dialogic, and action-oriented processes that have been described as 'essential' to the dissemination of authentic educational knowledge" (p. 745).

Tidwell (2002) provides an example of individual self-study. As a teacher educator, she explores her work with her students in her own classroom. She writes that her "interest in better understanding this connection between my teaching beliefs and my teaching practice served as the catalyst for [this] self-study . . ." (p. 31). This struggle of matching belief with action is a reoccurring one among the works of self-study. Over the course of a semester Tidwell focuses her attention on relationships she has with particular students whose interactions and actions raise questions about the beliefs she thinks she has about teaching and choice.

In Tidwell's study, when she reveals troubling aspects of conceptions of herself as a teacher as she analyzes her teacher behavior in interactions with her preservice students, she allows us several points of comparison and contrast with our own teaching and our own understanding of the research of teacher-student interaction and the impact of preservice teaching on teacher education students. Tidwell (2002) exposes the balancing act teacher educators experience as they attempt to value individual students and meet perceived goals as teachers. In their teaching, teacher educators must look beyond the students in their university classrooms to the effects their actions might have on those unseen students in public schools. As her *somehow* of teaching, Tidwell used self-study to look directly and unwaveringly at her choices as a teacher educator for ways to improve her practice.

Examples of individual work in self-study include Berry (2007), Craig (2006), Dinkelman (2003), and Kitchen (2002). But even in those studies others necessarily inform the inquiries. In short, no one works devoid of others' input, albeit to varying degrees.

In each example above, the *somehow* of teaching can be seen. Each example suggests that teacher educators examine their practices for the purpose of pushing their understandings of teaching to better facilitate learning for their students and for themselves.

Conclusion

Professional learning results in qualitative changes in both actions and thinking. For the teacher's actions this means more effectivity. Rather than simply acting, teacher educators make well-considered judgments about the how, when, and why of action as they widen, deepen, and enrich their professional knowledge. The self-study of teacher education practices, the *somehow* of teaching, can be a tool, particularly within the context of small groups. After defining the self-study of teacher education practices and describing the methodology to undertake such an endeavor, I offered a variety of examples of self-study that centered on collaboration and small groups. From these examples the value of self-study as a tool to explore the *somehow* of teaching and teacher education seems apparent. Engaging in small groups who use the self-study of teacher education as their methodology can be an important tool to the examination of practice and the development of teacher educators' professional knowledge.

References

Arizona Group (alphabetical order: Guilfoyle, K., Hamilton, M. L., Pinnegar, S., & Placier, P.). (1994). Letters from beginners: Negotiating the transition from graduate student to assistant professor. *The Journal, 8*(2), 71–82.

Arizona Group. (1995). Becoming teachers of teachers: The paths of four beginners. In T. Russell & F. Korthagen (Eds.), *Teachers who teach teachers: Reflections of teacher education* (pp. 35–55). London: Falmer Press.

Arizona Group. (1996). Negotiating balance between reforming teacher education and forming self as teacher educator. *Teacher Education Quarterly, 23*(3), 153–168.

Arizona Group. (1997). Obligations to unseen children: Struggling to walk our talk in institutions of teacher education. In J. Loughran & T. Russell (Eds.), *Pedagogy for reflective practice: Teaching to teach with purpose and passion* (pp. 183–209). London: Falmer Press.

Arizona Group. (1998). Negotiating balance between reforming teacher education and forming self as teacher educator. In A. Cole, R. Elijah, & G. Knowles (Eds.), *The heart of the matter* (pp. 171–192). San Francisco: Caddo Press.

Arizona Group. (2004). The epistemological dimensions and dynamics of professional dialogue. In J. Loughran, M. L. Hamilton, V. LaBoskey, & T. Russell (Eds.), *International handbook of self-study of teaching and teacher education practices* (pp. 1109–1166). Dordrecht, the Netherland: Kluwer.

Arizona Group. (2006). Exploring the concept of dialogue in teaching practice. In C. Kosnik, C. Beck, & A. Freese (Eds.), *Making a difference in teacher education through self-study: Studies of personal, professional, and program renewal* (pp. 51–64). Dordrecht, the Netherlands: Kluwer.

Barnes, D. (1998). Looking forward: The concluding remarks at the Castle Conference. In M. L. Hamilton (Ed.), *Reconceptualizing teaching practice: Self-study in teacher education* (pp. ix–xiv). London: Falmer Press.

Berry, A. (2007). *Tensions in teaching about teaching: A self-study of the development of myself as a teacher educator.* Dordrecht: Springer.

Bodone, F., Guðjónsdóttir, H., & Dalmau, M. (2004). Revisioning and recreating practice: Collaboration in self-study. In J. Loughran, M. L. Hamilton, V. LaBoskey, & T. Russell (Eds.), *International handbook of self-study of teaching and teacher education practices* (pp. 743–784). Dordrecht, the Netherlands: Kluwer.

Borko, H., Liston, D., & Whitcomb, J. (2007). Genres of empirical research in teacher education. *Journal of Teacher Education, 58*(1), 3–11.

Bullough, R. V. (1997). Practicing theory and theorizing practice in teacher education. In J. Loughran & T. Russell (Eds.), *Teaching about teaching* (pp. 13–31). London/Washington, DC: Falmer Press.

Bullough, R. V., & Pinnegar, S. (2001). Guidelines for quality in autobiographical forms of self-study research. *Educational Researcher, 30*(3), 13–21.

Bullough, R. V., & Pinnegar, S. (2004). Thinking about the thinking about self-study. In J. Loughran, M. L. Hamilton, V. LaBoskey, & T. Russell (Eds.), *International handbook of self-study of teaching and teacher education practices* (pp. 313–342). Dordrecht: Kluwer Academic Publishers.

Clarke, A., & Erickson, G. (2004a). The nature of teaching and learning in self-study. In J. J. Loughran, M. L. Hamilton, V. K. LaBoskey, & T. L. Russell (Eds.), *The international handbook of self-study of teaching practices* (pp. 41–67). Dordrecht: Kluwer Academic Publishers.

Clarke, A., & Erickson, G. (2004b). Self-study: the fifth commonplace. *Australian Journal of Education, 48*(2), 199–212. Retrieved online April 16, 2006, from *Expanded Academic ASAP.* Thomson Gale. University of Kansas Libraries. Thomson Gale Document Number: A119611997

Clarke, A., Erickson, G., Collins, S., & Phelan, A. (2005). Complexity science and cohorts in teacher education. *Studying Teacher Education, 1*(2), 159–177.

Clift, R., Brady, P., Mora, R., Choi, S. J., & Stegemoller, J. (2006). From self-study to collaborative self-study to collaborative self-study of collaboration: The evolution of a research team. In C. Kosnik, C. Beck, A. Freese, & A. Samaras (Eds.), *Making a difference in teacher education through self-study* (pp. 85–100). Dordrecht, the Netherlands: Springer.

Clift, R. T., Veal, M. L., Holland, P., Johnson, M., & McCarthy, J. (1995). *Collaborative leadership and shared decision making: Teachers, principals, and university professors.* New York: Teachers College Press.

Cochran-Smith, M. (2005). Teacher educators as researchers: Multiple perspectives. *Teaching and teacher education, 21*(2), 219–225. Dordrecht, the Netherlands: Springer.

Cochran-Smith, M., & Lytle, S. L. (2004). Practitioner inquiry, knowledge, and university culture. In J. Loughran, M. L. Hamilton, V. LaBoskey, & T. Russell (Eds.), *International handbook of research of self-study of teaching and teacher education practices* (pp. 601–649). Dordrecht, the Netherlands: Kluwer.

Cole, A. L., & Knowles, J. G. (2004). Research, practice and academia in North America. In J. Loughran, M. L. Hamilton, V. LaBoskey, & T. Russell (Eds.), *International handbook of research of self-study of teaching and teacher education practices* (pp. 451–482). Dordrecht, the Netherlands: Kluwer.

Connelly, F. M., & Clandinin, D. J. (1985). Personal practical knowledge and the modes of knowing: Relevance for teaching and learning. In E. Eisner (Ed.), *Learning and teaching the ways of knowing, the 84th Yearbook of the National Society for the Study of Education* (pp. 174–198). Chicago: University of Chicago Press.

Craig, C. (2006). Change, changing, and being changed: A self-study of a teacher educator's becoming real in the throes of urban school reform. *Studying teacher education, 2*(1), 105–116.

Dinkelman, T. (2003). Self-study in teacher education: A means and ends tool for promoting reflective teaching. *Journal of Teacher Education, 54*(1), 6–19.

Elbaz, F. (1983). *Teacher thinking: A study of practical knowledge.* London: Croom Helm.

Farr Darling, L., Erickson, G., & Clarke, A. (Eds.). (2007). *Collective improvisation in a teacher education community.* Dordrecht, the Netherlands: Springer.

Fendler, L. (2003). Teacher reflection in a hall of mirrors: Historical influences and political reverberations. *Educational Researcher, 32*(3), 16–25.

Freese, A. R. (2006). Transformation through self-study: The voice of preservice teachers. In C. Kosnik, C. Beck, A. R. Freese, & A. Samaras (Eds.), *Making a difference in teacher education through self-study* (pp. 65–79). Dordrecht: Springer.

Freese, A., Kosnik, C., & LaBoskey, V. (2000). Three teacher educators explore their understandings and practices of self-study through narrative. In J. Loughran & T. Russell (Eds.), *Exploring myths and legends of teacher education* (75–79). Proceedings of the Third International Conference on Self Study of Teacher Education Practices. Herstmonceux Castle, East Sussex, England. Kingston, Ontario: Queen's University.

Freidus, H. (2005). Through a murky mirror: Self-study of a program in reading and literacy. In C. Kosnik, C. Beck, A. Freese, & A. Samaras (Eds.), *Making a difference in teacher education through self-study* (pp. 167–183). Dordrecht, the Netherlands: Kluwer Academic Publishers.

Goodson, I., & Walker, R. (1991). *Biography, identity and schooling: Episodes in educational research*. London: Falmer Press.

Grossman, P. (2005). Research on pedagogical approaches in teacher education. In M. Cochran-Smith & K. M. Zeichner (Eds.), *Studying Teacher Education* (pp. 425–476). Washington, DC/Mahwah, NJ/London: AERA/Lawrence Erlbaum Associates.

Ham, V., & Davey, R. (2006). Is virtual teaching, real teaching? In C. Kosnik, C. Beck, & A. Freese (Eds.), *Making a difference in teacher education through self-study: Studies of personal, professional, and program renewal* (pp. 101–116). Dordrecht, the Netherlands: Kluwer.

Hamilton, M. L. (2004). Professional Knowledge, Self-Study and Teacher Education. In J. Loughran, M. L. Hamilton, V. LaBoskey, & T. Russell (Eds.), *The international handbook of self-study of teaching and teacher education practices* (pp. 375–419). Dordrecht, the Netherlands: Kluwer Academic Publishers.

Hamilton, M. L., Loughran, J., & Marcondes, M. I. (2008). Teacher educators, student teachers and the self-study of teaching practices. In A. Swennen & M. van der Klink (Eds.), *Becoming teacher educators*. Dordrecht: Springer.

Hamilton, M. L., & Pinnegar, S. (1998). Conclusion: The value and the promise of self-study. In M. L. Hamilton et al. (Eds.), *Reconceptualizing teaching practice: Self-study in teacher education* (pp. 234–246). London: Falmer Press.

Hamilton, M. L., & Pinnegar, S. (2000). On the threshold of a new century: Trustworthiness, integrity, and self-study in teacher education. *Journal of Teacher Education, 51*(3), 234–240.

Hamilton M. L., Smith, L., & Worthington, K. (2008). Fitting the methodology with the research: An exploration of autobiography, self-study and auto ethnography. *Studying Teacher Education, 4*(1), 17–28.

Hug, B., & Möller, C. (2005). Collaboration and connectedness in two teacher educators' shared self-study. *Studying Teacher Education, 1*(2), 123–140.

Johnston, J., Anderson, R., & DeMeulle, L. (1998). Prospects for collaborative self-study on the internet. In M. L. Hamilton (Ed.), *Reconceptualizing teaching practice: Self-study in teacher education* (pp. 208–223). London: Falmer Press.

Kelchtermans, G., & Hamilton, M. L. (2004). The dialectics of passion and theory. In J. Loughran, M. L. Hamilton, V. LaBoskey, & T. Russell (Eds.), *International handbook of self-study of teaching and teacher education practices* (pp. 785–810). Dordrecht, the Netherlands: Kluwer.

Kitchen, J. (2002). Becoming a relational teacher educator: A narrative inquirer's self-study. In C. Kosnik, A. Freese, & A. Samaras (Eds.), *Making a difference in teacher education through self-study* (pp. 36–42). Proceedings of the Fourth International Conference on Self-Study of Teacher Education Practices, Herstmonceux, East Sussex, England. Toronto, Ontario: OISE, University of Toronto.

Korthagen, F. A. J., with Kessels, J., Koster, B., Lagerwerf, B., & Wubbels, T. (2001). *Linking practice and theory: The pedagogy of realistic teacher education.* Mahwah, NJ: Lawrence Erlbaum Associates.

Korthagen, F., Loughran, J., & Lunenberg, M. (2005). Teaching teachers—Studies into the expertise of teacher educators: An introduction to this theme issue. *Teaching and teacher education, 21*(2), 107–115.

LaBoskey, V. K. (2004). The methodology of self-study and its theoretical underpinnings. In J. Loughran, M. L. Hamilton, V. K. LaBoskey, & T. Russell (Eds.), *International handbook of self-study of teaching practices* (pp. 817–869). London: Kluwer Press.

LaBoskey, V. K., Davies-Samway, K., & Garcia, S. (1998). Cross-institutional action research: A collaborative self-study. In M. L. Hamilton (Ed.), *Reconceptualizing teaching practice* (pp. 154–166). London: Falmer Press.

Lomax, P., Evans, M., & Parker, Z. (1998). For liberation . . . not less for love: A self-study of teacher educators working with a group of teachers who teach pupils with special needs. In M. L. Hamilton et al. (Eds.), *Reconceptualizing teaching practice: Self-study in teacher education* (pp. 167–177). London: Falmer Press.

Loughran, J. J. (2004). A history and context of self-study of teaching and teacher education practices. In J. Loughran, M. L. Hamilton, V. LaBoskey, & T. Russell (Eds.), *International handbook of self-study of teaching and teacher education practices* (pp. 7–39). Dordrecht: Kluwer Academic Publishers.

Loughran, J. (2006). *Developing a pedagogy of teacher education: Understanding teaching and learning about teaching.* Oxford, UK: Routledge.

Loughran, J. J. (2007). Researching teacher education practices: Responding to the challenges, demands, and expectations of self-study. *Journal of Teacher Education, 58*(1), 12–20.

Loughran, J. J., & Northfield, J. (1998). A framework for the development of self-study practice. In M. L. Hamilton et al. (Eds.), *Reconceptualizing teaching practice: Self-study in teacher education* (pp. 7–18). London: Falmer Press.

Louie, B., Drevdahl, D., Purdy, J., & Stackman, R. (2003). Advancing the scholarship of teaching through collaborative self-study. *Journal of Higher Education, 74*(2), 150–177.

McVarish, J., & Rust, F. (2006). Unsquaring teacher education: Reshaping teacher education in the context of a Research I University. In C. Kosnik, C. Beck, & A. Freese (Eds.), *Making a difference in teacher education through self-study: Studies of personal, professional, and program renewal* (pp. 185–201). Dordrecht, the Netherlands: Kluwer.

Pinnegar, S., & Russell, T. (1995). Introduction: Self-study and living educational theory. *Teacher Education Quarterly, 22*(3), 5–9.

Placier, M. (1995). "But I have to have an A": Probing the cultural meanings and ethical dilemmas of grades in teacher education. *Teacher Education Quarterly, 22*(3), 45–64.

Placier, P., Cockrell, K., Burgoyne, S., Welch, S., Neville, H., & Eferakorho, J. (2005). Theater of the Oppressed as an instructional practice. In C. Kosnik, C. Beck, A. R.

Freese, & A. Samaras (Eds.), *Making a difference in teacher education through self-study* (pp. 131–146). Dordrecht, the Netherlands: Springer.

Samaras, A., & Freese, A. (2006). *Self-study of teaching practices.* New York: Peter Lang.

Samaras, A., Kayler, M., Rigsby, L., Weller, K., & Wilcox, D. (2006). Self-study of the craft of faculty team teaching in a non-traditional teacher education program. *Studying Teacher Education, 2*(1), 43–57.

Schwab, J. J. (1978). The practical: A language for the curriculum. In I. Westbury & N. J. Wilkof (Eds.), *Joseph J. Schwab: Science, curriculum, and liberal education— Selected essays* (pp. 287–321). Chicago: University of Chicago Press.

Swennen, A., & van der Klink, M. (2008). *Becoming a teacher educator.* Dordrecht: Springer.

Tidwell, D. (2002). A balancing act: Self-study in valuing the individual student. In J. Loughran & T. Russell (Eds.), *Improving teacher education practices through self-study* (pp. 30–42). London: Routledge-Falmer.

Weber, S., & Mitchell, C. (2002). Academic literary performance, embodiment, and self-study: When the shoe doesn't fit: Death of a salesman. In C. Kosnik, A. Freese, & A. Samaras (Eds.), *Making a difference in teacher education through self-study* (pp. 121–124). Proceedings of the Fourth International Conference on Self-Study of Teacher Education Practices, Herstmonceux, East Sussex, England. Toronto, Ontario: OISE, University of Toronto.

Zeichner, K. (2007). Accumulating knowledge across self-studies in teacher education. *Journal of Teacher Education, 58*(1), 36–46.

Zembylas, M., & Barker, H. B. (2002). Preservice teacher attitudes and emotions: Individual spaces, community conversations and transformations. *Research in Science Education, 32*(3), 329–351.

CHAPTER 16

The Research Issues Table

A PLACE OF POSSIBILITIES FOR THE EDUCATION OF TEACHER EDUCATORS

Pam Steeves
University of Alberta

Ji-Sook Yeom
Konkuk University

Debbie Pushor
University of Saskatchewan

Carla Nelson
Tyndale University College

Bosire Monari Mwebi
St. Francis Xavier University

M. Shaun Murphy
University of Saskatchewan

Anne Murray Orr
St. Francis Xavier University

Florence Glanfield
University of Alberta

Janice Huber
University of Regina

D. Jean Clandinin
University of Alberta

Pam Steeves, Ph.D., was an elementary teacher and teacher librarian before completing her Ph.D. Her dissertation focused on a narrative inquiry into what it means to experience continual becoming in a situation of transition for a teacher and principal on a school landscape. As a Horowitz Scholar and currently as an assistant adjunct professor, Pam continues her association with the CRTED at the University of Alberta.

Ji-Sook Yeom, Ph.D., completed her doctoral and postdoctoral program at the Centre for Research for Teacher Education and Development (CRTED) at the University of Alberta. She is now an associate professor at Konkuk University in South Korea. Returning to CRTED in 2007 for her sabbatical leave, her research centered on the lives of Korean mothers and children who came to Canada temporarily for their children's education.

Debbie Pushor, Ph.D., is an associate professor in the Department of Curriculum Studies at the University of Saskatchewan in Canada. Her program of research centers on parent engagement and parent knowledge. Recent publications include articles in *Education Canada, Welcoming Parents: Educators as Guest Hosts on School Landscapes*, and in the *Journal for Teacher Education, Navigating Sites for Narrative Inquiry*, cowritten with D. Jean Clandinin and Anne Murray Orr.

Carla Nelson, Ph.D., is director of the preservice teacher program at Tyndale University College in Toronto, Ontario. As well as being an educator for many years, she completed her terminal degree at the University of Alberta. She has helped coordinate Canadian teachers to participate in programs of professional development for teachers in Kenya, Rwanda, Bolivia, and India, and continues to focus her research on teachers in transition.

Bosire Monari Mwebi, Ph.D., is an assistant professor of education at St. Francis Xavier University. He started his teaching career in Kenya as a teacher, inspector of schools, and administrator in the Ministry of Education. He has a Bachelor of Education from the University of Nairobi and obtained his advanced degrees at the University of Alberta. His research interests include: narrative inquiry; adolescent sexual health and HIV; and alternative placement and cultural diversity.

M. Shaun Murphy, Ph.D., is an assistant professor in curriculum studies at the University of Saskatchewan. He was a primary classroom teacher for twenty years. His current research focuses on narrative inquiry, teachers and children's curriculum making in schools, and the ways in which they take up identities in relation to subject matter.

Anne Murray Orr, Ph.D., is an associate professor of literacy and curriculum studies at St. Francis Xavier University, Nova Scotia. Her research program includes narrative inquiries with classroom teachers to better understand how children, families, teachers, and administrators experience life in schools.

Florence Glanfield, Ph.D., is an associate professor of mathematics education at the University of Alberta whose research interest is mathematics teacher development. Active in provincial, national, and international mathematics education organizations, her career has included opportunities to teach, work with students and teachers in all geographic regions of Canada, develop provincial mathematics curriculum, participate in implementation of curriculum, and develop student assessment materials.

Janice Huber, Ph.D., works in preservice and graduate teacher education at St. Francis Xavier University. She completed doctoral study in teacher education at the University of Alberta where she and Karen Keats Whelan coauthored a paper-formatted dissertation of their inquiries with teachers and principals into narrative understandings of identity and diversity.

D. Jean Clandinin, Ph.D., is professor and director of the Centre for Research for Teacher Education and Development, University of Alberta. Prior to completing her doctorate at OISE/University of Toronto, in 1983, she worked as a teacher, counselor, and school psychologist in Edmonton and Toronto. In 1993 she was awarded the American Educational Research Association Early Career Award and over the past fourteen years she has been honored with the CEA's Whitworth Award, the Gordin Kaplan Award, Division B (Curriculum Studies) of AERA's Lifetime Achievement Award, and a Killam Professorship. She was elected vice president of Division B in 1995 and served a two-year term.

ABSTRACT

In this chapter, we present a story of a voluntary gathering place where, over time, trusting relationships are shaped through storytelling as teacher educators continue to become. As Greene (1993) reminds us, these kinds of spaces need to be "deliberately created" (p. 219) so that in our continuous becoming as teacher educators and human beings we might live out what Dewey (1938) taught us so well, that is, that life *is* education. Our chapter unfolds as a multivocal account of teacher educators reflecting on their lives and learning experiences in this small-group setting. To provide an understanding of the learning in teacher education that happens in such a place, we story our living out of relational knowing, respectful listening, response, inquiry, "world" traveling, attending to tensions, learning to think narratively, and becoming teacher educators. What we open up in this chapter, then, is a subtle but radical shift in how teacher educators can be educated.

Over the past few decades, important study has been undertaken into the experiences of pre- and in-service teachers as they become teachers (Carter, 1993; Clandinin, Davies, Hogan, & Kennard, 1993; Craig, 2003; Hollingsworth, Dybdahl, & Minarik, 1993; Ladson-Billings, 2001; Lyons & LaBoskey, 2002; Miller, 1990; Vinz et al., 1996). The experiences of teachers as they compose their lives, in part through interactions with pre- and in-service teachers in undergraduate and graduate programs of teacher education (Hamilton & Pinnegar, 1998; Russell & Korthagen, 1995), have also become an increasing focus of study, as has the need for the ongoing professional development of teacher educators (Lunenberg, 2002). Yet, within this growing knowledge base, little attention has been turned toward the experiences of teacher educators as they become teacher educators, that is, little attention has focused on the fine-grained experiences, in particular places or spaces, that shape how teacher educators, in part, learn to become teacher educators in the midst of graduate study in postsecondary institutions. Indeed, Cochran-Smith (2003) outlines that for too long there has been a "lack of attention to a curriculum for teacher educators" (p. 6).

We, too, are interested in the education of teacher educators. Yet, what we open up in this chapter is a subtle but radical shift in *how* teacher educators can be educated. Our hope then is that our chapter brings to life how *our lives* as teacher educators have been shaped through a process of narrative inquiry in relationship. We invite you to travel with us, and through dwelling in the stories shared here, live through some of our experiences of being and becoming teacher educators.

What we share is a multivocal (Greene, 1995) account of teacher educators reflecting on their experiences of learning to become teacher educators in a small-group setting in higher education. We were not all in this place at the same time, but we all experienced the place at one point in our graduate work. Although the setting is small and has endured for many years, the ideas that shape this place are large and have a history of their own.

Embedded within our experiences within this setting are our living out of who we are and who we might become in relation with one another and with ideas such as the responsive community drawn from Dewey (1938); thinking and becoming narratively drawn from Clandinin and Connelly (2000); relational knowing drawn from Hollingsworth et al. (1993); respectful listening and response in dialogue drawn from Buber (1947) and Noddings (1993); "world" traveling drawn from Lugones (1987); and, becoming human beings (Greene, 1993) and teacher educators (Vinz, 1997) in a diverse world. While these ideas are not new in the broad curriculum of teacher education, in this chapter we show how our continuous laying of our lives alongside one another's lives with these ideas as a kind of language that mediates the discourse of our meetings has shaped embodied learnings that now reverberate in our identities as teacher educators.

A Place for Thinking Narratively about Our Becoming Teacher Educators

The place we each rekindled as we foregrounded our experiences of becoming teacher educators is a storied place known as the centre for Research for Teacher Education and Development (CRTED) at the University of Alberta in Edmonton. (This storied place was named and created the Centre for Research for Teacher Education and Development in 1991 with the support of former president of the University of Alberta, Dr. Myer Horowitz, and Dr. Bob Patterson, the dean of the Faculty of Education at the time. The director of the CRTED since its founding, Dr. D. Jean Clandinin, is acclaimed within the University of Alberta research community, as well as nationally and internationally for research in teacher education and the development of narrative inquiry as a research methodology. Over its eighteen-year history, the Centre has brought together diverse people, including graduate students from within the Faculty of Education and from across campus, teachers, principals, and administrators as well as national and international scholars from around the world. At the CRTED, interconnected office spaces offer a rich and shared environment for present and future teacher educators to work collaboratively for the purpose of furthering knowledge with a central focus on children's, teachers', parents', student teachers', and administrators' educational experiences. Please see Steeves, 2004, for a further account of the CRTED.) Central to the life of the CRTED is the weekly "research issues" table, which is a voluntary gathering for those associated specifically with the CRTED along with graduate students and faculty from other departments at the University of Alberta and visiting scholars who are interested in matters of research for teacher education and development (Steeves, 2004).

The meetings of around fifteen to twenty people are held at noon on Tuesdays from September to July and have been sustained over seventeen years. Research issues has no set agenda; rather it is a place where conversation and inquiry unfold according to the issues and interests of those who are willing and able to attend. The group is necessarily fluid in recognition of people's complex lives, but always there is a sense of invitation and belonging for participants, past and present. Some of the authors of this chapter have been associated with the Centre since its beginning; some of us have come to the Centre more recently.

The room where research issues is held is itself a kind of memory box alive with the spirit of those who have inscribed their lives in this moving community as years go by. Artwork and handiwork upon the walls, photo collages, a long-used tea service and other memorabilia evoke a sense that those who are there belong to a larger, ever more diverse, intergenerational community from close by and around the world.

The heart of this gathering room is the people who come to sit around a large "kitchen table" made up of many tables pushed together. On any given Tuesday, no one knows ahead of time who will join the table or what the conversation will bring forward. Instead, each research issues conversation evolves in unique ways because agendas are not prescribed but rather are drawn naturally from individual people's lives and research puzzles. While participants bring a range of research puzzles and methodologies to the conversation, each person is invited to share her inquiries in conversation. As this conversational inquiry moves gently around the table one to another, participants come to know the necessity of creating a safe and caring tone for sharing work and experiences in their lives, for inquiring and voicing concerns related to issues of research and teacher education.

Protocols of being part of a responsive community are learned through participation and are honed over time, yet have continued to shift with time. Traditions come into being as different participants leave their mark. Always, each conversation begins as a circle around the table where people name themselves one by one. Sometimes those gathered simply want to say their names and listen. Yet everyone knows they do have opportunities to speak of matters important in their lives as people and as researchers and educators in teacher education. As time goes on, participants become more skillful in voicing what is on their minds, while being respectful listeners of others in the community. Newcomers may allow themselves to sense the way of the table and join in. Attending through such a responsive community where a sense of belonging is experienced, participants deepen and broaden their knowing in becoming teacher educators. Now scattered across Canada and the world in diverse teacher education contexts, our learning through participation in Tuesday research issues tables pulsates in our lives and continuing learning as teacher educators.

In what follows, we show some of our "in the flesh" learning through living, which includes relational knowing, respectful listening, response, inquiry, "world" traveling, attending to tensions, learning to think narratively, and becoming teacher educators to provide an understanding of the learning in teacher education that happens in such a place. In authoring the narratives that bring to life our learning through living in relation with others at the research issues table and with each of these ideas, we each individually draw on our experiences of participation. These narratives then, cut across the eighteen-year history of the CRTED and the research issues table, and they show that the co-constructing of this space is much bigger than the ten of us. This space has been, and continues to be, shaped over time by many lives.

RELATIONAL KNOWING

Over the years, Hollingsworth et al.'s ideas (1993) about "relational knowing" have shaped the living and knowing at our table place. Her ideas suggest "structures that promote sustained conversation around teacher initiated issues," "a commitment to inquiry," and a "celebration of teachers' passion and commitment to altering relations of domination and subordination through relational knowing" (p. 32). It is at our research issues table that we begin to know what it might feel like to live with these ideas because, in coming to the table, participants are safe to bring their whole lives. As such, storied conversations are alive with passion, tensions, and imagining. Opportunities for sustained conversation over weeks, months, even years enable relational knowing as participants, over time, are able to share stories of their experiences and to relate to the lived experiences of others in ways that resonate or conjure questions or awakenings. Facts are not accumulated as separate things, but, rather, through relationships with one another, understanding deepens, broadens, and intertwines in complex ways. Let's begin with our first story.

COMING TO LIVE AND KNOW RELATIONAL KNOWING

I recall thinking that while I had a definition of relational knowing in my head, I was not quite sure what it looked like in practice. My years as a teacher in my classroom space had taught me to work on my own alongside children. Even the phrase "on my own alongside" suggests a kind of relational knowing. As a classroom teacher I was never on my own, but what kind of relational knowing was this compared to the relational knowing of working within an academic community? The power structure of the classroom shifted relational knowing away from what I experienced at the center and what I experienced at the center then shifted the relational knowing I experienced in my classroom.

The centre brought me to a deeper understanding of relational knowing. The relational knowing that took place at the center table was important in shaping my experience of knowing with others. At first I experienced this as a tension. What if I could not do it? What did it mean to work relationally? As my experience unfolded at the center I came to understand this meant more than doing your part of a project and then integrating it with the work of other group members. Relational work in this space meant relational knowing. I began to know with community, which was different from knowing in community.

Week by week, as I turned to face others at the center table in a pattern of speaking, listening, and response, I became aware of life stories unfolding, my own caught within others' inquiry threads. The relational knowing at the center table shaped my inquiries into the relational knowledge of teachers and children, it highlighted the nested knowledge of a community that is like a web of connected strands. In this web of knowing my location is along one of the strands, the center of the web is what we all hold in our minds and bodies, it is not a location or person, it is what we make together.

RESPECTFUL LISTENING

At the table, participants come to know a way of listening respectfully. Drawing on Noddings (1993), we consider engagement in dialogue at the table within the spirit of encounter. In this way, listening respectfully becomes a commitment "to the living other who addresses us"; a commitment to imagine what another "is going through" (p. 8). For Noddings, respectful listening requires attending with your heart. As we try to live out respectful listening and support at our research issues table, they become cohesive threads both binding people and freeing them to imagine in relationship. As participants become more attentive to one another's lives around the table, they become more sensitive to diverse situations shaping lives. Participants may hear and feel new imaginings of narrative inquiry and other methodologies, dilemmas around ethical concerns, and tensions around landscapes and the shaping of identities. Through all of this, rich and multiple perspectives from which to frame research, wonders and puzzles for education evolve alongside a sense of hopefulness from which to imagine new possibilities.

COMING TO LIVE AND KNOW RESPECTFUL LISTENING

One Tuesday afternoon when I returned to the table during my sabbatical leave after ten years of teaching in Korea, Yi Li, who emigrated from China to Canada to start graduate school, shared stories of feeling fear and disruption during her first teaching experience at the University of Alberta.

As I listened attentively to Yi Li's story of her experience, it reminded me of my first year teaching experience in Korea after seven years of studying at the University of Alberta. Soon after Yi Li shared her story, I shared a story of my struggle with uncertainty and ambiguity as I entered into a new professional knowledge landscape as a beginning teacher educator. Later in the circle of sharing, Jennifer Mitton also felt a resonant remembering as she listened to Yi Li's and my stories and recalled her experiences as a Canadian teacher learning to teach in a local high school in Turkey. Our listening to and connecting of our experiences through our stories became the seed of our continuing conversation of reflecting upon what our experiences might mean for us and other teachers in cross-cultural contexts. Through listening to each other's stories with mutual respect, sharing our own experiences and lives, and valuing different experiences in different cultures, the three of us were able to see how our identities as teachers were shaped through cross-cultural teaching experiences. This process also helped us to understand who we are now becoming as teacher educators. Listening respectfully to one another's stories was a reflective and relational experience. It enabled us not only to see possibilities in our own pasts, but also to imagine our future stories as teacher educators.

RESPONSE

At the research issues table, respectful listening as encounter leads naturally to response in an "I and thou" engagement (Buber, 1947). Following Noddings (1993), we embrace listening and response in dialogic relation as an embodiment of ethical practice because interwoven with stories of teacher education and research are the stories to live by of participants' lives (Connelly & Clandenin, 1999). Attending from these stories to live by enables unique patterns of response to evolve; a caring word of encouragement, a question to orient and see the situation differently. Perhaps another story is given as response, a story that resonates for the listener. Yet, often, response resides in silent grace; a felt sense of being in relation with one another is experienced; no words need interrupt.

COMING TO LIVE AND KNOW RESPONSE

Last spring, I was writing my doctoral proposal. Day by day, as the leaves gradually unfurled on the branches of the trees outside my window, this piece of writing began to unfold and take shape. I had begun by writing about my first year of teaching, far from home, and the memories that continued to trouble me, as I relived that experience. One day, Jean, my advisor, suggested that I read that part of my story to the group at research issues. Previously I had shared my thinking about my own inquiry and about a variety of issues at this table, but I had not read my own writing aloud before. I was a little nervous, although I knew others would respond to my words with respect and caring.

So, I took a deep breath and began to read my story. I read about four pages. Wayne Gorman was looking at me intently when I looked up. For a moment no one said much. Then Kris Wells commented on how he liked the way I return to the story from different perspectives over time. Vera Caine asked if my use of the word comfort will be a focus in my proposal, and I was not sure. At first I had thought so, but I seemed to be moving away from it. Wayne asked me if I was still in touch with Calvin, the child around whom I have told the story, and I regretfully told him that I was not. We wondered what Calvin would say about my memories of his short-lived experience of the second grade. Marni Pearce mentioned that this story reminded her of an experience from her first year of teaching, and she shared a short narrative about a boy who did not seem to fit easily within the story of school, as Calvin had not.

There was more talk around the table and I found I was not nervous now, but instead caught up in the conversation that arose within the space that my story had opened up. I felt ready to return to my writing with new perspectives and ideas dancing through my head.

A PLACE OF INQUIRY

Our table embodies Dewey's (1938) idea that education is a social experience and that experience is education. Through the responsive community we create and negotiate over time, we are given the opportunity, through interaction and continuity, to come to know educative experiences deeply. In this way, following Dewey, opportunities for continual growth and reconstruction emerge. Each weekly conversation evolves in unique ways because agendas are not prescribed but rather are drawn naturally from individual people's lives and research puzzles.

Research issues is not an answer place. The spirit of inquiry embodied at the table means there are no "right answers" to be accumulated as "things" to have more or less of. Rather, there are multiple perspectives from which to broaden and deepen understanding, from which newly imagined questions can be created. Graduate students and scholars in teacher education are welcomed to be uncertain, tentative, and unique. There is no separation by speeches one above the other. Everyone has something to offer. In being present with one another, accepting, listening, and learning from one another, those who gather can become comfortable enough to be vulnerable, to surrender some of their own ideologies and "expert knowing" as teacher educators. A transitioning from "certain to fluid researchers" (Schwab, 1978) takes place as participants begin to learn along the way.

COMING TO LIVE AND KNOW A PLACE OF INQUIRY

During my yearlong inquiry into the positioning of parents on school landscapes, I moved between the field—a large suburban elementary school—and the center table. I anticipated those Tuesday times when I could take my research stories, my questions, and my wonders to the center table and invite others to think or ponder alongside me.

As my inquiry unfolded, I came to see "welcoming families to schools" as a central and emerging theme in my field text. As I moved from field text to research text, though, and began to unpack more deeply the idea of "welcoming," I was troubled by assumptions I began to see as inherent in this concept. If the principal and educators are doing the welcoming, what does that imply about their power and position on the landscape—and that of parents? Because I knew the research issues table to be a place of multiple perspectives, one that would broaden and deepen my understandings through the sharing of diverse experiences and asking of thoughtful questions, I talked to others at the table about the sense of knowing I held previously and the uncertainty and tentativeness with which I was now thinking about "welcoming." In response, Wayne Gorman told stories of First Nations parents and families. ("The Constitution Act of 1982 specifies that the Aboriginal Peoples in Canada consist of three groups—Indians, Inuit and Métis. First Nations, Inuit and Métis peoples have unique heritages, languages, cultural practices and spiritual beliefs. The term First Nations came into common use in the 1970s to replace Indian, which some people found offensive." See the Assembly of First Nations website: http://www.afn.ca.) *He wondered whether all families are welcomed to school landscapes or if the welcoming is extended only to families who meet the expectations of the school. In adding this complexity, he asked me to keep thinking about the power and hierarchy inherent in educator-parent relationships. Heather Raymond, whose own inquiry focused on stories of her advocacy, alongside parents, for the education of children with developmental delays, raised questions about whether welcoming was a concept of hospitality or one of inclusion. The fluidity of the learning, as the conversation connected our multiple research puzzles and how each of us came to our knowing, called me to live as a researcher, awake to holding onto questions rather than seeking answers for them.*

"WORLD" TRAVELING

Lugones (1987) articulates for us the kind of learning we live through as we participate at the table. She calls us to stay at the work of shifting from "arrogant to loving perception through 'world' traveling," which she describes in the following way:

> The reason why I think that traveling to someone's "world" is a way of identifying with them is because by traveling to their "world" we can [begin to] understand *what it is to be them and what it is to be ourselves in their eyes.* Only when we have traveled to each other's "worlds" are we fully subject to each other. (p. 17, italics in original)

This kind of traveling involves imagination. Relationship ignites imagination. Many languages are spoken at the table, and other ways of being in the world are made meaningful through conversation and engagements with one another over time.

COMING TO LIVE AND KNOW "WORLD" TRAVELING

I have been wondering about the "world"—in Lugones's (1987) sense of "world," of teacher education. It is, at times, an unwelcoming world, a world that is inhabited by a select few whose sacred story of teacher development is well-entrenched. In certain spaces, it is a world "we enter at our own risk" and where "conquest and arrogance" are the main ingredients in its ethos (p. 17).

But, there are also spaces in teacher education wherein this is not the case. The table is one of them. The table is a place within the world of teacher education that encourages loving, even playful, travel. I write from experience.

At the table, I glimpsed the world of an early childhood educator in Taiwan in which pressure is countered with professional intentionality. I heard the powerlessness of the world of a teacher from Kenya who, along with the majority of his colleagues, lives the anguish of their students in the face of HIV/AIDS and the belief that classrooms can be restorative communities. I witnessed the loneliness of the world of an international student as she encountered the apathy of my world to strangers. I glimpsed the disillusionment of the world of a teacher/parent who lives in the tension of commitment to the public system of learning and to its inadequacy of providing effective learning for her challenged child. I was welcomed into the world of wisdom of an aboriginal teacher who understood my world with insightful clarity. I stumbled into the world of a gay teacher who confronted my traditional paths of knowing. I walked alongside an exceptional teacher whose navigation of the political world of education was crumbling her teacher identity.

A friend of mine says that there is a difference between tourists and travelers. Tourists go through worlds, but travelers let worlds go through them. Travelers "can understand what it is to be them and what it is to be ourselves in their eyes" (Lu-

gones, 1987, p. 17). The world of teacher education needs more places in which to travel.

ATTENDING TO TENSIONS

At research issues, participants live a relational landscape where joy and tension are present as participants attend their work in teacher education with their full lives. Joy is celebrated in playful interaction. Tension is not dismissed, but, instead, supports us "to keep . . . from positioning ourselves as fixing, as smoothing over or out, the complex, moment by moment interactions" (Huber & Clandinin, 2005, p. 332) as people's lives meet as human beings, educators, at the table, and so on. In this way, participants at research issues learn that rather than judging and blaming the lived and told stories shared, trying to understand their felt tensions creates a space for newly imagined possibilities to break through.

COMING TO LIVE AND KNOW ATTENDING TO TENSIONS

One Tuesday during Karen Keats Whelan's and my collaborative doctoral study, I came to the research issues table filled with questions about who I was as a teacher and researcher because of tensions I was experiencing in our research conversations with principal coresearchers. As the research issues conversation became shaped by the circle of people gathered that day, a thread emerged that foregrounded ethical dilemmas. When Nathalie Piquemal spoke she talked about how care and listening were becoming entangled with her understandings of living in ethical ways as she engaged in inquiry with members of a First Nations community. For Nathalie, living ethically as a researcher meant attending to her relationships with participants as well as honoring the sacredness of the cultural knowledge held within the partici- pants' community. Wayne Gorman spoke next, storying the tensions he was experi- encing as he worked with transcripts of stories participants shared of their experiences in residential schools. Wayne wondered who he was as a researcher if, in the writing of his thesis, he "cleaned up" the participants' stories by making standard the gram- mar that marked their tellings.

    Listening to Nathalie's and Wayne's stories of attending to the ethical dilemmas they were each experiencing supported me, in the short term, to work toward living differently in relation with the principal coresearchers with whom Karen and I were engaged in inquiry. In the long term, my learning to attend to participants' and my felt tensions in the midst of inquiry has been carried into my living as a teacher educator. Trying to stay at the living out of stories attentive to tensions in teaching and learning situations continues to keep me wakeful of my need to shift away from the ease of living stories of judgment and blame and toward living more difficult, liminal, and uncertain stories of working to understand conflicts between and among lives being composed in teacher education and public school classrooms.

LEARNING TO THINK NARRATIVELY

Participants bring their life stories, which inherently shape their inquiry wonders, to the table in all manner of ways, sometimes hesitantly, sometimes passionately. It sometimes takes time and deepening relationships to begin to know and to name these connections. In this way, a way that calls us to think about "life as a story," everyone at the table is called to "imagine who . . . [they] are, where . . . [they] have been, and where . . . [they] are going" (Connelly & Clandinin, 1994, p. 149). Those gathered in turn begin to wonder about the life story of the one speaking and how their concerns and interests are interwoven with their lives. Engaging in response, wonders surrounding past, present, and future situations begin to weave their way into conversations. Always, there is a sense that encounters with one another are "in the midst" (Clandinin & Connelly, 2000). And, it is within this midst that the possibilities shaped through thinking narratively emerge. Rather than

> regarding a story as a fixed entity . . . [we are called to] engage in conversations with our [and one another's] stories. The mere telling of a story leaves it as a fixed entity. It is in the inquiry, in our conversations with each other, with texts, with situations, and with other stories that we can come to retelling our stories and to reliving them. (Clandinin & Connelly, 1998, p. 251)

COMING TO LIVE AND KNOW THINKING NARRATIVELY

I would say that I spent a good part of my life looking for the order and the patterns in all things that I did. I remember the reading kit our teacher introduced to us when I was in grade 2. I remember the different "levels" in the kit, grouped by colors—magenta, blue, green, yellow—all waiting for me, a young girl, to read. My work was laid out for me; I would need to complete the whole kit by reading each card and answering the accompanying questions. Remembering this reading kit reminds me of other experiences, such as the many times when I yearned to work in the phonics and mathematics workbooks that were part of my life at school. I think I loved these books because they were books where I could "fill in the blank" with answers I knew. I loved the sense of completion and satisfaction when a whole page was complete. During summer vacation I would ask my mother to buy me the workbooks so that I could continue my studies. I shared this story of my childhood at the table one day and Jean asked, "How did you change?"

As I connect these experiences—my childhood love of the reading kit and of the workbooks with my noticing of and continued searching for order and patterns in my life—with Jean's question, I realize that my early movement toward thinking narratively began to take shape when I was teaching. As a former mathematics teacher, I liked order in my classroom, that is, until I noticed that children with whom I worked, lived complex lives. When I started to understand the complexity of the children's lives, I think I not only began to become a better mathematics teacher, but I also started to think narratively as a teacher. For example, I remember realizing one day that the children trusted me in such a way that they might do whatever I wanted—and this was a critical awakening for me in my life then as a teacher, and it continues to live with me now as a teacher educator. I realized that my life and the lives of the children were intertwined. Yet, thinking narratively as a teacher of mathematics is not a commonplace. Even though I was beginning to think narratively about my work as a teacher, I felt tension for the next number of years until I found myself at the center and at the table sharing and responding to my and colleagues' stories. As colleagues responded to my stories, I realized that my felt tensions were shaped in the differences between what I felt was commonly perceived as the world of a mathematics teacher alongside the world I was living with children.

As I participated in research issues I began to further understand that we, myself, the children I teach, and my colleagues, all live complex lives. I also began to further understand that our complex lives are intertwined. In this way, I began to realize that the way I came to know and understand was through relationships.

BECOMING TEACHER EDUCATORS

The trust that develops at the table enables thinking to become permeable as participants enter the storied worlds of everyone gathered there. It is as participants learn to be fully attentive and open to the stories to live by, of themselves and of one another, that they can genuinely learn from storied lives (Connelly & Clandinin, 1999). For in this way, participants let themselves go . . . allowing themselves to be vulnerable in the moment to becoming someone different, a process Vinz (1997) describes as living in a "dis-positioned" way. Little by little then, the research issues table becomes a place where we are each continuously held open to composing and recomposing our identities as teacher educators. Rather than being shaped by the more dominant institutional plotlines of remaining fixed in a script of teacher educator and researcher as someone who is finished or knows all, we are nurtured to "remain a moving form" by "continuously rethink[ing], reconceptualiz[ing], and reinsinuat[ing] ourselves into what it means to educate and be educated" (Vinz, 1997, p. 138).

COMING TO LIVE AND KNOW "BECOMING"

I came to live at the center table from a life filled with diverse experiences as a teacher, inspector of schools, education officer in Kenya, and graduate student in teacher education in Canada. I came with such a background wondering whether my lived experiences abroad would be validated or honored. I came not knowing whether it was wise to share my research puzzles imagined in those distant lands. Yet, as I participated at the table, I felt a sense of belonging. I was given space and I was listened to and honored.

Looking back, I think about who I was prior to joining the table. I lived as a teacher expert, transmitting knowledge without being receptive to others' ways of knowing. Joining the table, I realized my stories as a teacher educator were taking a different shape. I was listening and learning from table participants' knowing. In listening and in dialoguing with table participants, I began to awaken to their research wonders. I listened to Yi Li as she shared her research wonders about "where is home"; to Marni Pearce's wonders about "community as relationship"; to Anne Murray Orr's wonders about "book conversations as spaces"; and to Claire Desrocher's thoughts about "borderlands in teacher education for diversity." These dialogues between me and with table participants helped me gain deeper understanding of my practice as a teacher educator. I was living and learning in a way that was reshaping my becoming as a teacher educator, which Vinz (1997) calls an act of "continuous reformulation of the self as teacher" (p. 138).

I was coming to know my practice through listening and feeling a sense of connectedness as I dialogued with table participants on what I was hearing them telling. In other words, I was traveling into their worlds, while inquiring into their stories, which resonated with my lived experiences. In the process of trying to reach into one another's storied worlds, I was composing a new identity as a teacher educator, one who is attentive to people's storied lives to inform their own practice.

A Place of Possibility

Many years ago Buber (1947) said it is dialogue that embodies the true relation in education. At the CRTED and most centrally at the research issues table, dialogue as a way of living in relationship draws people to return over weeks, months, and years to create a condition of relational continuity from which graduate students, scholars, and others in the field of teacher education continue to compose their knowing and identities as teacher educators. As participants at the research issues table experience their own and one another's diverse lives attended to as people, there is a corresponding turn of attention to the lives of those who live on school and university landscapes, to wonder and imagine. As Greene (1993) reminds us, these kinds of spaces need to be "deliberately created" (p. 219) so that in our continuous becoming as teacher educators and human beings, we might live out what John Dewey (1938) taught us so well, that is, that life *is* education.

References

Assembly of First Nations (website: http://www.afn.ca).

Buber, M. (1947). *Between man and man* (R. G. Smith, Trans.). London: Collins.

Carter, K. (1993). The place of story in the study of teaching and teacher education. *Educational Researcher, 22*(1), 5–12, 18.

Clandinin, D. J., & Connelly, F. M. (1998). Asking questions about telling stories. In C. Kridel (Ed.), *Writing educational biography: Explorations in qualitative research* (pp. 202–209). New York: Garland.

Clandinin D. J., & Connelly, F. M. (2000). *Narrative inquiry: Experience and story in qualitative research.* San Francisco: Jossey-Bass.

Clandinin, D. J., Davies, A., Hogan, P., & Kennard, B. (1993). *Learning to teach, teaching to learn: Stories of collaboration in teacher education.* New York: Teachers College Press.

Cochran-Smith, M. (2003). Learning and unlearning: The education of teacher educators. *Teaching and Teacher Education, 19*(1), 5–28.

Connelly, F. M., & Clandinin, D. J. (1994). Telling teaching stories. *Teacher Education Quarterly, 21*(1), 145–158.

Connelly, F. M., & Clandenin, D. J. (1999). *Shaping a professional identity: Stories of educational practice.* New York: Teachers College Press.

Craig, C. (2003). *Narrative inquiries of school reform: Storied lives, storied landscapes, storied metaphors.* Greenwich, CT: Information Age Publishing.

Dewey, J. (1938). *Experience and education.* New York: Macmillan.

Greene, M. (1993). Diversity and inclusion: Toward a curriculum for human beings. *Teachers College Record, 95*(2), 211–221.

Greene, M. (1995). *Releasing the imagination: Essays on education, the arts, and social change.* San Francisco: Jossey-Bass.

Hamilton, M. L., & Pinnegar, S. (Eds.). (1998). *Reconceptualizing teaching practice: Self-study in teacher education.* Washington, DC: Falmer Press.

Hollingsworth, S., Dybdahl, M., & Minarik, L. (1993). By chart and chance and passion: The importance of relational knowing in learning to teach. *Curriculum Inquiry, 3*(1), 5–35.

Huber, J., & Clandinin, D. J. (2005). Living in tension: Negotiating a curriculum of lives on the professional knowledge landscape. In J. Brophy & S. Pinnegar (Eds.),

Learning from research on teaching: Perspective, methodology, and representation (Advances in Research on Teaching, vol. 11) (pp. 313–336). St. Louis: Elsevier.

Ladson-Billings, G. (2001). *Crossing over to Canaan: The journey of new teachers in diverse classrooms.* San Francisco: Jossey-Bass.

Lugones, M. (1987). Playfulness, "world-traveling" and loving perception. *Hypatia, 2*(2), 3–19.

Lunenberg, M. (2002). Designing a curriculum for teacher educators. *European Journal of Teacher Education, 25*(2 & 3), 263–277.

Lyons, N., & LaBoskey, V. K. (Eds.). (2002). *Narrative inquiry in practice: Advancing the knowledge of teaching.* New York: Teachers College Press.

Miller, J. L. (1990). *Creating spaces and finding voices: Teachers collaborating for empowerment.* New York: State University of New York Press.

Noddings, N. (1993). Learning to engage in moral dialogue. Paper presented to the Calgary Board of Education.

Russell, T., & Korthagen, F. (Eds.). (1995). *Teachers who teach teachers: Reflections on teacher education.* Washington, DC: Falmer Press.

Schwab, J. J. (1978). What do scientists do? In J. Schwab, I. Westbury, & N. J. Wilkof (Eds.), *Science, curriculum and liberal education: Selected essays* (pp. 184–228). Chicago: University of Chicago Press.

Steeves, P. (2004). A place of possibility: The Centre for Research for Teacher Education and Development. *ATA Magazine, 84*(4), 16–17.

Vinz, R. (1996). *Composing a teaching life.* Portsmouth, NH: Boynton/Cook.

Vinz, R. (1997). Capturing a moving form: "Becoming" as teachers. *English Education, 29*(2), 137–146.

CHAPTER 17

Voices from a Reflective Space

TEACHER EDUCATORS REFLECT ON PRACTICE

Helen Burchell
University of Hertfordshire, UK

Janet Dyson
University of Hertfordshire, UK

with Rosemary Allen, Mary Rees, and Marian Woolhouse
University of Hertfordshire, UK

with Pat Gidley
formerly University of Hertfordshire, UK

Helen Burchell, Ph.D., has a research leadership role within the School of Education at the University of Hertfordshire, UK, and is the Ed.D. program director. She is also a National Teaching Fellow (2005). Her teaching background is in continuing professional development programs and support for professional learning for schoolteachers and university faculty.

Janet Dyson, M.Ed., is a part-time researcher at the University of Hertfordshire, UK. Her research interests include narrative inquiry and reflective practice. She is also an educational consultant and teacher educator working with schools and local authorities, and the author of a number of publications and academic articles.

ABSTRACT

In this chapter we present a view "from the inside" of an action research project within which reflection was a key element. The project involves faculty in an education department exploring their practice as supervisors of dissertation students. Using an image of figures in an artist's studio to represent the group of supervisors, we explore key aspects of the "reflective space" established by the project: the importance of creating such a space, of opportunities for the supervisors to "surface" their understandings of their practice, to "think in dialogue with others," and to make meaning of their experiences of the project. The voices of five supervisors portray the quality of their reflections and show the importance of the reflective space amidst the busy-ness of their working lives.

Giacometti's Studio

In Sylvester's book Looking at Giacometti *(1994) there is a photograph of the artist's studio (p. 73). The floor is covered in plaster and stone; there are buckets, benches, frames and bottles, piles of papers, even a battered hat. The tall figures of his sculptures appear to stride purposefully across the foreground while large, brooding heads fill the background. In the middle of all this mess and apparent busy-ness, on a low table in a corner, is a group of small figures—some sitting, some standing; they convey a sense of stillness and reflection; it would be easy to overlook them.*

The small group of sculpted figures symbolizes a group of colleagues in a teacher education department. They are involved in a project looking at their practice as supervisors of students preparing dissertations. What is their relationship to what is happening around them in the studio? How can they ensure that what they have gained from the project is not overlooked, passed by, or lost?

In higher education today there are so many demands upon faculty that it is easy to settle into a way of working in which tasks and their completion become the major drivers; and where there are always new initiatives to attend to and seemingly new things to learn to put them in place. The purposefulness of this way of working—as seen in the striding figure sculptures of Giacometti—requires continual engagement with immediate issues and concerns. Professional learning is judged in terms of responsiveness to external demands and drivers. We also see in the photograph the artifacts of the artist's studio, representing perhaps the underlying "messiness" of these working lives, from which we create the order of our existence; a messiness that represents the uncertainties, unknowns, and ambiguities that are ever-present in our interactions with students and colleagues. The sense of stillness and reflection is perhaps unusual. When surrounded by the striding, purposeful activity of the everyday work environment, one of the hardest things to do is to find space for reflection, a place to stand back from engagement with the workplace routines.

And why should these figures not be overlooked? Because they can be thought of as engaging in a different kind of learning from that most easily recognized in the work environment. Their learning is based on a quality of reflection engendered when there is an opportunity to stand back from daily routines.

Overview

First an overview of the project is provided, followed by an exploration of key themes relating to the professional learning of those involved. The voices of the supervisors provide insights into their professional learning, together with the perspective of the project co-researcher. Our understanding of the place of collaboration in the supervisors' professional learning is developed through a collective reflection on the experience of being involved in the project some two years after it formally ended. To conclude we return to the questions raised in relation to the image of Giacometti's studio, and offer our response based on the experience of this project.

The Project

The yearlong project involved five supervisors and a coresearcher based in a university in the UK. The project became known as the Dissertation Action Research Project. Helen was the project leader; one of the supervisors, Janet, was the co-researcher; and Marian, Mary, Pat, and Rosemary were the other supervisors. In terms of an approach to professional development, this project had some distinctive features. The approach to learning was very much self-rected by the supervisors involved. It also offered more than a support group that discussed what practice might do, as there was a series of interviews with each supervisor over the year as part of the project structure, together with reflection on practice through writing in various forms. The project lies at the boundary between action research, reflective practice, and collaborative professional inquiry. We have discussed the way the project was carried out, and its impact on individual and collective reflection in general terms, in another paper (Burchell & Dyson, 2005). In this chapter the voices of the supervisors and co-researcher are brought more to the fore. We begin, however, with an account of how the project started and then developed over the year.

Helen introduced the project at a staff development conference for teacher educators within the university, inviting colleagues who were dissertation supervisors to meet to discuss the possibility of an action research group. Following this initial meeting, a further, longer meeting was arranged, and, at this point, Helen spoke of her own personal interest in inquiring into practice as a supervisor. She set out some questions regarding how a collaborative action research group might develop. The themes that were mentioned in a wide-ranging discussion of supervision practice highlighted the isolation of the role, and the feeling that it would be good to discuss issues with colleagues. At the end of this meeting, Helen invited colleagues to let her know if they wished to join an action research group. Four colleagues joined Helen as group leader and Janet as the co-researcher to form a project group of six.

At the first meeting of the action research group a month later, we took time for each person to outline the issues for them in dissertation supervision. The pattern for the development of the project over the rest of the year involved a series of six group meetings of normally a half-day, and Janet interviewed each supervisor on four occasions spread across the year.

Helen and Janet developed the interview strategy in consultation with the supervisors: Some of the themes for the interviews arose directly out of the group discussions, others from the literature on supervision. Janet's approach to interviewing rested in part on "interviews as conversations" (Rubin & Rubin, 1995), cocreating the interviews with the supervisors as opportunities to learn more about their practice (Mishler, 1986). At the end of the year, Janet wrote a "pen portrait" of each supervisor based on her interview responses for reflection and discussion at the final group meeting. These pen portraits form the basis for the supervisors' stories later in the chapter. The first supervisor interview explored expectations of dissertation students and strategies for supervision, particularly in early stages of the dissertation program. Subsequent supervisor interviews explored what was discussed in tutorials and the kind of guidance given to students. In the final interview supervisors considered the role of the project in facilitating their professional learning.

The group meetings took place in a light, spacious room, situated on a different part of the campus from supervisors' normal working environments. A list of topics that might be discussed was circulated in advance, but no formal agenda was provided. The aim was to encourage the openness needed for reflection. The discussions often had an exploratory quality, being directed by the concerns uppermost in supervisors' minds at that juncture. Helen acted as facilitator, shifting between participant in the discussion and the person who framed questions regarding the nature of supervision or how the project might be taken forward in light of the issues raised.

In addition to the opportunity to reflect provided by the interviews and group meetings, each supervisor continued to explore her practice through writing—through keeping a diary or writing stories, for example. As well as these "formal" elements of the project, there were numerous times in which supervisors engaged in informal discussion of their supervisor roles and of the project itself. At the end of the year each supervisor was invited to write about her experience of involvement in the project as well as commenting in the final interview. Supervisors both wrote and spoke at length in response to the question: How was it for you?

This group of colleagues had in common the fact that they were dissertation supervisors, reflective about their work, and were interested in exploring their practice in this role. They were also extremely busy people, and the issue of setting aside time for professional development through inquiry and research into practice was a significant one for each member of the group. These features of the context are important in defining the parameters of the project approach and in exploring how to sustain such a project in these circumstances.

We had no personal expectations regarding which aspects of the supervision role might be the focus for inquiry. There was an initial assumption that each supervisor might identify some element of practice that she wished to develop through trying out different teaching strategies, leading to a re-evaluation and possibly further such cycles. Elements of this approach did carry over into the project, but this did not become its core.

In our overview of the project as a basis for individual and collective reflection (Burchell & Dyson, 2005), we developed the concept of a reflective space, a space that embraced not only the group meetings and interviews, but also the various informal encounters between the members of the group. This represents for us the core of the project. Boud and Walker (1998) highlight the importance of a space for reflection through their image of a local context within an organization acting as an oasis (pp. 198–199). This resonates strongly with the participants' experiences of the project, and is reflected in the image of the small group in Giacometti's studio.

For the supervisors, an oasis might be seen as a space apart from normal routines in three different ways: firstly, in terms of physical space, as the place where group meetings were held and its separateness from the everyday working lives of the supervisors; secondly, in the sense of space in time: the meetings and the supervisor interviews provided "time out" from normal professional duties; finally, there was a qualitatively different space for professional dialogue in that the nature of the discussions that took place between supervisors, both within group meetings and outside them, was experienced as different from those that took place within the normal pattern of working life. These different aspects of the reflective space are highlighted in the stories in a later section.

Collaborative Professional Learning: Setting the Scene

In this chapter the views of those involved in the project are explored from the standpoint of collaborative professional learning within a small-group context.

There are two interwoven themes: first, the nature of the professional learning and reflection on practice for individuals; and second, the particular contribution offered by a collaborative project.

A number of studies have acknowledged the potential value of involvement in a small group of peers for the professional learning of faculty in higher education: action learning group approaches (e.g., Evans, 2004); research writing groups (e.g., Lee & Boud, 2003); self-initiated learning groups (Stefani & Elton, 2002); collaborative inquiry for staff development (Treleaven, 1994). Within the research traditions such as self-study in teacher education, where faculty are engaged in studying their own practice (e.g., Loughran et al., 2004) and some forms of action research in higher education (e.g., Zuber-Skerritt, 1992, 1996), some form of collaboration is acknowledged as a fundamental aspect. Some of the purposes offered are explored here.

ENGAGING IN PROFESSIONAL LEARNING THROUGH REFLECTION ON PRACTICE

Whenever "time out" from normal professional duties is provided in the context of a project such as this, it is hoped that it will help the practitioner stand back and examine her practice. The idea of "surfacing" (Schön, 1983) is a powerful image for describing the way in which someone can develop the capacity for reflection. Schön describes how, through reflection, a practitioner "can surface and criticize the tacit understandings that have grown up around the repetitive experiences of a specialized practice, and can make new sense of the situations of uncertainty or uniqueness which he may allow himself to experience" (p. 61). The two elements of reflection identified by Dewey (1933) are to be looked for, namely a state of uncertainty, balanced against a willingness to inquire in order to work toward a resolution of a problem. Such surfacing may reveal a number of dimensions of practice: its strategies and "ways of doing things," its value base, and its implicit theories (Clark, 2001). It may also be engaged in deliberately to provide a reflexive critique of that practice (Winter, 1989). The approach to reflection was holistic, engaging feelings and imagination as well as the more rational, cognitive aspects (Leitch & Day, 2000). In this regard it has parallels with Korthagen and Vasalos's (2005) idea of "core reflection," emphasizing core qualities rather than core competences in reflective practice.

This key concept of "surfacing" provides the basis for exploring the nature of reflection on practice in this project. There are many writers who have explored the nature and purpose of reflection on practice in the field of teacher education and more generally. Our intention here is not to review their work, but to highlight how through this project particular features of reflection on practice were deemed important by the supervisors involved.

In a collaborative project, it may become clear that others do things differently; and if so, surfacing may well present challenges to what we thought we knew, to practices with which we felt secure. The supervisors' stories suggest both a looking within and a looking outside of oneself. For each of the supervisors there is a strong orientation toward questioning of self and practice. What was important was the strong commitment of all members of the group to continue to engage with the project, and thereby to accept the challenges that it posed to themselves as supervisors. It is in the nature and strength of these challenges, and the willingness of the supervisors to engage with them, that their capacity for critical reflection is demonstrated. Moreover, these challenges were mostly revealed publicly, either in interviews or group meetings. Either implicitly or explicitly the supervisors were exploring others' views of what counted as good practice. In doing this they were provided with mirrors revealing their own practice, and the assumptions and values on which it was based. Arguably, this heightened the challenge and thereby the level of critical reflection.

Several features of the project aided this quality of reflection. Writing, being interviewed, being provided with a "pen portrait," and taking part in group meetings provided a range of experiences from which supervisors sought to create meanings for their roles, and for their professional learning within the project. For some supervisors the activity of keeping a diary contributed significantly to professional learning, exemplifying Bolton's (2001) view of a learning journal as "the cornerstone of reflective practice work" (p. 159). Writing stories was another form used by some of the supervisors, developing the "art of reflective writing" (Winter, Buck, & Sobieschowska, 1999), and emphasising the importance of narrative as a way of understanding experience (Clandinin & Connelly, 2000). Interviews provided a context in which individuals' stories of supervision could be told and heard (Mishler, 1986), and reflected back through the pen portraits created by the co-researcher.

These features of the project supported supervisors in bringing their practice to the surface for reflection and examination. In various ways the project provided a focus for a more sustained noticing of what was happening in practice, and an encouragement to pay attention to this aspect of their professional lives.

THE NATURE OF COLLABORATION WITHIN THE PROJECT

The second theme concerns the nature of the engagement with others within the project: through conversation, discussion, dialogue, interview exchanges, and the co-researcher's perspective provided through her pen portrait for each supervisor. Creating possibilities within the project framework for "thinking in dialogue with others" (Winter, 1998) was an important feature in that it embraces the "ideas of friends, colleagues, students, clients, etc., as well as 'the academic literature'" (p. 67). Supervision is largely a one-to-one activity, where supervisors do not often share their practice. The opportunity that was provided by membership of this group opened up a dialogue about supervision that was central to the professional learning of participants. Raelin (2001) highlights the importance of both introspection and public reflection, suggesting "reflection is fundamental to learning and can be brought out in the company of trusted others through dialogue" (p. 11).

When Winter (1998) writes that "thinking is also about understanding oneself in relation to the cultural traditions within which one finds oneself" (p. 67), she is identifying a fundamental part of the reflection process. The traditions that framed this project included assumptions and expectations concerning how to supervise students preparing dissertations. As supervision is generally a one-to-one activity, without an opportunity to explore how others engage in this form of teaching, we are very dependent on our own experience of being supervised, and these traditions and assumptions are likely to be deeply embedded in our practices.

The professional conversations that took place within the group meetings may be seen in the terms described by Clark (2001, p. 178) as necessary for professional learning: "Good conversations deal with worthwhile content; they resist narrow definition; they are voluntary; they flourish on common ground, in an atmosphere of safety, trust, and care; they develop over time, drawing on a shared history and anticipating a shared future." Key features of the way the project worked related closely to these characteristics—the focus on discussions of supervision practice; the openness of the group meetings and interviews; the development over time of a common ground of engagement with reflection on practice, which was seen as of value for its future development.

However, many conversations took place outside the "formal" elements of the project, where they provided a further context for professional learning in ways similar to those described by Haigh (2005), who highlighted the significance of a "conversation for learning perspective" (p. 8). We would suggest that these informal encounters as part of the reflective space are enhanced by the experience of paying attention to one another's stories and practice within the group meetings.

Taylor et al. (2006, p. 247) suggest collaboration can be viewed at least three ways within the literature on self-study in teacher education. Two of the views include the collaborator as critical friend and the collaboration that takes place when a number of colleagues are involved in a joint self-study. This project was conceived as a set of individual studies, rather than a joint study, and did not involve an explicit "critical friend" dimension. However, the third view is closer to the experience of the supervisors, namely where Taylor et al. (2006) refer to "collaborators as distanced 'authors'" (p. 247). They relate this to the observation by Loughran and Northfield (1998) that such collaboration involves a colleague who can "remain at a distance from the experience and see the trends developing over time" (p. 11). "Collaborators are distanced 'others' . . ." (Taylor et al., 2006, p. 247). This view has a particular relevance in relation to the co-researcher's role, as discussed below.

An interesting dimension underlying all these interpretations of the nature of collaboration concerns the significance of the "other" in professional learning. Penlington (2007) has drawn attention to the importance of "otherness" as part of collaboration, both as an element in professional conversation, discussion, and dialogue, and as an internal "other" in our own reflections on practice. There is a parallel here with Winter's assertion: "Other peoples' thinking, based on their experience, is a key resource in enabling us to think creatively about our own, to think critically about the thoughts we started with in order to construct a new cognitive space into which we might, provisionally, decide to move" (1998, p. 67).

Voices from a Reflective Space

Within Giacometti's studio we focus in on the small group of figures, to see what is going on. Who are they? What are they thinking or feeling? What do they have to say about the experience of being involved in the project? What differences do they perceive in their practice as a result of having had this experience?

Each supervisor's view of her involvement provides different insights into the project, and her professional learning around supervision. Through exploring the perspective of each in turn, we can engage with some of the key themes outlined above.

MARY'S STORY

Although time constraints made it difficult for Mary to attend all the group meetings, she maintained contact with the group mainly through informal discussion with colleagues and the regular interviews. She saw the value of being involved: *(it) has made me more conscious about the whole process (of supervision), the doing of it. I suppose the converse of that is the more you think about it the harder it is. . . . I think the obvious thing is it's really made me question and worry whether my role and the way I do it is . . . is good, I suppose.*

She explains why the opportunity to discuss aspects of supervision with colleagues was so valuable for her, the fact that discovering, through the group discussions, that there were many different ways of approaching supervision had somehow legitimated trying something different. Realizing that there is not a "right" way of doing it: *Although I always knew there was a variation in style, . . . that's been okayed by that group, acknowledged . . . And I think that was a huge thing and . . . I'm more confident in letting go a bit more in following sometimes a nonstandard (approach).*

For Mary the value of group meetings was the opportunity to discuss professional practice: *It's so valuable because we never discuss our professional lives.* She also found the experience of being interviewed regularly useful: *Being interviewed again is good because it makes you formulate what you think. And it gives it . . . status I suppose, that it's an important process.*

At first Mary did not feel that involvement in the action research had prompted her to be more reflective but, as she talked it through in interview, she began to explore some of the ways in which her involvement had resulted in continued reflection on practice: *Again I have to say it's limited to the meetings and just before the interviews and after the interviews. . . . though I suppose again, with the students I've got this year, all very different students, again, thinking more about the process. . . .* She describes what she learned from the other members of the group: *I learned more about the continuum (of supervisor practice) and that there are different models and different styles, so now I think with different students I vary my practice.*

Mary misses the professional dialogue that she felt was the main value of the action research group, but feels that, having been started, it continues on an informal basis: *That was the only (time) really where there was professional dialogue, I mean you have (some) but nothing so sustained and structured, so in that sense you miss it. But in another sense it carries on because you talk more to colleagues.*

MARIAN'S STORY

Marian is an experienced supervisor and has attended many meetings of dissertation supervisors to discuss aspects of the supervision process, including the need to discuss expectations with students at the beginning of the relationship, provide more structured tutorials, and encourage more independence (Woolhouse, 2002). However, she says, *But while one listens and thinks, "Yes, I should do that," without the structure of the project they remain "good ideas" that I might have incorporated if I had remembered.*

She identifies the structure of the project as important in keeping her engagement with reflection on supervision practice, against the backdrop of the inevitable difficulties encountered by busy professionals in engaging in any form of research: *Others, including myself, cannot maintain the focus if left alone. The practicalities of professional life—preparing for the next class, developing courses, and responding to all the varied demands that come our way—intervene and the less pressing desire to engage in action research gets lost. . . . For me, having time blocked out in my diary for meetings with colleagues and interviews with Janet was the only way that I could ensure that time was set aside for the action research. Deadlines act as a way to motivate the process, and not wanting to let colleagues down makes me stay at the computer.*

However, it was not only the fact of needing to make time available that was important. The involvement of others was very important in Marian's professional learning. *More importantly, engaging in discussion and debate, listening to colleagues and having the opportunity for them to listen to you, is essential. "In the same way as reading a good article can inspire thought and reflection in the reader and lead to questioning of one's own practice, so can open discussion and debate in a mutually supportive and collaborative atmosphere" (Woolhouse, 2005, p. 34). . . . Colleagues engaged in this action research project, including the research assistant, can often see things in what you say and write that you may not yourself have recognized, and by digesting what is reflected back it is possible to move your own thinking forward.*

Looking back on her involvement in the project, Marian says: *In conclusion, I need to ask whether the time and energy that went into being part of the action research group was beneficial and did it help develop my practice? My response in the early interview indicates that, while I did not feel that it had necessarily had an impact in terms of my supervision practice, it had prompted me to think much more about my role although, as I pointed out, "It has not necessarily changed what I've done." However (at a later stage in the project), involvement in the action research group was having an impact on my view of supervision and made me want to explore other views of practice in supervision.*

My involvement in the project showed me that I needed other people to help facilitate the process of reflection on my practice. I'm now open to different ways of supervising because the dialogue with colleagues, the engagement with some of the literature have supported my questioning of previously held assumptions. It's made me think about it more. Because before I'd do what comes naturally to me. And I have a good rapport with the students, I seem to get on well with them, and they generally do all right. But I think it has made me think much more about the style of supervision and I'd like to have the time to do some reading about supervision styles.

The involvement in the action research group certainly provided me with the motivation to question and develop my own practice, as well as gain greater knowl-

edge and understanding about many aspects of the supervision process. I would not have done this had I not been part of the group—for me "you can't do it on your own" has become an essential realization.

ROSEMARY'S STORY

Rosemary was extending her supervisor role to a new course, drawing on previous supervision experience where she very much enjoyed this aspect of her work. She used the information from the discussions that were taking place between the supervisors in the action research group meetings to help plan and structure her tutorials. This also provided the basis for some background work on learning styles to enable her to respond to students' needs.

In her interviews, Rosemary recounted in some detail her existing strategies for supervising students' projects, highlighting that the most important strategy is that of making the student feel safe: *Because I think once they've got some confidence then they are able to understand the process of working independently. If they are worried about seeking help they're not going to quiet their minds sufficiently to get at what they need.*

Reflecting generally on the experience of being involved with the action research, Rosemary indicated significant impact: *Being involved with the action research has had a huge impact on how I've been working with the range of people I'm working with, . . . I've been very clear and direct with the students I've been dealing with and I've felt much better about it . . . I've sort of devised, I don't know quite how to describe it, but I've got a philosophy about what I do as opposed to not being quite sure how I do it.*

Although she found fitting in group meetings and times for interviews placed pressure on her time, Rosemary has no doubt that belonging to the group provided a supportive framework for developing her skills as a supervisor. *At the time it was enormously valuable because it allowed me to focus on what I was supposed to be doing . . . having the group there meant that I could bring my anxieties and queries to the group . . . I think I'm the sort of person who needs to talk things over. I clarify things by talking things over.*

Although the group meetings were a vital element of the process, there were other vital ingredients such as thinking time. Commenting on the opportunity for reflection, Rosemary says: *I don't put by thinking time, I think about things as I'm doing something else. . . . But I think it gave it a particular focus, having the group, being part of the group. There's always the element of guilt that you'd be letting somebody else down if you didn't do your bit, and I think that's quite healthy in a way.*

Her involvement made her very conscious of how she supervised students, and the experience of working with other supervisors prompted consideration of matching style of supervision to the person being supervised: *that you match the style of supervision to the person. That you don't have a formula that you apply, you have a framework that you use. But I think what was very noticeable was that each one of us applied the framework to an individual as opposed to just going through your script, and I found that fascinating because I thought there would be a particular way that experienced people worked; and whilst there was, I could detect what it was, it was much more flexible than I'd realized, highly personal in fact, and I found that very interesting—that people didn't slip into "I know how to do it and this is how I do it."*

She also valued the sense of mutual professional respect that developed within the group. *Another thing I found really noticeable—I think it was a feature of this set of colleagues—is that nobody felt they had the answers, even when they quite clearly do. . . . I think when you get to know people you see their strengths . . . you get to know what peoples' experiences are, and you start to respect them for what they know and what they can do, so I think it's had quite an impact on how I see people and how I see myself as well.*

PAT'S STORY

Pat was a relatively new supervisor and identified many aspects of the supervision process that she had reflected on in the course of the action research process. From this standpoint, she questioned how far the action research process should replace a training mode for new supervisors. She also welcomed the team approach that provided a supportive framework to counter the "loneliness" of the supervisory role. She observed that through the reflection/discussion process she felt she had been taken through the same process as we do our students.

For Pat, the key aspect of the action research appears to have been the way it generated the writing of stories. She comments on its place within the overall experience: *I had not intended to use fiction, and had not realized that it was a vehicle through which to express research outcomes. . . . Since I wrote in the diary form, I was, I am certain, trying to make sense not only of the supervision process, but also of the culture of the institution and my own role within it, having only arrived a few weeks prior to meeting with my first dissertation student.*

This aspect of the research process highlighted for Pat key issues in the supervision process from the experience of supervising a number of teachers. The unresolved issues were pivotal points from which to reassess the realities of the supervisory process. *Normally it is in my nature to want to resolve questions and to relieve uncertainty and ambiguity for myself and others. Yet through this reflective process (which allowed for a closer than normal self-examination of my practice) I was not only keen to swiftly dispose of those issues that could be resolved more immediately, but also to focus on those that might never be able to be foreseen, or taught to either first-time or experienced supervisors. For example, the setting up of training initiatives, further support groups/networking opportunities, and more direct access to appropriate information could solve most of the initial fears or insecurities. . . . Without the aid of the fictional approach, I doubt that I would have allowed these niggling doubts, insecurities, and ambiguity to have crept in.*

Although, for Pat, this use of fiction was a significant focus for the professional learning associated with the project, the group meetings also provided a further support: *I had not thought that the element of collaborative discussion and enquiry had offered as much to me in terms of action research as did the use of fiction. However, I see now that this type of forum was rather like a testing bed at times, where one's ideas and thoughts could be rehearsed, checked, and given fresh "insights and scope for clarification" (Winter, 1989). It was at such sessions where professional themes and concerns were aired that I was again reawakened to the potential of the use of fiction as an evaluation tool.*

HELEN'S STORY

For Helen, her involvement in the action research group made a strong contribution to her reflection on and development of her practice. She valued the opportunities that the meetings of the group provided for sharing practice and raising issues. Helen also worked with another member of the group on peer observations of tutorials. She saw the benefits of the project in a number of ways. *The very fact of speaking in group meetings about how you look at supervision brings it to the surface so you can work on it, can hear other peoples' views. . . . the fact that we've picked up on peer observation as a real way of sharing practice and developing that. I suppose also hearing others' concerns that are different from mine, and acknowledging that each of us is an individual engaging in our supervision so the views we hold and the issues we raise will be unique because of who we are.*

She felt that her involvement with the group continued to have a significant impact on the way she viewed her practice: *It makes me think all the time about action research and dissertation supervision. It's made me much more thoughtful about ways in which I supervise, and how that might be different from other people's ways of supervising . . . so the group and the conversations around the project are important, because of course I chat with Rosemary, Pat, Mary, Marian from time to time, and often there's an element in those conversations around the project.*

She viewed it as fruitful for others too: *I suppose in a way we've got a legitimate topic of conversation on a regular basis that we wouldn't have without the project. So you might talk to a colleague about dissertation supervision from time to time, but the fact that you're in a project together legitimizes it. I think it keeps things alive.*

In addition to meeting regularly with the members of the group, keeping a reflective diary, and engaging in peer observations of tutorials, Helen also wrote a story through which she explored some of the dilemmas and tensions within the supervisor's role. She found the use of this form of writing to be a powerful means of expression providing both personal and professional insights: *So it's . . . a very powerful tool for showing you yourself and for allowing you to look at yourself and to say, "Do I want to use that as a basis for making some changes, doing some things differently?" It accesses a whole part of your being that isn't normally accessed in the research process, the imaginal, imaginative side of yourself.*

Helen's view of the effect of being involved in the project on her practice as a supervisor shows a growing awareness of how practice is changed or developed. *As I reflected further on the process, I began to define impact on practice as a new understanding, or a reconnection with an understanding I had had before. I saw it not as an earth-shattering shift, but more as a grounding experience. I described it as a way of seeing things—seeking to see more clearly what was already there but had been obscured in some way. So how did the action research help develop my understanding? Hearing my own voice in interview and diary presented me with the starting point. Analyzing and interpreting this evidence gave me a clearer picture of myself as a teacher.*

JANET'S STORY: A CO-RESEARCHER'S PERSPECTIVE

A powerful image from Clandinin and Connelly (2000) prompted a visualization of my role: "We see individuals as living storied lives on storied landscapes" (p. 24). This description made me think of a painting (an imagined one) that I called "Figures in a Landscape"; as a researcher I was, to use their image, entering a landscape and joining an ongoing professional life. I saw a series of "figures in landscape" pictures in which the groupings of the figures changed; sometimes I saw myself as part of the group, sometimes as a figure watching, apart from the group, sometimes I saw myself outside, watching with *Helen*.

The kind of role I held in this action research project is not easy to define. Somekh (1995) identifies the role of "an empathetic outsider" as "an invaluable resource in action research because of the different kind of experience and/or skills that the outsider brings to the work" (p. 341). She also refers to those who are not practitioners themselves but who have "a short term role" that is "peripheral to the main action," which would be an accurate description of my role in this case in the sense that I was not a supervisor. Somekh describes such people as "observers," "facilitators," and "critical friends" (p. 341).

I considered Somekh's descriptors and found them inadequate in relation to how I viewed my role. I felt that I could not be described as an "observer," certainly not a nonparticipant observer, except in the sense that I was not engaged in the supervision process. In discussion with Helen I suggested that perhaps a "go-between" would be a more accurate term, moving as I did between the supervisors and Helen, listening, reflecting, seeing issues and themes emerge and how these have been recognized and worked through during the year. Two supervisors' comments reflect something of this perspective. They described my role as:

> Almost as a catalyst, making things happen, prompting reflection in action.
>
> Pulling the bits together, feeding back to us, showing us the connections that we couldn't have made on our own, because you've got an overview. However much you talk about it you're still only getting little snapshots, and I think what you were able to do was point out connections for us. I think that once you've got connections you can start to build a picture that you can do something with.

I certainly always felt "part of the team" and, as the study progressed, I began to develop a sense of ownership of the action research and a feeling of "belonging" to the group in some way that went beyond the job description. A further consideration of the nature of narrative inquiry as defined by Clandinin and Connelly (2000) prompted me to reflect on how the role had developed during the course of the action research, and stimulated an imaginative response as to how this changing role might be captured in a visual way.

They describe narrative inquiry as "a way of understanding experience; . . . a collaboration between researcher and participants, over time, in a place or series of places, and in social action with milieus" (p. 20). This notion that a researcher is someone who comes into the middle of something and joins with those who are already there, linked strongly with a sense I had of my role in the action research process. I saw myself as a traveling companion joining a group of travellers on a journey, observing, and possibly sharing, their experiences for a time until the ways parted again: "an inquirer enters the matrix in the midst and progresses in the same spirit, concluding the inquiry still in the midst of living and telling, reliving and retelling, the stories of the experience that make up peoples' lives, both individual and social" (Clandinin & Connelly, 2000, p. 20).

Learning about Collaborative Professional Learning

The nature of the reflection within this project has been revealed through the supervisors' voices. Of central importance was their engagement with the project and the integral reflection on practice over a long time frame, through periods of questioning whether this engagement was having any effect, and, if so, of what kind. They were prepared to accept ambiguity and uncertainty; to move from a position of thinking that nothing much was happening to a later awareness that they were learning from involvement in the project; to acknowledge both a limited focus for reflection in and around the group meetings and interviews, and a recognition that the enhanced reflection was indeed very pervasive.

Professional learning through reflection, analysis, and evaluation takes time, as does developing new ways of thinking about and engaging in practice. As McEwan (1995) suggests:

> Reflection and study set in motion a circular process where old understandings are absorbed in a new synthesis that has the potential to inaugurate a qualitative change in the practice. . . . A new level of self-understandings and a concomitant change in practice results. . . . The process is a cyclical one because it has no beginning and no final end. New understandings impinge on old practices and become, to varying degrees, part of the language that constitutes the new practice . . . (p. 179)

Looking back at the supervisors' stories we can see the development of their self-understandings and how these impinge on their previous practices. For each of the supervisors this had a different meaning. Taken together, these new understandings had a range of foci: considering alternative supervision strategies; the development of confidence; articulation of a philosophy of supervising; the recognition of ambiguities and uncertainties; and the significance of deepening one's understanding of the long-held core dimensions of practice.

The stories show how the supervisors came to understand more about how professional learning within the project worked for them. This raised awareness made it possible for them to identify changes in their own practice as a result of being involved. Yet, there remains a question of how far such understandings and changes would continue beyond the timescale of the project. Hence we felt a need for a further dimension to our understanding of the impact of the project on professional learning, to show how this developed over time. Some two years after the project had officially "ended," four of the supervisors engaged in an e-mail exchange on their views of the project at that point. These are their voices in this online reflective conversation.

MARIAN

The experience of doing it stays with me. I often think back to the time we spent together in the Art Block engaged in discussion or just listening to someone else—

sometimes long silences as we all thought about what had been said and what we had to contribute. What we did must have been successful because here we are, how many years later? Still writing about it and talking to each other.

MARY

That was what was important for me too—the doing of it. The fact that discussing practice was firmly on the agenda and became a habit, more than administration or day-to-day practicalities or all the things you talk about in a day. Professional conversations—lone and with colleagues—became the grammar of my working life.

PAT

The setting aside of reflective time is still important to me. It was something I had engaged in both alone and with others in a previous role, but had forgotten within the higher education context. The culture of higher education somehow seemed to me as a newcomer not to be conducive to the creation of reflective space. (Yet I had imagined that I would find it being practiced even more within a research context.) I needed to be given "permission" to spend time thinking instead of doing and to have the value of reflection reinforced as part of a natural pattern of work.

MARY

I wonder where the "permission" came from? Was it that it was organized and therefore recognized? Or that we had to maintain some level of commitment (and I know mine was minimal!) for fear of letting others down? Or because Helen was always there saying come on—this is important—stick with it?

HELEN

For me the creating of this reflective space was something I remained uncertain about throughout the life span of the project. It felt very much as though I was trying to hold together something by the slimmest of threads. A gossamer thread, I called it. How do you create a space where something different from the "norm" of professional conversations can happen? And how do you recognize the difference anyway?

MARIAN

Progress was often slow—a whole morning or a whole day and what had we achieved? This has given me a much better empathy for students whose progress is often slow, and they don't have the luxury of a group of colleagues to work with— only me. I feel much better able to engage in dialogue with them, rather than be the tutor who knows all the answers. I never did know all the answers, but now I am more confident to say so and work with the student to make progress. I am better able to tolerate the slow progress because we made slow progress at times too.

PAT

My original feelings of naïveté and doubt as a newcomer to research supervision have long gone. This is no doubt partly attributable to the learning of new skills and competencies as I engaged in the practice. Nevertheless, I do believe that I only really began to have a real understanding of the depth of the supervision process and how to locate my own role within it through the opportunity to engage in dialogue (or silences) as a member of this "team." I began to understand that it is not enough to teach others how to do "it," or to point them to the sources of information. You have to help them internalize enquiry and unlock their own capacity for reflection and investigation—how else would I have learned this?

HELEN

As a supervisor I too learned a great deal about my practice, and the directions in which I wanted to develop this. Marian's comment about slowness resonates for me too. But isn't this in the nature of change, that we need time to "let go" our habitual patterns—whether of supervising or of discussing professional matters with colleagues. And Pat's observation about the importance of learning for oneself how to "unlock" a reflective and enquiring capacity as a necessary foundation for supporting others in doing the same rings so true.

MARIAN

For me the creation of space is perhaps one of the most important aspects of being part of the group. When the project was "active," the meetings (and the preparation for them—reading, writing, thinking) made me find the time to do what was necessary (I don't think I missed many). This commitment to the group has continued as

I sit here writing this all these years later. For me, time was certainly the most important, but place was also important. We met in a space I don't normally use, so it was special. It was like taking time out of my normal working life.

Making space is not only about time and place but also about what you do with "space." Ours was a mixture of what might have been considered long, rambling discussions—Janet's notes will confirm this—but underlying was a structure. Helen's way of letting us go and then bringing us back; the reading, the writing, as well as the meetings. All this contributed to a quality of reflection that I don't think any of us could have done on our own—I certainly couldn't.

PAT

When I reflect back I see that both Helen and Janet led us through their beliefs about reflection and narrative to finding our own. Both Helen and Janet legitimized the use of time, space, and narrative inquiry, and unlocked our sources of power. The process has much to offer the "culture" to be embedded in higher education.

HELEN

For me what remains fascinating is the way a project such as this can send out its threads across the years, and along pathways that one would not have anticipated. We continue to meet to discuss writing about the project, consulting one another as we develop our individual or joint papers and presentations. We also continue our collective reflections: Other "projects" have developed since this one "formally" ended. In various combinations, we five supervisors and Janet find ourselves involved in these new projects, bringing a quality to our professional discussions that I believe would not have been there had the first project not happened.

To End

Finally, we return to the question posed at the beginning of this chapter: Why should we not overlook or pass by the little group of figures in the corner of the artist's studio, individuals each standing in their own space, but also in relationship? There was no compulsion to be involved, and no strong institutional push behind the project. Each supervisor had decided for herself whether, and to what extent, she would take part. A strength of the project lay in the comradeship of the group, and the real interest of each supervisor in the focus on supervision.

However, we believe it is the distinctive nature of the reflective space established within the project that was key to its continuing impact. The ongoing attention to practice, one's own and that of others, provided a basis for the continuing reflection and engagement. In response to the question we have posed, we hope we have provided sufficient insight into what it was like to be a member of such a group to enable our readers to recognize the nature of their reflection and its importance in the midst of the busy-ness of their professional lives.

References

Bolton, G. (2001). *Reflective practice: Writing and professional development.* London: Paul Chapman Publishing Ltd.

Boud, D., & Walker, D. (1998). Promoting reflection in professional courses: The challenge of context. *Studies in Higher Education, 23*(2), 191–206.

Burchell, H., & Dyson, J. (2005). Action research in higher education: Exploring ways of creating and holding the space for reflection. *Educational Action Research, 13,* 291–300.

Clandinin, D. J., & Connelly, F. M. (2000). *Narrative inquiry: Experience and story in qualitative research.* San Francisco: Jossey-Bass.

Clark, C. M. (Ed.). (2001). *Talking shop: Authentic conversation and teacher learning.* New York: Teachers College Press.

Dewey, J. (1933). *How we think: A restatement of the relation of reflective thinking to the educative process.* Chicago: Henry Regnery.

Evans, C. (2004). The power of action learning groups to develop the HE organisation and its managers. *Educational Development, 5*(1), 17–20.

Haigh, N. (2005). Everyday conversation as a context for professional learning and development. *International Journal for Academic Development, 10*(1), 3–16.

Korthagen, F., & Vasalos, A. (2005). Levels in reflection: Core reflection as a means to enhance professional growth. *Teachers and Teaching: Theory and Practice, 11*(1), 47–71.

Lee, A., & Boud, D. (2003). Writing groups, change and academic identity: Research development as local practice. *Studies in Higher Education, 28*(2), 187–200.

Leitch, R., & Day, C. (2000). Action research and reflective practice: Towards a holistic view. *Educational Action Research, 8*(1), 179–193.

Loughran, J. J., Hamilton, M. L., LaBoskey, V. K., & Russell, T. (Eds.). (2004). *International handbook of self-study of teaching and teacher education practices.* Dordrecht, the Netherlands: Kluwer Academic Publishers.

Loughran, J., & Northfield, J. (1998). A framework for the development of self-study practice. In M. L. Hamilton (Ed.), *Reconceptualizing teaching practice: Self-study in teacher education* (pp. 7–18). London: Falmer.

McEwan, H. (1995). Narrative understanding in the study of teaching. In H. McEwan & K. Egan (Eds.), *Narrative in teaching, learning and research.* New York: Teachers College Press.

Mishler, E. (1986). *Research interviewing.* Cambridge, MA: Harvard University Press.

Penlington, C. (2008). Dialogue as a catalyst for teacher change: A conceptual analysis. *Teaching and Teacher Education, 24*(5), 1304–1316.

Raelin, J. A. (2001). Public reflection. *Management Learning, 32*(1), 11–30.

Rubin, H. J., & Rubin, I. S. (1995). *Qualitative interviewing: The art of hearing data.* Thousand Oaks, CA: Sage.

Schön, D. A. (1983). *The reflective practitioner: How professionals think in action.* London: Temple Smith.

Somekh, B. (1995). The contribution of action research to development in social endeavours: A position paper on action research methodology. *British Educational Research Journal, 21*, 339–353.

Stefani, L., & Elton, L. (2002). Continuing professional development of academic teachers through self-initiated learning. *Assessment and Evaluation in Higher Education, 27*(2), 117–129.

Sylvester, D. (1994). *Looking at Giacometti.* London: Pimlico.

Taylor, M., Coia, L., Hopper, T., Sanford, K., Smolin, L., & Crafton, L. (2006). Making collaboration explicit in self-study research in teacher education. In L. M. Fitzgerald, M. L. Heston, & D. L. Tidwell (Eds.), *Collaboration and community: Pushing boundaries through self-study* (pp. 247–251). (Proceedings of the Sixth International Conference of Self-Study of Teacher Education Practices, July–August 2006, Herstmonceux Castle, East Sussex). Cedar Falls, Iowa: University of Northern Iowa.

Treleaven, L. (1994). Making a space: A collaborative inquiry with women as staff development. In P. Reason (Ed.), *Participation in human inquiry* (pp. 138–162). London: Sage.

Winter, R. (1989). *Learning from experience.* New York: Basic Books.

Winter, R. (1998). Finding a voice—thinking with others: A conception of action research. *Educational Action Research, 6*, 53–68.

Winter, R., Buck, A., & Sobieschowska, P. (1999). *Professional experience and the investigative imagination: The ART of reflective writing.* London: Routledge.

Woolhouse, M. (2002). Supervising dissertation projects: Expectations of supervisors and students. *Innovations in Education and Training International, 39*(2), 137–144.

Woolhouse, M. (2005). You can't do it on your own: Gardening as an analogy for personal learning from a collaborative action research group. *Educational Action Research, 13*(1), 27–41.

Zuber-Skerritt, O. (Ed.). (1996). *New directions in action research.* London: Falmer.

Zuber-Skerritt, O. (1992). *Professional development in higher education: A theoretical framework for action research.* London: Kogan Page.

CHAPTER 18

The Faculty Academy
A PLACE FOR GROUNDING AND GROWTH

Lillian Benavente-McEnery
University of Houston–Clear Lake

Blake Bickham
Mesa State College

Christa A. Boske
Kent State University

Michele Kahn
University of Houston–Clear Lake

Andrea Foster
Sam Houston State University

Carrie Markello
University of Houston

Susan McCormack
University of Houston–Clear Lake

Denise McDonald
University of Houston–Clear Lake

Heidi C. Mullins
University of Arkansas at Little Rock

Angela López Pedrana
University of Houston–Downtown

Joy C. Phillips
East Carolina University

Rita P. Poimbeauf
University of Houston

Chris Witschonke
University of Houston–Downtown

Cheryl J. Craig
University of Houston

Lillian Benavente-McEnery, Ed.D., is an associate professor at the University of Houston–Clear Lake in the Language, Literacy, and Library Science Department. She serves as codirector of the Teaching Learning Enhancement Center on campus and codirects the Greater Houston Area Writing Project as well. Her passions include family literacy and the study of the socially shaped processes involved in literacy acquisition.

Blake Bickham, Ed.D., is assistant professor and secondary licensure coordinator at Mesa State College in Grand Junction, CO. He teaches both undergraduate and master's level students, and his interests include the moral dimensions of teaching, teacher education, and integrated literacy.

Christa A. Boske, Ed.D., is an assistant professor in educational leadership at Kent State University. She has eighteen years of experience in education as a principal, assistant principal, dean, residential treatment teacher, and school social worker. Her research interests include school-community relations, culturally responsive pedagogical practices, leading for social justice, and educational preparation programs.

Michele Kahn, Ph.D., is an assistant professor of multicultural education at the University of Houston–Clear Lake, serves as associate editor of the *Intercultural Education* journal, and is a board member of the International Association of Intercultural Education. A combination of her American Guatemalan background, linguistic and gender/sexual orientation studies, as well as a commitment to social justice, have led her to pursue a research agenda reflective of these issues.

Andrea Foster, Ph.D., is an assistant professor at Sam Houston State University, where she teaches science methods and other pedagogy-related classes. She is well known in the science community at the state and national levels and has received a number of awards as a classroom teacher and professor.

Carrie Markello, Ed.D., is a visiting assistant professor at the University of Houston, where she teaches courses in art education. She is an active member of the Houston arts community as an artist and founding member of Grassroots: Art in Action, a nonprofit organization that encourages connections between artists and art educators.

Susan McCormack, Ed.D., is an assistant professor of social education at the University of Houston–Clear Lake. She teaches social education methods to preservice educators focusing on pedagogy for social justice.

Denise McDonald, Ed.D., is an associate professor of curriculum and instruction at the University of Houston–Clear Lake, where she teaches undergraduate, graduate, and doctoral level courses in classroom management, instructional strategies, curriculum planning, and qualitative research. Her research interests include learning motivation, reflective pedagogy, and qualitative methodology.

Heidi C. Mullins, Ed.D., is an assistant professor in art and art education at University of Arkansas at Little Rock. She is a practicing artist, educator, and researcher in arts, and an active member of AATC, NAEA, AERA, and CAA. Her most recent publication that appears in *Curriculum and Teaching Dialogue* is titled "At the Crossroads of Pre-service Teacher Education." Her most recent exhibitions were held at the Washington State Convention and Trade Center and the Mobius Museum where she explores Native American iconography in contemporary culture.

Angela López Pedrana, Ed.D., is an assistant professor with the University of Houston–Downtown. Her personal and professional interests are varied, but her scholarship is centered on development of narrative authority of Latino teachers and how personal and professional experience of language and learning influence teachers of English language learners.

Joy C. Phillips, Ph.D., is an associate professor in the Department of Educational Leadership at the College of Education, East Carolina University, in Greenville. Her research interests focus on educational leadership, policy development and implementation, and school reform.

Rita Pokol Poimbeauf, Ed.D., was a school administrator for twenty-seven years and an executive director of a professional teachers' organization for eight years. Presently, she is teaching aspiring administrators and preservice teachers at the University of Houston. Her current interest is in preparing teachers for the realities of the classroom.

Chris Witschonke, Ed.D., is a new assistant professor at the University of Houston–Downtown. Prior to holding this position he worked as an eighth-grade social studies teacher for ten years in the Spring Branch Independent School district. In May 2007, he earned his doctoral degree from the University of Houston.

Cheryl J. Craig, Ph.D., is a professor in the Department of Curriculum and Instruction, College of Education, University of Houston, where she coordinates the Teaching and Teacher Education program and is the director of elementary education. Her research centers on the influence of school reform on teachers' knowledge development and their communities of knowing.

ABSTRACT

Using the rhizome metaphor, the Faculty Academy—a group of university professors brought together by virtue of a higher education reform initiative spearheaded by the Houston Annenberg Challenge—describes its origins and how a small group of dedicated professors have melded against the isolationist backdrop of members' respective university contexts. Along the way, the benefits of group interactions and how and what individuals learned in the midst are shared. Additionally, challenges the members of the Faculty Academy have encountered are made public and the future of the Faculty Academy is discussed.

Introduction: Planting Rhizomes

Professional development is the essence of all who aspire to grow in education, even those whose careers unfold in higher education. We all need it, we thrive on it, many of us have enacted it, and it is a necessary and huge part of our academic survival. It is where we learn our craft, share, and grow as individuals in order to make substantive contributions to our respective fields—whether they are science, art, music, social education, mathematics, language, literacy, multicultural education, special education, leadership, kinesiology, curriculum studies, or research.

There is critical need to support, nurture, and care for educators, particularly those whose primary responsibility is to develop others to be successful teachers. A long time ago, William Shakespeare said, "We know what we are, but not what we may be." The University of Houston Faculty Academy was the inspiration of a few dedicated individuals who envisioned the future of a group of academicians, realized their significance and potential impact on the educational enterprise, and farmed a rich soil of opportunity and growth to help its members become what they could be. The Faculty Academy provided a soft place in a hard world for aspiring educators to take root, interact, and reflect about purpose, focus, and contribution. This chapter chronicles the individual and collective stories of past, present, and future academy members. Their experiences outline a vast and rich outlook with regard to the professional development of educators who leave the sanctity of their classroom spaces for higher education. Through the use of the metaphor of a biological rhizome, the narrative of this chapter unfolds.

Meet the Academy

The Faculty Academy is comprised of a voluntary group of educators who transition in and out of permeable boundaries of relationship and association depending on specific needs, changing identities, and particular demands arising from their respective positions. Much like the organic rhizome found in nature, the Faculty Academy, which was seeded in the fall of 2002 by Annenberg dollars to propagate university and school district partnerships, continuously grows, producing new growths and offshoots that sprout in alternative directions and locations. The Faculty Academy, like a rhizome (i.e., a plant that grows and sprouts from itself), exists in many forms. It crops up unexpectedly and finds ways to survive and to produce beautiful short-lived blossoms; yet forms a solid, often unseen, organic infrastructure of possibility, endurance, and strength. The rhizomatous nature of the Faculty Academy not only allows for changes in membership, but for changes in identities as members transition from one role to another both within and outside the University of Houston. Over the Faculty Academy's five-and-a-half-year history, transitions include changes in members' roles and identities as they pursue new positions, establish new community connections, assume assigned university responsibilities, and affiliate with new institutions.

In bimonthly meetings, members of the Faculty Academy come together to deliberate our professional lives, to examine our own and others' scholarship, and to plot courses of action related to our practice and research agendas that result in a different way of thinking about reform along the continuum. Like the sporadic nature of rhizome growth, the Faculty Academy has, at times, a random unpredictable pattern of participation, even though what is accomplished is purposeful and directed. At any given meeting a new face may appear, or surface—a visitor, a contributing member, or someone simply in need of care and growth.

HISTORY: ROOTING RHIZOMES

The idea of a regional reform faculty was contained in Houston's original Child-Centered School Initiative, which was submitted to the Annenberg Foundation for major funding. Once named an Annenberg Challenge site in 1997 and gifted with $20 million from the Annenberg Foundation and matched locally with $40 million, the Houston Annenberg Challenge began rolling out its reform initiative that largely centered around networks of Beacon schools (eleven lead campuses) and Lamplighter schools (forty schools in different networks). In the meantime, the regional reform faculty concept was discussed as part of the reform movement's design but initially not brought to fruition. However, as the Houston Annenberg Challenge began to be formally evaluated, a position of director of higher education was created to specifically address the much-needed collaboration between higher education and Houston area public school systems. Louise Deretchin (coeditor of this yearbook) was hired into this position. As an outgrowth of her prior work at Baylor College of Medicine, she brought with her the concept of a faculty academy composed of professors from regional universities, coupled with community partners. This program became part of the funded higher education initiatives of the Houston Annenberg Challenge. Louise Deretchin approached Cheryl Craig (also coeditor of this yearbook) of the University of Houston who had been highly involved with the Beacon schools initiative. Craig's working example of collaborating with the campuses and reflecting and acting on their perceived challenges fit with the Houston Annenberg Challenge's mission as well as the University of Houston's College of Education mission of "collaboration through learning and leading."

When Louise Deretchin came to Cheryl Craig with the Faculty Academy opportunity, Craig drew upon her experience that was cultivated in the Research Issues Group at the University of Alberta (Chapter 16 in this volume)—a group founded by Jean Clandinin, Craig's doctoral advisor. Craig had experienced firsthand the power of faculty members and graduate students collaboratively examining their work in a sustained way in community.

A call was sent out to faculty members at universities in the Houston urban core to participate in the Faculty Academy, alongside a school-based educator or community partner of their choice. Prospective members were invited to complete a preliminary application that solicited a description of current individual research interests and professional goals. Originally, members who applied were aware that there would be a selection review or "pruning" process with only the hardiest of stock invited to participate. The application process was necessary for identifying matches of the reform initiative's purpose and potential members' field-based research goals, dispositions for long-term research interactions, and genuine interest in collaborative work toward a common objective.

Some of the original faculty members who answered the call imagined that belonging to the group would give them access to Houston Anneberg Challenge's generous funding stream. Unfortunately, since monies were not readily available, some initial members (and notably, all tenured) moved away from the Faculty Academy in search of funds in independent, conventional ways. The result was an organism of fledgling faculty longing for community, in the midst of the isolation perpetuated by research universities, especially those that are commuter campuses. Those who remained shared a desire to find new ways to live alongside schools, teachers, and community members. They wished to be co-teachers, co-learners, and co-researchers who preferred to examine shared dilemmas in a dialectical manner (McKeon, 1952). They wanted theory and practice to mutually inform one another. From its inception, the Faculty Academy operated in this horizontal interaction approach, following a pattern similar to rhizome growth.

However, when the group cohered, the plotline of the Faculty Academy encountered another bend in the road: the fact that those interested were primarily untenured, female professors and their school/community-based partners. This development seeded further questions. How could this faculty membership support the schools and the community if they could not meet promotion and tenure requirements and sustain their positions at the university? How could these individuals assist others when they themselves were in need of support?

As previously mentioned, the Faculty Academy was not formed for this specific membership base so it is worth noting the members the small group attracted and retained.

Despite the fact that female professors numerically dominate schools of education across the country (approximately 60 percent), academe is, and traditionally has been, a masculine field. According to the National Center for Education Statistics (NCES), 23.6 percent and 35.6 percent of women in schools of education are full and associate professors, respectively (2005). By extension this means that approximately 70 percent of tenured professors are male so the balance of power is tipped in that direction.

The Faculty Academy meetings unearthed this tenuous reality as many members confirmed their suspicions of a "good old boy" network, as well as the importance university departments afford male-dominated projects. For example, how and why funding was allocated often depended on who the applicant was as well as the type of activity it intended to support. Female faculty shared stories focused on how they interacted with male faculty and were often delegated to assuming "female duties" (i.e., assigned to serve as the secretary by taking notes for a meeting). The professional culture of the Faculty Academy has triggered participants' transcendence from just mulling through mundane tasks of academe and credulously accepting assigned "status quo" roles (as described above) to embracing challenging opportunities and augmenting individual capacity for creativity, problem-solving, communication, and collaboration. Additionally, this environment for professional growth is balanced with the nurturance, harmony, and recognition for honors and personal achievements that were seemingly dormant in our respective institutions. Also, the Faculty Academy respects the achievements of each member.

MEMBERSHIP: SEASONAL AND PERENNIAL FOLIAGE

The diversity of the members of the Faculty Academy is celebrated, and members are different in so many ways. Over time members have ranged in age from thirties to sixties with various amounts of experience and professional credentials. The group includes two males. Some members were born or lived outside the United States (Germany, several South American countries, Guatemala, and Canada). One member is a Native American (Eastern Oklahoma Delaware-Lenni Lenape), while three members are from Hispanic families. Four members speak Spanish, and other members have worked in Mexico and Uzbekistan. A number of Faculty Academy members have left the University of Houston's Main Campus and have accepted positions across the United States: East Carolina University in North Carolina, Eastern Washington University in Washington State, Mesa State College Center for Teacher Education in Grand Junction, Colorado, Sam Houston State University in Huntsville, Texas, as well as the University of Houston's Downtown, Clear Lake, and Victoria campuses.

Faculty Academy members represent a wide range of interests and teaching areas. Members are mainly working in educational leadership, teacher education, or curriculum and instruction with such diverse interests as art education, leadership and vision building, integrated literacy, moral dimensions of teaching, student teacher preparation, education of Latino students, narrative authority, sexual orientation and gender issues, science education, motivational theories, multicultural education, art and its relationship to daily life, school-based research, and social education centering on democracy and social justice. Hence, the Faculty Academy is a haven of diversity, which serves as the fertilizer for the grounded rhizomes; at the same time, a sense of common community binds the group together, as each living cell combines to provide support for the continued spread of the rhizome. This diversity enables a cross-pollination of ideas and information that promotes creative and critical thinking. While pushing the margins imposed by traditional academic practices, we always hold ourselves and one another to high scholarly standards.

CULTIVATING COLLEGIALITY: TRUE BUDS

To characterize who we are as a Faculty Academy, a deeper look into common community and diversity is necessary because these qualities provide the roots or grounding for the group. Major attributes of the group are the scholarly interests and the flourishing of knowledge both as a group and as individuals within the group. All members are educators, having influenced and reciprocally been influenced by the lives of elementary, secondary, and university-level students. When hours of direct instruction and student contact are calculated, Faculty Academy members have interacted with more than sixty thousand individuals. Who knows where they have been an influence and where their influence may continue to cascade? But one thing is for certain—the collective harvest of intellectual produce from the Faculty Academy's rhizome continues to increase.

Also, all members value the contributions of other members whether or not everyone agrees. Each member is respected for personal opinions and offerings as well as honors and triumphs in the academic world. Faculty Academy meetings have become a common experience in which members look forward to the exchange of ideas and thoughts; they find the Faculty Academy a safe place to develop ideas without jeopardizing their status, positions, or careers. Our meetings have become predictably unpredictable. This has evolved into the "Faculty Academy way."

MENTORSHIP: CROSS-POLLINATION AND COMPOST

Collaboration between and among faculty and institutions is one of the Academy's central themes and is embodied through our collective works. However, this process is most beneficial to newer Academy members as they negotiate the tenure process of higher education. All professional settings have unique requirements for their *apprentices*; university settings are no different and are notorious for their extremely complicated and competitive tenure processes. In too many instances new faculty are not properly nurtured to promote successful professional growth. In settings such as those, new faculty feel isolated and fail to thrive. The Faculty Academy reverses this "withering" process as the founding members serve vital roles in mentoring junior faculty to endure the tenure process.

In many mentorship situations, there is a hierarchy in which the most experienced personnel guide the least experienced through the intricacies of the given profession. The mentor/mentee relationship is blurred in the Academy. There are no separate meetings between perceived leaders. Each meeting is attended by all members. There is a sense that every member benefits and draws support through their mutual participation. There are ongoing dialogues to discuss professional expectations, issues, and concerns allowing ample time for each member to make contributions to the dialogic process. The scholarly discourse is strongly supported by samples of work and suggestions for ways to improve individual praxis. Collaboration is also strongly encouraged so new members are able to seed scholarly development and are accompanied by well-harvested support. Lillian, for example, writes:

> The continual growth nurtured and facilitated by the learning community we have in Faculty Academy is a complex and somewhat elusive phenomena to describe. To articulate fully what the group has meant to me, even at those times in my academic career when I have not seemingly been fully engaged, when life took me out of the mainstream, when I came to the meetings burdened with the day-to-day to-do lists of tasks that had little to do with real research and real scholarship, is a difficult task. In spite of this, each time I attend Faculty Academy, I come away refreshed, with my roots, which like the rhizome's may be spread in many different directions, watered and edified. Always.

Collaboration

Collaboration is strongly encouraged so new members are able to seed scholarly development and are accompanied by well-harvested support. From its inception, Cheryl Craig has guided and supported Faculty Academy members and has been central to its evolution as new filaments or threads continue to sprout. But what are these filaments? Why have they increased in importance? How are they connected to a faculty of interested novices? In seeking the answer to these questions, unique concepts come into focus: *collaboration, communication, connections, contacts, camaraderie, celebrations,* and *caring.* That they all begin with the letter C is coincidental. The linking threads of our community are produced slowly as we meet to create, to share, and to give feedback. As the threads grow, so does the bonding within our small-group setting.

Collaboration occurs as the group works on presentations or projects related to shared academic interests. In addition, individual members may be in touch with one another during times when meetings are not scheduled for further feedback. Some members of the group have worked in teams to write various articles for publication. A learning community of this type thrives when the differences and talents of all members are explored, sometimes critiqued, yet always appreciated. The stage is open to all, and the different collaborative opportunities and configurations are boundless.

PRODUCTIVITY: THE FRUIT OF OUR EFFORTS

Productive membership meetings have yielded multiple presentations at the American Educational Research Association conference, the American Association for Teaching and Curriculum conference, and the Invisible College. All presentations attended to the themes of voice, vision, reflection, collaboration, and professional growth through a melding of the practitioner/researcher worlds. Additionally, individual members have collaborated with field-based partners to conduct presentations at regional and national teaching and research conferences. Many of the presentations evolved into collaborative publications in national or international journals.

Members have also collectively authored book chapter introductions and summaries and individually authored or coauthored articles with their field partners. The Faculty Academy has also sponsored an Invited Speaker Sessions in which our field partners participated and has supported researcher/practitioner inquiry into a variety of school leadership roles and functions that include creating a shared vision, developing and sustaining teacher leaders, using current research to improve teacher practice and student outcomes, conducting collaborative research with field-based partners in the public schools, sponsoring or cohosting professional development opportunities, and fostering strategies that lead to development of professional learning communities.

VISIBILITY AND INVISIBILITY OF FACULTY ACADEMY VITALITY: BLOSSOMS AND SUBTERRANEAN GROWTH

Stories of our experiences as members of Faculty Academy poignantly illustrate the impact of what we describe as the "unseen, organic infrastructure of possibility, endurance, and strength." Cheryl Craig reminisces on one such memorable occasion.

> In the second year following the creation of the Faculty Academy, an issue arose at a faculty meeting. As probably the first female chair of the Graduate Studies Committee, I brought forward for discussion

and wrote a report that was not particularly well-received by certain faculty members who held a great deal of seniority, power, and sway in the department. While I cannot remember the nature of the issue, I do recall the heated discussion going on and on. In fact, I wondered when it would end. Finally, the matter was put to a vote. I felt certain that the committee's recommendation was a lost cause given the cantankerous debate. I hung my head low so as not to see how soundly the proposal was defeated. However, what occurred was one of the strangest outcomes that has ever taken place in my academic career. The proposal was accepted by a large margin! In a flash, I realized that among that majority were many Faculty Academy members. While it would have been perilous for them in their junior positions to openly express opposing views to those wielding power, they still held in their possession the power of their votes. On this occasion, they most certainly acted on it, and I personally felt the influence of the Faculty Academy in situations outside group meetings and presentations.

For some members, it may not be a singular significant event, but a melding of multiple, recurring informal episodes that inspire loyalty and continued participation with this community of learners, educators, and researchers. Denise shares:

> Getting rooted in academia is neither a natural nor easy growth process, especially with respect to the looming tenure "weeding out" contingency, which presents a perennial, unrelenting challenge. As a novice academic, I searched for campus colleagues with whom to share my budding thoughts about research queries, and found that communal dialogue was often directed by teaching responsibilities and service roles required by my entering position as assistant professor, rather than my personal desire and professional need to sprout a scholarly identity amongst seasoned researchers. Authentic and unrestrained voicing of views that served my developing identity and growth as an academic and researcher was not grounded in my own backyard.
>
> Fortunately for me, blossoming as a scholar progressed through regular and ongoing opportunities for dialogic exchange in a safe, well-cultivated "plot." More so, relational connections were generated by means of collegial discourse as members provided reciprocal recognition to one another's emerging scholarly identity. Not experienced as obligatory in nature, acknowledgments and affirmations occurred organically (without apparent forethought, deliberation, or intention), which assisted in the formation of mutual respect, recognition, and trust, providing hardy and "hearty" structure for our dialogic community.
>
> Having the opportunity to share research and pedagogical ideas,

listen to others' views, experiences, and stories and respond in an open, genuine fashion, significantly contributed to the meaningfulness I sought in higher education. I value the affirming process experienced in connecting with others and how that process feeds itself in propagating new, unexpected growth and knowledge. Individually and collectively, we have served as active epi*stem*ic agents for individual scholarly identities, but also have grown together and intertwined in an isomorphic empowered process; this is our garden with its own strategically positioned and aesthetically pleasing, self-reflective pond, albeit with encroaching weeds that continually need pruning.

Meanwhile, Andrea captures her story in the following way:

> My experience with the Faculty Academy was like a resurrection. I had a disheartening third-year review after my second year at the University of Houston. In the years I worked as an assistant professor in science education, I busied myself with developing new graduate and undergraduate courses, navigating a new and enormous city while teaching "in the field," and researching the impact of grant resources on school improvement. Unfortunately, I had neglected my writing and lost sight of what actually led to promotion and tenure—scholarly articles published in Cadillac journals. Fortunately, I received an invitation to participate in the newly formed Faculty Academy and was asked to write about my early experiences as an educational researcher. I found myself surrounded by like souls, by individuals who understood my plight. The constant nudging, interest, and interaction with exemplary educators and researchers led to numerous publications and opportunities that furthered my own professional development, and I am forever grateful.

Others delight in the empowering effects of group acceptance, professional support, and understanding unconditionally imparted by members. Joy describes the benefits of her involvement with the Faculty Academy:

> Because I was usually the only educational leadership faculty member, my research interests and agenda were typically different. Despite the different focus, my Faculty Academy colleagues graciously listened to my emerging thoughts about leadership in general, and leadership and vision building, in particular. Their encouragement and expertise bolstered my confidence to explore the vision concept in original conceptual and methodological ways. The group listened to preliminary ideas, developing manuscript drafts, and conference presentation previews. They offered consistently thoughtful, helpful feedback. They urged me especially to explore the creative aspects of leadership that are inherent in the vision building process. As a result of this productive exchange, I have developed a series of manuscripts

that delve ever deeper into the vision construct. These manuscripts, currently in the journal review process, contribute significantly to my developing body of scholarship.

Members have collectively endured many seasons and variable weathering conditions in the history of the Faculty Academy and have individually thrived in their own transforming and evolving professional roles and identities. Carrie's progression and growth are especially noteworthy as she expresses below:

> As a member from the very beginning, I may first appear as a constant; but with every year of membership my role and identity changed. My initial introduction to Faculty Academy came through assistant professor Sara Wilson McKay, who incidentally is the first person I heard speak of "rhizomes" and their spontaneous connected growth as conceptualized by Deleuze and Guattari (1987). At the time, Sara and I collaborated on projects while I worked as an art educator for the university's on-campus museum; through Sara, I gained entry into Faculty Academy as a community partner. Later, this role shifted when I became a graduate student. My doctoral studies fostered growth in exhilarating new directions. However, the change from community partner to graduate student caused me to feel uncertain about my new role as a graduate student Faculty Academy member. I questioned my place in a group composed of faculty. Not fully understanding the issues that faculty face, I wondered what my role should be as a student member. Could I become a full-fledged contributor as the sole student member?

Growth and change can take some unexpected turns. Sara moved to another university:

> With the loss of my mentor, my direction as a graduate student became unclear. Additionally, my classes interfered with Faculty Academy meeting dates, so for an entire semester I did not attend. I was challenged by these unforeseen twists of fate and felt unsure about my connection to Faculty Academy and my uncertain future in art education. Nothing on the academic landscape appeared as I thought it would or should be. At the time, I questioned my scholarly path because I felt that I was becoming detached from my art interests. These concerns caused me to seriously consider discontinuing Faculty Academy and my graduate work. Fortunately, rhizomatous growth is not easily snuffed out. I came back to Faculty Academy after a semester away. I was warmly welcomed and joined by other graduate students who were also faculty members. At that point, I wasn't a faculty member, but I felt a sense of camaraderie with both the new and old members. As we collaborated to prepare both collective and individual presentations and writings, I discov-

ered that I had missed the Faculty Academy members' nurturing support for scholarly development and that my views were respected. I did have something to offer. This realization led to a transformation. Thanks in part to the encouraging members of Faculty Academy, I was emerging as a scholar.

This story illustrates the fluid nature of individual membership within the academy. Another transitional aspect of membership includes academy "transplants" who participate in Faculty Academy initiatives at university settings across the United States. At this time, we have six attending members from system universities and three from the central campus. Most impressive is the far-reaching veining of five members in other geographic regions who investigate faculty academy possibilities and processes in higher education institutions that are located in Virginia, North Carolina, Colorado, Washington, and Louisiana.

TRANSITIONS OF ROLES AND IDENTITIES: SEASONS

Change experiences are fundamental to the growth and sustenance of Faculty Academy members. Affirmations have occurred for several of our members. One such individual, Heidi, describes how the haven of safety provided through Faculty Academy dialogues and interactions supported her development as an educator.

> I joined Faculty Academy as a doctoral student holding the full-time faculty position of visiting assistant professor, and as such, I often felt like an academic imposter, one who was supposed to have all the answers, knowledge, and know-how. My view quickly changed when I became a Faculty Academy member. I no longer had to sustain the illusion of "professor," but began to engage in who I was as an educator in a discipline wrought in subjectivity and ambiguity (art and education). The academy provided a place for questions and answers, an environment where I was protected and a place where I had the honor of protecting others in our quest to fulfill our destiny as educators. What moved me most was not only the process of continuous mentorship by our sponsor (Dr. Cheryl Craig), but the idea that each voice counted. The academy contributed to my well-being, development, growth, and questioning in a profession I hope to pursue for years to come.

Early season sprouts need the most protection, nurturance, and care, as evidenced in Heidi's continuing story:

> At first I remember watching the interaction of the members of the group wondering if I too would eventually feel that freedom, I did.

On several occasions I shared an idea, the beginnings of a paper, and even my doctoral candidacy paper, and received positive suggestions for taking each one to the next level. It was evident that my co-collaborators cared about whether I succeeded or failed in my endeavors. It rather reminds me of a story from the Bible where Moses had help holding his arms up so the fight would be won. The Faculty Academy held up my arms to help me be successful, and I was no Moses, but a visiting assistant professor struggling to understand my chosen profession. On the other side, I too had opportunities to help hold up the arms of others, to build them up and in turn cultivate a collaborative well-being. There is a reciprocal relationship in Faculty Academy, an interaction, where change takes place as everyone listens and shares.

Camaraderie is the greatest benefit in associating with the Faculty Academy. Young, aspiring faculty have a place to gain support and understanding. One is helped, not by the misery-loves-company cliché, but by the fact that suggestions and improvement come from the experiences of others who walk in the same shoes.

Chris reflects on his experience joining the Faculty Academy. He elaborates on his teaching transition from the classroom to the university setting:

Entry for the first time into this preexisting group leads to a strange mixture of fear and excitement. The fear is of the unknown, but the excitement is about the possibilities. The conversation begins with reports on what individuals are experiencing, working on, and struggling against. This alleviates much of the fear, for it illustrates that the experience of joining a faculty for the first time is not unique. It also increases the excitement for possibilities as ideas concerning research and presentations are discussed. As the group moves on to discussing previous meetings it became obvious that a vocabulary lesson is necessary. Words, ideas, concepts, and other such things were thrown about the room with a certain amount of authority, but without much explanation. However, a well-placed question or two provided the necessary context surrounding much of the conversation. When this introduction to the Faculty Academy comes to a close, it fills one with a sense of welcome and new found opportunities—opportunities that can spur a new professor to grow into his position rather than opportunities that left unfulfilled will bring about a quick cessation to his career in higher education.

So with this new challenge lying before me, I feel as though the Faculty Academy has helped equip me to put aside my old role as classroom teacher and begin to embrace my new position of university professor. No longer am I writing lesson plans trying to help students embrace different views of the content laid before them.

Instead I am designing lessons and assigning readings in an attempt to awaken realization within those choosing to enter the field of education. Research in my classroom has taken on an entirely new meaning. Instead of looking for better methods with which to teach teenagers a specific subject, I now strive to find patterns and underlying currents in the way students and teachers interact. As my view of the educational world continues to broaden, and as I continue to define my function within this world, a group such as the Faculty Academy will help me with this transition.

Chris further explains his expectations for the Faculty Academy as a support for career development:

A new professor is given several classes to teach, certain expectations to fulfill, and plenty of opportunity to bring about the end of his career. While striving to earn a doctoral degree the new professor is given a rigorous schedule of tasks to accomplish. This includes being introduced to new texts and interacting with them, finding and establishing research opportunities, and writing several papers at a time, all with the goal of publishing one or two pieces while at the same time completing the doctoral dissertation. However, now that check marks have been applied to each line, a faculty member is expected to develop and fulfill his own list. The problem is that transitioning from the secondary classroom to the university setting does not adequately prepare this professor for such a challenge. However, the Faculty Academy is supposed to provide a way to explore the role of a university professor and develop the skills needed to promote both career advancement and personal growth.

Carrie echoes Chris's comments on career development opportunities:

My personal transformation led to a new role as a visiting assistant professor. Currently in this position, I continue to be awakened to a greater sense of my abilities as a teacher and as a scholar. I gather sustenance and experience new growth as I work with my Faculty Academy colleagues sharing ideas, concerns, and experiencing transitions. Although my experiences are particular to my circumstances, other Faculty Academy members have experienced transitions that have led to rhizomatous growth in unique directions.

Rhizomatous transitions encourage members to assume new roles and identities, encouraging transformations in positive directions as contributing scholars. Faculty Academy offers the fertile soil to nurture the scholarly and personal growth to develop in new directions as members transition from their changing roles and identities.

NARRATIVE, VOICE, AND COMMUNICATION: POLLINATION

"Principles of connection and heterogeneity: any point of a rhizome can be connected to anything other, and must be. This is very different from the tree or root, which plots a point, fixes an order" (Deleuze & Guattari, 1987, p. 7). The Faculty Academy communicates much like a rhizome behaves, by creating connections, exploring differences, and discovering similarities. We often communicate through metaphor-sharing experiences that defy the rigid, often positivistic ideologies in which our respective institutions are rooted. In the past we have compared our group connections to spiderwebs, penguins, peacocks, and mobiles. We are comfortable with gray areas, with the "neither-nor messiness" that the merging of educational theory and practice brings.

Communication between members is greatest during meetings where most of the group's planning and interaction take place. It is not uncommon to hear members begin conversations with the phrases "I feel" and "it's like," which tend to lead into ideas for research projects and inspiration for writing. The large-group sessions become a means of fulfilling the group's purpose. If anything, these meetings build not only unity among the members, but also increase the members' productivity by offering challenges to all members to contribute work. E-mail is a way of keeping members within the circle of communication and is used as needed to pass along information. Cheryl Craig does a yeoman's job of keeping contacts alive. Her sensitivity and willingness to work with individual differences allow for a sense of connectedness that maintains the focus of the group. Members may leave the group due to physical distance, but they always are just an e-mail message away.

The linguistic diversity we use to explain our realities is shaped by our positions as teachers, researchers, students, writers, and artists. It stems from a shared belief in the power of narrative. We cross-pollinate personal and professional knowledge extracted from the mundane and extraordinary stories of our daily lives. The Faculty Academy is fertile ground, and at each meeting we are allowed to grow unhampered. This chapter is a fitting example of how we communicate. The very act of composing this manuscript began with seemingly random ideas expressed in our comfortable voices.

DISEASE, OBSTACLES, AND CHALLENGES: ROOT ROT, DRY ROT, AND FUNGUS

Rhizomes grow in different directions and thrive despite numerous threats from the environment. The threat of rot disease has the potential to cause one to abandon cultivation or production decline for rhizome crops (Myers, Elliot, & Young, 2002). This threat also diminishes drastically when systemic protection is induced (Ghosh & Purkayastha, 2003). Treating rhizome seeds with antibodies and immersing them in selected herbal abstracts protects seedlings from environmental threats. Faculty Academy provides a similar protection to its members or seedlings with opportunities for continued growth or sprouting despite the threat of institutional dysfunction or disease. Assisting members on developing the skills and knowledge to navigate through the realities of higher education and institutional dysfunction is not an easy task. Faculty Academy founders work diligently to carefully sift through the politics of higher education and predetermined agendas to minimize the threatening of the health of the seedlings or group members. Such threats include some administrators outside of Faculty Academy who attempt to change the research agendas of newly hired assistant professors and refocus them to alleged hot topics in education. Other threats to the health of its "seedlings" include departments outside of Faculty Academy making a concerted effort to schedule meetings at the same time Faculty Academy meetings are booked. Scheduling conflicts such as this prohibit professors from attending Faculty Academy.

Particular outliers, such as ones offered, who threaten the existence of Faculty Academy have the potential to stunt growth or seedling cultivation (Elliot, 2003). When faced with such obstacles, members of Faculty Academy discuss openly how they negotiate the realities of institutional disease. Members express their concerns that certain outliers attempt to stifle their creativity and threaten the existence of its membership and scholarly research. Outliers present unreasonable deadlines to members of Faculty Academy, attempting to dismiss seedlings to the will of bureaucratic systems. Through the wisdom of the Faculty Academy founders, seedlings have the opportunity to collaborate with members who know how to negotiate through bureaucratic structures.

As rhizome seedlings, Faculty Academy members also continue to work together to navigate through dysfunctional systems within higher education. Attempting to navigate through dysfunctional institutions is risky business. There are consequences associated with recruiting new members or planting seedlings in unwanted or infected areas. Infected areas tend to emerge when colleagues outside of Faculty Academy do not recognize or appreciate its vision. These outliers, in turn, attempt to diminish the benefits of scholarly collaboration and discredit the value of scholars adopting interdisciplinary investigations. Such infectious behaviors from pathogens better known as colleagues can be detrimental to the health of the Faculty Academy.

Comments such as "Faculty Academy does not count as professional development" or "It's not beneficial to tenure or your research agenda" are examples of pathogens attempting to impact the health of Faculty Academy. Other bacterium actions by colleagues outside of the Academy include persuading "seedling" recruits that the Academy is suspect to unfavorable conditions. Outliers suggest to recruited seedlings that the Academy stunts professional growth, research agendas, and future scholarship. Although the presence of outliers or pathogens does not seem to affect the Academy's healthy diagnosis, colleagues outside of the Academy continue to minimize its mission. These harbingers of disease are determined to impact the postharvest of high-quality rhizome seedlings who strive for collaborative scholarly outcomes. Despite the tremendous effort to suppress the academy's health, membership, and scholarly contributions, the academy prospers and demonstrates its hardiness to survive unfavorable seasons. Its cultivar resistance to institutional dysfunction and disease is pertinent to preserving its vision, mission, and core values.

NETWORKS: OFFSHOOTS AND STEMS

"A rhizome may be broken, shattered at a given spot, but it will start up again at one of its old lines, or on new lines. . . . These lines always tie back to one another" (Delueze & Guattari, 1987, p. 11). We have several members who have left the area, but who continue to participate in the Faculty Academy long distance. Here are their stories, from Joy, Heidi, and Blake respectively.

JOY

> I left UH in summer 2007 to join the faculty of East Carolina University (ECU) in Greenville, North Carolina. When I left, I was determined to take the Faculty Academy concept with me. Thus, in fall 2007 I established a new Faculty Academy chapter using the philosophy, structure, tone, and substance of the UH Faculty Academy. Presently, eight faculty in my Educational Leadership Department meet once a month to share research agendas, present manuscript drafts, and preview conference presentations. As we develop, we look forward to inviting experienced scholars to visit with us in "fireside chats." And, we anticipate experimenting with innovative uses of technology (webcasts, etc.) to broaden our access and horizons.

HEIDI

> Listening was a key element in Faculty Academy; it pushed my development as an "individual" within a collaborative environment. I had

many opportunities to not only listen to my more experienced peers, but renowned scholars as well. One such visit included Dr. Tom Barone, a renowned scholar in the arts and education, where he planted seeds that would germinate and grow and helped me direct my scholarly future. These seeds came in the form of words. He spoke about moving toward research that does not focus on certain declarative truth, but rather one that focuses on the heuristic, asking questions. He emphasized perspectives (the multiplicity of views) and encouraged asking questions that engaged multiple answers, to engage in the narratives of life. He was describing research, but in many ways he was also describing the Faculty Academy.

Today, Faculty Academy still resonates and impacts who I am as an educator, artist, and scholar. I graduated and moved 2,300 miles away to take a position as an assistant professor in art education. I am in many ways a broken-off piece of the rhizome that is now connected to the old and new. I am empowered by knowing that I am still connected to Faculty Academy's past, its present, and my ability to further new lines of the rhizome in my present appointment. Faculty Academy birthed in me an understanding that no one perspective is privileged in academia, but a heteroglossia, a coexistence of diversity within a commonality and is a chronotype, a meeting place, "a place where the knots of narrative are tied and untied" (Bakhtin, 1981, p. 250). It has taught me that ambiguity is implicit in who we are as researchers and educators. There are no imposters, only ways of knowing, where congenial conflict and collaboration give rise to new ways of understanding academia and our place in it. There is no final author or "version of the truth, but what makes sense to all those invested" (Tom Barone, Faculty Academy meeting, personal communication).

BLAKE

Upon graduating with my doctorate, I remained at the University of Houston as an instructor for a semester and was invited to become a member of Faculty Academy. Having been peripherally involved as a student, I felt very welcome by the other members and treated as an equal right away. This warmth and encouragement provided by the members of Faculty Academy make it a strong and powerful force.

Though I am now living and working in another state, I still feel the presence of this force in my working life. The rhizome metaphor is particularly apropos because I sense the roots of the organization beneath me as I continue to develop as a junior faculty member. As an assistant professor at a teaching-focused institution in western Colorado, I learned that most of the experienced faculty work on their scholarship activities in the summers and during holidays. Everyone either writes in isolation or else they have developed smaller support groups within their departments; as a new faculty member, I cannot be sure which the more likely scenario is. In short, I have not yet established a support group like Faculty Academy in my current environment.

Most recently, I realized how deeply and how far the Faculty Academy's rhizome reaches. Since I left Houston about six months ago, I have only kept in touch with Faculty Academy through the grapevine. However, over the holiday I began thinking about writing and submitting to different journals. I wondered who might read my writing. Maybe, I thought, Faculty Academy would be willing to review some of my writing. Any uncertainty about whether I might still be considered a member was erased the next day when I received an e-mail asking if I would like to contribute to this piece. Others have written about the blooms that have sprouted from the Faculty Academy rhizome. Though I do not feel that I have quite blossomed, I do believe that the continued support and encouragement of Faculty Academy will lead to another bloom here in Colorado.

Goals and Future Direction?

The goals and future direction of the Faculty Academy have been imagined by both individuals and the group. Lillian's words capture well the sentiment of the group and particular group members. She writes:

Some plants have rhizomes that grow above ground. This can be likened to the clearly articulated focus we determine each semester in Faculty Academy—the theme or project to which we choose to devote our time, attention, and resources. Many rhizomes do their work underground, however. I connect with this version. The idea that, like the development and growth of the rhizome, my professional development and nourishment take root in very "underground" ways, in quiet unassuming ways, in ways that set me off on a current unforeseen. This development is facilitated by the cross-fertilization of ideas, by the willingness of the members of our learning community to listen attentively, the ability of the members to pose thoughtful, reflective, and provocative questions, and a collaborative spirit that embodies what it means to work shoulder to shoulder as colleagues. It strikes me that we often seek to explain complex concepts and ideas through metaphors and representations that help us see what is there more clearly. Perhaps, just as importantly, metaphors help to shed light on that which we were not aware existed. In many instances, the rhizome acts as the "seed," and is used to propagate the plants by vegetative reproduction, such as in the case of asparagus and ginger. The ideas generated in this safe place serve to plant the seeds that help spur us on, not only in fulfilling our respective research agendas, but in living fuller and richer lives as scholars, thinkers, and writers. The process is not seamless. As with rhizomes, our paths are sometimes blocked. We veer, then, in different directions. Obstacles don't signal an end, just a readjustment in our thinking.

Natural extensions of the camaraderie are the celebrations and caring for each other that the group exhibits. Celebrations are in order when members relate their successes in having publications accepted or new job offers. The pats on the back are genuine in wishing the academy member continued professional success and career advancement. The caring for each other becomes greater as the group becomes more familiar with each other, their circumstances and problems. At times, members share stories of misfortune, frustrations, or personal tragedy. The academy has become a place to voice these issues in that "what happens in the academy stays in the academy." Hence, it has become a safe haven to vent and yet be valued. Feelings of respect and understanding that flow for one another within the academy walls are, at times, so needed and necessary for the psyche. With the academy, there is a place to care and be cared for. Whether or not the founding members envisioned the Academy spawning these specific threads of support is not significant; what is important is that the concept that was created to help novice faculty members bloom has taken on a life of its own. In the sometimes unyielding, always ruthless field of academia, we have become a live, productive organism that is continuing to grow and evolve. Who knows what direction the next filament will take?

Concluding Statements

As a model of small-group learning in higher education, the Faculty Academy of which we are a part exemplifies the kind of growing that takes place on the edges of academia. While begrudgingly recognized, the initiative has not been officially recognized as self-directed professional development for university professors nor funded as a faculty priority. Rather, it has been tolerated, not championed. This constitutes both an advantage and a disadvantage. The advantage is the group is not co-opted into administrative fiats, nor populated by placeholder professors. The disadvantage is that all members are not credited for participation, nor funded for travel for collaborative presentations. In fact, some are chastened for cross-institutionalized collaboration (cross-pollination). Also, the Faculty Academy at times is isolated from decision-makers, and members are occasionally viewed as suspect by those whose isolationist practices are deeply embedded in tradition and feel no need to change.

The future of Faculty Academy cannot be plotted on a flowchart because the work is situated, collaborative, and relational. It will emerge as both individual Faculty Academy members and the group grow, develop, and respond to the ever-shifting higher educational landscape. One branch to which the group is committed is to propagate a Graduate Student Faculty Academy because master's level and doctoral students have already identified themselves and indicated a dire need for community. And a second thing is a certainty: Passion and possibilities will continue to generate a place for grounding and growth for present and future Faculty Academy members.

References

Bakhtin, M. (1981). *Dialogic imagination.* Austin: University of Texas Press.

Deleuze, G., & Guattari, F. (1987). *A thousand plateaus: Capitalism and schizophrenia.* Minneapolis: University of Minnesota Press.

Elliot, S. M. (2003). Rhizome rot. Ministry of Agriculture and Lands Research and Development. Retrieved on November 15, 2007, at www.moa.gov.jm/tsd/randd/plant/misc/ginger_rhizome_rot.pdf.

Ghosh, R., & Purkayastha, R. P. (2003). Molecular diagnosis and induced systemic protection against rhizome rot disease of ginger caused by pythium aphanidermatum. *Current Science, 85*(12), 1782–1787.

McKeon, R. (1952). Philosophy and action. *Ethics, 62*(2), 79–100.

Myers, L., Elliot, S., & Young, F. (2002). Pre-plant treatments in the control of rhizome rot disease of ginger in Jamaica. *The Jamaican Agriculturist, 14,* 74–87.

National Center for Education Statistics. (2005). Retrieved on November 28, 2007, at http://nces.ed.gov/programs/digest/d05/tables/dt05_231.asp.

Summary and Implications

Cheryl J. Craig

Louise F. Deretchin

We conclude our discussion of teacher learning in small-group settings by drawing attention to higher education practices that were intimately linked to what was underway in teaching (Division 1) and teacher education (Division 2).

In Chapter 15, Mary Lynn Hamilton discussed the "somehow" of teaching, which she equated to the self-study of teaching and teacher education practices. Readers quickly came to see that self-study as practiced in small groups fruitfully merged teacher educators' interests in both practice and theory through creating a space at the intersection of self, practice, and context. At the same time, readers learned that this space could be long-distance or face-to-face or a combination of the two and could include students, focus on teacher education programs, or be of an individually driven variety.

The exemplars Hamilton provided formed rich narratives on which other teacher educators could draw. She told of how the membership of the Arizona Group—which was once geographically connected—then became scattered across the United States. She also featured the small-group self-study work that Peggy Placier, a member of the Arizona Group, had embarked on with her colleagues at the University of Missouri. In both instances, the sense of real professors in real institutions dealing with real-world challenges emerged. Then, the example of Freese working with her students was highlighted, along with the University of British Columbia method of studying the CITE teacher education program, which Clarke and Erickson themselves described in Division 2. Finally, several individual self-studies were spotlighted, some of which also suggested collaborative work. Through these multiple small-group possibilities, the value of the self-study of teaching and teacher education practices shone through.

In Chapter 16 of the higher-education group of essays, Murray Orr et al.

centered on the research issues table as a place of possibility for the education of teacher educators. The team of ten professors offered a multivocal account of a place—the research issues table—that all experienced in their respective graduate work. As the chapter unfolded, readers were introduced to qualities integral to the practice of teacher educators as understood by these authors. These included coming to live and know relational knowing, respectful listening, and response. Further to that, participants also valued coming to live and know a place of inquiry, "world" traveling, and the need to mindfully attend to tensions. Finally, coming to live and know included thinking narratively and the process of becoming, which, together with the aforementioned qualities, opened up a radically different plotline of how teacher educators could be educated and situated in the academy.

We then moved from Canada in Chapter 16 to the United Kingdom in Chapter 17. Here, the focus on higher education pertained to the cultivation of those supervising students' dissertation research. Through metaphorically using the figures in Giacometti's studio, Burchell and Dyson situated their action research project and the reflective space they created with a group of lecturers at the University of Hertfordshire amid the hubbub of other activities underway at their institution. In a nutshell, learning about self, other instructors, and dissertation students provoked changes in practice over time. Also, the sustained reflective conversation concerning the supervision of students' dissertation studies hung with the advisors long after the action research project concluded, productively informing their mentoring of new cadres of doctoral students.

Finally, we return to the United States and the concluding chapter, Chapter 18, authored by Lillian Benavente-McEnery et al. Also, a collaboratively authored piece, the essay told of a relatively stable group of teacher educators who met bimonthly as a way to support one another, cultivate relationships in schools and the community, and develop their scholarship in ways that would allow the members to continue to live their academic lives in higher education. In the chapter, readers were afforded insights into how the academy was experienced by new professors and some of the struggles with which they contended. More than that, the need for cultivation and sustenance in community was articulated personally, institutionally, and beyond the boundaries of one's place of work.

Placed alongside one another, each of the four chapters in Division 3: Higher Education illuminated how small-group learning has unfurled internationally at four different sites of inquiry. The unique efforts—albeit on the edges of the academy—speak of the rich possibilities yet to be tapped in higher education, despite the considerable challenges still to be faced.

Afterword

Cheryl J. Craig

Louise F. Deretchin

In Chapter 16, Murray Orr et al. introduced the concept of world traveling (Lugones, 1987), which is the ability to enter into others' experiences and to understand them in those individuals' own terms. To conclude this edited volume, we would like to borrow Lugones's concept from Murray Orr et al. and suggest that readers world-traveled as they took up the authors' invitations to enter into their experiences of how teacher small-group learning was lived in their particular teaching, teacher education, and higher education practices. Further to that, ideas also traveled across the pages of this book. For example, Kooy, in Chapter 1, set the context for small-group learning, citing literature and ideas that were echoed in subsequent chapters. Next, Orland-Barak's Chapter 2 focused intently on conversation as many other authors did, particularly Ensign in Chapter 8 and Meijer and Oolbekkink-Marchand in Chapter 10. Then, Ballock in Chapter 3 introduced critical friends group (CFG) work, which was not only evident in Yendol-Hoppey and Fichtman Dana's Chapter 4 and Kelley, North, and Craig's Chapter 5, but in Patrizio's Chapter 9 as well. Moving on, Rath in Chapter 6 spoke of a funded research project, which was also the case with Yendol-Hoppey and Fichtman Dana's Chapter 4; Kelley, North, and Craig's Chapter 5; and the Faculty Academy's Chapter 18. Rath's chapter additionally fit with Burchell and Dyson's action research approach in Chapter 17, which was conducted in a higher education setting. Next, Clarke and Erickson, in Chapter 7, opened up a discussion of cohorts as sites of small-group inquiry, an idea implied by Patrizio's Chapter 9 and present in Halquist and Novinger's Chapter 11. At the same time, Clarke and Erickson's self-study of their CITE teacher education program was also a part of Hamilton's Chapter 15, and Hamilton's concept of self-study was similarly foreshadowed in Meijer and Oolbekkink-Marchand's Chapter 10. Then, Gallavan in Chapter 12 described small groups as places where diversity could be recognized and fostered, an idea that further unraveled in Merino and Ambrose's Chapter 13 and Tompkins and Orr's Chapter 14. Yet, the diversity topic also found expression in Kooy's Chapter 1 (feminist thought) and Kelley, North, and Craig's Chapter 5 (racial, socioeconomic, and linguistic diversity). Meanwhile, Merino and Ambrose's teacher research idea in Chapter 13 blended with Yendol-Hoppey and Fichtman Dana's Chapter 4 and Kelley, North, and Craig's Chapter 5. Clandinin and Connelly's work at the intersection where curriculum and narrative inquiry meet was consistently referenced throughout the entire volume. What also surfaced was the critical tradition, which was especially evident in Rath's Chapter 6 and Tompkins and Orr's Chapter 14. As can be seen, this book cumulatively conveys a rich tapestry of approaches that crystalize teacher learning in small-group settings. Together, the eighteen chapters form an insightful volume from a mere kernel of an idea. Combined, the forty-five authors illuminate how small-group work found expression in their teaching, teacher education, and higher education practices.

Reference

Lugones, M. (1987). Playfulness, "world-traveling," and loving perception. *Hypatia,* 2(2), pp. 3–9.